Understanding Deviance

Paul C. Higgins
University of South Carolina, Columbia

Richard R. Butler
Benedict College

McGraw-Hill Book Company

New York   St. Louis   San Francisco   Auckland   Bogotá   Hamburg
Johannesburg   London   Madrid   Mexico   Montreal   New Delhi
Panama   Paris   São Paulo   Singapore   Sydney   Tokyo   Toronto

In loving memory of my brothers, Carl and Earl,
of whom I will always be so much a part

P.C.H.

To Kay, Beattie, and Kathy

R.R.B.

This book was set in Times Roman by Black Dot, Inc. (ECU).
The editors were Eric M. Munson and Barry Benjamin;
the production supervisor was Leroy A. Young.
The cover was designed by Janice Noto.
Fairfield Graphics was printer and binder.

UNDERSTANDING DEVIANCE

1 2 3 4 5 6 7 8 9 0 FGFG 8 9 8 7 6 5 4 3 2 1

ISBN 0-07-028776-7

Library of Congress Cataloging in Publication Data

Higgins, Paul C.
    Understanding deviance.

    Bibliography: p.
    Includes index.
    1. Deviant behavior.   I. Butler, Richard R.
II. Title.
HM291.H5257   302.5   81-8321
ISBN 0-07-028776-7   AACR2

Contents

Preface

Social scientists have long been interested in deviance. Consequently, there are many textbooks on the subject. Many of these texts have great appeal. They contain interesting discussions of various kinds of deviance and deviants: prostitutes, homosexuals, drug use, criminals, and so forth. Why then is another textbook needed? Because despite their strengths and appeal, the existing textbooks present a limited understanding of deviance.

In the past several years some sociologists have begun to emphasize in textbooks the basic issues and activities which underlie deviance no matter what that deviance may be. We agree with that approach. While it may be fascinating to read about different and often dramatic forms of deviance, when we are finished we are typically left with a disparate collection of facts and figures. We sense little coherence to the study of deviance. An examination of the basic issues and activities which underlie deviance can provide us with that coherence. Students can then apply their understanding of those basic issues to whatever particular kinds of deviance interest them. The facts and figures change. An understanding of the basic issues remains. However, why is another book still needed if there are some recent ones that explore the basic issues? Because despite their approach, these textbooks are limited too.

Deviance is an integral feature of our lives. In the study of deviance there has been too much emphasis on "those people over there," the deviants, and us conventional people over here. All of us are both deviant and conventional, though not in the same ways and to the same degree. We are all involved in the phenomenon of deviance in various capacities. Further, deviance and respectability are intimately linked. To understand one necessitates that we understand the other, and both should be understood within the same framework of concepts, ideas, and explanations. Thus, in *Understanding Deviance* we not only try to *thoroughly* explore the basic issues and activities which underlie all of deviance, but we also try to demonstrate how all of us are involved in deviance in various ways.

At the end of the book is a glossary of some of the terms used throughout the book. The "definitions" provided take into account how the terms were used in the book. A knowledge of "key" terms and their definitions is no substitute for a complete understanding of deviance. The terms should not become an end in themselves. They are only a tool to help us achieve that understanding.

At the end of each chapter are suggested projects. Some can be carried out as stated. Others may need to be scaled down or to be elaborated. Many will need to be specified, to be given added details, in order to be carried out in specific situations. We feel that making the projects workable in concrete situations is part of the process of understanding. Therefore, we have left that task up to those who undertake the projects. Individuals may work on some of the projects; groups on others. Some projects may take only a few days to complete. Others may take most of a semester. We have provided a wide range of activities which can be tailored to the needs of and the constraints faced by teachers and students. These projects may stimulate teachers and students to develop other projects. The ones listed here, as well as others that they may give rise to, are "hands-on" activities through which we can better understand deviance.

ACKNOWLEDGMENTS

Books are a social creation. Even when they bear the name of only one author, they are the product of the activities of many people. Without the stimulating work in the study of deviance by our colleagues, this book could not have been written. Though we have questioned at times what our colleagues have written, we have profited by it. The citations throughout the book are one small indication of how great that profit has been. More specifically, we thank Professor John Johnson, Arizona State University at Tempe; Professor John Delameter, University of Wisconsin; Professor Jeffrey Riemer, Wichita State University; Professor Charles McCaghy,

Bowling Green College, Professor Earl Rubington, Northeastern University; Professor Marvin Krohn, University of Iowa; Professor T. F. Courtless, George Washington University; Professor Martin Kozloff, Boston University; and Professor John A. Humphrey, University of North Carolina, Greensboro for commenting on previous drafts of this book in part or in whole. Their comments have increased our understanding of deviance and in turn, we hope, will increase the reader's understanding. We also appreciate the patience of our students, upon whom we tried out various ideas contained in this book.

Writing a book is also a very practical matter. The manuscript must be typed and proofread again and again. We thank Linda Adams, Brenda Crapse, Darlene Ellison, and Marcilla Holmes for their help here. We thank the University of South Carolina, Department of Sociology, for providing us with that assistance.

Eric M. Munson, our editor, provided continued support for our book. He shepherded the work from its beginning as a proposal to its completion as a textbook. We also appreciate the help of his assistant, Catherine Libby.

The encouragement of our families has made this project enjoyable. We have greatly appreciated Leigh's and Kay's patience during the many hours we devoted to this book and despite our occasional preoccupation with it.

To all those who have been a part of this social creation, thanks.

Paul C. Higgins
Richard R. Butler

Chapter 1

Understanding Deviance

What do the following have in common?

Recent legislation restricting where one can smoke has drawn heavy opposition from many groups, the tobacco industry being one. In several states, laws dealing with prostitution have been modified to enable the arrest of the patron as well as the prostitute.

A prominent politician's history of mental illness is discovered by investigative reporters. Upon examination of a bright student's term paper, a teacher finds evidence of plagiarism. What later turns out to be a case of child abuse is overlooked and the child dies.

An Air Force officer is dishonorably discharged following public disclosure of his homosexuality. Following burglary of a local grocery store, a cooperative juvenile is remanded to the custody of his prominent parents.

A runaway high school dropout becomes a hooker. A physician bills the government for Medicaid services that were never performed. Not wanting to appear different from others at a party, a teenager smokes his first marijuana cigarette.

Tired of the stares and laughter of others and of self-doubts, an overweight person joins a weight-loss group. Following release from prison, an ex-convict seeks a conventional way of life. In protest against how they are treated, gays demonstrate in various cities.

These events seem at first and even second glance to be quite different. Some are dramatic. Others are very routine. Some events involve the setting of rules and standards, others the recognition of a "problem" or the reactions to such "problems." All of these events and more are part of the *phenomenon of deviance.* It is this phenomenon, the actions and reactions of many people, which we will try to understand in this book.

In this chapter we will briefly outline the phenomenon of deviance. The following chapters will examine in detail each process which makes up that phenomenon. Before we sketch out the phenomenon of deviance we need to discuss the perspective used here. In doing so we will contrast our perspective with other perspectives on deviance that have been or still are used in sociology. Perspectives are neither right nor wrong. Rather, they are more or less useful. Throughout the book we will examine various views about deviance, changes in those views, and reasons for the changes. As will become evident later, just as deviance is dynamic, so is our understanding of it.

WHAT IS DEVIANCE?

Deviance is behavior, ideas, or attributes of an individual(s) which some, though not necessarily all, people in a society find wrong, bad, crazy, disgusting, strange, or immoral—in other words *offensive.* If *known about,* deviance is likely to lead to some kind of negative reaction: epithets under one's breath, avoidance, criticisms, warning to the deviant or to others, punishment, treatment, (perhaps self-reactions by the deviant, such as feelings of shame or guilt), and so on. If there is no negative reaction, not even a covert reaction (i.e., negative thoughts or feelings), then the behavior was not deviant to the observer. Thus deviance can be what people do or are alleged to have done, their *behavior;* what they think, their *ideas;* or even how they appear, their *attributes.*

Objective and Subjective Views

Traditionally social scientists viewed deviance as any serious behavior that violated the standards of society. Moral standards and legal rules were usually emphasized. These rules were taken for granted, and it was assumed that they reflected how society *naturally* should be. Since anyone who violated the rules and standards was obviously immoral, impoverished, or imperfect, deviance was *objectively* given (Rubington and Weinberg, 1978, p. 3). That is, certain behaviors, such as crime, drunkenness, or improper sexual behavior, were thought of as inherently deviant.

Their very nature made them so. Deviance was also absolute. It was unquestioned and unchanging.

Instead, we view deviance as *subjectively problematic*. The "nature, causes, and consequences of deviance are neither simple nor uniform" (Rubington and Weinberg, 1978, p. 4). Deviance is a complex phenomenon of social creation. It arises out of the many activities of the people involved, activities that we will explore in this book. Thus, behaviors, ideas, or attributes are not inherently deviant. Instead, as Howard Becker (1963, p. 9) has suggested: "social groups create deviance by making the rules whose infraction constitutes deviance, and by applying those rules to particular people and labeling them as outsiders." What standards are created, how they are interpreted, and who they are applied to is problematic, not simple or obvious.

In a very important sense deviance is in the eye (and the actions) of the beholder (Thio, 1978, p. 17). While there may be much agreement about some behaviors' being offensive—for example, murder—there is also a great deal of disagreement about other behaviors—for example, smoking marijuana. What is repugnant to some may be acceptable to or even praised by others. Thus, deviance is relative. Whether behaviors, ideas, or attributes are deviant or not depends. What it depends on will be examined particularly in Chapter 3 as well as throughout the book. Deviance is also a matter of degree (Goode, 1978, p. 31). We are more or less offended by the behavior, thoughts, and attributes of others.

By saying that deviance is subjectively problematic or relative, we do not mean that we feel deviance necessarily should be relative. Instead, we feel that a subjectively problematic or relative view of deviance is a more useful approach for understanding what people are doing with and to one another than is the traditional, objective approach. Even various members of the general public (and social scientists) who hold to a traditional approach, in which some people and behaviors are inherently offensive, are likely to consider different people and behaviors as obviously deviant within their different absolute views.

The Dramatic and the Routine

Until recently the predominant view of deviance stressed the presumably dramatic and even exotic nature of deviance. It was something alien to conventional people and conventional sociologists. Deviance was the study of "nuts, sluts and preverts" (Liazos, 1972, p. 103). Students were and still are invited to visit the "strange territory" of deviance, almost as if they were Dorothy awakening in the Land of Oz (Goode, 1978, p. 19). Sociologists became big game hunters who captured the exotic animals and displayed them for the amusement and thrill of the visitors (Gouldner, 1968, p. 106).

Many textbooks on deviance continue to embody the dramatic

approach to deviance. Some textbooks are a collection of chapters about different, presumably dramatic types of deviant behavior: alcoholism, crime, mental illness, drug addiction, homosexuality, and so on. Little attempt is made to examine the basic processes in deviance. The textbook covers symbolically advertise this dramatic and bizarre characterization of deviance. Abstract designs often include a geometrical figure glaringly out of place: a circle among squares or a wavy line among straight ones. Shadowy images or distorted human figures are displayed. Colors are sometimes garish. Thus the "marquee" lures the customers with the promise that inside they will find pleasure in the exotic and bizarre goings-on.

Similar to sociologists' emphasis on the dramatic nature of deviance is the public's fascination with exotic activities and people. Tabloids capitalize on mass murders, sexual crimes, religious cults, the occult, and other unusual happenings to attract customers. Sensational murders, graphic details of the ordeals of a teenage runaway, and the pornography business have become best-selling books, television programs, and movies. Investigative reporting of fraud, embezzlement, swindles, drug operations, teenage hookers, and other attention-getting activities propelled an hour-long television news program into top national ratings. Though we may not engage in such activities and are often appalled by them, we also enjoy such portrayals of deviance (Simmons, 1969). Thus, being "banned in Boston" can assure a book or movie of a great deal of publicity and therefore sales. In a very real sense, deviance is a main theme in entertainment in this country. Because it is, it becomes relatively easy to collect a wide variety of examples from the mass media to use in illustrating various points throughout this book.

New York City officials have certainly recognized that we are fascinated by deviance. In fact, they want to capitalize on that fascination. The city comptroller of New York feels that the city should consider promoting its gay community as a tourist attraction. As he told a gay business group:

> Your role in the city's economic recovery is a large one. . . . It might make sense—dollars and cents—to include the gay community in the national promotion of New York City, along with Chinatown, Little Italy, the Statue of Liberty and the Empire State Building. (*Columbia Record*, September 20, 1979, p. 10-A)

While deviance may be dramatic and exotic—mass slayings, religious cults, or mental illness—it is also routine. People are often defined as offensive in ordinary situations: outperforming the informal standards of a work group, disavowing one's previous religious beliefs, making cynical and critical statements about one's colleagues, wearing the "wrong" clothes, and so on. Even where the deviance is dramatic, leading to intervention by the police, the courts, or mental health officials, it is typically called to the attention of official agents by ordinary citizens, colleagues, or family members. What we consider dramatic depends upon the observer. For some, being arrested or incarcerated is a routine feature of their lives. For others, being singled out as unprepared or incompetent in school can be quite traumatic.

Sociologists have given most of their attention to dramatic deviance. Consequently, many of our examples and explanations in this book will necessarily involve discussions of crime, mental illness, homosexuality, and so on. Others will involve more routine deviance. However, whether it be dramatic or not, it is important to understand the phenomenon of deviance. Both dramatic and routine forms of deviance involve similar processes. They are woven of the same fabric.

Crime and Deviance

Although crime has traditionally been stressed in the study of deviance, there is not a one-to-one relationship between deviance and illegal behavior (Sagarin, 1975, pp. 24–33). Deviant behavior may or may not be illegal. Conversely, illegal behavior may or may not be deviant. Murder is both illegal and deviant. Being a Communist is not illegal but is likely to be deviant among most Americans; so too for outperforming the informal standards of a work group. An unmarried couple who live together are breaking the law in most states, but they raise few eyebrows among many people. Thus deviant behavior is not the same as illegal behavior. In fact, crime is only a very small, though highly dramatized, part of deviance.

Voluntary and Involuntary Deviance

Some sociologists have restricted the concept of deviance to "voluntary" deviants. Some have even prepared special texts on voluntary deviants (Sagarin and Montanino, 1977). To Albert Cohen (1966, p. 36) a deviant is someone who "knows what he is doing and is capable of doing otherwise, but who *chooses* to violate some normative rule, and so may legitimately be held accountable for his behavior." Thus, the disabled, the retarded, and the mentally ill, to name a few, would not be included.

Such an approach is too restrictive for several reasons. Deviance is more or less voluntary. It is a matter of degree, as is deviance itself. Further, whether deviance is more or less voluntary depends on the viewer. Most of us would probably not view blindness as something a person chose. Historically, however, those who were disabled were often viewed as responsible in some way for their impairment. Their impairment was a punishment for something immoral their parents had done or for their own sins (Hanks and Hanks, 1948; Meyerson, 1948). More subtly, some people *seek* a disabled role as a way of coping with other problems (Haber and Smith, 1971; Cole and Lejeune, 1972).

While many people would probably say that most criminals voluntarily chose to commit their crimes, others may not view them as voluntary actors. A significant trend in criminology (and not a recent one) is to see criminals and particularly delinquents as influenced by social forces and thus only partially responsible for their behavior. Such is clearly the case in the traditional view that juvenile delinquents are immature youths who lack proper adult guidance. Further, whether one was a voluntary actor or not is the center of contention in many cases, especially in insanity cases. More routinely, mitigating factors which "reduce" a defendant's responsibility for a crime often lead to less severe punishment. Thus we do not restrict deviance to voluntary actions. Rather, deviance may be more or less voluntary. As we will see in Chapter 5, the notion of responsibility, or whether behavior is voluntary or not, strongly influences how society reacts to deviants.

Being Different and Being Deviant

Many people think of being different as being deviant. The sociology of deviance is not the same as the sociology of being different (Freedman and Doob, 1968). Deviance is not a statistical term which covers those who are few in number or who differ from some mythical average person. The key to deviance is society's negative reaction (real, imagined, or potential). As in the case of illegal behavior, there is no one-to-one relationship between being different and being deviant. Few people become President of the United States, but that does not mean that presidents are deviant. On the other hand, many people, perhaps a majority of teenagers, have shoplifted. Yet those who shoplift may be arrested, fined, or put in jail. Thus deviance and being different are not the same.

Deviance and differentness, however, are related in several important ways. Persons with some visible differences may be reacted to negatively. Unattractive people may be avoided, and men who wear earrings may be ridiculed. The strained interaction which follows may enhance deviance. Further, as we will see in Chapter 4, the behavior of those who are different from the observer is more likely to be called deviant than is the behavior of those who are similar to the observer. Finally, those who are defined as deviant—homosexuals, for example—are often viewed as different and deviant in other ways as well.

What may at first glance be thought of as being different in a *positive* way may be deviant on closer inspection. For example, being smart is highly valued in our society. Those with IQs above 160 are rare. Yet some children who are geniuses are laughed at, ridiculed, and picked on, just as are those who are "slow" or retarded. Thus, if what might seem to be a positive behavior or quality is treated in a negative way in a certain group, then within that group the supposedly positive quality or behavior is deviant (see Scarpitti and McFarlane, 1975, for a slightly different approach).

Sociologists' and Citizens' View of Deviance

Sociologists are not the only ones who use the terms "deviance" and "deviant." As members of the general public we all use these terms though perhaps we are more likely to use such terms as "weirdo," "loony," "pervert," "crazy," "sick," "pothead," and so on. How sociologists use the terms "deviance" and "deviant" may not be the same as how the general public uses the concepts. In fact, both among sociologists and among the general public there are likely to be different understandings of what is meant by "deviance" and "deviant." As sociologists, though, we must define our concepts in the ways which we think will be most useful for understanding the world around us, in this case the world of deviance. Sociological concepts are neither right nor wrong. Rather, they are more or less useful.

Asking the general public who and what they consider deviant will lead to a wide range of responses. In a survey of 180 people in the 1960s, Jerry Simmons (1965) found that homosexuals, drug addicts, liars, reckless drivers, atheists, career women, the retired, perpetual bridge players, liberals, conservatives, girls who wear make-up, know-it-all professors, and another 240 kinds of persons and acts were considered deviant. One could do the same survey today and no doubt arrive at a diverse range of responses. However, asking people who and what they think is deviant will only give us a partial sociological understanding of the phenomenon of deviance. Such questions may tell us how people use and understand the term "deviant," but they are not a very accurate way of determining which people and behaviors offend others in concrete situations or why they offend others. That, however, is what we mean by deviance in this book. Even if the general public used the term "deviant" just as it is used in this book, what people say and what they do are not always the same (Deutscher, 1973). While it can easily become confusing when people use the same terms but actually refer to different ideas (often without our realizing that at first), it is important to have as clear an understanding as possible of what we are studying. Deviance is that which offends us.

Deviance: An Integral Feature of Society

We often think of deviance as something only "those" people do; something that only touches our lives through the mass media. Nothing could be farther from the truth. We are all involved in some way. We are the ones who sign petitions, write our representatives, agitate for new standards and rules or for the reform of old ones. We are the ones who spot a robber, suspect that a child is blind, or fail to see that a friend is an alcoholic. We are the ones who do or do not report a deviant to the police, the mental health specialist, the doctor, our supervisor, or some other official. We are the ones who cheat, do drugs, steal, have "crazy" thoughts, break rules, are incompetent and unprepared, are physically disabled—in other words, who are deviant. We are the ones who hide what we do, rationalize it, join other offenders who are like-minded, and so on. As Jerry Simmons (1969, p. v) noted, when it comes to deviance, "there are no 'thems,' there is only us." Of course, this does not mean that we are all equally involved in all kinds of offensive behavior or in the phenomenon of deviance. Yet, we all are involved in some way.

The phenomenon of deviance is an *integral* feature of society. Deviance is not just found on the "lunatic" fringe of society. It is not confined to serious legal or moral violations. Rather, deviance is an important dimension of everyday life. It is everywhere in both dramatic and routine forms: in education, in government, in athletics, in the arts, on the street and in the home, among the affluent and among the poor. Even among saints some are singled out as sinners. The phenomenon of deviance is *pervasive*. Criminals are punished, but so are unruly students. There is corruption and cover-up in government and in big (and small) business. Recruiting violations occur in athletics and in the military. Church members are excommunicated because of their beliefs, but so are fraternity and sorority members. The pervasiveness of deviance will be explored throughout the book.

Deviance is an integral feature of society in another respect. Deviance and respectability are "flip sides" of the same coin (Douglas, 1970). We often know what is respectable or moral by contrasting it to what we consider deviant or immoral. Much of our concern about deviance is an expression of our concern about conventionality, respectability, morality. Deviance and respectability are tightly interwoven in our lives. Many of the important issues concerning deviance can be viewed, often should be viewed, in terms of respectability. We engage in respectable behavior, enforce respectable behavior, legislate respectable behavior, discipline others for not being respectable, give the impression of being respectable, and so on. However, most of us take respectability for granted and then focus on those who are deviant. One could turn the issue upside down, however, by asking, for example: Why do people engage in respectable behavior (Hirschi, 1969)?

There may be particular offensive behaviors and people which we would like to be rid of. There may even be a consensus about these offensive behaviors and people. However, the *phenomenon* of deviance is not like a cancerous sore, something alien to the body which needs to be cured or excised. Instead it is an integral part of society. The fact that we want to get rid of certain offensive behaviors is part of the phenomenon of deviance itself. And as we will discuss in Chapter 3, no society ever has been, nor does it seem possible for any future society to be, free of deviance. It is an essential part of our lives.

If deviance is an integral and essential feature of our lives, and if it is tightly interwoven with respectability, then our explanations of the phenomenon of deviance should also be explanations of the phenomenon of respectability. We should not need separate sets of concepts, hypotheses, and explanations in order to understand deviance and respectability. As Robert Scott (1969, p. 14) noted in his study of how visually impaired people become helpless, dependent, blind people; blind people "are made, and by the same processes of socialization that have made us all." Thus, understanding deviance necessarily means that we must understand respectability, and to understand respectability we must understand deviance.

Further, deviance has some important ties with other *subordinate* statuses. Homosexuals, women, and blacks all have relatively little power in society. All are restricted to some degree by other people's standards. Many people in society are antagonistic toward cultural minorities as well as toward deviants (Simmons, 1969). The disvalued, the disenfranchised, and the deviant are watched more closely by control agents than are others. Therefore, examining deviance may help us understand others who occupy subordinate statuses in society.

THE PROCESSES OF DEVIANCE

The phenomenon of deviance is dynamic, not static. It comprises the interrelated activities of many people. These activities concern various issues. As the following chapters explore in detail, we conceptualize the phenomenon of deviance as composed of several processes: *imagining* and *observing deviance; creating deviance; recognizing deviance* and *identifying deviants; dealing with deviance; becoming deviant;* and *deviants' coping with conventional society.*

We must be sensitive to the *multiple perspectives* of the many people involved in the processes of deviance. They play different roles and have different interests, ideas, and values. We should not deny the differences among the actors nor should we overlook their similarities. We need to understand the processes of deviance from the viewpoint of each of the participants. Therefore, a complete understanding of prostitution would take into account the perspectives of the prostitute, the patron, the pimp, the police, the public, and many other people. This need not mean that we sympathize or agree with their views, but only that we try to understand them (Matza, 1969, p. 18).

It is somewhat arbitrary to say that any one of these processes necessarily precedes or follows another in a fixed order. These processes are interrelated, occur simultaneously in various arenas, and at times are difficult to separate. But textbooks must be written in a sequence, one chapter after the next, even if social processes do not always follow that pattern. Nevertheless, by the end of the book the interrelatedness of these processes should be apparent.

Imagining and Observing Deviance

The general public and social scientists have long observed and attempted to understand deviance. Through their efforts, they have created images of deviance. The images of deviance involve four basic themes: pathology, differentiation, causality, and determinism. These four themes are played out in different ways, depending on whether a traditional, biological, psychodynamic, or sociological perspective is used. Our images of deviance lead us to observe it in certain ways. Our observations in turn may lead us to change our images. Therefore, our observations and images are interwoven features of our understanding of deviance. In fact, deviance only exists through our understanding of it and through the actions that we take based on that understanding. Our observations and images are continually being challenged and are changing. Some are refuted, new ones appear, and old ones may be dusted off and may reappear with a fresh coat of paint. Only through examining where we have been can we better know where we are and where we may be going in our understanding of deviance.

Creating Deviance

Deviance is neither absolute nor given, though people often treat it as such. Rather, deviance must be created. People develop standards, rules, and laws for what is appropriate or inappropriate behavior. How such "definitions of deviance" develop concerns us here. Further, deviance is created within cultural, historical, and social contexts. To take deviance out of those contexts is to distort it. Finally, when deviance is created, so too are mechanisms for dealing with deviance. Therefore the creation of deviance also involves the creation of social control.

Recognizing Deviance and Identifying Deviants

Before people can react to deviance, they must *recognize* deviant behavior and *identify* those who are deviant. We must discover who is doing what. Recognition of deviance involves ideas or conceptions of what deviance is like, its signs and symptoms, and acquiring information about a suspected case and then interpreting the information. Recognition of deviance is in many ways analogous to the medical diagnosis of an illness.

Once deviant behavior is recognized, how is it to be interpreted? What are the causes and motives for the deviance? Is the suspect a deviant person? One may commit a deviant act without being *identified* as deviant. Deviant behavior does not necessarily imply a deviant identity. Both recognition and identification occur not only within organizations that officially deal with deviants but also in everyday life.

Dealing with Deviance

When behavior or people are recognized as deviant, they are dealt with in some way. The deviant may be severely punished or "sympathetically" treated; given a warning or ignored; ostracized or dealt with in many other ways. Such reactions are part of social control. Yet social control is aimed not only at offenders. It takes many forms and serves many purposes. Much of it is designed to keep conventional people conventional (Buckner, 1971). We deal with deviance and deviants in different ways for various reasons. How we handle deviance has changed over the years. Although we all deal with deviance in our everyday lives, we have empowered certain people to handle deviance for us—police officers, mental health professionals, members of disciplinary boards, and so on. They are official agents of social control. Finally, our reactions to deviance are not merely responses to offensive behavior. They *emerge* within the interaction between the accusers and the accused.

Becoming Deviant

Becoming deviant is a gradual process of changing attitudes and behaviors. We will examine the basic approaches to understanding why people engage in deviance. Deviance can also be viewed as a *career:* a sequence of movements from one position to another in deviance (Becker, 1963). For most people deviance is episodic; it is engaged in only once or twice or only sporadically. For others it becomes a more regular activity. For some it becomes a way of life. Though some occupations are deviant—stripteasing or the job of a masseuse, for example—the career model of deviance is not limited just to work. Becoming and being gay, deaf, or a "failure" can also be viewed within a career model.

Deviants' Coping with Conventional Society

Deviants cope with the real, imagined, or potential reactions of others and of themselves. Through various strategies deviants confront their accusers, live with their deviant identity, or try to change their deviant status. Whether by coming together with other deviant people—for example, in self-help groups like Alcoholics Anonymous or in deviant communities like the deaf community—or by going it alone, deviants try to deal with conventional society. Deviants may struggle, sometimes successfully, to have their deviant behavior redefined as conventional or acceptable, and perhaps to have other behavior defined as deviant. If so, then we have returned to the creation of deviance.

An important feature of the phenomenon of deviance pertains to how social scientists (and the general public) conceptualize an issue. How we think about an issue leads us to ask some questions and ignore others. In the past several years sociologists have begun to realize that the phenomenon of deviance involves more than a discussion of why people engage in deviance or of different types of deviant behavior and people. An understanding of deviance also involves an examination of the interrelated activities of many people which make up the phenomenon of deviance (Hawkins and Tiedeman, 1975; Rubington and Weinberg, 1978; Schur, 1979; Pfuhl, 1980). Thus, this book is both an examination of the phenomenon of deviance as well as a small part of the phenomenon.

CONCLUSION

One of the primary benefits that a sociological imagination can provide is the ability to see old issues in new ways (Mills, 1959). A sociological imagination can liberate us from viewpoints which we have taken for granted for a long time without critically questioning them. Certainly the history of the study of deviance has been full of assumptions that went unexamined for much too long. Even those who are now critically questioning earlier assumptions and approaches have overlooked much themselves. No doubt we will too. Our sociological understanding is really just beginning. As a discipline, sociology is an infant compared to such well-established disciplines as mathematics or biology. Further, the task of sociology is enormously difficult. We wish to understand the social world—the world of people and their interaction with others. Yet that world is continually being created and changed by people. Or to put it another way, rocks do not think, talk, or act, but people do.

Therefore, in the following chapters we will examine issues without discussing everything one might want to know about the issue. Part of the incompleteness will be due to selectivity. We do not plan to cover "everything under the sun" in this book. Much of the incompleteness of our answers and explanations will be due to our incomplete understanding of deviance. It is very misleading to give the impression that sociologists, or anyone else for that matter, have all the answers, in this case all the answers about deviance. Clearly they do not, and the perceptive reader will soon recognize this. Thus, we will raise questions which we cannot answer to our satisfaction or, probably, to yours. Yet that is part of the challenge and the promise of understanding deviance. To raise important questions is a beginning, and often a much more difficult task than might be imagined. To try and understand the questions is the challenge and the reward of understanding deviance. To understand deviance is to better understand ourselves.

PROJECTS

1 Collect copies of recent textbooks on the sociology of deviance (hardback editions may not have the same covers as paperback editions). Compare the covers with the covers of textbooks in another area of sociology (e.g.,

introductory textbooks or sociology of the family) or in another field (e.g., chemistry). What similarities or differences do you notice? Ask friends to examine the covers of the deviance textbooks. You may want to cover up the title. What impression do the covers make on them? Ask them to speculate about what the books are about.

2 Ask a group of people what they consider to be bad, wrong, sick, immoral—in other words, offensive. Try to make them be specific. For example, if they think drinking is offensive, do they think so for all situations or only under certain circumstances? Can you check their words and deeds? Are different groups of people (e.g., young vs. old or teachers vs. students) offended by different behaviors? Note how many of the offensive behaviors are dramatic as compared to routine. Compare your results with your colleagues' results.

3 Outline the process of deviance in an everyday setting that you are interested in—for example, athletics, your dorm or fraternity or sorority, your office, and so on. Try to identify who the actors are and what the issues are concerning deviance in that setting. A particular incident, such as an athlete being kicked off a team, the blackballing of rushes for a fraternity or sorority, or a debate over new university regulations, could serve as the basis for your project. Use the outline as a reference point as you read through the following chapters. Fill in the outline with details and with your analysis as you learn more about the phenomenon of deviance and as you examine the selected everyday setting more thoroughly.

4 Examine the mass media for their presentation of deviance. You can examine newspapers (even your college newspaper), magazines, or TV newscasts. You might even examine talk shows, comedians' routines, or letters to the editor. Notice the kinds of stories presented (e.g., dramatic or routine), the slant used for the stories, the space or time devoted to them, where they are located in the newspaper or on the telecast, and so on. You might compare the media's presentation of deviance for different time periods. You could compare the same newspaper twenty years ago or even longer ago with today's paper. Or you could compare large newspapers with small ones, rural ones with urban ones, and so on. Do newspapers that present a great deal of dramatic or bizarre deviance have a large circulation? See if you can find out. Deviance is an integral feature of the mass media.

Chapter 2

Imagining and Observing Deviance

One hundred years ago people imagined that criminals were biologically inferior to noncriminals. Criminals were a throwback to an earlier stage of human development. They were atavists (Reid, 1979, pp. 136–138). Later, scientists believed that criminals and delinquents were feebleminded or that they had different body types. Those with a muscular body type, called "mesomorphic," were thought more likely to be delinquent than those with a skinny or fat type of body (Glueck and Glueck, 1956). In the past, the mentally ill have been viewed as possessed by the devil, the physically disabled as atoning for their parents' sins or their own sins, and (male) alcoholism as an expression of unconscious homosexuality (Davison and Neale, 1978, p. 250). Today, of course, we know better. Or do we?

Our understanding of deviance is an important part of the phenomenon of deviance. It needs to be investigated, just as do the issues presented in the other chapters in this book. It should not be taken for granted. Thus, this textbook is not just *about* the phenomenon of deviance, but in a very small way it is *part* of that phenomenon. Our understanding is a result of the interplay between our images and observations of deviance. It arises out of the many activities of people concerned with deviance. Our understanding must be created and recreated. Our understanding of deviance is not absolute or objective, even though we may treat it as if it were. It changes as our images and observations change. What was taken as understanding one hundred years ago or even ten years ago may be dismissed today as ignorance. Previous understandings may be seen as the result of perhaps well-intentioned, but misguided and poorly prepared, investigators who had their own biases to build on. On the other hand, some previous ideas may be seen as brilliant. No doubt the same may be said in the future about much of our present-day understanding of deviance.

To an important extent, deviance only exists through our images and observations. Deviance exists because for various reasons people are concerned about it. Ultimately that concern grows out of the desire to understand deviance. For example, prostitution exists through the images and ideas (i.e., the understanding) that patrons, pimps, the police, professionals (e.g., social scientists), and prostitutes themselves have about prostitution, as well as the activities of those people which are based on their images and ideas. Of course, the reasons for understanding prostitution and the activities based on that understanding may be quite different for the various concerned people. Prostitutes and pimps develop their understanding so that they can make a living with as few hassles as possible. The police develop their understanding so that they can control it better. Social scientists develop their understanding so that they can enlighten others, and so it goes. Where does that understanding come from? It comes from observation and reflection. It comes from the direct experience of police officers, from the advice of experienced hookers, from the research of social scientists. Thus, deviance exists through the activities of concerned people, and those activities reflect the images and observations of those people.

In this chapter we want to examine our images and observations of deviance, primarily our scientific images and observations. The images and observations of the general public will be investigated in Chapter 4. In order to fully understand deviance, we need to analyze our understandings of deviance. What are our understandings? How have they changed? In particular we want to examine various perspectives for understanding deviance: the *traditional, biological,* and *psychodynamic.* Dominant themes emerge in each of these perspectives. What are the themes? The sociological perspective, of course, makes up this book. While much of the traditional sociological view of deviance will be found in Chapter 7, we do not want to totally ignore it here. Instead, we will briefly show how the traditional sociological perspective is quite similar to the other three perspectives.

We are also interested in how images of deviance are created. Thus, we will examine research strategies through which social scientists have sought to understand deviance. These strategies, which have their counter-part in everyday observations, are part of the basis for our images of deviance. The strategies, like much else in deviance, are the source of conflict.

Finally, we want to explore the relationship between our images and observations of deviance. To some degree, a reciprocal relationship exists. Our images of deviance influence how and what we observe. In turn, we may modify or recreate our images of deviance based upon our recent observations. Robert Merton (1957) has urged sociologists to establish a reciprocal relationship between their theory about social life (i.e., images) and their research into it (i.e., observations). As we will examine later, however, there is no simple reciprocal relationship between our images and observations of deviance. At times our images are based on precious few observations or our observations are interpreted to fit our existing images. Similarly, our observations do not necessarily lead us to modify or abandon our images. Those images may be discarded due to a lack of interest rather than to observations which do not support the images. Nevertheless, our images and observations of deviance have influenced and continue to influence each other.

IMAGINING DEVIANCE

By "imagining" we do not mean that we create our understandings of deviance through "flights of fantasy." Some critics might argue, however, that our earlier as well as our present understandings of deviance could only be the result of such fanciful trips. We do not mean that our understanding is imaginary, false, or unreal. It is not make-believe except to the extent that all beliefs must be made. Instead, "imagining" denotes the creation of mental images or pictures, in this case, images of deviance. We use the term, as we use the terms in all the chapter headings, to emphasize the active involvement of people in the phenomenon of deviance. People are actively involved in creating their understanding of deviance, in imagining or constructing images of deviance.

Throughout the traditional, biological, and psychodynamic perspec-tives for understanding deviance, four basic themes have emerged: *pathol-ogy, differentiation, causality,* and *determinism* (see Matza, 1969, chaps. 1–3, for a discussion of related issues in sociology). Deviance was seen as evidence of harmful, diseased, aberrant, or dangerous conditions. Devi-ance was like a cancerous sore on the body. It was an affliction. Because deviance was pathological, deviants were clearly different from normal, healthy, respectable members of society. Deviance set apart or differenti-ated the offensive from the conventional. Never shall the two meet. There were no similarities between them. In Chapter 4 we will discuss the everyday counterpart of differentiation when we examine one feature of stereotypes, disjunctiveness. If deviance was harmful to society, then how could we control it? That concern led to the emphasis on causality. Why do deviants do such offensive things? If we could answer that question, then perhaps we could better control deviance and deviants. We might be able to prevent it or to correct it. Questions of causality were typically answered with deterministic explanations. Each perspective and each specific approach within the various perspectives located the origin of deviant behavior in a particular force, condition, or event. These "prime movers" caused deviant behavior. They propelled people into deviance. It could hardly be otherwise. As we will mention throughout the book, people's active invovement with the world—their action, reaction, and interaction (Scarpitti and McFarlane, 1975)—tended to be overlooked. Instead, deviants were viewed as possessed or afflicted by some evil force which caused them to be offensive. Each perspective chose different evils.

Traditional Perspective

People are forever trying to understand the world around them. Understanding has not waited for the development of science and the pronouncements of scientists. Traditional sources of truth, such as religion, those in power, or common sense (folk wisdom), have been the basis for people's understandings of their complex world. These traditional perspectives include an understanding of deviance. Everyday views of deviance were and still are an integral part of people's views of the world around them, of themselves, and of others. These understandings are taken for granted and rarely questioned. They are obviously so. Such views influence the social scientist as well.

The traditional view of deviance, which for thousands of years was the primary understanding of deviance, has often involved a mystical or supernatural component. Deviance is intimately linked with evil forces or demonic possession. For example, in the New Testament, Jesus encountered a man who lived in the tombs. The man cried and cut himself with stones. His strength was so great that he broke the chains by which others tried to tame him. Jesus cast out the legion of devils from the man and sent them into a herd of swine which then ran violently into the sea and drowned. The man was miraculously restored to normal health (Mark 5:1–20). Similarly, in some North American Indian tribes, possession by the spirit of Wiitiko, a cannibalistic giant, was used to explain a male's homicidal, cannibalistic, "monsterlike" impulses. Gastric symptoms, such as loss of appetite, chronic nausea, and vomiting, were viewed as early signs of the spirit's invasion. Such individuals might ask to be killed immediately even though they had not yet expressed any cannibalistic behavior. Typically they were strangled and their bodies burned in order to prevent the escape of the evil spirit (Hallowell, 1959, pp. 38, 50).

Witches, of course, have been seen as important actors in the drama of deviance. Many social ills in Europe from the fifteenth century to the seventeenth century were blamed on witches, on those in league with the devil. Poor crops, leaky roofs, broken fences, high taxes, sick and dying children, and other calamities were blamed on witches. More than a half-million people were executed for "practicing" witchcraft. The major result of this witch craze, which we will examine from a different angle in the next chapter, was that the "poor came to believe that they were being victimized by witches and devils instead of princes and popes. . . . Preoccupied with the fantastic activities of these demons, the distraught, alienated, and pauperized masses blamed the rampant Devil instead of the corrupt clergy and the rapacious nobility" (Harris, 1974: pp. 237–238). Witches appeared again in Puritan Massachusetts in 1692 (Erikson, 1966). They appear among the Navaho of the southwestern United States. Any excessive behavior, such as too much prosperity or an attempt to acquire glory, was defined as a sign of witchcraft, and as elsewhere, witches were generally killed (Kluckhohn and Leighton, 1946).

Although mystical views of deviance are less prevalent today because of the development of science, they are not completely absent. Recently, Billy Graham (1979), a well-known and widely-traveled minister, claimed on a television talk show that "crime, moral degeneracy and widespread corruption are obviously evidence of forces of evil at work in the world today." Another religious spokesman explained that the mass suicide-homicide of more than 900 members of Jonestown in Guyana was due to the "demon possession" of their leader, Jim Jones (Pat Robertson, "700 Club," January 1979). The drama of deviance still centers even today on the contention between the forces of good and the forces of evil.

Less spectacular, but more pervasive, is our religious heritage of viewing offensive behavior as sin (Conrad and Schneider, 1980). Any sampling of sermons or religious books reveals a great deal of concern with a wide array of problems, such as adultery, alcohol and drug abuse, and corruption. Our moral orientations, which are derived from Judaic-Christian ethics, lead us to dichotomize the world into good and evil. Offensive behavior becomes sinful behavior.

Thus, in the traditional view of deviance, evil forces, spirits, or the devil take center stage. They are the causes of offensive behavior. Those possessed are different from those not possessed. And clearly the possessed are pathological.

The mystical, religious, or traditional perspective for understanding deviance reigned supreme for hundreds, if not thousands, of years. However, church authority and doctrine had to increasingly compete with the authority of the developing nation states in the sixteenth and seventeenth centuries. The church had to compete with the crown. As scientific thought became more well established, the traditional understanding of deviance declined. The traditional understandings have not disappeared, but they have strong competitors—competitors which have eclipsed them in the Western world.

Scientific approaches to understanding the world around us emerged as an alternative to the traditional or folk view of the world, in this case the view of deviance. Traditional views were seen as uncritical and unsophisticated. Scientific approaches were seen as objective. They were based on hard data, not personal opinion. They were self-correcting, not self-perpetuating. The continual formulation and checking of ideas through the research of many investigators made it possible to cast aside inadequate and unsupported ideas in favor of increasingly accurate understandings. Yet, there are interesting parallels between the scientific and traditional approaches to deviance. The four themes in our images of deviance—pathology, differentiation, causality, and determinism—appear in the scientific approaches as well. To a great extent, the scientific approaches have developed out of the traditional views of deviance.

BIOLOGICAL PERSPECTIVE

In the nineteenth century European and American social scientists became increasingly committed to developing their discipline by utilizing the same approach that was applied in the physical and natural sciences, such as physics, chemistry, and biology. Emile Durkheim (1966), a French sociologist of the late nineteenth and early twentieth century, spoke of *social facts*. Social facts were to be treated as "things" which were to be related to other social facts or things in order to understand the social world around us. According to Durkheim (1966, p. 27), "To treat phenomena as things is to treat them as data, and these constitute the point of departure of science." Social facts, like physical or biological events, were determined by specific forces. Then, as well as today, many social scientists have attempted to pattern their disciplines after the physical or natural sciences. The latter sciences have been developed over thousands or at least hundreds of years. They have widespread respectability. By paralleling the "hard" sciences, the social scientists hoped to increase respect for their own, much younger discipline.

Social scientists began to think of societies as biological organisms which were composed of interdependent parts, developed through various stages, and were susceptible to disease. Crime, mental illness, suicide, and other forms of aberrant behavior were viewed as pathological conditions in otherwise healthy organisms (Martindale, 1961, pp. 35–122). Social Darwinism became a popular view among both scientists and lay people in the late nineteenth century and early twentieth. According to this philosophy, the fittest people survived and thrived. Differences in wealth, power, or prestige, as well as racial differences, were attributed to biological superiority or inferiority (Hofstadter, 1955).

Within this context, biological approaches to understanding deviance were developed (Voss and Peterson, 1971, p. 6). Cesare Lombroso, a nineteenth-century Italian physician, is often called the "father of criminology," even though others interested in the systematic study of crime and deviance preceded him. As a prison physician he collected data on thousands of Italian prisoners. Based on his investigations, he concluded that criminals were a distinct type of people. They were biologically different from law-abiding citizens. Criminals were atavists, or throwbacks to an earlier stage in human development. They were biologically inferior. Since their brains were less developed, they were more primitive in their thoughts than conventional people. Their lack of development was the basis for their criminal behavior. Born criminals could be distinguished from others by physical characteristics or stigmata, such as a low, narrow forehead, large jaws and cheekbones, outstanding ears, hairiness, left-handedness, and excessively long arms. Lombroso initially estimated that almost all criminals were born criminals. Later, he revised his estimates downward as he began to take psychological and social factors into account. While he developed other categories of criminals, it was his biologically inferior born-criminal that received the greatest attention and criticism from others (Reid, 1979: 136–138).

One of Lombroso's leading critics was a British psychiatrist and philosopher, Charles Goring. Goring compared 3,000 English convicts with noncriminals, such as college students, hospital patients, and soldiers. He found no differences in physical traits as enumerated by Lombroso. Although Goring rejected the idea of there being a distinct, physical, criminal type, he concluded that convicts were shorter, weighed less, and were more often characterized by "mental defectiveness" than noncriminals. Using statistical measures of correlation which were new at the time, Goring found a high degree of association between fathers and sons on physical features as well as on criminal behavior. He concluded that selective inbreeding led to inherited physical differences in the "criminal class" (Goring, 1913; Reid, 1979, pp. 140–142). Although Goring heavily criticized Lombroso, especially for his failure to be scientific, Goring was also working within a biological perspective.

Defective People   At the turn of the century American social scientists became concerned with social pathology. Crime, mental illness, drunkenness, laziness, and other social ills appeared to be on the increase. While the social pathologists were aware of the unsettling social changes that were taking place, such as industrialization, urbanization, and the arrival of millions of immigrants, they were less concerned with the effect of these changes on individuals than with the problem of "defective" people in society. While "bad" environments were recognized, the focus of the social scientists was on the individuals involved in crime, drunkenness, and other pathological activities. The concern was that defective people who caused problems would themselves produce more defective people who would create additional trouble for society (Smith, 1911, pp. 24–25; Neubeck, 1979, pp. 3–4).

This defective-people image of deviance was given support by the research of Henry Goddard. Goddard reconstructed the lineage of the Kallikak family. During the Revolutionary War Martin Kallikak, a young soldier from a respectable family, met a barmaid who was thought to be feebleminded. They had an illegitimate son whose 480 descendants included 143 who were feebleminded, 36 who were illegitimate, 33 who were sexually immoral, 24 who were alcoholics, 3 who were epileptic, 3 criminals, and 8 prostitutes. Following the war Martin Kallikak married a woman from a respectable family. Most of their 496 descendants were doctors, lawyers, educators—conventional, upstanding citizens. None were feebleminded or criminal (Goddard, 1912).

With the development of intelligence tests in the early 1900s, Goddard began a second study of the relationship between mental deficiency and crime and delinquency. After administering tests of intelligence to adults and juveniles in prisons and reformatories, Goddard (1920, p. 73) concluded that the "greatest single cause of delinquency and crime is low grade mentality, much of it within the limits of feeble-mindedness." Goddard had tested the residents of the New Jersey School for the Feeble Minded. No resident had a mental age over 13 years of age. Thus, he concluded that a mental age of 12 was the upper limit of feeblemindedness since only feebleminded people would be committed to an institution for the feeble-minded. Tests of criminals and delinquents by Goddard and others revealed that as high as 89 percent or as low as 28 percent, with a median of 70 percent, of incarcerated offenders were feebleminded (i.e., they scored below a mental age of 13) (Vold, 1958).

The intelligence testing of recruits during World War I led to the questioning of the relationship between feeblemindedness and crime and delinquency. Before this widespread intelligence testing, it had been assumed that a mental age of 16 was the average for the adult population. The median mental age of World War I draftees was slightly more than 13 years. Almost one-third scored below a mental age of 12. Incarcerated offenders differed only slightly from Army draftees in terms of intelligence. Did this mean that one-third of the draft army of World War I were feebleminded? Clearly not. Scientists had greatly overestimated the intelligence of the general population. However, it was only gradually that scientists abandoned the idea that feeblemindedness was related to crime and delinquency (Vold, 1958).

Edwin Sutherland, one of the most influential figures in the development of the sociological study of crime and delinquencey, was also an influential opponent of the view that illegal behavior and intelligence were related. In 1931 he severely criticized both the previous research and the "mental testers," claiming that they tried to outdo one another in finding a large percentage of delinquents to be feebleminded. While other reviewers of that early research, as well as of more recent research, found significant IQ differences between delinquents and the general population, Sutherland's conclusion became the standard position in sociology during the next five decades. Only recently have some sociologists again become interested in the relationship between intelligence and illegal behavior. The relationship is not seen as a simple one where "dumb people do dumb things." Instead, IQ may be linked to delinquency through its impact on performance in and adjustment to school. Nevertheless, Sutherland's opposition has been the dominant position among social scientists. Why? By opposing and then ignoring the possible relation between IQ and illegal behavior, sociologists were able to claim that crime and delinquency needed to be studied from their own still young perspective instead of the prevailing biological perspective, which was dominated by physicians. The presumed relationship between intelligence and illegal behavior was not dismissed solely because of a lack of evidence. Instead, it was refuted and then ignored in order to enhance the status of sociologists and their perspective concerning crime and delinquency (Hirschi and Hindelang, 1977). However, social scientists are not the only ones who have tried to "corner the market" in deviance. Today, medicine is increasingly taking a larger portion of deviance under its control, as we will see in the next chapter (Conrad and Schneider, 1980). Thus images of deviance are no more objective than is deviance itself.

The demise of the belief that illegal behavior was the result of low intelligence did not sound the death knell for the then widespread belief that hereditary factors were major contributors to the social problems in America. Social pathologists frequently suggested that various defective ethnic groups should be denied entry into the United States. Their efforts, as well as the efforts of others, resulted in the Immigration Act of 1924, which drastically reduced the entry of Poles, Jews, Italians, Greeks, Hungarians, and others who were considered to be "racial defectives" (Chase, 1977, pp. 138–175). More drastic measures also emerged to deal with biological sources of undesirable behavior. Harvard anthropologist Earnest Hooton (1939, p. 388) maintained that it was "impossible to improve or correct the environment to a point at which these flawed and degenerate human beings [i.e., criminals] will be able to succeed in honest competition." He recommended a program of eugenic sterilization as the most effective solution to the problem of crime. He was not the only one to recommend such action.

Sterilization was practiced in numerous state institutions even before such operations were authorized by law in twenty-six states. Since the turn of the century some 70,000 individuals have been involuntarily sterilized in the United States. The sterilization laws were aimed at the mentally ill, the mentally deficient, epileptics, and "hereditary criminals." Seven states permitted involuntary sterilization of sex offenders and "moral degenerates." In the late 1930s the superintendent of the Kansas Industrial School for Girls had sixty-two juveniles sterilized because of their insubordination (Kittrie, 1971, pp. 312–325). Since deviance was held to be biologically based, sterilization was viewed as an effective way to deal with it.

Continuing Search for Biological Clues Biological approaches for understanding deviance have not died. Like the other approaches, they continually reoccur in different guises. In the mid-1960s biological perspectives were rejuvenated by an interest in the possible connection between chromosome patterns and deviance. Each individual has twenty-three pairs of chromosomes in each cell of the body. One of the twenty-three pairs contains genes which determine the sexual characteristics of the individual. In women, this pair of chromosomes is termed an XX pair. Most males possess an XY pattern. The Y chromosome leads to masculine sexual characteristics. Although several different and atypical chromosome patterns have been discovered (e.g., XXY and XXYY males), the XYY or "super male" pattern stirred the most controversy.

The first XYY male, whose behavior and intelligence happened to be normal, was discovered in 1961. Shortly after this discovery some evidence was developed which seemed to link the XYY chromosome pattern with criminal behavior. Several criminal cases involving offenders with an XYY pattern received a great deal of publicity. It was used as a defense in criminal cases but without success. Subsequent investigations of several groups of prisoners revealed a small but unexpected percentage of inmates with atypical chromosome patterns. The XYY pattern was found in 3 percent of prison inmates as compared to only 0.15 percent of males in the general population (Fox, 1971, pp. 62–63). A review of a series of studies indicated, however, that XYY "super males" were not prone to violence or bizarre antisocial behavior. Some studies indicated that they were less aggressive than XY males (Sarbin and Miller, 1970, p. 199). Several criminologists have speculated that XYY males are overrepresented in prisons and mental hospitals because they tend to be relatively tall. Their size may work against them when they are dealt with by official agencies (Fox, 1971, p. 370). While the XYY chromosome pattern has received a great deal of attention, it does not have a major impact on crime. It occurs too rarely to help us understand much of criminal or deviant behavior (Gibbons, 1977, p. 150).

No doubt the search for biological clues to deviance will continue. Current interest in the relationship between brain chemistry and predisposition toward violence is evidence of this continuing search. Kenneth Clark, a past president of the American Psychiatric Association, recently suggested that an "advanced" development of the part of the brain associated with empathic feelings leads to altruistic and self-sacrificing behavior (like that of the late Martin Luther King, Jr.). However, those whose development of the empathic part of the brain has been stunted are perhaps most prone to callous or criminal behavior (Cory, 1979). Also, a recent investigator has concluded that certain kinds of sensory deprivation during infancy, such as a lack of touching or rocking by the mother, result in the impaired development of the system of nerves which influence centers in the brain associated with violence. Consequently, infants who are deprived of such stimulation "may have difficulty controlling violent impulses as adults" (Prescott, 1979, p. 124). The search for biological clues goes on.

These biological approaches to understanding deviance have been transformed into potential future systems for monitoring possibly troublesome people. Several "futuristic" social scientists have proposed systems of physiological monitoring and control of persons with "criminal tendencies." Electrical devices may be implanted in the brain to provide continuous surveillance and to block a criminal act through electronic stimulation of the brain (Ingraham and Smith, 1972). The advocates of "telemetry incapacitation" contend that these "techniques would remove the offender's ability to choose to harm others," but would not affect the performance of constructive activities (Lehtinen, 1979, p. 54). In any case, it is argued that incarceration is more limiting than this kind of electronic surveillance and control.

Psychodynamic Perspective

Both the traditional and the biological approaches locate the source of deviance within the individual offender, whether it be demonic possession or biological inferiority. While external influences, such as evil forces or selective inbreeding of defective people, are recognized as leading to these internal states of pathology, the focus is on the individual offender. This focus on locating the source of deviance within the individual is also found in numerous psychodynamic approaches to understanding deviance. Some form of psychological disturbance or personality maladjustment is seen as the important force in causing deviant behavior. While the environment may contribute to the producing of pathological mental states, it is the "sick" mental condition of the offender which is emphasized (Gibbons, 1977, p. 155). Offensive behavior is an expression of these psychological problems.

Psychodynamic approaches began to gain prominence in the United States about the time that feeblemindedness as an explanation for deviance began to be reevaluated. If criminals and delinquents were not less intelligent or biologically inferior to conventional citizens, then they

"must" be different and defective in some other way. Personality disturbances might be that way.

Freud's Psychoanalytic Approach   Perhaps the most influential statement on human behavior in general is Sigmund Freud's psychoanalytic
approach. The psychoanalytic approach, a specialty within psychiatry, has
had a pervasive influence on the images of deviance held by social scientists
as well as the general public (La Piere, 1959). Freud developed his theory
of personality from his work with upper-class Viennese patients in the late
nineteenth century. He contended that people are born with strong drives
concerning sex and aggression. Society's task is to control human nature by
either suppressing these drives or channeling them so that they will be
more appropriately expressed. Freud's emphasis on unconscious sexual
motivations shocked the citizens and scholars of Europe. Theories of social
evolution had convinced respectable people of their hereditary and moral
superiority. "Freud disturbed Europe's sleep by showing . . . that the
moral barrier between 'normal' and 'pathological' scarcely existed and that
the sexual underground was much higher than anyone was willing to
admit" (Collins and Makowsky, 1972, pp. 123–124). Despite initial public
ridicule and the defection of some colleagues in psychiatry, Freud's
psychoanalytic theory of personality was to become a cornerstone of many
of our ideas about offensive people and offensive behavior.

According to Freud, personalities are made up of three interacting
components. From birth and throughout life a basic component called the
id operates as a phenomenal "energy system." Our basic drives and
instincts are an expression of the id, which operates on the *pleasure
principle* (i.e., immediate gratification). Unrestrained expression of the id
is selfish, infantile, and insensitive to others. The *ego* develops in order to
mediate between the demands and limitations imposed by the environment
and the basic urges and drives to which the id attempts to give immediate
expression. The ego makes no moral judgments. It operates on a *reality
principle* in controlling and deciding how, when, and what drives and
instincts will be satisfied in order to minimize pain. The ego develops out of
the id's confrontation with the world about it. The last component of
personality is the *superego,* which begins to develop out of the ego in
childhood. The superego represents the moral values of parents and others
which are internalized by the individual. It is our conscience, though it is
not a conscious component of our personality. The superego is a "psychic
police officer" who lays down rules and punishes the ego for violating those
rules through shame, guilt, and anxiety (Bischof, 1964, pp. 44–47).

A healthy personality exists when the three components are in
harmony or balance with one another. However, that may not always be
the case. Deviance is viewed as the result of an imbalance or conflict
among the three components of personality. Deviance "may be the direct

expression of original urges; it may be symbolic expression of repressed desires; or it may be the result of an ego which has become maladjusted because of the conflicting forces exerted on it by the id and the superego" (Sutherland and Cressey, 1978. pp. 175).

A too dominant id might lead to aggressive, hedonistic, or callous behavior. An overly strong superego may create guilt feelings and anxiety about repressed urges. Thus, arson, armed robbery, and burglary may be due to unconscious sexual motivation (Fox, 1976, chap. 9; Revitch, 1978). Such offenses are thought to be *symbolic* behaviors substituted for the underlying instincts and conflict which have been repressed and cannot be given direct expression. Further, the offender leaves clues because of an unconscious desire to be caught and punished. The punishment becomes an atonement for the unconscious and repressed conflict and urges. It alleviates guilt and anxiety and at least momentarily restores the balance among the components of the personality (Vold, 1958). Thus, in a popular account of "Why Writers Plagiarize," one psychiatrist suggested that "deliberate theft" is an attempt "to get caught and be punished. It derives from lack of confidence, and a feeling that they don't deserve the success they are striving for" (*Newsweek,* November 3, 1980, p. 62).

Where does the conflict and personality disturbance come from? Mainly from a disturbed relationship between the child and its parents. This disturbed relationship leads to mental conflict, which is repressed initially, but is later expressed through offensive behavior. Thus, some investigators in the late 1930s and 1940s argued that alcoholism among males could be traced to an "overprotective mother" and was an expression of "unconscious homosexuality" and symbolic "self-destructiveness tendencies" (Davison and Neale, 1978, p. 250). Others argued that male alcoholism was due to insufficient mothering and was an expression of need for oral gratification and of latent homosexuality (Neubeck, 1979, p. 394). Similarly, some argued that the "violent sex assaultist is the product of a family pattern of repressive sexual notions, seductive mother-son interaction, or similar conditions" (Gibbons, 1977, p. 390). Male homosexuality has been attributed to a combination of mothers who are intimate with, but also rigidly control, their sons, and fathers who are hostile to, but detached from, their sons (Bieber et al., 1962). Thus, deviance is seen as a result of personality disturbances which arise out of inappropriate parent-child relationships.

The Search for Deviant Personalities   An outgrowth of the psychodynamic approach was the personality testing of criminals and delinquents to see if and how they differed from conventional people. In 1950, after a review of twenty-five years of such research, Karl Schuessler and Donald Cressey (1950), the later a former student and colleague of Sutherland, concluded that the research did not demonstrate that illegal behavior and personality elements were related. Their conclusion, like Sutherland's conclusion twenty years earlier concerning intelligence and illegal behavior, was aimed in part at establishing the importance of a distinctly sociological perspective for understanding crime and delinquency. Nevertheless, personality studies of offensive people continue.

The search for distinctive personality types which could explain involvement in deviance is expressed in the historical search for the "criminal mind." In the early 1900s, this search was characterized by such terms as "constitutional psychopathic inferiority" and "moral imbecility," which reflected the influence of a biological perspective for understanding deviance. By the 1940s and 1950s the terms "psychopathic" personality and "sociopathic" personality (the latter reflecting the influence of social factors) were used to refer to those who were insensitive to the feelings of others, did not learn from experience, were impulsive, felt no remorse after hurting someone, and were not deterred by punishment (Gibbons, 1977, pp. 172–173; Sutherland and Cressey, 1978, p. 162). They became "catch-all" terms which were applied to offenders engaged in repetitive or seemingly bizarre behavior or who did not respond to rehabilitation as society would have liked. In a recent historical review of the search for the criminal man, Ysabel Rennie (1978, p. 270) concludes: "It is time we gave a decent burial to the concept of Criminal Man. In the grave next to him we should inter the Dangerous Offender."

Still the search goes on. Based on fifteen years of research, Samuel Yochelson and Stanton E. Samenow (1976) conclude that a criminal personality is formed at an early age and is characterized by chronic lying, adamant unwillingness to change, and the mastery of self-justifications to account for criminal behavior. Those who possess a criminal personality cannot be rehabilitated, because rehabilitation assumes a return to a conventional style of life, but most people with criminal personalities never led a conventional life to which they could return. While hundreds of hours of voluntary therapy might enable a few to create a conventional personality, most may have to be confined for life.

Thus, psychodynamic approaches focused on personality disturbances in understanding offensive behavior. The four themes which we identified earlier—pathology, differentiation, causality, and determinism—are contained in the key element of this perspective, the sick or maladjusted personality. A sick personality is pathological. The terms "psychopath" and "sociopath" are extreme examples of that view. Disturbed personalities differentiate the sick from the healthy, and deviance is a result of these disturbances.

Parallels Among the Perspectives

While there are differences among the traditional, biological, and psychodynamic approaches, the parallels among them are striking. While each takes into account the environment in which the deviant lives, each ultimately locates deviance within the individual. Offensiveness resides within the individual and may appear at any time. The problem springs from some internal pathology, whether it be demonic possession, biological and physiological inferiority, or psychological disturbances. For example, in several criminal cases the XYY chromosome pattern has been offered as a defense (Reid, 1979, p. 153). The implication is clear: "The devil made me do it."

If the trouble lurks within the offender, then some form of either exorcism or containment is called for to cure or control the offender and the offense. Thus the devil may be exorcised, but if that is not possible, the possessed may be strangled and/or burned in order to prevent the evil spirit from escaping. If biological inferiority is the problem, exorcism will not work, but containment may, to ensure that others are not contaminated. Thus, we have a long history of involuntary sterilization of troublesome people. Or, the XYY "super male" becomes the object of a modern-day witch hunt in the suggested genetic screening of all male babies in order to identify those with a propensity for violence (Walzer et al., 1969). Psychoanalytic approaches attempt to make conscious a conflict which is unconscious. If the conflict can be brought out into the open, it can be dealt with by the patient. The parallel with exorcism is striking: take the source of pathology, which is hidden inside the offender, and bring it out into the open.

At times the approaches may be merged in order to deal with the deviant. Psychosurgery and electroshock therapy are prime examples of the intertwining of biological and psychodynamic attempts to understand and control deviance. Psychosurgery—for example, lobotomies—involves the surgical removal of parts of the brain associated with aggressive, compulsive, or uncontrollable behavior. Some 50,000 of these operations were performed in the United States between 1935 and 1955. Electroshock therapy, in which the patient's brain receives an electrical stimulation or shock, continues today, but on a reduced scale. Both were based on the rationale that they changed helpless, uncontrollable patients into cooperative, self-sufficient individuals who could live in the community. However, research on the effects of psychosurgery also revealed that the patient's capacity for abstract thought and planning, ambition, and conscience were damaged (Goldstein, 1950). The passivity induced by surgery apparently was intended not just for the patient's benefit, but also for the relief of the hospital staff (Kittrie, 1971, pp. 305–307).

Finally, each approach offers an explanation for society's lack of success in preventing, controlling, or correcting deviance. Each approach also absolves the respectable members of society from any part in the deviance. Because deviance is located within the individual, and because it is due to powerful forces of evil, biological inferiority, or deep-seated conflicts and disturbances, respectable members of society should prepare for the worst in dealing with deviance while they also try their best. It rarely occurred to respectable members that they were important actors in the drama of deviance with many roles to play. We will examine these roles throughout the book.

Sociological Approach

To a large extent the previous approaches to understanding deviance focus on the issue of causality. Why do offensive people act the way they do? Until recently the sociological approach also focused on causes. The major difference between the sociological approach and the other three concerned the relative emphasis on where the causes of deviance were located. The traditional, biological, and psychodynamic approaches ultimately located deviance within the individual offender, though the importance of the social world around the offender was recognized. The sociological approach focused on the social world in order to explain why some acted offensively. While the early social pathologists focused on defective people, later sociologists, in the first half of the twentieth century, strongly emphasized that causes of deviance resided in the social environment, but were manifested in individual, offensive behavior (Matza, 1969, pp. 45–49). We will wait until Chapter 7 to discuss the traditional sociological approaches to understanding deviance.

However, we do not want to give the impression that we have first discussed the traditional, biological, and psychodynamic approaches in order to criticize and debunk them in favor of the "obviously" superior sociological approach. In fact, sociologists have also worked with biological and psychodynamic perspectives, though they were not the major proponents of those perspectives. While we feel that sociologists have a great deal to offer in understanding deviance, the sociological approach also has its limitations.

The sociological approach has paralleled the other three perspectives. Until recently, the four themes of pathology, differentiation, causality, and determinism were also the bases for the sociological approach. American sociologists of the late nineteenth century and early twentieth century were predominantly from small-town, Protestant backgrounds. Many had been religious leaders, had considered religious vocations, or were sons of religious leaders (Gouldner, 1970). Consequently, behavior which departed from small-town Protestant morality was considered pathological. Further, much of the early sociological interest in troublesome behavior stemmed from its assumed relationship to changes in American society in the last half of the nineteenth century and early twentieth century. Industrialization, urbanization, and immigration were viewed as traumatic. Small-town, middle-class, Protestant life was being threatened by the rise of the big, boisterous, and often impersonal cities (Simmel, 1903; Wirth,

1938; Mills, 1943). City life was viewed as the breeding ground for social pathology. The poor lived in squalid tenements. Immigrants to the city often found it difficult to adjust to the new way of life. Children went unsupervised. Out of this unhealthy environment arose crime, delinquency, mental illness, and other pathological behavior (Shaw and McKay, 1942, 1969). Thus, pathological social environments produced pathological and offensive behavior. It was the quality of the social environment that differentiated conventional people from offensive people and determined who would become which. Gradually, during the 1950s, the term "deviance" replaced "social pathology," but the emphasis on the pathological and abnormal nature of deviance lingered.

Thus, in important ways the sociological approach has paralleled the traditional, biological, and psychodynamic perspectives. For example, just as there has been a call for genetic screening or physiological monitoring of potential deviants, so has there been the development of social scientific instruments for detecting "predelinquents" and programs to work with those so identified (Glueck and Glueck, 1959, 1972; Craig and Glick, 1963; Toby, 1965). In the past twenty years, however, sociologists have broadened their approach to understanding deviance. In doing so they have tried to move beyond the four pervasive themes in understanding deviance.

OBSERVING DEVIANCE

While our images of deviance may sometimes be based on pure speculation, they are also based to some degree on our observations of deviance. One of the hallmarks of the scientific method of investigation is to observe the phenomenon to be understood rather than merely to speculate about it. However, as Charles McCaghy (1976, p. 8) warns us, while the

> . . . use of scientific method appears superior to mere conjecture, methodology alone carries no assurance that truth is just around the corner. Inaccurate assumptions, misinterpretation and misapplication of findings, and intellectual arrogance can all conspire to make the . . . [scientific] approach not only misleading but dangerous.

We would add that for many people truth is just around the corner, but what is one person's truth need not be another's.

While we will concentrate on the observations of deviance made by scientists, the traditional approach has also been based on observations. There are similarities between scientific observations of deviance and everyday observations. Everyday observations, which themselves can be part of the phenomenon of deviance, will be explored in Chapter 4. Here, we want to describe the major modes used in observing deviance and then discuss the relationship between observing and imagining deviance.

Methods of Observation

Social scientists use many methods of observation for investigating phenomena, whether deviance or something else of interest. These methods of investigation include participant observation, questionnaires, laboratory experiments, in-depth interviews, and the analysis of official records (e.g., census data or business records). There are many ways of classifying the various methods of observation. A classic distinction is between qualitative research, such as participant observation, in-depth interviewing, and the analysis of historical records (e.g., diaries), and quantitative research, such as structured questionnaires and laboratory experiments which lead to the statistical manipulation of observations. Observational strategies are also sometimes classified on the basis of the degree of control or preprogramming versus the degree of flexibility (Douglas, 1976). Experiments, questionnaires, and polls are quite controlled. Informal interviews are fairly flexible. Researchers, of course, argue the merits of various approaches. Because this is not a textbook on research methodology, we will not explore all the various methods of observing a phenomenon.

The distinction between *official* and *unofficial* observations is important in investigating deviance. By official observations we mean those that are based on officially designated cases of deviance. An analysis of police, court, or prison records involves observations of officially recognized deviance. So does an examination of mental hospital records. Case studies of homosexuals or prostitutes who are patients of psychiatrists also involve observations of officially designated or identified deviants. Unofficial observations are those which are not confined to officially designated deviants or official cases of deviance. Field research into the gay community would be an unofficial observation of deviance, as would a self-report study of delinquent behavior among high school students, in-depth interviews with members of the general population concerning their sexual behaviors, or a survey of citizens of a community concerning mental health problems. As is probably obvious to most of us, though it was not so obvious thirty or more years ago, a great deal of deviance is hidden.

Changing Observations, Changing Images

During the first half of this century, social scientists primarily investigated deviance through official observations. It was not merely coincidental that these social scientists were using a traditional framework in conceptualizing deviance. Deviance was objective. It was obvious to all what was and what was not offensive. Official agencies, such as the police, courts, or mental hospitals, had the responsibility for dealing with offenders. Thus, whoever showed up in the official statistics were obviously offenders, and those who did not were clearly conventional members of society. Today, many of us may see that as somewhat naive. No doubt, though, future generations will criticize some of our assumptions and understanding as naive. Further, officially designated deviants were a captive audience. The researcher did not have to go to the trouble of rounding up people to investigate. The official agencies had already done that. Thus, for practical reasons as well, investigations of deviance were typically, though not totally, confined to official deviance and official statistics.

The Pervasiveness of Deviance   Gradually social scientists began to recognize that official observations of deviance overlooked a great deal of deviance. As early as the 1930s and 1940s investigators discovered that only a very small percentage of the offenses committed by urban, slum youth were reflected in police arrest records or court statistics (Robison, 1936; Murphy et al., 1946; Schwartz, 1946, pp. 157–181). These findings, however, were interpreted to mean that delinquency was a "way of life" for many youths in urban, slum areas. What could you expect of kids from disorganized areas? Slowly, though, the extent of hidden deviance was recognized, as self-report or questionnaire studies concerning crime, delinquency, mental illness, and sexual deviance were conducted, beginning in the 1940s and becoming widely used by the 1960s. The findings of these unofficial observations of deviance led social scientists to question the view that deviance was confined to those "nuts, sluts, and perverts" over "there." Instead, unofficial observations indicated that deviance was pervasive even among people who otherwise would be considered very conventional.

For example, self-report studies on juvenile delinquency indicated that almost all youths had been involved in illegal behavior, though some much more than others (Empey, 1978, p. 146). Similarly, the pioneering research in sexual behavior by Alfred Kinsey and his colleagues (1948, 1953) stunned American society. They found that 85 percent of all men had engaged in premarital intercourse, 70 percent had visited a prostitute, 90 percent had masturbated, 60 percent had engaged in heterosexual oral-genital sex, half had been adulterous, and more than one-third had some homosexual experience. Kinsey was not prepared for such findings. He (1948) noted that a call for a cleanup of sex offenders would mean that 5 percent of the male population would round up the other 95 percent. Nearly half of the women in Kinsey's 1953 survey had engaged in premarital intercourse, although for most their only partner had been their prospective husband. One-fourth had committed adultery, 60 percent had masturbated, 60 percent had engaged in heterosexual oral-genital sex, and 13 percent had some homosexual experience. Recent research corroborates Kinsey's observations of the widespread nature of what many conventional people would consider sexual deviance (Goode, 1978, pp. 313–321). Finally, interviews of citizens in various communities indicate that mental illness is not confined to the patients of mental hospitals. Interviews with a sample of New York City adults led researchers to conclude that only 18 percent were mentally healthy. Almost 25 percent were incapacitated or showed severe symptoms of mental illness. The remainder expressed moderate or mild symptoms of mental illness (Srole et al., 1962). Similar studies in other cities indicated that between 1 percent and 60 percent of the population had some mental health problems. The typical figure was 10 percent, though that may be a conservative figure (Neubeck, 1979, p. 329). Deviance was everywhere. It extended far beyond the boundaries of officially designated deviance.

Unofficial observations of deviance led researchers to question the assumption that deviant behavior was confined to a small segment of pathological or perverted people. Instead, social scientists began to realize that there was a continuum of deviance, with some people heavily involved and others lightly involved. There was no simple dichotomy between those who were offensive and those who were conventional, because many otherwise conventional people were involved in offensive activities.

Questioning Official Observations of Deviance   Social scientists began to question the meaning of official statistics. If official statistics were not a complete indication of deviance, then what were they an indication of? Gradually social scientists realized that official statistics and official designations of deviance are the result of many people's activities. They are a *social construction* (Pfuhl, 1980, pp. 97–118). Official statistics are "produced by *the actions taken by persons in the social system* which define, classify and record certain behaviors as deviant" (Kitsuse and Cicourel, 1963, p. 135). For example, prison statistics are the result not only of people who violate the law, but also of citizens who may or may not complain to the police, police officers who may arrest a suspect or handle the case informally, prosecuting attorneys who decide what charges to bring against the defendant, negotiations between the prosecuting and defense attorneys, judges who sentence the defendant, and, in a small percentage of cases, juries who decide the guilt or innocence of the defendant. All of these activities and more lead to prison statistics. The same can be said of other official records and officially designated deviants.

If official statistics are social constructions, what influences their construction? Social scientists as well as concerned citizens wondered whether officials were biased against the poor, against blacks, and against other segments of society. This concern predated the questioning of official statistics, but became heavily expressed when unofficial observations conflicted with official statistics. For example, suppose blacks were more likely to be arrested by the police even if they committed the same offenses as whites. If so, then official statistics not only overlooked a great deal of deviance, but also gave a distorted image of who was involved in deviance. The construction of official statistics involves recognition, identification, and reactions to deviance. Chapters 4 and 5 will help us understand what is involved in the social construction of official statistics on deviance. While neither chapter focuses on this issue, Chapter 4 explores how we recognize deviance and identify deviants, and Chapter 5 examines how we deal with deviance.

Official statistics are also the result of record-keeping activities. As these activities change, so may official statistics. Improved record-keeping may lead to a sharp increase in the official statistics. For example, following reforms in 1959 in Kansas City, its volume of crime increased 200 percent in two years (Glaser, 1978). Record-keeping may also be influenced by pressure upon the record-keepers. In 1969 the Nixon administration made Washington, D.C., its showcase for crime-control programs. A new police chief was hired who allegedly threatened to replace police commanders who could not reduce crime in their districts. A brief decline in the city's crime index occurred. At that time larceny over $50 was one of the crimes that constituted the crime index. The drop in the index may have been mainly due to the police recording as under $50 thefts which in the past would have been designated as over $50 and therefore part of the index (Seidman and Couzens, 1974). Thus record-keeping activities also influence the creation of official statistics.

A questioning of the official data also led social scientists to question their theories of deviance. If official statistics and official designations of deviance did not accurately reflect who was involved in offensive behavior, then theories about why people engaged in deviance that were based on the official observations of deviance might not be very useful. Theories which explained the offensive behavior of *captive audiences* of deviants may not usefully explain the offensive behavior of deviants in general, whether officially recognized or not. For example, if we find that juveniles who are incarcerated in state training schools are likely to come from broken homes, does this mean that broken homes lead to juvenile delinquency, or might it mean that juvenile court judges are more likely to incarcerate delinquents ("for their own good," of course) who come from broken homes? The latter seems to be the case (Sanders, 1976). Similarly, studies of homosexuals based on psychiatric case histories indicate that nearly 70 percent have been reared by "close-binding, intimate" mothers and by distant, hostile fathers who were dominated by their wives (Bieber et al., 1962, pp. 44–84). However, are homosexuals who go to psychiatrists representative of homosexuals who do not seek psychiatric help? If not, then theories of homosexual involvement which are based on the case histories of those who went to psychiatrists are probably not useful for explaining homosexual involvement in general.

As social scientists began to question the meaning of official statistics and officially designated deviation, they broadened their view of the phenomenon of deviance. They became interested in how officials deal with deviance. This concern, which developed out of the concern for how official statistics were constructed, became an issue of interest in its own right. How did officials and official agencies, such as the police or a mental hospital, operate? Further, what impact did arrest or commitment to a mental hospital have on the offender? Did it have the impact that was intended? Finally, social scientists began to question the theories which were based on official observations of deviance. They proposed revisions or new approaches which were based on unofficial observations. As observations changed, social scientists changed their images of deviance as well as the issues to be investigated.

If the use of official data fits well with the objectively given framework for understanding deviance, then the use of unofficial observations, and in particular of participant observations, fits well with the subjectively problematic approach (Kitsuse, 1972; Becker, 1974). Unofficial observations and field research allow the investigator to observe the phenomenon of deviance as it is constructed by the people involved, whether those people happen to be mental health officials, drug users, police officers, or delinquents. Such observational strategies allow the researcher to confront the full complexity of deviance rather than be limited to that which is officially presented for inspection. In connection with the causes of deviance, Howard Becker (1974, p. 52) notes that "It is easier to construct mythical wrongdoers, and give them whatever qualities go best with our hypothesized explanations, if we have only such fragments of fact as we might find in an official folder." Thus, while changing observations may lead to changing images, a change in perspective may support different observational strategies.

Who Are Delinquents?

Perhaps no other area concerning images and observations in the field of deviance is as full of controversy as the conflict over the social characteristics of juvenile delinquents. For two decades social scientists have argued that how we observe delinquency has a profound impact on our image of delinquency, in this case our image of who is and is not a juvenile delinquent. The controversy among social scientists centers on the apparent conflict in the images of delinquency presented by studies using official records versus self-report (i.e., unofficial) data. The two methods of observation seem to present different indications as to whether and in what way race and social class are related to involvement in juvenile delinquency. A discussion of this controversy will highlight our previous discussion of images and observations of deviance. This discussion illustrates that images and observations of deviance are dependent upon one another. It also illustrates that our images of deviance are a social construction, whether they are based on official statistics or unofficial observations. Either way, we construct our images and understanding of deviance.

For many years now we have realized that much delinquency goes undetected or unreported. Official statistics only "capture" part of the picture of delinquency. Perhaps more importantly, critics of official statistics argue that the image of delinquency that is based on official statistics is distorted. Critics claim that official statistics may tell us more about the activities of police officers and other officials than about who is involved in delinquency. In particular, the controversy centers on the relationship, if any, between race, social class, and, to a lesser extent, sex and delinquent behavior.

This is not an idle controversy. Various theories of or orientations about delinquency are based on particular images of delinquency, images which themselves are based on official and unofficial observations of delinquency. Criticism and research about how juveniles are handled by police and other juvenile justice officials stem from this controversy. The call for reform of the juvenile justice system is partially based on the assumption that the system is biased against certain segments of youth. This assumption of bias is based on the apparent conflict between the images of delinquency resulting from official as opposed to unofficial observations.

Put simply, research based on official statistics, such as police arrest records, has been interpreted as indicating that black youth are more heavily involved in delinquent behavior than white youth. This varies somewhat by the type of offense. Further, until recently social scientists tended to conclude that official statistics indicated an inverse relation between social class and delinquency. Lower-class juveniles were assumed to be more involved in delinquency than middle-class or upper-class youth (Hindelang et al., 1979; Elliot and Ageton, 1980).

Those who observe delinquency through self-report studies (e.g., a questionnaire, administered to students in a high school, which includes a list of delinquent activities to be checked off) question such images of delinquency. Many claim that self-report studies provide a more accurate indication of who commits delinquent offenses. Further, they claim that self-report studies question the relationship of race and social class with delinquency. They argue that self-report studies show that race is not as strongly related to delinquency as official data seem to indicate. Instead, the "overall *frequency* of law violation may be slightly higher for blacks than for whites, but if it is higher it is not much higher" (Empey, 1978, p. 158). According to self-report studies, social class is at best minimally related to delinquency (Tittle et al., 1978). Some researchers have found middle- and upper-class youth to be more delinquent than lower-class teenagers (Empey, 1978, p. 155). In summary, studies based on self-report studies suggest that race and social class are much less related to delinquency, if they are related at all, than is indicated by official observations of delinquency. Different observations produce different images—or do they?

Resolving the Discrepancy in Images of Delinquency?   Two recent studies attempt to explain the apparent discrepancy between the images of delinquency produced by official observations and unofficial observations (i.e., self-report measures). Michael Hindelang and his colleagues (1979) argue that there is only an illusion of difference between official and self-report measures of the social correlates of delinquency. They suggest that when thoughtfully used and interpreted, both ways of observing delinquency produce similar pictures of which juveniles are involved in illegal activities. The illusion of differences is due to several factors. Self-report studies tend to ask questions concerning involvement in less serious offenses, such as running away from home, skipping school, drinking beer, wine, or liquor, or taking things worth less than $2. Self-report studies have primarily tapped trivial offenses. The FBI's Uniform Crime Report, a compilation of statistics from law enforcement agencies throughout the country, includes information on what many people regard as the most serious offenses—murder, rape, robbery, assault, and so on—as well as less serious offenses. Thus, self-report researchers, primarily observing trivial offenses, are comparing their results to official data for serious offenses as well as some minor offenses. That would be like comparing apples and oranges—it cannot be done. Hindelang and his colleagues argue that official measures and self-report measures present similar images of the relationship between race and delinquency if the type of offense is taken into account. The few self-report studies that include some serious offenses in their checklists do show a racial difference. Black youth are more involved than white youth in serious offenses. These self-report findings have been partially overlooked because involvement in delinquency was not reported on an offense-by-offense basis, and instead total involvement in illegal activities, combining serious misconduct with less serious misbehavior, was reported. Conversely, official data for less serious offenses show few differences between black and white youth. For some less serious offenses, such as drinking violations, official data show a reverse trend—white youth are more involved than black youth. Thus the discrepancy between official and self-report measures is due to the fact that the two observational approaches tap different domains of delinquency. When they tap the same domains, they present similar images of delinquency.

The discrepancy concerning the relationship between social class and delinquency is also illusionary according to Hindelang and his associates. Global comparisons of involvement in delinquency for youth from different social classes are too crude for meaningful results. Comparisons for involvement in specific offenses would be appropriate, but as yet there has been no adequate research in this area. The comparisons which have been made between official and self-report measures of the relationship between social class and delinquency have been faulty. The data have been misinterpreted. Inappropriate statistical techniques have been used. Results have been overlooked. According to Hindelang and his colleagues, a reanalysis of previous studies does not show any significant differences between studies using official statistics and studies using self-report observations. Each method of observation generally indicates that social class is weakly related at best to involvement in delinquency. Thus, Hindelang and his colleagues conclude that the discrepancy in the images of delinquncy that has been attributed to our different observations of delinquency is illusory. Self-report studies need not contradict the findings of studies using official statistics. If used thoughtfully and carefully, official measures and self-report measures both provide valid and similar indications of who is involved in delinquent behavior. Yet didn't the earlier researchers believe that they were thoughtful and careful?

Delbert Elliott and Suzanne Ageton (1980) reconcile the apparent differences between the images of delinquency based on self-report and official measures in a way that is similar to that of Hindelang and his colleagues, though with slight differences. Elliott and Ageton suggest that self-report measures have been plagued by the trivial nature of the offenses included, by overlap among the items included (e.g., shoplifting is one item and theft under $5 is another), and by the limited or ambiguous responses available for the respondents to check (e.g., "often," "sometimes," or "three or more times"). Using small samples of students in one community can limit the generality of findings from self-report studies. Through their national youth survey with a new self-report measure of delinquency, Elliott and Ageton feel that they have overcome the unnecessary limitations of previous self-report research, limitations which led to the apparent discrepancy between self-report and official images of delinquency.

They find that race and class differences do exist for specific offenses. The differences are greatest at the high end of the frequency continuum. Youths between the ages of 11 and 17 were asked to indicate how many times during the past year they had committed various acts. This open-ended format allowed the researchers to discriminate better at the high end of the frequency continuum. Rather than lumping together all respondents who responded "three or more times," the researchers could differentiate between those involved in an offense a few times, eight times, twenty-three times and so on. Thus, there may be few differences between black and white youths, or between lower-class and middle-class youths, in the percentage who have committed a group of similar offenses, such as predatory crimes against persons, less than four times in a year, but relatively greater differences exist in the percentage who have committed more than thirty or even fifty such offenses in a year. Yet it is the most frequent offenders and the most serious offenders who are most likely to be arrested and therefore be included in official data. Consequently, while there may be race and class bias in how police or other officials handle juveniles, Elliott and Ageton argue that such bias cannot completely account for the differences between official and self-report images of delinquency. By including a wider range of offenses in self-report studies, and by being more precise in measuring the frequency of involvement in offenses, Elliott and Ageton conclude that self-report studies do present images of delinquency similar to those presented by official observations.

The controversy concerning the apparent discrepancy between images of delinquency based on official observations and those based on self-report observations illustrates the complex relation between images and observations. The controversy highlights the contention that our understanding of deviance is a social creation. It is a result of concerned people's investigative activities. Understanding is no more objective or absolute than is deviance itself. Some social scientists were eager to criticize officials and to argue that official observations were misleading but were less willing to recognize that their own unofficial observations were also a social construction. Being liberal and taking an "underdog" perspective, social scientists were much more willing to accept an image of delinquency in which race and social class did not have much of an impact than to accept an image in which race and class made a difference (Cohen, 1955, p. 42). Thus, they uncritically embraced self-report studies. No doubt, however, the latest contention that self-report studies and official measures can lead to similar images of delinquency is only the most recent shot in the continuing conflict over official versus unofficial observations. This controversy foreshadows the conflict and controversy which is an integral feature of deviance and which we will discuss throughout the book.

To return to our initial question: who is involved in delinquency? All we can say is that the answer depends on how you observe the issue and interpret the results. Even Elliott and Ageton, who support Hindelang and his colleagues in reconciling the apparent differences between official and self-report measures, contend that social class is related to delinquency. Hindelang and his colleagues found no evidence for more than a minimal relationship at best. Our interpretation is that social class and race are related to delinquent behavior, but not in any simple way. More importantly, we feel that merely looking at the social characteristics that correlate with delinquency is of limited use. Our discussion in Chapter 6 should help explain why. The drama continues.

CONCLUSION

Our understanding of deviance is created. Many of us take this understanding, this "textbook knowledge," for granted. It is something to be learned. Maybe it is even helpful. Where it came from, though, is rarely seriously considered. Yet, isn't the creation of understanding, especially in so sensitive an area as deviance, important to examine in its own right? Based on our understanding of deviance we engage in various activities. Different understandings may lead to different activities. For example, the search for causes of deviance has been a practical one. It is ultimately aimed at developing better ways of preventing, controlling, or correcting deviants. Different understandings of the causes of deviance may lead to different strategies. But how are our understandings of deviance created? While much more research is needed, we know that images and observations of deviance are related to one another. Based on observations we create images. Based on our images we may make new observations. And based on our new observations we may alter our images. However, images and observations do not determine each other.

In the preceding pages we examined three major perspectives for understanding deviance: the traditional, biological, and psychodynamic. Each of those approaches is based on four common themes: pathology, differentiation, causality, and determinism. Until recently, the sociological approach paralleled the others. It too was based on these four themes. The primary difference between the sociological approach and the other three was that sociologists put the main emphasis on locating the causes of deviance in the social world within which the offender lived rather than within the offender.

We also explored our observations of deviance. While research strategies can be classified in many ways, the distinction between official and unofficial observations of deviance is an important one for the creation of our understanding of deviance. The recognition of the possible limitations of official observations, and the subsequent use of unofficial observations, led social scientists to question previous images of deviance as well as to broaden their view of the important issues in the phenomenon of deviance. Unofficial observations of deviance, however, do not necessarily guarantee any better than official observations that useful images of deviance are developed. *All* observations are the result of the ongoing activities of the observers. How observations are constructed, why they are constructed, and the implications of their use for our understanding of deviance need to be examined. These issues should not be taken for granted, because ultimately deviance exists in our understanding of it and in the activities we engage in which are based on that understanding, whether we happen to be police officers, concerned citizens, or social scientists.

PROJECTS

1 Our images of deviance are not static. They are changed, reworked, abandoned, and then sometimes dusted off again after receiving a fresh coat of paint. Our images also vary depending on the perspective we use. Pick a particular

form of deviance, such as mental illness, homosexuality, drug use, or perhaps a more routine or mundane type. Trace our changing images of that deviance within one particular perspective—its nature and its causes. You can trace the changing images by examining scholarly works (textbooks might be one type of scholarly work) or popular works, such as magazines and newspaper articles. You might pick a *few* works from the 1970s, 1950s, 1930s, and so on. How have those images varied? How have they remained similar? Or, compare images of your selected kind of deviance which are presented by different perspectives during the same time period.

2   We develop our images of deviance at least partially out of our observations of deviance. Different observations may lead to different images. Conduct a self-report study of deviant behavior in your class. On the anonymous questionnaire also ask whether the respondents have ever been *officially* designated as deviant (e.g., arrested, suspended, and so on) for the behaviors they committed. Asking respondents whether they have ever been officially designated deviant is a time-saving and less cumbersome (as well as potentially less accurate) way of attaining official observations. Compare your unofficial and official observations of deviance. How are they similiar and how are they different? Various modifications of this project which are more involved, more time-consuming, and perhaps more challenging can be developed.

Chapter 3

Creating Deviance

Both lay people and social scientists have traditionally viewed deviance as absolute and objective. Deviance was inherent in the very nature of the behaviors that were called bad, disgusting, or perverted. Since the 1960s social scientists have begun to emphasize, though certainly some realized it earlier, that *definitions of deviance*—rules, regulations, laws, or common understandings—are created through the activities of people. Deviance does not inhere in the behavior which is offensive. Rather it adheres to the behavior through people's actions. As we noted in Chapter 1, "social groups create deviance by making the rules whose infraction constitutes deviance" (Becker, 1963, p. 9). In the past twenty years social scientists have become increasingly interested in how standards of respectability, and conversely notions of deviance, are created. Much of this research has been addressed toward the creation of criminal law. William Chambliss (1974, p. 7) notes that it is now generally recognized that the "starting point for the systematic study of crime is *not* to ask why some people become criminal while others do not, but to ask first why is it that some acts become defined as criminal while others do not." This perspective, as well as the research into the establishment of criminal law, can be applied to the creation of deviance in general.

If definitions of deviance are not absolute, how do they vary? What is the context within which deviance is created? What is the basis for defining some behavior as respectable and other behavior as deviant? Will differentiation between good and bad ever be absent from any society? How do social scientists view the construction of deviance? What models or perspectives do they use in trying to understand the defining and redefining of deviance? Our understanding of the creation of deviance is itself a creation resulting from the activities of social scientists. Since deviance is that which offends people, it is likely that people will do something about deviance. As we will see in Chapter 5, deviance is dealt with in various ways. But who is to deal with deviance? In our complex society only certain people and agencies are charged with the responsibility of dealing with deviance. Different agencies and institutions are empowered to deal with different kinds of deviance. Thus, the creation of deviance also implies the creation of social control. These are the questions and issues which we will pursue in this chapter.

THE CONTEXTS OF DEVIANCE

As we noted in Chapter 1, deviance is relative. It varies from one context to another. Standards of respectability are not absolute (i.e., unchanging), even if some of us talk as if they were and wished that they were. According to Erich Goode (1978, pp. 32–36), there are three broad types of relativity: *audience, actor,* and *situational.* Another way of stating it is that the audience, the actor, and the situation are three key features of the context within which deviance is defined. As each varies, so may the standards of respectability and the definitions of deviance.

Audience

We defined deviance in Chapter 1 as a behavior, an idea, or an attribute which offends others. Those others are the audience. They are the observers who sit in judgment on the respectability of people's activities. As audiences vary, so will their standards of respectability. Audiences can be composed of *individual* observers, groups or *subcultures* of people, or a *society.* The audience's standards may vary over time. Thus the *historical* context of the audience becomes important as well.

What is considered offensive may vary from individual to individual. One person may be offended by the use of certain words (i.e., cuss words or "dirty" language), whereas another may not even notice them. A manager in one store may allow the employees to dress however they please (within "limits"), but another manager may require employees to dress according to a particular code. A few years ago the new owner of a once-powerful baseball team set standards for the personal grooming of his players as one small way of rebuilding a winning tradition. To give another example, some parents may be upset if their children behave in a certain way, whereas other parents may consider the same kind of behavior harmless. Individual variation does not just concern the mundane and the routine. Witness the very heated disagreements over abortion, the use of marijuana and other drugs, and income tax cheating.

The observer, of course, can also be the individual who is involved in the possibly deviant behavior. Those involved in deviance may or may not find their own behavior offensive. As we will explore in Chapter 7, many do see their behavior as offensive. They feel ashamed or guilty about what they have done or only anticipate doing. Consequently, they engage in deviance only a few times and then give it up. Those who become more regularly involved in deviance must manage such feelings of shame. They are likely to change their views concerning the offensiveness of their activities.

Audiences may also be conceptualized as groups or subcultures of individuals who share to some degree a general orientation about the world. Part of that orientation consists of standards of respectability. Social-class or ethnic differences in deviance are a reflection of subcultural variation. In this regard, Ruth Cavan (1961) has indicated that degrees of tolerance for juvenile behavior vary by social class. Similarly, Jane Mercer (1973) suggests that definitions of mental retardation vary from one subculture to another. What middle-class whites may consider mental retardation is likely to be quite different from what lower-class blacks or Mexican-Americans consider retardation. Regional variations within a country often reflect subcultural differences. For example, until recently a small town in Oklahoma banned public dancing within the city limits. The new ordinance, however, is still quite strict. License fees ranging from $300 to $500 are required, and no dance hall can be located within 300 feet of an establishment which sells alcohol or within 500 feet of a church, school, or residential neighborhood where more than half of the residents object (United Press International, 1979). The city's new ordinance does not make it a libertine town, though no doubt some citizens became upset at the decline of public morality. Morality, however, varies from group to group.

Groups and subcultures bound together create societies. What is acceptable within one society may not be in another. In many African tribes women carry out their everyday activities nude from the waist up. A popular magazine seems to have capitalized on that fact. In American society such attire, or lack of it, would be both outrageous and crowd-drawing. In the same vein, public nude bathing has long been accepted in certain coastal areas of France, but is still relatively limited and meets with a great deal of opposition in America (Douglas et al., 1977). Similarly, while premarital and to a lesser degree extramarital sex is relatively commonplace in America (Goode, 1978, pp. 314–316), in 1977, a Saudi

Arabian princess and her lover were executed for wanting to live together. Further, a British television program on the incident in 1980 caused a diplomatic incident between Saudi Arabia and Great Britain. Several weeks later, a few public broadcasting stations in America decided not to televise it. Societies also vary in regard to their concern about drug use. For example, Paul McCartney of Beatle fame claimed that his drug bust in Japan in 1980 was due to his subscribing to America's now relaxed attitude about marijuana. He did not realize that Japan was so strict. Moreover, in some societies self-destructive behavior, such as suicide, is not considered deviant (Edgerton, 1976, p. 43). Thus, deviance and respectability vary from society to society.

Finally, the judgments of audiences are likely to change over time. What is considered deviant today may not be tomorrow, and vice versa. The changing laws concerning the use of drugs, and in particular marijuana, are testimony to the historical context within which deviance is defined. Before and during the Civil War, as well as at the turn of the century, opiate use was widespread and tolerated (Edgerton, 1976). However, as recently as the early 1970s, users in some states were given harsh penalties if convicted of marijuana use. Now marijuana use is being increasingly decriminalized. In many jurisdictions, the possession of under an ounce results in nothing more serious than a penalty similar to a traffic ticket. More than half the states have legalized the use of marijuana for medical or research purposes. To cite another example, forty years ago women's swim suits typically covered everything from their shoulders to their knees. Uncovering a knee in public was shocking, and the "flapper" bathing suits of the 1920s, even though they still covered the thighs, were scandalous (Douglas et al, 1977, p. 27). Today, of course, knees and thighs are not the only parts of the body which are bared at the beach. Deviance is continually being defined and redefined.

Actors

The context within which deviance is defined also includes the actors who are involved in the possibly deviant behavior. What offends us varies according to who is engaging in the activity. What might be offensive if committed by one actor may be seen as quite ordinary if committed by another. Thus parents have traditionally had the right to punish their children. Such punishment has often been quite harsh. As we will see later in the chapter, the historical context of parental treatment of children has changed as notions of child abuse slowly emerged in the 1950s and 1960s (Pfohl, 1977). Children's "punishing" their parents (e.g., striking them, hitting them, or talking back to them), though, is quite another matter. Such behavior is grounds for disciplinary action and in some cases might lead to incarceration in a state training school for juveniles. Similarly, babies are expected to babble, but adults who do so are likely to be viewed as mad. Women are allowed, and in some contexts required, to wear skirts, though many fewer do nowadays than in the past. Men who wear skirts, however, may be viewed as transvestites or strange, unless you are in Scotland (which is an indication of the societal context of deviance). Conversely, for a long time it was disreputable for women to smoke, though that is certainly changing.

We often assume that those with higher status or more resources can "get away" with more than those with less status or fewer resources. If this is true, it could be the result of two factors. Different standards may exist for those in high places or we may react differently (i.e., less harshly) to offensive people in high places. The latter possibility will be examined in Chapter 5. Here, we are concerned with the former. Social psychological theorizing suggests that those with high status, either through contributing to the focal concerns of the group or through possession of characteristics which are routinely valued outside of the group, can draw on an "idiosyncrasy credit" in order to behave in ways which would not be sanctioned if engaged in by members with little status or credit (Hollander, 1958). However, we do not necessarily create more lax standards for those with high status. Officers in the armed services can be court-martialed for fraternizing with enlisted personnel, whereas male and female enlisted personnel who fraternize with each other cause much less concern for the military (Bryant, 1979, pp. 149–156). Priests who drink too much are more likely to offend us than construction workers who drink too much. Thus our definitions of deviance vary according to the actor, but not in a simplistic way.

Situation

Finally, the situation or circumstances within which people act influences whether observers are offended or not. Drinking alcoholic beverages in a bar or restaurant is to be expected. Drinking in a classroom or in a church (except for certain ceremonies which entail a different set of circumstances) may be quite offensive to others and grounds for dismissal from both places. Being nude in private is no one's business, but public nudity often becomes everyone's business. The distinction between public and private behavior is important for understanding standards of respectability and deviance (Stinchcombe, 1963). A great deal of behavior that is acceptable when conducted in private becomes offensive or illegal if carried out in public. Further, as we will see in Chapter 4, whether people have access to private places or not is important in who will be recognized as deviant. Circumstances can legitimize what would otherwise be deviant. Killing during war may lead to a hero's medal. Killing a family in cold blood may lead to the electric chair. Thus, situations provide the framework within which people structure their interactions with others. Those who jeopardize or disturb the framework are often viewed as deviant.

Deviance can only be understood in a social context, but the social context varies according to the observers, the actors, and the situation. As far as we know, there is no behavior that has been universally condemned by all people, at all times, and in any situation when engaged in by anyone. Any activity is respectable or has been respectable depending on the context within which it occurs or occurred. Conversely, any activity can be offensive depending on the context in which it takes place. Deviance is created in specific contexts. But why and how? To those issues we now turn our attention.

DIFFERENTIATION AND DEVIANCE

In our everyday life we continually create differences among the objects in our environment: among people, behaviors, beliefs, and so on. These differences are indicated by the words we use to name them. We are likely to consider the differences important, otherwise we would not have named them, and we will educate the next generation of people about them. To take a mundane example, we have differentiated the color spectrum into colors that we call purple, blue, green, yellow, orange, red, and so on. Other societies may differentiate the color spectrum differently. For example, some societies only differentiate between the blue-green end of the spectrum and the red-orange end (Brown, 1965, p. 315). In the Philippine Islands, the Hanunóo name ninety-two varieties of rice. To us, those varieties would all simply be rice (Brown, 1965, p. 317). Closer to home, many people see sociology as just sociology, but sociologists differentiate many important specialities and approaches within the total field and endlessly debate their relative merits. To modify an old saying, a rose is not just a rose is not just a rose to aficionados of flowers. In myriad ways we differentiate the world about us. We create heterogeneity. Edwin Schur (1979, pp. 48 ff.) calls this practice the "urge to differentiate." An urge sounds very biological, as if it were an instinct. We would simply say that in living our lives we create differences among that which we encounter in our environment.

What is differentiation based on? Why do the Hanunóo create ninety-two varieties of rice, while most Americans are satisfied to name all of those varieties merely rice? Roger Brown (1965, p. 317) suggests that "cognitive domains that are close up are more differentiated than are remote domains." The areas of life that are more central to us are likely to be more differentiated than those that are peripheral. Rice is a staple among the Hanunóo, and thus small differences among varieties become important to them. To someone with little interest, a baseball player is just a baseball player. To the avid fan, and even more so to managers, coaches, and owners, baseball players are differentiated into the positions they play, the type of hitter they are, how well they field, what situations they are most effective in, and so on. Or, to give an example from deviance, to many of us mental illness is just plain craziness. Some of us may use terms like "neurotic," "psychotic," and "schizophrenic" without really understanding what they mean. To psychiatrists and psychologists fine distinctions among forms of mental illness are quite important, and thus diagnosis of the illness may be debated.

As distinctions are made, specialists and "experts" proliferate to deal with the increasing differentiation and complexity. This occurs in the sphere of respectability as well as deviance. Witness the specializations among professors at a university or among medical personnel. Within the field of deviance there are law enforcement officers, psychologists, psychiatrists, counselors, social workers, and so on (with, of course, many specialists in each area). These experts develop an interest in preserving the differentiations because in large part their livelihood depends on them.

Thus, the differences which we create arise out of the context of our everyday lives. However, we do not create differences and simply leave it there. Instead, we typically *evaluate* the differences. We evaluate them in terms of how costly, efficient, beautiful, powerful, threatening, and so on, they are. Evaluation implies worth. We attach more or less worth to the differences that we create. We call some of the differences with high worth "good," "moral," or "respectable." Others, to which we assign little worth, may be called "bad," "wrong," or "deviant." We share these evaluations with each other to various degrees. Remember the context within which deviance varies. They are established in rules and laws. They are taught to succeeding generations. Yet they are also changing, as we have seen, and as we will see in this chapter and later. The evaluation of differences is thus the basis for the creation of deviance. What underlies such evaluations is not completely clear, but we will take that issue up later in the chapter.

UNIVERSALITY OF DEVIANCE

If we continually create differences and then evaluate them, and if the evaluation of differences is the basis for definitions of deviance, then is it possible for a society not to have deviance? Several sociologists have answered no. The phenomenon of deviance is universal. Human beings will always regard some behaviors, beliefs, or attributes as wrong. Humans will always be offended by something.

According to Emile Durkheim (1966), we will always have a category of acts that we call crime. If we do away with crime as it is presently defined, then we will elevate what used to be considered trivial offenses or bad taste to the level of serious offenses, of crimes. Durkheim (1966, p. 67) argued that crimes are those behaviors which offend "certain very strong collective sentiments." By collective sentiments, he meant the basic values and beliefs of a group. Criminal behavior, he said, results from the actions of individuals who do not firmly believe in the community's collective sentiments. Durkheim argued that if there were no murders, for example, this would mean that the collective sentiment throughout the community, and particularly among those most likely to murder, must have grown stronger. Collective sentiments govern our behavior. However, if the sentiments related to murder grow stronger, those related to more trivial offenses will grow stronger too. Thus, what may have simply been considered bad taste in the past will now be considered a criminal offense. Society's standards have become stricter. As Durkheim (1966, p. 68) suggested concerning theft and the sentiments related to it:

> If this sentiment grows stronger, to the point of silencing in all consciousness the inclination which disposes man to steal, he will become more sensitive to the offenses which, until then, touched him but lightly. He will react against them, then, with more energy.

No matter how morally upstanding a community is, according to Durkheim, it will always evaluate some behaviors as offensive. While no one in its midst may murder or rob, the morally upright community will be outraged at behavior that other communities consider trivial. Even among saints there will be sin, but what is a sin among saints will be much less scandalous or even barely noticed among ordinary citizens (Durkheim, 1966, pp. 68–69).

From a slightly different standpoint, Jack Douglas (1970) argues that deviance is also universal. How do we recognize what is good, moral, or respectable? We recognize it because it is *not* evil, immoral, or deviant. These basic categories with which we evaluate ourselves and others are interdependent. In Western society, at least, neither seems able to exist without the other. It is by the contrast to what offends us that we know what pleases us. As Kai Erikson (1964, p. 15) notes, deviants inform us of "what shapes the devil can assume," and in doing so, they show "us the difference between the inside of the group and the outside." Thus, even if we "eradicate our present evils, we will simply construct new ones" (Douglas, 1970, p. 5). We "need" deviance in order to establish our own moral worth in contrast to those who are unworthy. Though some may wish that it were not so, we gain in worth to the extent that others lose, and vice versa. To the extent that we downgrade others by placing them in the unworthy category of deviant, we upgrade ourselves in contrast. Thus, not only are notions of respectability dependent on ideas of deviance, but our own worth is dependent on the lack of worth of deviants. Or as Barry Adam (1978, p. 42) notes, deviants serve as a "*foil* to ideals of health and the good." Consequently, deviance will always be with us.

In this regard, Kenneth Gergen (1972, p. 33) suggests that "we need slobs." In a "Mr. Dirty, Mr. Clean" experiment, male applicants for a summer job were seated alone in a conference room. After the applicant began working on a battery of forms and tests, one of which was a self-evaluation questionnaire, another applicant was sent in. The second applicant was actually a confederate of the experimenter. In half of the cases the confederate was "Mr. Clean," a striking figure in a well-tailored business suit and gleaming shoes, with an attaché case from which he took a dozen sharpened pencils and a book on Plato. In the other cases the confederate was "Mr. Dirty," dressed in a torn sweatshirt and pants torn off at the knees, with a day's growth of beard, no pencils, and a popular paperback, *The Carpetbaggers*. What were the results? Mr. Clean produced a sharp drop in self-esteem among the applicants. They felt sloppy, stupid, and inferior in contrast. However, "Mr. Dirty" gave the applicants a moral lift. Applicants felt more handsome, confident, and optimistic. Says Gergen (1972, p. 35): "We might conclude that the slobs of the world do a great favor for those around them: They raise self-esteem."

THE CONSTRUCTION OF DEVIANCE

As social scientists have become interested in the creation of rules, laws, or definitions of deviance, they have developed various approaches or models for explaining the construction of deviance. Most of the research and the perspectives have been aimed at explaining the creation of criminal law (See Berk et al., 1977, chap. 1, for a succinct overview). Clearly, many expressions of deviance are not embodied in criminal law. Thus, social scientists need to broaden their investigation in the future.

We will not examine all of the various approaches. Instead, we will focus on two dominant themes in explaining the creation of deviance: the *consensus* approach and the *conflict* approach. Nowadays, the latter approach has received the greatest attention from social scientists. In examining it, we will discuss several related and more specialized approaches which in various ways spell out the possible nature of the conflict leading to the creation of deviance.

Consensus

Put simply, the consensus approach suggests that rules, laws, and definitions of deviance are the reflection of widespread agreement (i.e., consensus) among the members of society as to what is appropriate or inappropriate. People are assumed to have basically the same values and beliefs. Thus Chambliss (1974, p. 34) notes that until recently both legal and social science thought focused on five models of law creation. Three of the five approaches can be subsumed under a consensus approach. Laws represented the value consensus of society, the values or perspectives fundamental to social order, or the values which it was in the public interest to protect.

Emile Durkheim (1964, 1966) proposed a consensus approach to the creation of deviance which influenced a large number of succeeding sociologists. As we noted earlier, he argued that crimes were acts that offended very strong collective sentiments. The "only common characteristic of all crimes is that they consist . . . in acts universally disapproved of by members of each society" (Durkheim, 1964, p. 73). Crime "shocks sentiments which, for a given social system, are found in all healthy consciences" (Durkheim, 1964, p. 73). Law was the formal reflection of those healthy consciences. As Durkheim (1964, p. 65) suggested, "Normally, custom is not opposed to law, but is on the contrary, its basis." This approach has been termed the "incipient law" perspective (Berk et al., 1977, p. 3).

A consensus approach views society as primarily a harmonious system of interlocking people and institutions which is in equilibrium. The harmony, or lack of conflict, is held to account for society's stability. Society is not completely static, however. Processes do take place, but they are recurrent processes which help reproduce and support the prevailing society. For example, since people are mortal, society must develop arrangements by which biological and social reproduction takes place. Children must be born, cared for, raised, taught and trained, and finally funneled into various positions or roles in society. This is an ongoing, yet recurring process. Change seems to be absent from such harmonious societies. Conflict is merely a momentary aberration, perhaps the result of imperfect socialization, while deviance comprises acts that are considered disruptive of the harmonious social order. As Ralf Dahrendorf (1958) has suggested, such a view of society seems to resemble a utopia, which means "nowhere." Nowhere do utopias or such societies exist.

We find that a consensus approach provides limited insight into the creation of deviance. It may have had more utility for explaining the construction of definitions of deviance in simpler societies, though even in simpler or "primitive" societies conflict was not or is not absent (Edgerton, 1976). It may be useful for understanding what have been called *mala in se* crimes as opposed to *mala prohibita* crimes (Reid, 1979, p. 41). *Mala in se* crimes are considered to be evil in themselves—murder, robbery, rape, aggravated assault, and so on. *Mala prohibita* crimes are behaviors which are evil because they are prohibited by the government. Traffic offenses and gambling offenses would be such crimes. *Mala in se* crimes presumably reflect the consensus of society. They clearly recall the traditional approach to deviance, which assumed that acts considered deviant were inherently offensive. Upon greater reflection, however, it is not at all certain whether there is general agreement that *mala in se* crimes are clearly evil by their very nature. Each act listed above as a *mala in se* crime has been legal and even acceptable in different contexts. For example, children have long been assaulted as part of parental discipline. Only recently, as we will see later, have such beatings and other assaults been considered abuse. Also, since there are so many well-recognized exceptions to the idea that killing another person is reprehensible (though not necessarily universally agreed upon exceptions, which is part of the point), it is difficult to claim that killing is evil in itself.

We would argue that within some very broad and often vaguely defined consensus (e.g., that the rights of others should be protected or that people should be allowed to pursue their own goals as long as they do not endanger others), conflict and disagreement reign supreme. Even when a consensus momentarily exists among a large segment of society—as is currently the case in regard to child abuse—the consensus approach cannot adequately explain the rise and fall of the consensus. The consensus approach assumes that consensus always exists. We would argue that if it does exist, it had to be created and later may be modified or destroyed. A consensus approach is based on the view that people are fundamentally captives of their society, in this case a harmonious society (Wrong, 1961). It does not adequately allow for people interacting with one another on the basis of possibly divergent interests and perspectives. It does not allow for the continual creation and re-creation of deviance. A broader view points to the great historical changes in deviance. It corrects our nearsighted view that what may be agreed upon today (and even then not by all people) has always been and will always be agreed upon.

By criticizing the consensus approach we do not mean to imply that there should not be a consensus on various issues. Nor do we mean to suggest that conflict and disagreement are necessarily healthy or productive. Nonetheless, as a description of how deviance is created—not necessarily how we or you would like it to be created—a conflict approach seems more useful than a consensus approach. We turn our attention to that now.

Conflict

A conflict model of society emphasizes that change is an integral feature of all aspects of a society. It assumes that social conflict among various segments of society (e.g., between employers and employees or between the "haves" and the "have nots") is a creative force for this change. Finally, conflict sociologists assume that societies are primarily held together through constraint and not consensus (Dahrendorf, 1958).

As applied to the creation of deviance, the conflict approach assumes that people are likely to develop different interests and viewpoints related to their different locations in society. Consequently, they may disagree about numerous issues, including standards of respectability and deviance. People occupy different positions. Some are wealthy. Others are poor. Some are merchants, Others are customers. Some are law enforcement officers. Others are citizens. Some are landlords. Others are renters. Some are employers. Others are employees. Due to these different positions, people are likely to develop different perspectives about the world and different interests to protect. Think about your own situation. Do you have the same interests as your professors? If you rent an apartment, do you see the landlord-tenant relationship the same way the landlord does? Probably not. Thus, the construction of deviance is the ever-changing result of different people and groups pursuing their own interests in competition or conflict (i.e., disagreement) with one another.

William Chambliss (1974, pp. 38–39) echoes this sentiment when he notes that:

> modern, industrialized society is composed of numerous social classes and interest groups who compete for the favors of the state. The stratification of society into social classes where there are substantial (and at times vast) differences in wealth, power, and prestige inevitably leads to conflict between the extant classes. . . . It is out of the conflicts generated by social class divisions that the definition of some acts as criminal or delinquent emerges.

We would simply add that the conflict is not always tied to social-class differences, nor are the views of the seemingly most powerful groups always reflected in definitions of deviance.

Recent research into the changes in the California Penal Code between 1955 and 1971 indicates that they can be best explained, though not totally so, by the "shifting political fortunes of various interest groups and the two political parties" (Berk et al., 1977, p. 279). While such interest groups as an association of law enforcement officers and a civil liberties lobby dominated the legislative scene, no one group consistently dominated the others. Issues were typically multidimensional, so that the interests of the contending groups were rarely in total opposition to one another. The groups that were involved, however, rarely reflected broader public opinion. What emerges in this investigation of routine changes in the California Penal Code is what was found in an investigation of a revision of the New York State Penal Law on prostitution. Revisions (i.e., re-creations of definitions of deviance) involved "numerous efforts on the part of a relatively small number of interested groups" to affect the behavior of others. Further, the "groups which exercised power with respect to any particular section of the law changed over time, and at most instances in time different groups exercised power over different sections of the law" (Roby, 1969, p. 109). It is to a description of this case study that illustrates the conflict position that we now turn.

Prostitution, Patrons, and Penalties   In 1961 a Penal Law and Criminal Code Revision Commission was established in New York to revise the out-of-date and cumbersome 1909 Code of Criminal Procedures. In 1964 the Commission published a proposed penal law which was introduced as a study bill at the 1964 legislative session in order to elicit the opinions of legislators and citizens but not to be voted on. The Commission's proposed revision of the law on prostitution did not include patrons, but explicitly referred to prostitutes as female or male. Prostitution was also made a "violation" rather than a crime, and it carried a maximum sentence of fifteen days rather than a year in jail or three years in a reformatory as previously mandated. The Commission felt that prostitution had to be kept "on the books," but that the punishment could be lessened in keeping with the practice in New York City, where prostitutes were generally given five to thirty days.

In November 1964 the Commission held public hearings about the proposed penal law. It was assumed that only interest groups which had already made their views known to the Commission would appear. The general public would be relatively ignorant of what was happening. A main issue concerning the proposed changes in the prostitution law and later the controversy after its enactment was whether patronizing a prostitute should be an offense. At the hearings three people presented views that it should be an offense. A president of the American Social Health Association argued that both the prostitute and the patron were involved in the spreading of disease. A retired chief probation officer of the New York City Magistrates Court felt that prostitution should be handled under the Public Health Law, but since it was not, and since prostitution could not exist without customers, it was unequal treatment to arrest the prostitute and not the patron. A third person, who represented no organization, testified that both the prostitute and the patron were equally guilty. However, other New Yorkers argued against a patron clause because the city's police typically used customers to testify against prostitutes, and a patron clause would make this practice, and thus the obtaining of convictions, more difficult. Following the hearings, the Commission added the offense of patronizing a prostitute. The new sections passed the State Legislature without comment in 1965, but the revision was not to take effect until September 1, 1967.

The new law slightly altered the status of prostitutes, but greatly changed the position of patrons and the legally permissible practices of the police. The law prohibited the police from using customers as witnesses and "*technically* prohibited plainclothesmen from obtaining solicitations from and subsequently testifying against prostitutes" (Roby, 1969, p. 93). The only legal procedure for officers was to observe a patron and a prostitute strike a deal. As September 1967 approached, it was not clear what the police would do regarding prostitution.

In May 1967 the New York City police stopped their practice of having the arresting officer of the prostitute act as prosecutor in Women's Court. During early summer they relaxed their pickups of prostitutes, either in anticipation of the new law or due to a shift of manpower because of the racial unrest which developed in the city during the summer of 1967. An alleged influx of prostitutes occurred, but it may be that businessmen, some politicians, and the police fueled the rumors because of dissatisfaction with the new law that was soon to go into effect. Due to pressure from businessmen, politicians, and the city government, a "cleanup" campaign aimed at prostitution began on August 20. Between August 20 and September 30, there were 2,400 prostitution-connected arrests, many of them for loitering or disorderly conduct. This was only 200 fewer prostitution arrests than in the previous six months. Some judges and civil liberties officials argued that the arrests were harassment and an abridgement of the constitutional rights of the alleged prostitutes. After the new penal law went into effect on September 1, it became unclear whether alleged prostitutes could, as in the past, be arrested for loitering. The loitering statute required that the arrested person be suspected of committing a crime, but prostitution was now legally defined as a violation, a different category from a misdemeanor or a felony, which are crimes. On November 9, after threatened legal action, a judge dismissed loitering charges against forty-one women, declaring that they had been arrested illegally. That ended the crackdown on prostitution.

During the cleanup campaign only 6 percent of the new prostitution and patronizing arrests in September and October were for patronizing. Less than 1 percent of the convictions were for patronizing. The newspapers did not report the names of patrons. High-priced call girls were also ignored in the crackdown. After November the arrests for prostitution declined to typical figures.

The police department, the hotel association, and business people opposed the new law. The New York Commission on the United Nations Secretariat allegedly complained about arrests of foreign visitors who did not know that patronizing a prostitute was illegal. In September the police department prefiled draft amendments to the Penal Law to be considered by the 1968 State Legislature. The amendments would allow the police to arrest those who were loitering for the purpose of prostitution or for any offense, and not just those suspected of committing a crime. The police also urged that prostitution be made a Class B misdemeanor, a crime, with a maximum sentence of ninety-one days which was still less than the previous maximum sentence of three years.

In November a Mayor's Committee on Prostitution was formed due to pressure from hotel-owners and businesspeople. In January 1968, the Committee recommended and sent to the State Senate a proposed amendment to the Penal Law, reclassifying prostitution as a Class A misdemeanor with a maximum penalty of one year imprisonment. The Committee disapproved several pending bills, including the police department's proposal. The Committee felt that a three-month maximum penalty was too short for rehabilitation and that the present fifteen-day maximum penalty supported neither rehabilitative nor preventive aims. Reclassifying prostitution as a Class A misdemeanor would allow greater rehabilitation through possible placement on probation or sentence to a halfway house. It might also have a greater deterrent impact.

In April the State Senate committed the Mayor's Committee's proposed amendments to the Senate's Committee on Codes, which later decided not to send it back to the Senate for a vote. The counsel to the Committee on Codes detailed three reasons why the proposed amendment was killed: the initial revision by the PLCCR Commission was well considered and the law had been in effect too short a time to assess its effectiveness and impact; giving prostitutes a one-year jail sentence might overcrowd the jails; and finally, prostitution did not warrant such a penalty. Coincidentally, all sixteen committee members were lawyers, and the lawyers in New York supported and respected the PLCCR Commission, which was also composed of lawyers. Further, one member of the Senate's Committee on Codes had also been a member of the PLCCR Commission. Thus, the changes in the laws governing prostitution, an early effort to include patrons as violators, were the result of a relatively small number of groups pursuing their own interests. Conflict over the law as well as over its enforcement was the order of the day.

Three Conflict Perspectives Within a broadly conceived conflict approach there are several specific perspectives on the construction of deviance: moral entrepreneurs, bureaucratic interests, and ruling elites. These specific perspectives point to a narrower body of interests or actors as the important features in the creation of deviance. While we view the following within a conflict approach, those who work within these specific areas may take offense about how we have characterized them. Thus there is conflict about what constitutes a conflict approach.

Moral Entrepreneurs Howard Becker (1963, p. 147) notes that rules are the results of the initiatives of a category of people that he calls moral entrepreneurs. They seek to define deviance and respectability for the rest of us. While we may think of them as meddlesome busybodies, many are deeply humanitarian. They may be sincere crusaders who notice a profound evil which they feel must be publicized and corrected.

The Women's Christian Temperance Union may be seen as a group of moral entrepreneurs who, especially during their heyday in the late nineteenth and early twentieth centuries, were successful in banning alcohol. Joseph Gusfield (1963) argues that the prohibition movement was primarily a symbolic crusade through which middle-class, small-town, and rural Protestant society, which saw its economic and social position threatened by the changing times—by the rising urban, immigrant, and Catholic segment of society, where alcohol was an integral part of life—could reassert its now-diminishing importance and morality. Alcohol was the symbol of the conflict. The temperance movement was much more interested in the passage of the Eighteenth Amendment—in effect, public support for its way of life—than in the enforcement of the law, which was lax. "If the law was often disobeyed and not enforced, the respectability of its adherents was honored in the breach. After all, it was *their* law that drinkers had to avoid" (Gusfield, 1963, p. 8). Many might call Anita Bryant a moral entrepreneur because of her crusade against homosexuality in the late 1970s. The members of the American Civil Liberties Union might be considered a group of moral entrepreneurs because of their support for due process in the criminal justice system. The tobacco industry viewed Joseph Califano, former secretary of what was then the Department of Health, Education and Welfare in the late 1970s (there is now a separate Department of Education and a retitled Department of Health and Human Services), who urged a national campaign to help smokers quit their "slow-motion" suicide, as a born-again nonsmoker with a "prohibitionist mentality" (AP, 1978). A focus on moral entrepreneurs, however, may entail the danger of overlooking the historical and social context within which deviance is created in favor of psychologizing the phenomenon.

Bureaucratic Interests   The interests of those who work within institutions and agencies to maintain or enlarge their scope of operations has been pointed to as an important feature in the designation of deviance as well as in dealing with deviance. For example, the emphasis on witches and the control of witchcraft in Renaissance Europe has been viewed as a form of deviance which was "created and sustained largely through the efforts of a self-sustaining bureaucratic organization dedicated to its discovery and punishment, and granted unusual powers which, when removed, dealt a final blow to that entire conception of deviant behavior" (Currie, 1968, p. 24).

Especially on the Continent, the prosecution of witches was a profitable business. The prosecution of witches in Renaissance Europe was based on religious prohibitions against making a pact with the devil. Interestingly, between 1000 and 1480 A.D. it was forbidden to believe that rides with the devil could take place. After 1480, those who claimed that such rides were an illusion were viewed by the Catholic Church as in league with the devil (Harris, 1974, pp. 213–214). Priests, judges, executioners, torturers, and other bureaucratic agents were becoming wealthy from trying and executing witches. Because they were paid well, and because after convicting wealthy citizens and landowners they confiscated their property, the bureaucratic officials had a vested interest in the deviance of witches as well as in a continuing supply of them. Several hundred thousand people were burned in Continental Europe during this mania. When confiscation and/or torture, which was used to extract the confessions necessary for capital punishment and also provided new suspects for further trials, became illegal, the incidence of witches decreased dramatically.

Similarly, in the late fifteenth and early sixteenth centuries, many leprosariums in Europe became emptied, perhaps due to the end of the Crusades, which had helped to spread the disease. These hospitals and their staffs stood unused or were soon to be unused. Instead, through royal decisions the institutions now began to house beggars, criminals, the insane, and the diseased—the refuse of society, who could not be productive members of the labor force and would only help to increase the number of unemployed, idle people. Until this time madness had been considered a touch of divinity. The mad existed on another plane of reality. They were fools or geniuses, but were not thought to be depraved. With the conversion of leprosariums into institutions housing all kinds of problem people, madness took on a different definition. Confinement to an institution, which itself was typically debilitating, led the mad to be seen as depraved and degenerate. There was still a touch of divinity, but there was also a touch of doom. Thus, in order to use existing bureaucracies and facilities, laws were created which in turn created a public perception about a particular behavior, madness (Chambliss, 1974, pp. 27–28).

Not all situations concerning the impact of bureaucratic interests on the creation and control of deviance are so dramatic or so far removed from the present. For example, law enforcement agencies are often intimately involved in promoting legislation to support their interests (Berk et al., 1977). We will examine one case of this shortly when we explore the origins of the Marihuana Tax Act of 1937.

In regard to bureaucratic interests, Becker (1967) argues that there is a "hierarchy of credibility." Those with the most power or highest rank are given the greatest credibility, by sociologists and lay people alike, in telling how things are. They are the near-monopolizers of reality. Until our recent widespread dissatisfaction with those at the top, law enforcement agencies, medical associations, and government bureaucracies often had the greatest credibility in defining what the problems were and how to deal with them. However, they may selectively present a case in order to promote their own self-serving (and possibly also self-sacrificing) version of reality, in this case a reality concerning deviance (Altheide and Johnson, 1980; Conrad and Schneider, 1980, chap. 5).

Ruling Elite Some sociologists and criminologists have rediscovered a Marxian or critical approach to understanding deviance (Quinney, 1970, 1979; Taylor et al., 1973; Spitzer, 1975). As we will see in Chapter 5, this approach is not limited to the investigation of the creation of criminal law or definitions of deviance. However, it has been applied to the understanding of the construction of deviance. Put simply, a Marxian approach suggests that "in every era the ruling ideas are the ideas of the ruling class" (Chambliss, 1974, p. 8). Definitions of deviance can only be understood in terms of the prevailing mode of production and who controls production in a given historical period. At present the ruling class is made up of capitalists, the owners of the means of production—factories, businesses, land, and so on. The capitalist ruling class uses laws and definitions of deviance as tools to enhance or support its position.

For example, in a provocative investigation with which others disagree (Hagan and Leon, 1977), Anthony Platt (1977, p. 177) argues that to a great extent the invention of the concept of delinquency and the creation of juvenile courts in the late nineteenth and early twentieth centuries

> . . . served to reinforce a code of moral values which was seemingly threat-
> ened by urban life, industrialism, and the influx of immigrant cultures. In a
> rapidly changing and increasingly complex urban society, the child-saving
> philosophy [of the reformers] represented a defense against "foreign" ideol-
> ogies and a proclamation of cherished values.

Further, Platt argues that liberals who criticize the juvenile courts for failing to rehabilitate delinquents and reduce crime miss the point. If the juvenile courts are seen as a tool of class and racial oppression which emerged in a "specific period of this society's historical development to regulate the children of the urban working-class and to attune them to the realities and discipline of industrial life under advanced capitalism," then their "failures," such as overrepresentation of minority juveniles within the juvenile justice system, are quite understandable (Platt, 1977, p. 192).

Chambliss (1974, pp. 25–27) argues that because the protection of private property is the basis of capitalism, it is not surprising that criminal law reflects that concern. In feudal times, laws concerning theft were largely "unsophisticated" and not very subtle because feudal landowners were in complete control of society's resources. As feudal landowners lost control, and as commerce and trade developed throughout Europe, laws of theft began to take the shape they presently have. The *Carrier's Case* in England (1473) was an important basis for the development of modern laws of theft (Hall, 1952). The defendant in the case, the carrier, was hired to deliver merchandise to Southampton. Instead, he took the merchandise for his own use. He was caught, tried, and convicted. In the process the court reached a new definition of theft. Until then trespass had been necessary in order to be convicted of theft. However, since the defendant was given the merchandise and therefore had not committed trespass, he could not be guilty of theft as it was then defined. The judges, though, created a distinction between "custody" and "possession." While the carrier was in custody of the merchandise, the merchant had never given him legal possession of it. Thus, the carrier was found guilty of theft through a decision which had no legal precedent, but which fundamentally altered the definition of deviance. To understand why the judges reached that decision, it must be noted that the judges served the crown. Commerce and trade were growing throughout England and Europe as the old feudal order broke down. It was in the interest of the king, a merchant himself, to guarantee the safe passage of goods throughout the country. Taxes on them went to the crown. Thus, a new law was established which was extremely important for the emerging class of traders and industrialists as well as for the king.

While the *Carrier's Case* decision and the extensions of that decision which have led to our present laws concerning theft may seem obvious or natural, critical criminologists would argue that those laws are created to serve the interests of the ruling class, presently capitalists. Further, they seem natural to us because we have been fully and subtly indoctrinated into the morality of such a class structure and because many of us have an interest in maintaining that class structure. However, laws concerning theft have not always been interpreted to the benefit of the economic elites (Chambliss, 1974, p. 26). For example, in 1799 an English court ruled that a bank clerk, who took a deposit of 100 pounds without even putting the money into the drawer and later withdrawing it, was not guilty. Here, as elsewhere, the ruling elite is not all-powerful. A narrow view which focuses only on it may lead us to overlook the shifting fortunes of various interest groups.

The Marihuana Tax Act of 1937 Since the early 1960s several social scientists have investigated the creation of the Marihuana Tax Act of 1937, the first federal attempt to control marijuana in the United States (Becker, 1963; Lindesmith, 1965; Dickson, 1968; Musto, 1973; Bonnie and Whitebread, 1974; Reasons, 1974). A recent review of the research and a reinterpretation of the origins of the act indicate that the researchers reached different conclusions concerning the creation of the law (Galliher and Walker, 1977). We would like to briefly discuss the divergent thoughts about a particular creation of deviance, the Marihuana Tax Act of 1937, in order to highlight two points. First, all of these pieces of research point to a broadly conceived conflict model of the creation of deviance. Each takes a slightly different view which underscores some of the specific perspectives within the conflict approach that we have just discussed. Second, the divergent conclusions clearly indicate that our understanding of deviance, in this case our understanding of a particular piece of legislation, is itself a creation. It arises out of the activities of people. Our understanding is not absolute. There may be disagreement about our understanding just as there is often disagreement concerning various features of the phenomenon of deviance.

Becker (1963), Lindesmith (1965), and Reasons (1974) attribute the enactment of the Marihuana Tax Act of 1937 to the publicity campaign conducted by the Federal Bureau of Narcotics under its director, Henry J. Anslinger (Galliher and Walker, 1977). The Bureau and, more specifically, Director Anslinger are viewed as moral entrepreneurs who were concerned to put properly what they felt was an area of wrongdoing within their jurisdiction (Becker, 1963, p. 38). According to Becker (1963, p. 136), three values are the basis for the moral opposition to drugs, and thus for attempts to suppress them (both intoxicants and narcotics): (1) people should not do anything to lose self-control; (2) activity solely for the purpose of producing ecstasy is wrong; and (3) humanitarian opposition to any kind of enslaving practice. Thus, as Reasons (1974, p. 146) states, "Largely because of public concern, primarily induced by the Bureau of Narcotics, the Marihuana Tax Act was passed in 1937 placing a prohibitively high tax on marihuana and creating a whole new class of criminals."

Dickson (1968) suggests, however, that the efforts of the Bureau of Narcotics were not due primarily to moral concerns, but rather to bureaucratic interests. The bulk of the publicity inspired by the Bureau occurred *after* the passage of the act, not before it. Faced with a declining budget, the Bureau and its director were interested in appearing to be a much-needed agency and in increasing their scope of operation. Striking parallels with the efforts of the Narcotics Division of the Internal Revenue Bureau of the Treasury Department to enforce the Harrison Act of 1914 are interpreted as support by Dickson for his emphasis on bureaucratic interests in the 1937 act. The Harrison Act of 1914 did not make narcotic addiction illegal, but merely required addicts to obtain their drugs from registered physicians who would record the transaction. The Narcotics Division was intended by Congress to have limited scope. It was to enforce registration and record-keeping concerning narcotics. The Division, however, launched a two-pronged campaign in order to broaden its support in Congress and among the public. The campaign involved a "barrage of reports and newspaper articles which generated a substantial public outcry against narcotics use" where little had previously existed and the sponsorship of a series of "test cases in the courts which resulted in a reinterpretation of the Harrison Act and substantially broadened powers for the Narcotics Division" (Dickson, 1968, p. 149). Approximately twenty years later, the Bureau of Narcotics, faced with an unsupportive environment, engaged in similar efforts to protect its interests.

Musto (1973) argues that the Bureau did not create the marijuana scare of the early 1930s. Fear of marijuana was primarily confined to the southwestern United States, where Mexican immigrants had brought with them customs concerning its use. It was not until the depression of the thirties that hatred for the Mexican immigrants, who were willing to work for low wages and created greater competition for jobs, arose. During the 1920s their cheap labor had been welcomed. With the increased concern about the Mexicans came an increased concern about their customs, in particular, the use of marijuana. The political pressure from the southwestern states, and not the moral entrepreneurship of the Bureau, was the basis for the act. Further, the act was not seen by Director Anslinger as a boon to the Bureau. The lack of increased appropriations to the Bureau after the passage of the act supports Anslinger's contention.

Bonnie and Whitebread (1974, p. 117) see little public concern about marijuana in particular or narcotics in general during the 1930s. "Apathy was the norm." They note that Director Anslinger tried to convince Americans of the danger of marijuana, but was not particularly successful. Further, they, as well as Musto, suggest that the Bureau and Anslinger felt that uniform state laws could adequately handle the problem. Moreover, Anslinger questioned whether a federal law would be helpful or constitutional, but went along with pressure from the Department of Treasury, the Bureau's parent agency, for a federal law. The real marijuana issue pertained to the intricate legal question of how a federal law could be framed which would be constitutional and provide effective social control (Bonnie and Whitehead, 1974, p. 126).

Galliher and Walker (1977), who have remarked on the conflict among the previous interpretations of the creation of the Marihuana Tax Act of 1937, have developed their own version. They argue that Director Anslinger and the Bureau did not institute a massive propaganda campaign in order to secure passage of the act. "Blaming a government official for what many, including liberals, see as a ridiculous law is not unexpected, except in sociologists trained to analyze structural conditions rather than individual characteristics" (Galliher and Walker, 1977, p. 374). Before the Bureau's campaign to secure uniform state drug laws, many states had laws prohibiting the sale and possession of marijuana, and all states had such laws prior to the first federal hearings. Thus, the Bureau cannot be credited with arousing the public's interest. Moreover, there seems to have been something less than a national crisis over marijuana, and not even a local one in the Southwest. The ease with which the bill passed in Congress indicates the prevailing commonsense opinion that marijuana was bad. Consequently, the Marihuana Tax Act of 1937 was primarily symbolic reassurance for that commonsense feeling in the country. No great legal change was made through the act. It was a technical change so that federal law could reflect existing state laws. However, it was good public relations for Congress and federal law enforcement agencies, since it reflected existing opinion. Galliher and Walker, however, do not investigate how this prevailing commonsense opinion was created.

The point of this description of the conflict over the origins of the Marihuana Tax Act of 1937 is not that any of the researchers presents a more insightful analysis of the creation of deviance as compared to the others. Much more research is needed. Instead, the conflict over the creation of the act is an indication that our understanding of deviance, which is itself part of the phenomenon of deviance, is the result of divergent activities and interpretations.

Rule-Making We have examined the basic approaches for understanding the construction of deviance. These basic approaches focus on key issues in the construction of deviance, but do not examine the process by which rules are made. Erdwin Pfuhl (1980, chap. 4) analyzes the process of making rules as a moral enterprise. Rule-making involves the creation and establishment of a morality favored by some but opposed by others.

The creation of rules begins with a dissatisfaction over some aspect of the prevailing scene. Some people or some group of people become *aware* (more accurately, develop an awareness) that something is troubling them. They decide that something must be prevented or corrected so that their own interests are not threatened. Thus, a "sense of distress and a lack of a ready means for its resolution underlie the efforts of rule creators" (Pfuhl, 1980, p. 125). The threatened person or group, however, must gain a wider audience to share their view. They must try to transform their personal trouble into a public issue (Mills, 1959, pp. 8–11). They will likely need to overcome opposition and to create support where only indifference or ignorance prevails.

In order to develop a broader base of support or respectability for their position, potential rule-creators may try to enhance their public image through alliances with already well-respected organizations and people (witness the practice of listing the names of prominent supporters or board members on the stationery of action-oriented organizations) as well as through testimonials and endorsements. The support of already respectable people provides legitimacy to the position of the potential rule-makers. They may use the media in order to bring their views to a wider audience. Through a careful manipulation of what is presented, potential rule-creators may be able to present their perspective in a favorable and convincing manner. In this regard, it has been alleged in the capital of a southern state that the sheriff is called "Captain Video" by his deputies for being in the media so often.

Potential rule-creators must construct a moral story about the evil of whatever troubles them. This story—or myth, as it is termed by Pfuhl—may couch the putative deviance in terms of a moral framework already well accepted by the wider audience. The new, putative deviance is presented as intertwined (or congruent) with well-established evils. If the would-be rule-creators are successful, the audience needs to restructure its existing moral framework only slightly in order to accommodate the new evil. For example, at the turn of the century prostitution was presented as white slavery whereby unsophisticated girls of foreign heritage were bound into prostitution through drugs and coercion (Reasons, 1970, in Pfuhl, 1980). The notion of white slavery depicts prostitution as opposing "premarital chastity, the purity of womanhood and the sanctity of home and hearth," the dominant morality of turn-of-the-century America

(Pfuhl, 1980, p. 143). Similarly, the "dope fiend" stories of the 1930s and 1940s, which were disseminated in articles, movies, and government announcements, helped link the use of marijuana to "obviously" immoral and degenerate behaviors, such as killing, rape, theft, and insanity. These stories surrounded the creation of the Marihuana Tax Act of 1937. Such myths also enhance the moral superiority of the rule-creators and of those who agree with them. Finally, the personal troubles which have been transformed into public issues must be enacted into public policy. As Pfuhl (1980) notes, this is typically a matter of conflict and power. We would argue, however, that power is an overused concept which glosses over the negotiations, trade-offs, and bargains underlying such legislation. And, as we noted earlier, the most powerful do not always have their interests promoted in the creation of deviance.

Deviance and Social Control The creation of deviance and the creation of social control are intimately tied together. Social control agencies are institutions which are given the authority to deal with deviance. We will have more to say about control agencies in Chapter 5. Deviance demands some kind of handling, and in turn social control agencies may seek to widen their scope of power by creating or bringing additional forms of deviance within their purview. We have already touched on this phenomenon in examining bureaucratic interests in the creation of deviance. The forms of deviance that are brought within the boundary of a control agency may be a *redesignation* of existing deviance. By designation is meant what kind of deviance. "Is the offending conduct a sin, a moral problem, a crime or a sickness?" (Conrad and Schneider, 1980, p. 25). As we saw in the previous chapter, our images or designations of deviance have historically varied. Deviance was designated as a sin, then as a crime, and nowadays much of it is seen as an illness. As definitions of deviance developed, and as designations and redesignations were created, social control agencies garnered for themselves the authority to deal with deviance. When existing institutions gain the "power and authority to define deviance, that is, to say what kind of problem something is, the responsibility for dealing with that problem often comes to that institution" (Conrad and Schneider, 1980, p. 8).

Thus, as our designations of deviance have changed, so have the institutions which deal with deviance. For a long period throughout the Middle Ages, the church defined deviance and dealt with it. As nations and states developed and central governments gained power, deviance became an offense against the state—a crime to be handled by government-sponsored law enforcement and judicial agencies. Presently, the medical profession is increasing its influence over the designation of and dealing with deviance.

For example, the disease concept of deviant drinking—alcoholism—is a social creation which seems to be linked to the Yale Center for Alcohol Studies, Alcoholics Anonymous, and the formulation by E. M. Jellineck, medical researcher and director of the Yale Center. The American Medical Association, in 1956, recognized alcoholism as an illness, restating an earlier, less significant endorsement of the concept (Schneider, 1978). Today, alcoholism is much more likely to be handled by the medical profession than by law enforcement agencies. This dramatic change is illustrated by the declining proportion of arrests for drunkenness by law enforcement agencies. In 1960, more than one-third of all arrests by law enforcement agencies were for drunkenness. The figure would be even higher if traffic offenses were excluded from the figure for total arrests. In 1970, the proportion had decreased to less than one-fourth with traffic offenses excluded. By the end of the 1970s, the figure had declined even further, to less than one-eighth of all arrests, even though drinking problems seem to be on the rise (Hoover, 1961, 1971; Webster, 1980). The "discovery" of child abuse in the late 1950s and early 1960s is further testimony both to the intimate relation between the creation of deviance and social control and to the medicalization of deviance.

The Creation of Child Abuse   Stephen Pfohl (1977) suggests that child beating, a traditional and legitimate form of parental discipline of children, became defined as deviant through the efforts of pediatric radiologists in the late 1950s and early 1960s. Until that time, social and legal reactions to child beating were sporadic. In the mid-1960s all states passed laws prohibiting the abuse of children. How did this occur?

Violence toward children has traditionally been legitimized under the philosophy that beatings were necessary for discipline. From the early 1800s into the early 1900s three reform movements—the "house-of-refuge" movement, the turn-of-the-century crusades of the Society for the Prevention of Cruelty to Children, and the rise of the juvenile courts—directed attention to beaten, neglected, and delinquent children. However, "in each case the primary objective was not to save the child from cruel or abusive parents, but to save society from future delinquents" (Pfohl, 1977, p. 311). Children would be taken out of "bad" homes and put into institutions so that they would not become bad themselves.

This preventive penology, or society-saving philosophy and approach, weakened due to the perceived failure of institutionalization, the impact of the depression of the 1930s, and changes in the meaning of adult vices. The effectiveness of institutionalizing juveniles was seriously questioned, as it is today. Thus the juvenile court's role, which is based on intervention and institutionalization, was also questioned as it is today. With its role questioned, one barrier to seeing abuse as victimization rather than only as a potential basis for future delinquency began to crumble. During the depression many "good" families became poor, and this weakened the presumed link between poverty and immorality which was at the heart of preventive penology. Finally, such adult vices as drinking or failing to provide a Christian home were slowly viewed no longer as quite so unacceptable or as the precursor of the child's delinquency. Thus, there began a reorientation toward seeing child beating as the beating of a victim rather than as the beginning of a threat to society.

Interest in the problems of children grew during the first half of the twentieth century. A White House Conference on Children was held in 1909, and in 1930 the Children's Bureau was established in what until recently was the Department of Health, Education and Welfare. Child labor was regulated, as were other practices concerning the young. Even with an increasing concern for children, however, child abuse was not viewed as a major issue and was widely tolerated.

In the 1950s, pediatric radiologists began to discover many cases of children with long bone fractures of "unspecified origin." Later, the traumas showing up on x-rays were linked to childhood accidents, parental carelessness, parental conduct and misconduct, and deliberate injury. By the late 1950s increased concern about battered children had developed. Yet, why were pediatric radiologists the discoverers of child abuse and not someone else?

Pfohl (1977, p. 316) suggests that legal and social welfare agents either were outside the "scene of abusive behavior" or, in the case of social workers, were using a psychoanalytical framework in which they attempted to understand and correct the personality disturbances of parents and, in effect, buttress the parents' power within the family. What of hospital physicians and pediatricians? First, physicians may have been unaware of the possibility of abuse as a diagnosis. It did not exist at the time. Of course, the signs of the often massive trauma were much more evident to the physician than to the pediatric radiologist, who went by lines on an x-ray. Second, many were unwilling to believe that parents could inflict such abuse upon their children. Third, the possible legal liability for violating the patient's confidentiality (and the parents were viewed as the patient if the child was injured) would lessen the likelihood of doctors' creating the concept of abuse. Finally, if doctors discovered abuse, they might lose control over their work to, as well as have to be involved with, law enforcement and criminal justice agencies.

Research radiologists would not be hampered by a lack of a diagnostic category. In part their work consisted of creating such categories. Second, they are removed from the horror of the child's trauma and therefore would be more willing to see the parents as possible culprits. Third, radiologists are less likely than physicians or pediatricians to view the parents as their patients. Confidentiality becomes less of an issue. Finally, discovering child abuse and successfully establishing it as a clinical condition enabled pediatric radiologists to raise their marginal status in the field of medicine. They would become involved in issues of risk and responsibility, and this is the basis for status in the medical profession. By aligning themselves with pediatricians and psychodynamically oriented psychiatrists in this discovery, professionals who had more prestige than pediatric radiologists, the radiologists could increase their status. Similarly, pediatricians and psychodynamically oriented psychiatrists were somewhat marginal themselves. The mission of the former was being narrowed through the development and use of preventive drugs and treatments for previously dangerous infant diseases. The marginality of the latter arose in their mission of dealing with nonphysical problems, problems which could not be seen and therefore whose existence was often questioned. The status of each group could be enhanced by cooperating with and supporting the growing concern of pediatric radiologists.

In labeling the problem as the "battered child syndrome," radiologists, pediatricians, and psychiatrists defined it as a "clinical condition" due to "unrecognized trauma" caused by "psychopathic" perpetrators. The editorial board of the American Medical Association endorsed this position in the same 1962 issue of its journal in which the article appeared. The report was also endorsed before publication by a Children's Bureau conference which included not only doctors, but also social workers and law enforcement officials. This designation of deviance provided physicians with a diagnostic category to orient their behavior. It allowed physicians to separate the healthy parents from the pathological ones who could inflict such trauma on their children. Confidentiality became less of a problem because the parents themselves needed help. Finally, the designation of child battering as a clinical condition due to "sick" perpetrators allowed the problem to be kept to a great extent within the medical profession. Pfohl would not argue that the professionals involved consciously examined the situation as he did and then acted accordingly. Instead, the considerations that Pfohl outlined are important features of the social context within which the designation of child abuse was developed.

This particular designation of deviance has had a profound impact on the handling of abusers. Offenders are prosecuted at a low rate, and the reporting of offenders has gradually shifted from reporting to law enforcement agencies to reporting to child protection agencies or to "helping services," such as the medical profession itself. Thus, for a variety of organizational concerns and within a particular historical context, pediatric radiology, with the later support of the medical profession, helped to create the deviance of child abuse and designate it as a certain form of deviance to be controlled by particular agencies.

THE TRIALS AND TRIBULATIONS OF TOBACCO

In the past two decades there has been a growing concern over the hazards of smoking tobacco. In the past decade there has been an increasing number of attempts to regulate cigarettes and their use. The trials and tribulations of tobacco, though, have been going on in Western society for approximately 400 years. The trials and tribulations concerning what is now a multibillion-dollar industry provide us with an example of the dynamic creation of deviance and at times of its vindication (i.e., making it respectable) that includes many of the issues we have discussed in this chapter: the historical context of deviance, conflict, bureaucratic interests, moral entrepreneurs, and so on. It is a fitting conclusion for this chapter, though the trials and tribulations of tobacco are not concluded. The following discussion is based on Joel Best's (1979) work on tobacco in seventeenth-century Europe, Elaine Nuehring and Gerald Markle's (1974) analysis of the concerns about and subsequent changes in the television advertising of cigarettes in the late 1960s and early 1970s, and Markle and Troyer's (1979) discussion of the growing conflict over cigarettes in the middle to late 1970s.

In England

Tobacco was indigenous to the Western Hemisphere. Thus, Europe had no contact with tobacco until it was introduced into several countries in the mid-sixteenth century. By the beginning of the seventeenth century tobacco was well known and used as a medical drug. Physicians claimed it could cure a wide variety of diseases, and therefore Europeans began to grow it. By the beginning of the 1600s Europeans had also discovered a recreational value in smoking it. However, during the first decade of the 1600s, moral entrepreneurs in England, headed by King James I, attacked tobacco. Its recreational use was seen as irresponsible and similar to drunkenness. Critics argued that excessive use of tobacco was hazardous to the smoker's health. It lead to "insanity, sterility, birth defects, and other maladies" (Best, 1979, p. 173). It was "religiously offensive," a habit of "low prestige," and because the best tobacco was imported from Spanish colonies, it was viewed as foolish to trade English gold for a rival nation's product which was to be burned anyway. Similar criticisms were voiced in other European countries.

Those criticisms led to public policy. King James added a 4000 percent increase on the standard import tax on tobacco. He did not want to make it illegal for those who intended to use it medically, but he did want to discourage the recreational user. Other Northern European countries, such as Austria, France, and Denmark-Norway, established laws after 1630 which forbade trading in tobacco and/or smoking it. Violation typically carried a penalty of a small fine, though in Russia a violator might be whipped, tortured, deported to Siberia, or executed. Interestingly, Southern Europe and the states that now comprise Italy never legislated against tobacco. They were the first countries to learn of tobacco. Perhaps their already profitable trade in tobacco before the rise of criticism against it kept those countries and states from criminalizing its use.

In spite of public policy, the use of tobacco spread throughout Europe. Smuggling flourished. Thus, tobacco became a social problem. However, by the end of the seventeenth century tobacco was legal throughout Europe. Slowly, it was redefined as a revenue-producing substance. This redefinition led to tobacco's respectability. It had been *vindicated.* How did that happen?

King James had tried to tax the recreational use of tobacco out of existence. He failed. While officially the amount of tobacco that was imported declined, the amount smoked did not. Tobacco smuggling was profitable. During this period, the taxes on tobacco and other imports were collected by agents who paid a fee to the king to do so. With the high rate of smuggling, the agents were unable to make a profit from taxing the legitimately imported tobacco. They asked the king to lower the import tax on tobacco or allow them to give up the right (called a "farm") to tax imports which they leased from the king. In 1608 James lowered the import tax dramatically. This began the process of redefining tobacco as a revenue-producing crop. Tobacco imports rose rapidly. In 1615 the tax collectors surrendered their leases to collect taxes to the king for a payment of several thousand pounds. After two years, during which royal agents collected the taxes, the "farm" was leased again at four times its previous rent. Tobacco was becoming a money-making crop. This redefinition was tied in with England's colonization of Virginia.

In comparison to Spain, England had not succeeded well in colonizing the New World during the sixteenth century. The seventeenth century might be different. Virginia was initially hoped to be a source of metals and other important products which England had to import from foreign countries. However, the colony could not provide those products. Instead, it was well suited for growing tobacco. Thus, the colonists in Virginia and in later English colonies turned to tobacco farming. Virginia's exports rose dramatically, from 2,500 pounds to an estimated million and a half pounds, between 1616 and 1636. However, the English crown was upset that the colonists had not found precious metals and that they were becoming increasingly committed to what might be only a fad. Both James and his successor, Charles I, complained to the Virginia leaders about their investment in tobacco. Similar complaints would be made to the colonies for almost sixty years.

During the seventeenth century most European nations were experiencing financial problems. While trying to increase the scope of their authority, which entailed additional costs, they were also unable to raise more revenue through exchange economies with other countries. The tobacco trade was one measure, albeit a small one initially, for easing the financial difficulties of the king. At the same time, Virginia had become a one-crop colony. The crown, of course, was vitally concerned about Virginia's welfare as well as about the growth of its other colonies. That welfare and growth depended on a flourishing tobacco trade. Therefore, even while James and Charles were writing angry letters to the colonists to stop concentrating on tobacco, they were protecting their income as well as the welfare of the colonies through such practices as controlling Spanish imports, examining imports for quality, minimizing smuggling through policing and tax adjustment, and controlling the colonies' production of tobacco in order to avoid glutting the market. Tobacco policy continued to be debated for much of the 1600s. Continually the crown morally objected to tobacco and the colonies' dependence on it while also protecting the tobacco industry.

By the middle of the 1600s the market for tobacco in England had become stable. Thus, new markets had to be found. Tobacco was exported from the colonies to England, taxed for revenue, and then reexported to European countries. Reexporting soon became the largest part of the export trade. Over half of the tobacco exported to England from Virginia and Maryland in 1669 was reexported. New markets, however, depended on the elimination of laws against tobacco in the other European countries. Therefore, England sent representatives to these countries to encourage them to "repeal their laws and profit through the taxation of legitimately imported tobacco" (Best, 1979, p. 178). The rest of Europe soon realized the profits to be made from encouraging the use of tobacco and followed in changing their policies toward it. By the end of the seventeenth century tobacco was vindicated. It was defined as a recreational drug whose taxation was an important source of government revenue. However, the trials and tribulations of tobacco were not over.

In America

The scene shifts to America in the late 1850s (Nuehring and Markle, 1974). At that time cigarettes were brought back to the States by American tourists visiting England. During the Civil War, cigarettes became a standard military ration. Controversy concerning tobacco—in this case cigarettes—continued, however. In the 1870s cigar manufacturers claimed that cigarettes were "drugged with opium, their paper bleached with arsenic, their contents derived from garbage, and their makers Chinese lepers" (Nuehring and Markle, 1974, p. 514). Religious and moral opposition to cigarettes developed by the turn of the century. Cigarette smoking was blamed for male delinquency and failure in school. A member of the WCTU nearly waged a 1920 presidential campaign based on a moralistic antitobacco stance. And, as had happened 300 years earlier, a wide variety of physical ills were claimed to be the result of the "little white slavers" or "coffin nails."

Between 1895 and 1921 fourteen states, primarily Midwestern, completely banned cigarettes. Laws which regulated the sale of cigarettes to minors and the possession of ciagrettes by minors were passed in all other states except Texas. Around the beginning of this century antismoking campaigns were going strong and quit-smoking clinics were established in several cities. Part of the anticigarette sentiment may have been due to the fact that the early users were urban immigrants, a disreputable group anyway. The "status of the group who practices the behavior can influence whether behavior is seen as deviant" (Nuehring and Markle, 1974, p. 515). In this respect remember Musto's discussion of the use of marijuana by Mexican immigrants in the Southwest in the 1930s or its later use by other marginal members of society, such as blacks and jazz musicians.

Even with the opposition to cigarettes, sales increased, and after World War I public opinion began to change. Cigarettes were seen as suited to the fast pace of urban life. States "rediscovered" the revenue potential of taxing cigarette sales. The tobacco industry began to advertise on a massive scale. It appealed to weight-watchers, to women, and even to those concerned with their health. One cigarette was advertised as bringing cooling relief to irritated throats. By 1927 all fourteen states which had prohibited cigarettes had repealed those laws. By the end of World War II smoking was accepted and even expected.

During the early 1950s health concerns were being increasingly voiced. A link between cigarette smoking and various diseases, including lung cancer and heart disease, was suspected. In 1964 the Surgeon General's Office released its "landmark" report, "Smoking and Health." The tobacco industry was threatened again. For example, some states, such as Florida, passed anticigarette laws which instructed schools to teach students about the adverse effects of cigarette smoking. The Federal Trade Commission ruled that by July 1, 1965, cigarette packages would have to carry a warning label. However, the tobacco industry successfully lobbied to dilute the intent of this proposal. In 1965 the Cigarette Labeling and Advertising Act was passed. It required a health warning on packages, but more importantly it prohibited the FTC and other federal agencies from regulating cigarette advertising and nullified all similar state and local efforts. Most members of Congress from the tobacco-growing states supported the measure.

In 1967, through the efforts of John Banzhaf III, a young New York lawyer, the Federal Communication Commission, under the equal time doctrine, ordered radio and television stations to broadcast antismoking advertisements. While some members of Congress and network officials protested, the antismoking advertisements appeared on television in 1968. With the 1965 Cigarette Act due to expire in 1969, the antismoking faction in the Senate was growing stronger while the powerful alliance between the television networks and the tobacco industry was unraveling. When the failure of the networks to monitor cigarette advertising, as they claimed they had been doing, came out in congressional hearings, the networks offered to phase out advertisements of high-tar and high-nicotine cigarettes. The tobacco industry was shaken. The antismoking forces in the

Senate pushed for more concessions from the networks. The broadcasters agreed to phase out all cigarette advertising by 1973. The tobacco industry retaliated by threatening to withdraw all of its advertising by September 1970, which would have meant a potential loss of $200 million to the networks. They also requested antitrust immunity. Instead, the Senate Commerce Committee decided to ban all cigarette advertising on the air by January 1, 1971. The Public Health Smoking Act of 1970 was a victory for the antismoking senators.

Winners and Losers   Various people and groups were involved in or affected by the drama surrounding cigarette smoking and its advertising. The antismoking forces were led by John Banzhof, who might be considered a moral entrepreneur. While state and federal governments have taken in enormous amounts of money through taxations of cigarettes, they have also discouraged its use through legislation. More specifically, the Federal Trade Commission had been sparring for years with the tobacco industry over advertising violations. Broad legislation would aid it in controlling the industry as well as in answering its critics. Such legislation would also help the FTC and the FCC to assert their regulatory powers vis-à-vis encroachments by Congress. The American Heart Association and the American Cancer Society increased their organizational basis for existence through antismoking campaigns. Not too surprisingly, they did not want to directly attack the tobacco industry and the television networks until the alliance unraveled. For example, the American Cancer Society did not offer the FCC direct support in 1967 due to a fear of losing free public-service advertising from the networks. Clinics, smoking therapists, and manufacturers of stop-smoking products have benefited from the controversy. On a broader scale, organized crime has benefited from the unequal taxes imposed on cigarettes in various states by smuggling cigarettes across state lines and then selling them without having paid the second state's higher taxes.

The tobacco industry has been threatened by the reemergence of tobacco and smoking as deviant. While women, particularly teenage women, have increased their use of cigarettes, beginning in the late 1960s the amount of cigarette tobacco consumed dropped dramatically. However, some have charged that the tobacco industry has made up for the loss by dumping the most hazardous cigarettes on the Middle East. In order to protect its image (and profits), the tobacco industry points to its contributions to health research, aid to disaster areas, and other public services. Advertising companies and broadcasters were the big losers according to Nuehring and Markle. Cigarettes were the most advertised product on television before 1971. The broadcasters lost almost $200 million per year and advertisers as much as 25 percent of their pre-1971 business due to the 1971 legislation. We wonder, though, whether broadcasters and advertisers really lost much. Cigarette advertising has been replaced by other advertising on television and radio, and the tobacco industry has merely shifted its advertising to other media, such as newspapers, magazines, and billboards.

The American Medical Association, which received $18 million in research subsidies from the tobacco industry, supported the tobacco forces during the 1960s. The AMA felt that Congress, not the more aggressive federal commissions, should regulate the tobacco industry. It argued that warning labels would be ineffective. Until 1971 it was absent from membership in a national coalition of government agencies and health organizations, the National Interagency Council on Smoking and Health, established in 1964. When the tide finally turned against tobacco, the AMA jumped aboard.

Continuing Controversy   The trials and tribulations have continued throughout the 1970s and will continue into the 1980s. Both antismoking forces and prosmoking forces can claim victories. Larger and more prominent health warnings on cigarette packages are required. Nonsmoking seats are required on interstate buses and on airplanes and are to be found in restaurants. Government agencies and firms have banned smoking in conference rooms, auditoriums, and eating areas. Approximately thirty states and many cities regulate smoking to various degrees. In various states smoking is banned in such places as elevators, museums, and physicians' offices. Clean Indoor Air Acts are being passed throughout the nation. These new regulations are "coercive." Rather than bring the repentant smoker back into the fold, as earlier approaches tried to do, these recent attempts treat the unrepentant smoker "more as enemy than friend" (Markle and Troyer, 1979, p. 612).

Prosmoking forces can claim victories as well. More than 150 bills that would have affected the cigarette industry have been introduced into Congress since 1966, but none has been passed since 1970 (Markle and Troyer, 1979). In 1978 a referendum in California concerning a wide-ranging but inconsistent ban on smoking was defeated. Millions of dollars were spent by the tobacco industry in order to present its views to California's citizens. Similar referenda to ban smoking in enclosed places failed for the second time in a year in Dade County (Miami), Florida, and failed again in California in the Fall 1980 elections. The continuing trials and tribulations of tobacco attest to the dynamic and ever-changing creation of deviance.

In light of the trials and tribulations, we wonder what the future will be concerning marijuana. Already, more than one-third of the states have legalized the therapeutic use of marijuana. Its use has been decriminalized in many jurisdictions. Its revenue potential for governments (as well as legitimate businesses) is astounding. For example, officials in Tennessee have estimated that marijuana is the state's fifth-largest cash crop (*Columbia Record,* October 12, 1979, p. 1-A). What might it be if it were legal? If the parallels with tobacco are instructive, marijuana will undergo a continuing redefinition of its status as deviant or respectable.

CONCLUSION

Deviance is not inherent in the behaviors that offend us. Rather, through our activities we create standards of respectability and deviance. If deviance is not absolute, it must vary according to the context in which it is created and maintained. The audience, the actor engaged in the behavior, and the situation in which the behavior occurs are three important features of that context. The creation of deviance is related to a basic process in society: differentiation. We create differences between people and objects on various criteria. We evaluate these differences and decide that some are respectable and others offensive. In contrast to those whom we view as deviant, we build up our own self-worth. Thus, definitions of deviance are likely to always be with us. They serve an important function for society.

Social scientists have developed two basic models for the construction of deviance: the consensus model and the conflict model. The former emphasizes agreement and similarities, whereas the latter focuses on disagreement and differences. Within the conflict approach the possible importance of moral entrepreneurs, bureaucratic interests, and ruling elites has been explored. Further, conflict also exists within our understanding of the creation of deviance.

The creation of deviance is a process of moral conversion. Those who are personally troubled by some situation must convert others to their viewpoint if they are to be successful in defining what is deviant. With the creation of deviance also comes the creation of social control. If we are offended, we are likely to try to do something about that which offends us. Broadly conceived, social control is that something. As our designations of deviance change, so do our institutions for dealing with deviance. If deviance is a sin, the church is the appropriate control agency. If it is a crime, the state is appropriate. But if it is an illness, medicine must have its say. Thus, the creation of deviance is an ever-changing, ongoing accomplishment of people.

Once we have defined what is offensive, we will likely be concerned about spotting it and those who engage in it. It is to that concern, the recognition of deviance and the identification of deviants, that we turn our attention.

PROJECTS

1 Examine the context of deviance for a particular activity, belief, or characteristic which interests you. Try to detail who are offended by the phenomenon, in what situations they find it offensive, and whether their finding it offensive is

dependent on which people engage in the phenomenon. You can explore the context of deviance through library research, informal interviews, observations, and even staged demonstrations, though the latter should be carefully considered.

2 Definitions of deviance often change over time or vary from one community to another. Examine the present and past code of laws for your state as it concerns one particular behavior. Have the definitions of deviance varied? If so, how did they vary? Or, compare several states' codes of law. How are they similar and how are they different? A similar project can be done using dress codes for a school, university regulations governing student or faculty activity, city ordinances, and so on.

3 Investigate the ongoing creation of deviance on your campus or in your local community. Follow a proposed rule or law and the various parties involved in the proposal. Who is involved? What interests are they pursuing? What maneuvering is taking place? How are the issues resolved? You might find Pfuhl's analysis of the process of rule-making helpful for understanding your specific case.

Recognizing Deviance and Identifying Deviants

What leads a wife to suspect that her husband is mentally ill? How do store detectives know which customers to watch out of the thousands that may enter the store during a day? What tips off a professor to students who cheat? Why did many middle-class parents overlook the use of drugs and alcohol by their sons and daughters in the 1960s and 1970s? Why do many people who engage in homosexuality, prostitution, and so on, go unnoticed? Why are some offenses, like burglary, unlikely to be solved, while others, such as criminal homicide, likely to be solved? Why is one juvenile seen as a delinquent, as a "truly" bad kid, while another youth is viewed as an ordinary teenager, even though both may have committed similar offenses? These are the kinds of questions that we want to pursue in this chapter.

In this chapter we are concerned with how we recognize deviance and identify deviants. Recognition and identification are a prelude to, and intertwined with, our dealing with offensive behavior and people. We cannot deal with deviance until we have observed it. Once we have recognized deviance, we may notify others. Notification is an instance of dealing with deviance. Those whom we notify are likely to want to satisfy themselves that the behavior or person in question is deviant. They will evaluate the situation, perhaps using a different set of criteria as to what is deviant. Thus, our recognition of deviance may lead to reactions which in turn set the scene for a new set of evaluations and perhaps recognition. For example, think of parents who suspect that their child is mentally retarded. They *deal* with it, perhaps, by taking the child to a physician. In turn, the physician may confirm their suspicions. If the suspicions are confirmed, the child may be sent to a school for the retarded, a further way of dealing with this deviance. Or, imagine police officers who arrest a suspect for committing a crime. The prosecuting attorney, who concurs with the officers that the suspect committed a crime, prosecutes the case before a jury. However, the jury cannot reach a verdict. Recognitions and reactions are often intertwined. For the purposes of our discussion, however, we have separated them into two chapters.

We have also separated the recognition of deviance from the identification of deviants. In separating the two processes, we have in mind the distinction between *doing* and *being,* between behavior and identity. Later in the chapter we will explore how observers, after noticing that an individual has *committed* deviant behavior, claim that the person *is* a deviant. There are reasons why observers may make such claims. It is also clear that we will not necessarily call an individual deviant just because he or she engages in deviant behavior. For example, even though shoplifting is an illegal behavior, we are not likely to think of a senior citizen who shoplifts some food as a criminal. Depending on the circumstances, though, we may feel that a juvenile who shoplifts some items is "truly" a delinquent. A business executive who bribes foreign officials has committed a crime, but do we think of this executive as a criminal? Perhaps increasingly we do. The processes of recognizing offenses and identifying offenders are best kept separate in order for us to have a clearer understanding of the phenomenon of deviance. As will become clear in the next chapter, the distinction between the two has a great impact on how we deal with offenders.

RECOGNIZING DEVIANCE

The recognition of deviance occurs in everyday life as well as in formal control agencies established to deal with deviance: police departments, courts, mental health facilities, and so on. As we explore in the next chapter, official control agencies, in order to have deviants to deal with, depend to a great extent on the recognition of deviance by citizens and then on the citizens' summoning the agents. Once the agents have been summoned, they too are concerned with recognition and identification. Thus the recognition of deviance by citizens is often a prelude to the appearance of formal agencies and agents in the drama of deviance.

Moreover, the general processes by which citizens and officials recognize deviance and identify deviants are similar. Thus, we do not want to concentrate just on the recognition of deviance within control agencies, though certainly that is important. We also want to examine the everyday, informal settings within which our involvement in recognizing deviance is most likely to occur.

The recognition of deviance involves two basic activities: (1) noticing an offense, and (2) linking that offense to an offender, or what is typically called "identifying" the offender. Identifying an offender is more or less difficult. Often, when we notice an offense we also notice the offender. Parents who suspect that their child is retarded, married people who think that their spouses are mentally ill, or teachers who suspect that a student has plagiarized a paper are recognizing the offense and the offender in the same process.

There are also a host of offenses in which it is difficult to establish a link between the offense and the offender. Offenses such as property crimes—burglary, vandalism, and so on—are easily noticed even though the offender may never be. As we will see later, offenders who are not seen in the act of committing the offense, or whose offense is not a quality or characteristic of themselves, often are not identified. We are not very successful in recognizing offenders apart from noticing their offenses. Of course, offenders typically want it that way. In this chapter we will primarily concern ourselves with cases where recognition of offense and offender occur together. We will devote some discussion to "picking out" offenders. Let us begin our discussion of the recognition of deviance with an analogy to medical diagnosis.

"Diagnosing" Deviance

How do doctors diagnose an illness? Briefly, what typically happens is that a patient comes to a doctor. The patient complains of certain pains and uneasiness. The doctor will probably ask the patient for additional information, perform some tests, and examine the patient in various ways. After consultation with others, perhaps, the doctor will make a diagnosis. This brief description contains three essential elements in diagnosing an illness: knowledge of illnesses—their signs, symptoms, and so on; gathering information about the complaint; and finally, interpreting that information to reach a diagnosis. These three features also seem to be the important ones in recognizing deviance. Therefore, the three features of our model for recognizing deviance are: *conceptions* of deviance, *checking out* the situation, and *interpreting* information in order to reach a decision. Our recognition of deviance always includes these three features. We will explore them shortly.

This model is useful for understanding the recognition of deviance for two major reasons. First, deviance nowadays is more and more being seen as sickness. The general image of deviance has changed over the years. Deviance was once predominantly viewed as sin, then as crime, and now is beginning to be viewed as sickness (Conrad and Schneider, 1980). The case of habitual drunkenness is a good example (Schneider, 1978). Thus, as a useful model for understanding the medical diagnosis of illness, our approach also seems useful for understanding the recognition of deviance.

More importantly, we view deviance as an integral feature of society. It is the "flip side" of respectability. Therefore, understanding an issue in deviance should not require a radically different approach from understanding the same issue in terms of respectability. The model we will be using in this chapter can help us understand both the recognition of deviance and the recognition of respectability. For example, how do we recognize that someone is a business person? We have general conceptions of what business people are like—they wear certain styles of clothing, carry briefcases, work late in office buildings, and so on. We gather information about particular individuals who walk past us. We check out what they are wearing, what they are carrying, where they may be heading, and so on. We then interpret that information in order to conclude what those people are. We may conclude that a man walking past us and into an office building who is wearing a three-piece suit and holding a briefcase is a businessman. Of course, we could be mistaken. The man could be a thief who is giving the appearance of a businessman. The important point, though, is that how we recognize deviance is similar to how we recognize (or think we recognize) respectability. That such a model is useful for understanding the recognition of deviance and of respectability underscores the belief that deviance is an integral feature of society. Now let us explore the three features of recognizing deviance: conceptions, checking out, and interpretation.

Conceptions of Deviance Our conceptions of deviance involve two basic features: *definitions* of deviance and *typifications* of deviance. Since in the previous chapter we explored in detail the development of definitions of deviance, we will only make some brief points here about them. Definitions of deviance are more or less precise understandings of what constitutes offensive behavior, ideas, or attributes. Laws are fairly specific in stating what constitutes different crimes, but even here there is often disagreement as to what the law means. Interpretation, the third key feature of our model, becomes problematic because the definitions themselves are unclear. For example, laws concerning juvenile delinquency have included, and still do include, such terms as "incorrigibility," "immorality," "growing up in idleness," "habitual truancy," and so on (Griffin and Griffin, 1978). What do these terms mean? The definitions of deviance that we use in everyday life are likely to be even more imprecise. What constitutes incompetence, ugliness, disloyalty, malingering, "doing" drugs, and so on? Even though we may have general and partially shared notions of what we mean by them, it is typically in specific situations that these offenses are concretely defined. Definitions of deviance can be written, as in the case of laws, rules, regulations, and procedures, or they can be more informal, as in the case of cultural values, common understandings within a group, and so forth.

Even when people "agree" as to what is deviant, the specific definitions of what constitutes deviance may be quite different. Police officers typically know the law better than do citizens (Gibbs and Erickson, 1979). Therefore, what citizens call an assault may not be an assault according to police officers. The officers and the citizens are not disagreeing that assaults are wrong, but they are disagreeing as to what constitutes an assault. Similarly, both lower-class and middle-class families may feel that retarded children need special education and services, but what one family considers retardation may not be what another family considers retardation. Definitions of retardation may differ according to social class (Mercer, 1973). People who use the same terms may actually be referring to different phenomena even if they agree that their respective phenomena are deviant. Definitions of deviance are understandings of what constitutes offenses and offenders. They are more or less precise and are more or less shared.

Typifications of Deviance   Typifications are "simplified, standardized categories or labels used to place other people or things" (Hawkins and Tiedeman, 1975, p. 82). In dealing with the world around us, it is impossible to take into account all of the information that we can gather about people and objects. There is too much for us to make sense out of all of it, so we emphasize some characteristics and exclude others. We create categories of people and events and then develop essential, usual, general, or *typical* features of those categories. In doing so, we are likely to overlook or be unconcerned with unique characteristics of particular people or objects that we put into such categories. Thus we create and learn from others what a typical football game is about, a typical lawyer, a typical test, and so on. We also develop typifications of homosexuality, prostitution, criminality, disability, and so on. We typify deviance and respectability. Typifications are known as stereotypes if they concern people. As Erich Goode (1978, p. 89) notes, stereotypes are "mental cartoons" of people. However, we typify phenomena other than people. Thus, typification is a more general concept than stereotype, though certainly the two address similar issues.

Typifications have two basic features. In part, they are *characterizations* or descriptions of the people or objects that we place within categories. Typifications are also *indications* enabling us to recognize people and objects that "belong" in those categories. Typifications help us place people and objectes into categories. Typifications are likely to influence how we deal with deviance. As Goode (1978, p. 92) notes, the "basic purpose of deviant stereotypes is instant recognition and denunciation of the deviant." We would argue that denunciation is only one way of dealing with deviance. In the next chapter we will explore how typifications and stereotypes influence our handling of deviance. Here we want to examine the two basic features of typifications: characterizations and indications.

Characterizations of Deviance   Characterizations of deviance and deviants will not be universally agreed upon, just as what is deviance is not. However, there seem to be some broad characterizations of different forms of deviance and kinds of deviants. For example, Russell Ward (1979) has uncovered three major dimensions of our attitudes toward homosexuality. He calls these *sinful lust*—sinful, oversexed, immoral, and so forth; *sensitive intellectual*—intelligent, artistic, and such; and *sick deviant*—sexually abnormal, perverted, and maladjusted. People do not equally hold to these three factors. Their social background and experiences, as measured by income, education, and age, are related to how strongly they view homosexuals in terms of these three factors. As another example, the blind are viewed as helpless, dependent people who live in a dark world but are also artistic (Scott, 1969). Marijuana users have been characterized as escapist, insecure people who are looking for kicks (Simmons, 1965).

Our characterizations of deviance are strongly related to our characterizations of minority groups and of the disabled (both of which could be usefully viewed within the framework of deviance). Those who hold negative attitudes toward deviants tend to hold negative attitudes toward racial and ethnic minorities (Simmons, 1969). Further, those who have unfavorable opinions about the blind or the deaf tend to have unfavorable opinions about minority groups in general and blacks in particular (Cowen et al., 1958, 1967). As we mentioned in the introductory chapter, deviants, minority groups, the disabled, women, and so on, have relatively little power in society. They have been put into subordinate statuses. Therefore, our understanding of deviance can help us better understand others who occupy subordinate statuses. In this case, those who are hostile and intolerant toward deviants also tend to be hostile and intolerant toward racial and ethnic minorities and toward the disabled.

In this respect, Barry Adam (1978) suggests that we have created a composite picture of three "inferiorized" groups: blacks, Jews, and homosexuals. While the specific descriptions for each group may vary, the composite picture depicts the three groups as (1) animals—foul smelling, brutish, uncivilized people; (2) hypersexual—unrestrained passions, uninhibited sensuality, links to witchcraft and the supernatural; (3) heretics and conspirators—faithless corruptors, seducers, susceptible to treason; and

(4) overly visible—noisy, flashy, loud, pushy, conspicuous in their consumption, and so forth.

Whatever their specific content, such characterizations seem to possess certain general features. Adam (1978, p. 43) suggests that the composite portrait of the three inferiorized groups is based on three factors. They are seen as a "problem," they are "all alike," and they are "recognizable as such without exception." Taking a different approach, Goode (1978, pp. 93–102) outlines six basic features of our stereotypes or characterizations about deviants: *exaggeration, centrality, persistence, disjunctiveness, homogeneity,* and *clustering.* The most extreme or exaggerated instances of people and behavior are seen as typical of all who are placed into the same category. The offense is viewed as central to the lives of those who engage in it or are characterized by it. The deviance becomes a "master status" (Hughes, 1945; Becker, 1963). Thus a blind person is first and foremost blind, and only later do we consider his or her other characteristics. A homosexual is seen as continually preoccupied with sex, and so on. We assume that once a deviant, always a deviant. Offenders are persistent in their identity. We feel that there is a radical separation, a disjunctiveness, between deviants and conventional people. Deviants live in separate worlds from respectable people. We assume that all those within a category are the same, they are homogeneous. Finally, we assume that a cluster or group of offensive characteristics describe a particular kind of deviant. Homosexuals are not just degraded because of their sexual preference, but we may also characterize them as perverted, mentally ill, maladjusted, lonely, and so on (Simmons, 1965). Remember Adam's (1978) *composite* portrait of inferiorized groups. We describe deviants with a cluster of traits (typically negative) and not just one.

Sources of Characterizations   We develop typifications of deviance in general and characterizations in particular through interaction with others, both conventional others and deviant others. Since our interaction with deviants is likely to be minimal or very impersonal, what we learn from conventional others will have a greater impact on our characterizations of deviance. (We will come back to this point later.) In fact, we may hold strongly to certain typifications of deviance without having interacted (or at least not being aware that we have) with the deviants. According to Hawkins and Tiedeman (1975, pp. 82–87), there are several major sources of our typifications and, in particular, our characterizations of deviance: *everyday words and phrases,* the *mass media, public education campaigns,* the activities of *moral crusaders,* official labeling *ceremonies,* the work of *control agencies,* and the activities of *social scientists.*

Sayings such as "queer as a three-dollar bill," "blind as a bat," "falling down drunk," "deaf and dumb," "dope fiend," "screaming fairy," "stark raving mad," and so on, imply a certain picture about those we consider deviant. The mass media capitalize on our ambivalence about deviance. As we noted in Chapter 1, while we may be repelled by deviance, we are also fascinated with it. Thus, the mass media may present sensationalist pictures of deviance in order to keep readership high (Dominick, 1978). And even when they are not trying to sensationalize, they are likely only to portray certain aspects of deviance. Violent crimes are emphasized by the mass media more than other illegal offenses (Dominick, 1978). Newspapers present stories of ex–mental patients who commit horrible crimes, but rarely do they present stories of ex–mental patients who lead quiet, respectable lives. Yet, fewer ex–mental patients are involved in crime as compared to the general population (Scheff, 1966). In the middle to late 1970s, the "disturbed Vietnam veteran" was a popular theme in the mass media. We partially develop our characterizations of deviance based on the images of deviance presented in the mass media (Dominick, 1978).

Through public education campaigns concerned groups disseminate to a wide audience their views of troublesome people and behaviors. They also often present the indications by which such offensive behavior and people can be recognized, the second basic feature of typifications. Child protection agencies inform us of the characteristics of abusing families. A brochure distributed by one agency states that abusing or neglecting families may be characterized by immaturity, lack of "parenting knowledge," social isolation, frequent crisis, and drug or alcohol problems. Moral crusaders—such as Anita Bryant in terms of homosexuality, Joseph Califano, former HEW secretary under President Carter, in terms of smoking, Joseph McCarthy in the early 1950s in terms of Communism, or Ralph Nader in terms of waste and corruption in business and government—also spread the word as to what shape the devil comes in and how the devil should be handled. Local figures may also act as moral crusaders. Reformed deviants who take to the lecture circuit often crusade against deviance and in doing so present a portrayal of offenses and offenders. They often tell "horror" stories about what they were like until they "saw the light," and by implication about what other deviants are still like.

During official labeling ceremonies, such as trials, commitment proceedings, court martials, and disciplinary hearings, images of deviance and deviants are presented. In order to be successful, these *status degradation ceremonies* must set the offender apart as a different kind of person (Garfinkel, 1956). When successful, the accused has been transformed into a devalued type of person. We denounce the deviant, and in doing so we depict what "evil" lurks within such people. We place the offender outside the boundaries of respectability. In large part official ceremonies are morality plays in which the opposing sides try to cast the accused as good or evil. And even when those in charge decide that the accused is not deviant, that the accused should remain among us, they do so by arguing that the accused is not like the deviants whose image was presented. Thus a successful defense still involves the presentation of images of deviance.

Control agencies also help to create and disseminate typifications of deviance. Their personnel, in order to routinely do their jobs, develop conceptions of the offenders they work with. This notion of routinely doing their jobs will be discussed in the next chapter. Control officials "share" their views with the deviants themselves, with the families and friends of the deviants, and with the public through interviews, guest lectures, public appeals for cooperation and support, and so on. Thus, the blind are depicted as likely to be helpless and dependent without the services of blindness agencies (Scott, 1969). Alcoholics Anonymous portrays alcoholics as always carrying the disease of alcoholism within them. Prison inmates may be portrayed as sadistic criminals or as people who need a second chance. In a newspaper article, a Southern sheriff linked topless clubs with organized crime and other undesirable activities. Whether accurate or not, the pronouncements of official agents are another source of our characterizations of deviance.

Finally, through their research, writing, public speaking, and teaching, social scientists help to create our conceptions of deviance. As we noted in Chapter 2, scientific images of deviance often parallel public images of deviance. Until recently, these images emphasized the absolute, inherent, and pathological nature of deviance. More specifically, social scientists develop pictures of deviance—a "profile" of assassins, the danger signs of suicide, the characteristics that presumably correlate with delinquency, and so on. For example, as we explored in Chapter 2, it has long been assumed by sociologists and criminologists that black youth and lower-class youth were the adolescents most likely to be involved in illegal behaviors. Recently, investigators have questioned the accuracy of such correlates of crime, and others have questioned the questioners (Hindelang, 1978; Tittle et al., 1978; Hindelang et al., 1979; Elliott and Ageton, 1980). Whether these and other recent images are more accurate than Cesare Lombroso's contention, during the nineteenth century, that many criminals were atavists, or throwbacks to an earlier stage in human development, and thus were characterized by excessively long arms, ears of unusual size, a large jaw, retreating forehead, and so forth (Reid, 1979; Hartjen, 1978; Sykes, 1978), is not the point. Hopefully, these images are more accurate. More importantly, the work of social scientists today, as in the past, influences our characterizations of deviance and deviants, and in turn how we handle such behavior and people. For example, Stanton Wheeler (1968) and his colleagues found that juvenile court judges who read social science literature were more likely to handle juveniles severely than those not familiar with such research. Or, educational programs for the deaf have moved toward total communication (signing, speaking, and any other effective means) in the past fifteen years and away from oralism (speaking and lip-reading), in part due to the research by social scientists (Higgins, 1980). Thus, social science research influences how we characterize and deal with deviants, though perhaps not as much as or in the ways social scientists would like.

Characterizations and Change Characterizations of deviance and deviants are likely to be resistant to change. This is so for several reasons. Our contacts with those who are felt to be offensive are likely to be minimal, socially distant, or stylized. We are likely to be ignorant of, indifferent toward, or hostile to deviants. Such limited relationships make it easy to stereotype people and not have our stereotypes challenged (Goode, 1978, pp. 89–90). The kinds of relationships we have with deviants support the development and perpetuation of our characterizations of offensive people. Our typifications of deviance and deviants support our morality (Goode, 1978, p. 92). To change them is, necessarily, to change our views of morality and immorality, of respectability and deviance. If homosexuals are not perverted, sexually abnormal, and mentally ill, what does that say for those of us who claim moral superiority because we are not homosexual? The same question can be asked of those who feel superior because they are not disabled, incompetent, on drugs, or alcoholic, and therefore are not characterized by the negative traits assumed to cluster with those kinds of deviance (Douglas, 1970). Do we create such a wide gulf between us and deviants as a way of reassuring ourselves of our own moral worth? If so, then changing our characterizations of deviance necessarily involves changing our conceptions of our own moral worth.

Finally, the coping strategies of deviants, which we will explore in detail in Chapter 7, may further inhibit our changing our characterizations of them. Out of fear of what may happen, many deviants do not disclose their offensive characteristics, behaviors, or identities. They keep secret their drug use, their homosexuality, their prison record, their "disloyal" feelings, and so forth. Consequently, we treat such people as respectable. If we knew that they were involved in deviance, some of us would be shocked and would apply our characterizations of deviance to them. Others of us, though, would slowly revise our notions about deviants because our deviant colleagues or friends simply belie the stereotypes. Some, though, might argue that the exception proves the rule. Thus the coping strategies that many deviants use do not provide conventional folks with the opportunity to revise their conceptions of deviants. Of course, some deviants flaunt their offenses as a way of ridiculing the morality of conventional people or in order to make conventional people uncomfortable. Some gays may "go out of their way" to camp it up in public in order to mock heterosexual morality. Such behavior may be useful for those who engage in it, but it is likely to help reinforce the stereotypes with which conventional people regard them as well as upset the "conventional" deviants within that particular group of deviants (Warren, 1974). Neither hiding one's deviance nor flaunting it will help lead conventional people to revise their characterizations of deviants.

However, while our characterizations of deviance may be resistant to change, they are not static. They are part of our broader images of deviance, and as we noted in Chapter 2, those images do change. So do our characterizations of offensive behavior and people. For example, as we noted earlier, Ward (1979), uncovered three features of our characterization of homosexuals: sinful lust, sensitive intellectual, and sick deviant. Compared to research more than a decade earlier (Simmons, 1965), Ward found that his respondents were less likely to characterize homosexuals in terms of sinful lust, were more likely to describe them in terms of sensitive intellectual, and had not changed much in their views of them as sick deviants. The emphasis on homosexuals as sick continued to be the predominant image. However, even here there was some change. According to Ward, we are more likely nowadays to view the presumed psychological problems of homosexuals as consequences rather than causes. We are less likely to see homosexuality as mental illness, though we may still see homosexuals as frustrated or maladjusted as a consequence of being homosexual. Similarly, while deaf people are still viewed as typically less competent than hearing people by the very nature of their being deaf, they are no longer seen as unable to think, as was the case in biblical times, or as incapable of driving a car, as was the case in the early part of this century (Higgins, 1980). Thus, our characterizations of deviance do change even if the changes are gradual.

Indications of Deviance Our typifications of deviance are not only descriptions or characterizations of the people we place in different categories. They are also the signs and symptoms, the indications, by which we recognize offenses and offenders. Often we do not directly observe offenders in the act of committing an offense—prostitutes engaging in prostitution, homosexuals engaging in sex with a same-gender person, or a drug user using a drug. In other cases, the offense is seen as a quality of the person, something inside them—mental illness, alcoholism, incompetence, and so forth. In these cases what we take to be indications of deviance are likely to be *indirect* signs and symptoms, observable clues of an underlying or unseen offense. The signs and symptoms that doctors use to diagnose illnesses and diseases are medical versions of what we have in mind. We all carry around with us notions about how to recognize an alcoholic, a homosexual, a cheater, and so on. We learn these through the people around us, through the sources of typifications that we discussed earlier. Let us present a few examples.

A nationally distributed magazine tells us that there are eight symptoms of depression that we should be aware of and concerned about (*Good Housekeeping,* October 1979). The article provides a self-test. If you check four of the symptoms, whether as mild, moderate, or severe, then according to the article you are suffering from some degree of clinical depression and should seek treatment; if you check one of the symptoms as severe, you should also seek treatment. In abbreviated form, the symptoms are: (1) loss of appetite or suddenly increased appetite; (2) problems sleeping; (3) loss of energy; (4) nervous agitation or the opposite—listlessness; (5) inability to enjoy normally pleasurable activities—decreased sex drive; (6) feelings of guilt; (7) difficulty in concentrating or in making decisions; and (8) recurrent thoughts of suicide or wishing to be dead.

Here is another example. Alcoholics Anonymous distributes a twelve-question self-report test to be used as a screening device for those who have trouble with alcohol. According to AA, an individual who answers yes to four or more of the questions is probably in trouble with alcohol. Why does AA say this? Because that has been the *experience* of its members. The self-report questions can also be used to spot alcohol problems in your family members and friends. Some of the questions are: (1) Do you wish people would mind their own business about your drinking—stop telling you what to do? (2) Have you had a drink in the morning during the past year? (3) Has your drinking caused trouble at home? (4) Do you ever try to get "extra" drinks at a party? (5) Have you missed days of work because of drinking? (6) Do you have "blackouts"? (7) Have you ever felt that your life would be better if you did not drink?

Official agents are trained to look for the signs and symptoms of deviance, whether it be crime, mental illness, drug dependence, and so on. Some may even write books to enable fellow agents, as well as the general public, to acquire the skills to better observe deviance. David Powis, a deputy assistant commissioner for Scotland Yard, has written a field manual for police, *The Signs of Crime,* for just that purpose. Powis (1977, p. 2) suggests that police officers "should study and observe in all circumstances the behaviour of ordinary, innocent people, as well as the behaviour of criminals. Once differences have been analyzed, there will be development towards instant recognition." Among Powis's tips are the following: Watch for a man sitting in the front passenger seat of a parked car. He may be a lookout for a crime in progress. A man sitting in the driver's seat arouses suspicion, but an observer may assume that a passenger has to wait for the driver to return. Watch for a man without an overcoat in the winter who is in the part of the store that sells overcoats. He may be a shoplifter. Watch for the false disturbance (how does one know it is false?) that may be a cover for theft. This too may indicate a crime in progress.

The Supreme Court seems to support the use of these signs of crime.

In 1980 it overturned a lower-court ruling which had struck down as unconstitutional the Drug Enforcement Administration's five-year-old program of stopping airline passengers who show "characteristics" of being drug couriers. The following case was involved.

> On February 10, 1976 two DEA agents at Detroit's airport observed _____get off a commercial flight from Los Angeles. The agents later testified that they grew suspicious because Ms._____was the last passenger to leave the plane, appeared nervous, claimed no luggage and changed airplanes for a connecting flight to Pittsburgh. Ms._____was stopped and questioned, and then asked to accompany the agents to their private office. Two bags of heroin were found in Ms._____'s undergarments. She was arrested, eventually convicted and sentenced to 18 months in jail. (*Columbia Record*, May 27, 1980, p. 4-A)

While organizations and officials may create and distribute guides to what they consider the signs and symptoms of deviance, citizens may use commonsensical, everyday characteristics as indications of deviance. John Kitsuse (1962) suggests that we are likely to infer that a person is a homosexual based on vague behaviors "which everyone knows" are indications of homosexuality. In his research in the early 1960s, Kitsuse found that students used such behaviors as a person's expressed interest in psychology or a career Navy man's lack of interest in girls during leave as indications of homosexuality. Whether the individuals concerned were homosexual or not is another issue. Interestingly, Kitsuse found that there were relatively few characteristics which students took as indications of female homosexuality.

    Signs and Symptoms   While we cannot provide a list of all the signs and symptoms that are used as indications of deviance, we can briefly explore the *kinds* of signs and symptoms that are likely to be used as indications of deviance. *Clothing, appearance, behavior, location,* and *social relations* are all used as indications of deviance. Tight pants as an indication of homosexuality or fishnet stockings as an indication of prostitution is what we mean by clothing. A bedraggled appearance may be taken as an indication of being a drunk. Unattractiveness in general is used as an indication of deviance, whether it be crime or epilepsy (Shoemaker et al., 1973; Hansson and Duffield, 1976). During a local trial, a police officer testified that the behavior of the defendant, who was driving slowly past parked cars and looking from side to side, aroused the officer's suspicion. The defendant was driving along some streets where cars had been parked for an athletic contest and where previous complaints of break-ins had been made. Thus the defendant's location and behavior both aroused suspicion. Similarly, a woman's standing on a certain street corner may be taken as an indication that she is a prostitute. Finally, those who are friends of homosexuals may be suspect themselves. Those who associate with "known" criminals are thought to be up to no good. Thus the social relationships which people have with others may be taken as indications of deviance.

Most likely we will not use individual, isolated characteristics as indications of deviance. Instead, our suspicions may be aroused through a *constellation* of several characteristics which together are taken as an indication of deviance. For example, we will probably not infer that a woman is a prostitute just because she is wearing fishnet stockings, but if she is wearing fishnet stockings, is "made up," and is standing on a certain corner, we are likely to infer that she is a hooker or maybe a decoy. So too with the officer who testified at the trial that the defendant was driving in a certain way in a certain location. It is because we infer deviance through a constellation of signs and symptoms in concrete situations that it is fruitless to try to come up with a list of the signs and symptoms of deviance.

The signs and symptoms that we use as indications of deviance will differ based on our background and experiences. For example, what the police use as signs of crime is *presumably* more sophisticated, subtle, and accurate than what citizens take to be indications of crime. The training and experience of police officers influence the kinds of signs and symptoms they use as indications of crime.

The signs and symptoms that we use are relative, as is deviance itself. For example, the lower classes are not as quick as those of higher status to recognize mental illness or mental retardation in their family members. When lower-class individuals are recognized as mentally ill or mentally retarded, they are more likely to be recognized by official agents, such as police officers or teachers, than are those from higher classes (Mercer, 1973; Clausen and Huffine, 1975). There are many complex reasons for this. For the purpose of our discussion, the important point is that lower-status families are farther removed from the experiences and orientations of professionals than are middle- or upper-class families. Professionals are members of the middle and upper-middle class, and the signs and symptoms they have created for recognizing mental illness and mental retardation are probably more familiar to middle- and upper-status families than to lower-status families. Consequently, if those signs and symptoms are helpful for recognizing mental illness or retardation, lower-status families would be slower to recognize such deviance. The point is not so much that lower-status families use less accurate signs and symptoms of mental illness and retardation than middle-class families, but rather that, because of their experiences, they use different ones. A great deal more research needs to be done concerning the development and use of indications of deviance.

In this respect, deviants are likely to develop signs for recognizing fellow deviants that are more subtle than the signs used by the general public. The techniques that deviants use to pass as respectable people—hiding their blemish, as it were—may give away their identity to those who are familiar with such tricks (Goffman, 1963). (We will have more to say about these coping strategies later.) Thus, a child of hearing-impaired parents, through being familiar with the mechanisms that his or her parents used to pass as hearing—soft voices, sentences that trail off, or monopolizing the conversation—may be able to recognize others who are hearing-impaired (Warfield, 1948). Similarly, Edward Delph (1978) speaks of the silent community of public male homosexual encounters where, through body language, fellow homosexuals make their intentions and therefore their identity known to one another. Clandestine groups are likely to develop means by which fellow members can recognize each other, but not be recognized by the larger social world. Thus, deviants too use signs and symptoms by which to recognize fellow deviants or to inform fellow deviants who they are.

Checking Out Deviance

In order to recognize deviance we need to gather information. In a very broad sense, we check out what is happening or what we think may happen. We can gather information actively or passively. We can go out and try to "dig up" information, or we may just happen to be in a situation where we cannot escape noticing that deviance is occurring all around us. For example, stores use "integrity shoppers," employees of an outside detective firm, who make purchases and observe the behavior of salespeople. Employee theft is most likely to be discovered this way. Yet, employee theft may also be discovered by a co-worker who cannot help but notice the dishonest behavior of a fellow employee (Robin, 1969). Even a passive approach, however, requires some effort on our part. Thus, active and passive stances are a matter of degree. The most extreme form of the active approach to gathering information might be where we try to *induce* others to engage in deviance and therefore observe them "red-handed." Not only do we actively seek out information, but we also set the stage for the deviance. The recent FBI undercover "sting" operations, such as the Abscam investigation of corruption among politicians and other officials, is an example of what we mean. The FBI rented a house in Washington, D.C., arranged for politicians to attend meetings there, and recorded the transactions with sophisticated electronic gear. Many people argued that the FBI went beyond pursuing an active stance in gathering information. Instead it created the deviance and entrapped the politicians. Some of the accused have made just this point in their defenses and have successfully used it in appealing guilty verdicts.

In checking out deviance we can gather either *direct* or *indirect* information. We can observe the offensive behavior and the offenders through our senses, or we can detect deviance indirectly through the signs and symptoms discussed above. If we indirectly become aware of deviance, and if we are concerned with the matter, we will probably continue to check out our suspicions. In checking out our suspicions we may gather additional indirect information and also search for direct information concerning the deviance. The police continue to check out suspects, parents check out their fears that their child is retarded, and teachers may check out their hunches that a student is cheating on tests. If we have direct information about the offenses and the offenders, then we likely will not do as much additional checking out. Checking out is thus a process of gathering information and also implies that the information is being *interpreted* in order to decide what to do next. Thus checking out deviance and interpreting the information uncovered are tied together. As will become evident shortly, conceptions of deviance, checking out deviance, and interpreting the information—the three features of our model for recognizing deviance—are closely linked. Each influences the other.

Visibility   The visibility of offenses and offenders is a crucial issue in recognizing deviance. Offenses and offenders that are relatively invisible will require greater checking out than those that are visible. Checking out is a way of making deviance visible. Instead of "visibility," Erving Goffman (1963, p. 48) uses the term *evidentness*. While most deviance is observed through our sense of sight, not all is. We see a robbery, but we *hear* a stammer, and may *taste* an awful meal which leads us to say that the chef is incompetent. However, for ease of discussion, we will use the term "visibility." Some deviance is more visible than other types. The victims of a robbery are quite aware that they are being robbed even if they may not recognize the robber. That is a matter of identifying the offender, which we will discuss later. However, computer theft—for example, the illegal transfer of funds from other accounts to one's own—is relatively invisible. A facial disfigurement or missing limb is quite visible, but deafness in an infant may not be. In general, the more visible the deviance, the more likely it is that we will recognize it.

However, those engaged in offensive behavior realize this very point: the more visible their behavior, the more likely they will be recognized. Therefore, offenders are likely to engage in offensive behavior behind locked doors, under cover of night, in secluded spots, when no one is looking, and so on. Not too surprisingly, more than 40 percent of all personal crimes occur in the nighttime, from 6 P.M. to 6 A.M. (U.S. Department of Justice, 1977). Those who do engage in offensive behavior in such a way that everyone can see may not care whether others know of their deviance, may not be concerned about what others will do, or may want others to find out. College students have staged "smoke-ins" to protest laws against the use of marijuana. Williams and Weinberg (1970) found that homosexual servicemen who had received less-than-honorable discharges, as compared to those who avoided recognition, were more likely to have sought to identify themselves as homosexual in order to be discharged or had increased the risk of discovery through a high level of homosexual behavior or through an "unwise" choice of partners. Making their behavior and orientation visible served other purposes for these servicemen. Coping strategies of deviant groups may entail their becoming visible as they demand more just treatment. Often, though, those who engage in offensive behavior will attempt to hide it, which makes it all the more difficult to recognize.

Private vs. Public Places   The place in which deviant behavior is committed influences whether we recognize it or not. Offensive behavior carried out in private places is less likely to be observed, except by fellow participants, as compared to similar behavior taking place in more public areas. Can you imagine a police officer routinely checking out a country club? What about a public bar, though? In fact, many behaviors that would be regarded as offensive if they took place in public are seen as inoffensive or less offensive if they occur in private. The idea of situational relativity comes into play here. As Arthur Stinchcombe (1963, p. 157) has noted: "Individual disorder in public places consists mainly of doing things that would be entirely legitimate if done in private, such as getting too drunk to stand up, or sleeping on park benches."

Those who have access to private places are better able to engage in deviance without being observed than those who only have more public places in which to act offensively. As has often been noted, access to private places generally implies the possession of resources, and it is those with the fewest resources who will have the least access to private places. Privacy does not come cheaply. A company's executives can "goof off" behind closed doors, but the secretaries who "goof off" in the large typing pools run a much greater risk of being caught (Palmer, 1977). Similarly, as William Chambliss (1973) found in a study of two gangs, which he called the Saints and the Roughnecks, one reason why the Roughnecks were handled more harshly by the police and were more likely to be seen as delinquent, as compared to the Saints, was that their behavior was more visible. The Saints, an upper-middle-class group of boys, could drive away from the watchful eyes of the community. The Roughnecks, a lower-class group, congregated near a drugstore in a crowded, heavily traveled area of the city. Since the members did not have cars and were scattered throughout the city, a central meeting place was a necessity. However, teachers and law enforcement officers passed by frequently. Even those with few resources may have some privacy. Earl Rubington (1978) found that members of a West Coast bottle gang, men who pass around a bottle, were much less likely to be hassled by the police or citizens than an East Coast gang. The West Coast gang had established a territory—they stayed within it and others kept out. The East Coast gang had no such "private" territory, and therefore in procuring and drinking alcohol they were more visible to police and citizens.

In general, it is those within the lower strata of a community, an organization, or a group who have the least access to private places, and thus their deviance will be the most visible. Interestingly, the impact of private places on visibility has greatly influenced who and what sociologists have studied. Sociologists have focused on deviance which is visible and to which they have had relatively easy access (Thio, 1973). They have focused more on public deviance than on private deviance. They have focused on the deviance of the lower class and the less powerful. Since the deviance of the more powerful in society is less accessible, sociologists have tended to overlook in their work the deviance of corporate executives, military brass, high-ranking law enforcement officers, the upper class, and so on. The lack of visibility due to the offender's access to private places has influenced whose deviance both sociologists and others have observed.

The visibility of people and their behavior is further increased by the number of contacts or tie-ins they have with official agencies. While providing services to clients, agencies gather information and monitor the client's behavior. The agencies may pass incriminating information on to other agencies. Again, it is generally those with the fewest resources who are tied into official agencies which provide services to them, such as public housing agencies, welfare departments, public health services, and so forth (Hawkins and Tiedeman, 1975). For example, in a California city, 40 percent of the statutory rape cases that came to the attention of the police were referrals from welfare agencies. The cases became known during routine investigations of poor, often young mothers who were applying for ADC (Aid for Dependent Children), and the information was turned over to the police (Skolnick and Woodworth, 1967). Thus, the more agencies which keep track of your behavior, the more likely your deviance will become known.

Hide and Seek   Because observers know that much deviance will be hidden, how observers deploy their resources will have a great impact on whom they observe. Where observers choose to search for deviance will clearly influence what offenses and which offenders they uncover. Where observers look will likely be influenced by their *typifications* of deviance and by the often conflicting *interests* of themselves and others.

Typifications of deviance will influence observers, whether they be police officers, IRS auditors, public health officials, or the general public, to look in some places and not others, and to watch some people closely and not others. Typifications not only help us to recognize deviance but they also inform us of where to look for it. Thus, more police squad cars are deployed in certain sections of the city than in others, store detectives watch some shoppers more closely than others, and so on. Observers often deploy their resources as efficiently as they think possible. Typifications influence that deployment.

However, to the extent that observers' typifications of deviance are inaccurate, their deployment of resources will be less useful. Further, to the extent that the typifications are themselves offensive to others, the deployment of resources will create conflict. Thus, minority-group members often complain that they are stopped on the street for no apparent reason. Are they stopped simply because police officers are prejudiced against them? Possibly. Or are they stopped because police officers, through their experience, training, and background, have developed typifications which suggest to them that minority members need to be watched more closely? As David Matza (1969, pp. 180–195) has noted, not all people are equally suspect. In doing their job, law enforcement officers use a "method of suspicion" which influences whom they watch and where they look. It is this bureaucratic suspicion, or what we have called typification, and not incidental suspicion or individual prejudice, which is the more important factor in where observers look for deviance. In general, our typifications of deviance lead us to watch more closely those with fewer resources, the poor, the disadvantaged, and so on, rather than the powerful.

In this respect, Johnson (1977) and his colleagues analyzed the arrest probabilities for marijuana users in three localities—Chicago, Omaha, and Washington, D.C. While there were some differences among the three localities, Johnson and his colleagues found that males as compared to females, blue-collar workers as compared to white-collar workers, and to a less consistent degree, blacks as compared to whites, and those 25 and under as compared to those over 25, had higher probabilities of arrest for marijuana use. The differences in the probability of being arrested could *not* be simply accounted for by males, blue-collar workers, and so on, being more likely to use marijuana than females, white-collar workers, and so forth. Instead, Johnson and his colleagues argue that either *differential visibility* or *differential law enforcement* accounts for the difference in the likelihood of being arrested. The arrests tended to take place on the "street," or in cars and during routine patrols by officers. Perhaps blue-collar workers, the young, and blacks are more likely to smoke in such public places, as compared to white-collar workers, those over 25, and whites. Thus the visibility of the marijuana use may have influenced who was arrested. Or it may be that during routine patrol not all people are equally suspect or watched equally closely. Police give differential attention to passers-by. Perhaps characteristics associated with being young, black, male, or a blue-collar worker are taken as cues by officers to be more suspicious of such people than others. Thus the marijuana user's access to and use of private places as well as the officer's conceptions of where to look probably influenced who was arrested for using marijuana.

Our typifications of deviance are not the only factors that influence how we deploy our resources for observing deviance. In a world of conflict, the personal interests of the observers and of other concerned parties will have an impact on where observers look for deviance. For example, as we noted in the previous chapter, during the summer of 1967, the New York City police were pressured by politicians, business people, and City Hall to "clean up" the Times Square area in terms of prostitution (Roby, 1969). They did so by arresting more than 1,000 prostitutes in a one-month period. Call girls, who served well-connected men, went about their business unnoticed. Similarly, the IRS has been accused in the past of being "out to get" certain taxpayers on orders from the White House. The FBI for a long time, primarily under J. Edgar Hoover, was interested in keeping a polished image with high arrest statistics for auto theft, but did not actively pursue a policy of using undercover agents to catch crime among the higher-ups. The recent "sting" operations signal a definite shift in policy within the FBI. Thus, while typifications of deviance influence where observers look for deviance, other factors do too.

In seeking deviance and deviants, observers will often create new *strategies* and *technologies* which allow them to observe better. Police officers now use radar "guns" to spot speeders and lie-detector tests to observe criminals. Mental health specialists develop what they hope are sophisticated diagnostic tools in order to recognize mental illness. Airport security personnel use metal detectors and x-ray devices to detect potential hijackers and trained dogs to sniff for contraband or explosives. Banks and other businesses use hidden and sometimes clearly displayed cameras in order to record all transactions. There are two basic problems with such strategies or technologies.

First, they are rarely 100 percent accurate. Of course few methods of observation are. The new technologies are only designed to be better than the old, not to be perfect. However, because of their potential inaccuracy, information gathered with them may not be viewed as acceptable by others. Thus, the results of lie-detector (polygraph) tests are generally not admissible as evidence. Now, the accuracy of radar is being questioned. A third of all radar readings may be in error according to a former San Diego police officer (Associated Press, 1980). Consequently, some judges have ruled that such evidence is inadmissible, and no doubt more motorists will seek to suppress such information at their trials. In California, a federal judge has ruled that using IQ tests to place black children in classes for the mentally retarded violates the Fourteenth Amendment's equal-protection clause. The judge presumes that the tests are biased against certain minority groups (*Newsweek,* February 18, 1980).

Second, offenders realize that control agents are likely to develop better devices for detecting them. Consequently, offenders are likely to become more sophisticated (or is it devious?) in hiding their offenses. Motorists now use radar detectors or "fuzz busters" in order to detect the presence of a police officer with radar and therefore to be able to go undetected themselves. The use of CBs serves a similar purpose. Or, as airport security has increased dramatically in the past ten years, the strategies of hijackers have become more sophisticated. Through the use of fake weapons that seem real to the people on the plane but are not detected, through the use of gasoline or lighter fluid, or through smuggling a real weapon in a baby's metal carrying seat with the baby in it, individuals still manage to hijack planes. In turn, as the offenders become more sophisticated, so do the observers, and an ever-increasing escalation of sophistication by both sides continues. Police officers now monitor CBs with their own CBs, and there is talk of developing a radar detector which cannot be detected. Where will it all end? Does this sound similar to the arms race between countries?

Picking Out the Offender   An additional task in recognizing deviance is to identify the offender. In everyday talk "identify" means to "pick out," as in: "The victim identified the suspect in a police lineup." Remember, later we will discuss the identification of deviants, by which we mean the decision of observers as to the "true" character of the offender. As we mentioned earlier, in some cases when we recognize an offense we also recognize an offender. Such is not always the case, however, In some situations the offender may directly confront the victim-observer, as in robbery, but the observer may not be able to identify the offender. There are also situations in which the offender does not directly confront anyone, though the offense is very evident. Property crimes, such as burglary, auto theft, and vandalism, fall into this category. In either case, additional effort or checking out will be necessary in order to identify or pick out the offender.

Picking out an offender is generally a great deal more difficult than noticing an offense. When observers do not identify offenders at the time that they recognize the offense, a successful identification later is unlikely. Often there are few leads to go on. If there are no leads upon which other observers—say the police, for example—can act, then they typically will not pursue the case further. Police generally have enough cases to work as it is. From experience, they feel that cases with few or no leads will simply be a waste of their time. Unless victims complain that nothing is being done, detectives primarily investigate "big" cases and those with good leads (Sanders, 1977). Thus, in a malicious mischief case where someone had shot a BB pellet through a window, the juvenile detectives in a West Coast sheriff's department spent little effort on it because there was nothing to go on in the case (Sanders, 1977, p. 134). Property offenses often have no good leads. For example, burglary, by definition, involves going inside a building. Thus burglars are invisible to observers unless they were seen entering the building. Further, most burglaries are committed when no regular occupant is present, so the victim does not observe the burglar either (Sanders, 1977). The same can also be said of other property offenses. Thus, it is not too surprising that of the eight Part One offenses, also called the Crime Index by the FBI, three property offenses—burglary, larceny-theft, and motor vehicle theft—have the lowest clearance rates (i.e., "solved" by arrest or exceptional means): 16 percent, 20 percent, and 15 percent respectively for 1978 (Webster, 1979). The same was true the following year as well (Webster, 1980).

However, even when offenders are observed while committing offenses, it may still be difficult to identify them. We can pick out or recognize people's *social* identities and/or their *personal* identities. Social identity means the general social characteristics, such as age, sex, race, and social class, by which we categorize people (Goffman, 1963). Personal identity refers to the unique biography of an individual with which we associate a name, such as John Jones or Mary Smith. Ultimately, we want the offender to be personally identified, not socially identified. Even when an offender directly confronts the victim-observer, as in a robbery, typically the two are strangers. In such cases the social identity of the offender may be recognized, but not the personal identity. Consequently, robberies too have a low rate of being solved. Only 26 percent of reported robberies were cleared in 1978 (Webster, 1979). Why?

The more that control agents must rely on information concerning the social identity of the offender and not the personal identity, the less likely they will be able to locate the suspect. The reason is relatively simple. Social identities and personal identities only loosely correspond to each other. Many people have similar social identities but are, of course, different individuals. Thus, when minority members charge police harassment, the trouble in part may be that officers are relying too much on social identity in order to personally identify a suspect. Of course, it may be harassment too. Only in limited cases will knowing the social identity of the offender help us much in personally identifying the culprit. For example, in a former all-girls school which now has a few male students, knowing that an offense was committed by a male will eliminate most of the suspects. The problem then becomes to distinguish among the males. In this and similarly limited cases, the social identity of certain people may be enough information by which to personally identify them.

Finally, in our society filled with conflict, the cooperation necessary for personally identifying offenders may be difficult to obtain. Through mistrust, fear, or conflicting interests, citizens may fail to cooperate with officials or officials may not cooperate with each other. Thus, in one London police district, an identification parade (lineup) was held in the tube (subway) station. It was held there because black residents of the community are reluctant to go to the police station as participants in identification parades. To be fair, though, the suspects in this case had to be paraded with other blacks and not just with whites. If they were not, their social identity would have made them easier to pick out. As one official commented, the practice may become routine (*Guardian*, 1979). Thus, even if offenses are noticed, it may take additional effort to identify the offenders. And once identified, offenders may still have to be located.

Interpreting the Information

As we gather information, as we check out what is happening, we will interpret that information. Based on our interpretations we may decide to do a number of different things: gather more information, look in a different place, decide that our suspicions are unfounded, confirm our suspicions, and so on. As we noted earlier, checking out and interpreting are interwoven features of our recognition of deviance. Our interpretative work is aimed at making sense out of what is often an unclear or confusing situation.

In many situations the interpretative work seems relatively straightforward. In fact, we may not even realize that we are engaging in it because what is happening seems so obvious. For example, while standing in line at a bank teller's window you notice that people have suddenly become quiet. You develop a suspicion that something is wrong. A few seconds later as you lie on the floor you have confirmed your suspicion: the bank is being robbed.

Many times, however, there may be a delay of several hours, days, weeks, even months, or longer between your suspicion and your final interpretation of what is and was happening. In these more problematic cases (i.e., not as clear-cut for the observer), the interpretative aspect of recognizing deviance becomes clear. The delay itself is a result of the interpretative work, as people check, recheck, consult with others, sort out, and piece together information before reaching a decision. For example, as William Sanders notes (1977), since detective work is routinely problematic, a study of detective work can greatly help us to understand different features of the interpretative aspects of recognizing deviance. Detectives themselves classify criminal homicide cases as either "whodunits" or "walk-throughs." The distinction refers to whether or not the officers have any idea as to who the suspect is (Sanders, 1977). Of course, in other cases it may not even be clear whether a criminal homicide has been committed. The death may have been due to suicide. For example, in testing the victim's shotgun in one case, West Coast detectives decided that what they had considered to be a possible homicide was in fact a suicide and not a homicide. The detectives had been initially puzzled because the "breach of the pump-action shotgun was opened and the shell casing was in a wastebasket on the other side of the room" (Terry and Luckenbill, 1976, p. 85). By testing the shotgun, the detectives concluded that the shell would eject from the chamber. The fact that it landed in a wastebasket was just chance. Thus, even in detective work, some cases are more problematic than others. But whether problematic or not, interpretative work is necessary to solve the case.

From Suspicion to Confirmation Our interpretations are aimed at making sense out of what is happening. Through checking out we try to reduce our uncertainty as to what is going on. We may decide that our suspicions are unfounded. We may change our suspicions or our sense of what is happening. We may just let "everything drop" and go on to other matters. Or we may confirm our suspicions. We will use this last path, from suspicion to confirmation, as the basis for our discussion of various features that influence our interpretative work. Very little research has been done concerning this issue. Much remains to be done. However, we can suggest several important features of interpretative work: *information;* the *familiarity* of the deviance to the observer; and the *relation* between the observer and the observed.

Information From the information available, observers may be able to make more than one interpretation of what is happening. For example, store detectives may not be sure whether a certain shopper is stealing some merchandise. Perhaps the shopper absent-mindedly put the item in a coat pocket. There is uncertainty as to what is happening; a suspicion that must be checked out further. Or, the parents notice that their young child has not responded to their voices. Perhaps the child is deaf, or perhaps the child was only tired. Or, in most cases during William Sander's (1977) observation of a sheriff's department, there was more than one possible interpretation of the information the detectives had. Information is often incomplete, ambiguous, or inconsistent. Additional checking out and interpretation will be necessary.

The information that observers acquire about a possible case of deviance is often inconsistent. With inconsistent information, confident interpretations of what is happening may be difficult. Inconsistent information (of course, inconsistency is a matter of interpretation too) primarily comes from two sources: the suspect's behavior and the *opinions of others.* The behavior of possibly offensive people is likely to be both offensive and acceptable, both deviant and respectable. Even those who are greatly involved in serious deviance also engage in very routine activities: eating, buying clothes, talking normally, and so forth. Alcoholics are not always drinking and are not always drunk. Homosexuals do not spend their entire day pursuing sex. Those who commit crimes also watch TV, go to the grocery store, and have their hair cut. Thus, while our stereotypes may suggest that there is a wide gulf between deviants and conventional people (disjunctiveness), the behavior of deviants is often very conventional. Thus, with conflicting information, interpretative work becomes more difficult.

In checking out our suspicions we often ask for the advice, opinion, or interpretation of others as to what is happening. Because of their different backgrounds and different experiences with the suspect, they may provide interpretations (i.e., more information) at odds with what we believe is happening. Of course, they could help confirm our suspicions. Parents who suspect that their infant or young child has a disability may be told by doctors and other health officials not to worry: it is too early to tell, their fears are ungrounded, the child will grow out of the symptom, and so on (Freemen et al., 1975). Or, a married person who suspects that his or her spouse is having mental difficulties may get conflicting information from others. Some may discount the likelihood of there being reason for alarm. Others, however, may encourage the view that the problem is a psychiatric one (Yarrow et al., 1955). Thus, our interpretations are likely to be influenced by the information that others provide us.

Familiarity with the Deviance   Deviance may be more or less familiar to us. We may have no knowledge of some types of deviance and therefore could not possibly interpret what is happening in terms of those categories. For example, how many of us knew what hyperkinesis or hyperactivity was a few years ago? Other categories may seem unreasonable. The category of "witch" is known to many of us, but does not seem very reasonable. The same continues to hold true for many physicians who cannot believe that parents could abuse their children (Pfohl, 1977). Finally, we are more sensitive to some categories of deviance than to others (Lofland, 1969, pp. 131–136).

Prior experience and training will increase our knowledge about deviance and sensitize us to it. Thus, one spouse may have difficulty in interpreting the disturbing and puzzling behavior of the other, whereas a psychiatrist might quickly conclude that such behavior is a result of mental illness (Yarrow et al., 1955). In this regard, Sanders (1977, p. 25) argues that through experience and training detectives develop skills that are similar to the

> ability developed by a jigsaw-puzzle master. However, whereas the puzzle-doer is given a jumble of pieces which he knows are parts of a single puzzle, and he also knows what the puzzle is supposed to look like on completion, the detective at the outset of a case has numerous pieces but does not know which pieces fit which puzzle or, indeed, whether any of them belong in any puzzle at all.

Prior experience and training, though, can both sensitize us to deviance and create blinders for us. We may become so sensitized to deviance that we recognize it when it does not exist. As we will discuss shortly, psychiatrists may be prone to interpret behavior as an indication of mental illness when "in fact" the patient is not mentally ill. Prior experiences and, especially, training may also act as blinders. While they open our eyes to some events, they close them to others. Information may be interpreted in standard ways, and other information may be overlooked or ignored. As we will see in the next chapter, official control agents develop and learn standard ways of routinely dealing with deviance. However, those standard procedures also serve a useful function.

Relationship Between the Observer and the Observed   The relationship that we as observers have with the observed will often influence our interpretation of what is happening. Relationships can vary in many different ways: the reason for the relationship, how close the involved parties are, how often the involved parties see each other, and so on. For our purposes here, relationships between observers and observed can be *positive* (e.g., love, respect, friendship, etc.) or *negative* (e.g., hate, dislike, etc.). Obviously relationships are a matter of degree, and there may be both positive and negative aspects to any relationship. In general, the more positively observers feel toward the observed—toward the suspect—the less likely and less quickly will they confirm their suspicions of deviance in the observed. The more negative the relationship, the more likely and quicker will be the confirmation.

The impact of the quality of the relationship between the observer and the observed on interpreting information and recognizing deviance can best be understood in terms of *cognitive consistency*. In general we like the world to be consistent; the different parts of it should fit together. Good should go with good, and bad with bad (Brown, 1965, chap. 11). A great deal of research shows that we like to create consistency out of inconsistency. For example, two people who like each other would tend to feel better if each knew that the other held similar views about a particular issue. If one of them liked a certain movie but the other did not, that would be inconsistent. However, two people who dislike each other might feel it quite consistent for each of them to have a different opinion about the same movie—each might feel that the disliked person would, of course, not know any better. Whether people think a situation is consistent or inconsistent usually becomes important only when the issue is significant to them. If the issue is relatively unimportant, then whether their feelings are consistent or not becomes less troublesome.

There are many ways of dealing with inconsistency, such as ignoring the situation, changing one's view about the other person in order to make the situation consistent, changing one's view toward the issue, or trying to differentiate the issue into several issues. A husband who disagrees with his wife about a movie may reinterpret the situation such that although his wife did not like the acting, he was really speaking about his enjoyment of the plot.

This notion of cognitive consistency and how we deal with it can be applied to the relationship between observers and suspects. Observers who have a positive relationship with the observed will likely feel that it is inconsistent for the observer to be engaging in deviance. Good is being associated with evil. Further, in some cases, to recognize deviance in a person we are close to is to possibly implicate ourselves in the deviance or threaten our own security. Think of the wife who begins to suspect mental illness in her husband or the parents who suspect that their child is doing drugs.

How can such observers deal with this inconsistency? The wife may ignore the disturbing behavior, may deny that anything is wrong, may interpret it as not all that different from what other husbands do, or may try to explain it away (Yarrow et al., 1955). Parents of children who are later suspected of hyperactivity may do the same thing:

> Parents accommodate to the deviant behavior within the family system. . . . They would ignore what they could. . . . Families seem to have a relatively high tolerance level for deviance. Parents talk in terms of "accepting things" and "We could handle it" when asked why they did not earlier identify their child's behavior as deviance. They often only identify deviance after it has come to outside (especially school) attention (Conrad, 1976, pp. 35–36).

In this respect the tendency to use denials and self-deception instead of admitting deviance in oneself becomes understandable. Alcoholics are often likely at first to deny that they have a problem (Rubington, 1973). To admit it is to associate yourself with "evil." Similarly, a young woman who is a lesbian and who is often a guest speaker in one of our classes mentioned that she suspected she was gay when she was a teenager, but did not admit it to herself until more than ten years later. Many gays and other deviants have also delayed for a long time before admitting to themselves who or what they are.

In contrast, neutral observers presumably would not face the same kind of difficulty in recognizing deviance as do observers who have a positive relationship to the observed. And to go one step further, observers who have a negative relationship with the observed would more quickly suspect and confirm deviance. In fact, they may be eager to do so.

Retrospective Interpretation   In confirming our suspicion and in supporting our confirmation we are likely to retrospectively interpret past events (Kitsuse, 1962). In order to document our belief that a particular individual is offensive and has been that way all along, we reinterpret past incidents and events which had no special significance at the time they occurred. In light of our present belief about the offensive individual, we give meaning to past occurrences. Retrospective interpretation is a way of bolstering our beliefs, making a case, or trying to create consistency out of what we think has happened and is happening. Kitsuse (1962) argues that this process is particularly likely to occur when the prior relationship between the observer and the offender is more than fleeting. As Kitsuse (1962, p. 253) notes, observers search for "subtle cues and nuances of behavior which might give further evidence of the alleged deviance." Generally, the observers are able to "find" such cues in order to support the conclusion that the person was engaging in offensive behavior all along.

For example, while in graduate school one of the authors developed a friendship with a new professor at the university through playing tennis with him. After being told later by the professor that he was gay, the author retrospectively interpreted the situation. The author remembered that the professor was in his early thirties, but not married. Before the disclosure the author has assumed that in pursuing a Ph.D. over several years, the professor simply had not found the right woman. Now it made even more "sense." The author also remembered that the new professor had expressed interest in a book by another sociologist about the gay community in San Diego which the author had compared to his own research about the deaf community. After the disclosure, the author interpreted that interest as "obvious" and consistent with the professor's being gay. The retrospective clues need not be subtle, however. The friends of Mark David Chapman, the accused killer of ex-Beatle John Lennon, said that "in retrospect . . . the signs of Chapman's final disintegration had been all too clear—and altogether missed" (*Newsweek*, December 22, 1980, p. 35). And what were the signs? They were the divorce of his parents, a nervous breakdown, two failed suicide attempts, testiness with his wife, and a feud with a church across from his job. They *became* signs, however, only after and in light of Chapman's alleged murder of Lennon.

Official agents often engage in a process very similar to retrospective interpretation. As Kitsuse has used the concept, it implies that the observer was aware of the past incidents when they occurred, but only later attributed special significance to them. Official agents, however, are often not aware of the past incidents when they occur. Such incidents may concern the behavior of a suspected mentally ill person, an alleged delinquent, a retarded child, and so on. What official agents may do, however, is *search* through the biography of the suspected offender—the offender's past behaviors—in order to find incidents which support the belief that the offender is indeed offensive. Many times, the agents not only find information to support their belief, but actively try to present a case against the individual to other agents. This construction of a moral character or a deviant identity will be developed later. And as Kitsuse noted in terms of retrospective interpretation, agents are routinely successful in finding information in a suspect's past to support their beliefs about the suspect.

For example, in a now classic piece of research, D. L. Rosenhan (1973) had eight *sane* people gain admission to twelve different psychiatric hospitals. Each patient called the hospital for an appointment and was admitted after talking with admission officers. The pseudopatients all complained of hearing voices which were unclear but seemed to say "empty" or "hollow." Except for hearing the voices and for giving false names, job information, and employment histories, the pseudopatients answered honestly about their lives. Upon admission, the pseudopatients stopped simulating any symptoms of mental illness. All were admitted with a diagnosis of schizophrenia except one, and all were released with the diagnosis of schizophrenia "in remission." None of the pseudopatients was detected by the staff even though they remained in the hospitals from seven to fifty-two days.

The staff interpreted the past events of these "normal," healthy people in conformity with the diagnosis of the individuals as ill. The question to be asked is: How did this happen? Rosenhan argues that the meanings attached to the pseudopatients' histories were influenced by the belief (i.e., diagnosis) that the pseudopatients were ill. Past incidents were interpreted (some, such as Rosenhan, would say unintentionally distorted) in order to support the diganosis that the pseudopatients were ill. For example, in one case a pseudopatient had a

> close relationship with his mother but was rather remote from his father during his early childhood. During adolescence and beyond, however, his father became a close friend, while his relationship with his wife was characteristically close and warm. Apart from occasional angry exchanges, friction was minimal. The children had rarely been spanked. (Rosenhan, 1973, p. 253)

Rosenhan suggests that such a history is not particularly unusual. Remember, though, that his words are also an interpretation of that history. Rosenhan suggests that the interpretation of the patient's history in the case summary prepared after the patient was discharged was consistent with a popular theory of the dynamics of schizophrenia. The summary states in part that the patient:

> . . . manifests a long history of considerable ambivalence in close relationships, which begins in early childhood. A warm relationship with his mother cools during his adolescence. A distant relationship to his father is described as becoming very intense. Affective stability is absent. His attempts to control emotionality with his wife and children are punctuated by angry outbursts and, in the case of the children, spankings. And while he says that he has several good friends, one senses considerable ambivalence embedded in those relationships also. (Rosenhan, 1973, p. 253)

According to Rosenhan, the doctors interpreted the patient's history in such a manner as to keep it consistent with or supportive of the original diagnosis.

The point is not that psychiatrists, probation officers, doctors, teachers, and other officials are incompetent. Many are well-trained and hardworking, though others may not be. Of course, even this is a matter of interpretation, of judgment. The important point is that official agents as well as ordinary citizens (and sociologists too as they do their work) are likely to reinterpret past incidents, or search out past incidents to interpret, in ways that support their beliefs about what has happened and is happening.

The mass media use a technique similar to the retrospective interpretation that official agents may use. When some kind of newsworthy deviance occurs, the media sift through the deviant's biography in order to find information with which they can present a consistent story that the person was always like that or was obviously "on the road" to such an occurrence. For example, newspapers tried to present a consistent picture of Richard Speck, the man found guilty of murdering eight student nurses in Chicago in July 1966. Interviews with people who described him as sensitive and intelligent were placed on the back pages of one large newspaper. Four days after his apprehension the "appropriately" evil biography was presented on the front page of the same newspaper. Under the headline, "Richard Speck's Twisted Path," the report read:

> Charged with the brutal slaying of eight student nurses, Richard Speck was trapped by the tattoo that bore his credo: Born to Raise Hell. Here is a special report on the man accused of mass murder, a report on the twisted path that led to tragedy. (*Detroit Free Press,* July 24, 1966, p. 1, in Lofland, 1969, p. 150)

The report noted that Speck was a " 'murder suspect' in another case who 'had been hating for a long time,' and 'had been arrested 36 times.' In his youth he was already 'a reckless tough . . . with the leather jacket crowd' who 'would drink anything.' 'A high school dropout' who was 'divorced,' he had served three years for burglary and was 'woman crazy' " (Lofland, 1969, pp. 150–151). It is when the media people cannot "find" such information that they, as well as others, remain puzzled. This "search and destroy" operation by the media, of course, further enhances the general public's typifications of deviance (Cromer, 1978).

Overlooking Deviance

In recognizing offensive behavior and people, observers are likely to make mistakes, often well-intentioned mistakes. The observers may later recognize their mistakes or they may not, at least not in time, as in some capital cases (MacNamara, 1969). And, of course, what one observer considers a mistake another observer may not. Mistakes themselves are not objective, absolute, or inherent. When we disagree, we may begin to realize that mistakes are dependent upon people's judgments. Think of tests that you have taken and the disagreements that could have occurred over the "correct" answer.

We are likely to accuse some people and later discover they were not engaged in offensive activity. We are also likely to overlook much deviance that takes place. If you think about it, observers are much more likely to make the second mistake, overlooking or failing to recognize deviance, than they are to make the first mistake, falsely accusing innocent people (Goode, 1978, p. 53). Why would this be so?

First, our typifications of deviance will often lead us astray. Research is needed, but we suspect that the vast majority of those involved in deviance are not adequately characterized by our typifications of deviance. No doubt, some offenders and offenses fit the signs and symptoms by which we recognize deviance. However, many do not. Our experiences, though, are unlikely to greatly challenge our belief in the usefulness of the typifications we hold. Those who fit our typifications and "prove" to be deviant give further support for our beliefs. Many who fit our typifications will be assumed to be deviant without our checking further. Those who do not fit our typifications—the vast majority, we suspect—will likely go unrecognized and therefore will not be a challenge to us to rethink our conceptions of deviance. Those who do not fit our typifications but are discovered to be deviant may be seen merely as the exception to the rule. Further, we may interpret information so that it fits our typifications of deviance even if "objectively" the information does not (Chapman and Chapman, 1967). Because we believe in our typifications so stongly, we interpret information about people and events in ways that support them. For all these reasons, our typifications of deviance may often lead us astray. They may lead us to falsely accuse people, but more likely to overlook a great deal of deviance.

Second, a false accusation can often lead to unpleasant consequences for the observer-accuser, such as charges of libel or slander, embarrassment, suspicions of the observer's own motives, monetary fines, and so on. A young woman in New York City was recently awarded $10,000 in damages because of being falsely arrested by police officers as a prostitute and because excessive force was used (Associated Press, 1979). Our legal system is established on the principle that it is better to let many guilty people go free than to falsely convict one innocent person. Many criticize the courts for just that reason, that too many "guilty" people are getting off on technicalities. Nevertheless, observers realize that the consequences of a false accusation can be great.

Interestingly, this same principle that it is better to overlook deviance than to falsely accuse someone does not seem to hold for medicine (Scheff, 1963). In medicine, especially nowadays with increased malpractice suits, doctors do not want to overlook any possible medical problem. The feeling among the medical profession seems to be that it is much better to treat some people who perhaps did not need the treatment than to let others who need medical services go unnoticed. Yet even in medicine, doctors and others are beginning to question the assumption of "treat when in doubt." Rising medical bills, unnecessary surgery, treatment that leads to illnesses, and so on, are causing the medical profession to reexamine its assumptions (Illich, 1976). If we are beginning to see deviance as a disease, what does that imply? Will we become more concerned about overlooking some deviance as opposed to unnecessarily treating others who later turn out not to be deviant?

Finally, because those engaged in deviance typically do not want to be discovered by unsympathetic observers, they hide their activities. While we may seek for them, clearly some offenders will remain hidden. For all these reasons, we are more likely to overlook deviance than we are to falsely accuse people of being involved in deviance.

IDENTIFYING THE DEVIANT

Recognizing deviant behavior and those who committ offenses is only part of the interpretative process that precedes how we deal with deviance. Many of us would agree that there is something fundamentally different between the following two situations. How we handle them is likely to be different too. A 68-year-old woman on social security, who is having difficulty making ends meet, is caught shoplifting some food from a grocery store. A 19-year-old male, who has been in trouble with the law several times before, is caught shoplifting some items from a department store with the intent to sell them for a profit. Although the two offenses are very similar, we are likely to view the two offenders in much different ways. The 68-year-old woman might be seen as an upstanding but hard-pressed citizen who shoplifted due to circumstances. The 19-year-old male, however, might be viewed as basically a bad person who is committed to a life of crime. The important difference between the two cases is the difference between *doing* and *being*. People may *do* deviance without our necessarily saying that they *are* deviant.

People may engage in similar offenses, but we may attribute to them different types of identities. That is what is meant by identification. What sort of person is the offender? What is the offender's "true" character? Is the offender *essentially* a respectable person or a deviant person? Identification is important in the phenomenon of deviance because how we deal with deviance is based to some degree on what types of people we think the offenders are. For example, citizens, police officers, and parole officers recommend harsher penalties for offenders who are felt to be responsible for their actions (Kidder and Cohn, 1979). We will pursue the impact of identification on our reactions to deviance in more detail in the next chapter. The following example, however, clearly illustrates that how we identify an offender influences how we handle that offender.

While investigating a West Coast police department, Irving Piliavin and Scott Briar (1964) found that the police officers' judgments of youths affected how the officers handled the youths. In one case, a sergeant intended to charge a youth with statutory rape. During the interrogation, however,

> three points quickly emerged which profoundly affected the sergeant's judgment of the youth. First, the youth was polite and co-operative; he consistently addressed the officer as "sir," answered all questions quietly, and signed a statement implicating himself in numerous accounts of statutory rape. Second, the youth's intentions toward the girl appeared to have been honorable; for example, he said that he eventually wanted to marry her. Third, the youth was not in fact a member of the gang in question. The sergeant's attitude became increasingly sympathetic, and after we left the interrogation room he announced his intention to "get 'A' off the hook." (Piliavin and Briar, 1964, pp. 142–143)

However, another youth, also brought to the station for having sex with a minor, answered questions slowly and with disregard. He gave no indication of being concerned about his situation. One of the officers commented that the boy was "simply a 'stud' interested only in sex, eating, and sleeping" (Piliavin and Briar, 1964, p. 143). Further lack of concern led the officers to make out an arrest report and the youth was taken to Juvenile Hall.

We identify in order to understand and control our environment. If we feel that someone is "truly" deviant, we know always to be cautious and watchful about that person. However, if we feel that a person is offensive due to certain circumstances, then it is the circumstances that we need to be concerned about, In part, identification is a way of deciding why someone engaged in deviance. If we understand that, we can better predict the person's future behavior and perhaps control it. Or, we can better fit our reactions to the offense and the offender.

> Clearly, the punishment of individuals who are not intentionally responsible for violations or who are blamed for violations which are instigated by uncontrollable or unknown agents inside or outside the person would lead to a chaotic existence, difficult to cope with. (Pepitone, 1975, p. 201)

We would add that often the situation is clear as to who is at fault, but clear in different ways to different observers. Nevertheless, identification gives meaning and order to our world, in this case the world of deviance.

From Doing to Being

To judge whether or not someone is "truly" deviant involves many considerations about the offender and the offense. We are likely to be concerned with whether the offender's offense was due to internal (i.e., dispositional) or external (i.e., situational) reasons. Was it intentional or not? Is the cause for the offense stable or unstable? If the behavior was outside the control of the offender, did the offender engage in some prior behavior (e.g., drinking) which led to the loss of control? All of these are considerations in deciding what sort of character the offender is and where the blame should be placed (Pepitone, 1975; Carroll, 1979).

What people do is not the only information that we take into account in deciding what they are like. While much more research is needed, we can outline several important principles in how we, as observers, attribute a deviant identity to someone who has engaged in deviant behavior: accentuating the negative; the relationship between the identifier and the offender; and the prior behavior of the offender.

Accentuating the Negative   In deciding what a person is like, we give more weight to negative information about that person than to positive information (Kanouse and Hanson, 1972). Rather than merely average the negative and positive information we have about people, we slant our impressions toward the negative. By its very definition, deviant behavior is that which is offensive to the observer. Consequently, there is a general tendency to focus on the offensive behavior of offenders in deciding what the offenders are like. The positive qualities may be ignored or given relatively less weight.

This tendency is enhanced by the finding that when people engage in behavior which is expected of people in their positions, that behavior is not very informative to observers about what types of people those individuals are (Jones and Davis, 1965). Further, when people engage in behavior which we think they should not engage in, we will give even more weight to whatever cause we think explains their behavior (Kelley, 1971). The implication of these two findings is that deviant behavior, which is rarely expected of people, is more informative to us than conventional behavior. Further, we can think of reasons why people should not engage in deviance (e.g., they might get caught). Thus, if they do, whatever reason we feel explains their offensive behavior will be emphasized. Therefore, "we tend to read [people] through [their] deviant acts" (Hawkins and Tiedeman, 1975, p. 92). We think of deviance as out of the ordinary, and thus we try to make sense about why the offender committed the offense and what type of person the offender must be.

Further, there is a "bias" among observers such that they are likely not to take the situation sufficiently into account in deciding why people did what they did. Instead, observers are likely to "overemphasize" personal dispositions (Mischel, 1968; Jones and Nisbett, 1971). We are prone to conclude that people did what they did because that is the type of people they are rather than because that is the kind of situation they were in. This "bias," coupled with the previous tendency to read people by their deviant behaviors, leads to the general tendency to attribute deviant behavior to deviant types of people. The offensive behavior is seen as the outcome of truly offensive types of people. The *"present evil* of current character must be related to *past evil* that can be discovered in biography" (Lofland, 1969, p. 150).

Identifier and Offender   The general tendency to attribute a deviant identity to those engaged in deviant behavior is greatly modified by the relationship between the observer and the offender (Jones and Nisbett, 1971). In general,

   1   If the observer has a favorable opinion of the actor, the observer will attribute the offensive behavior to external or situational factors: "My friend John was under a great deal of pressure from his parents. That's why he cheated on the exam."
   2   If the observer has an unfavorable opinion of the actor, the observer will even more heavily emphasize the offensive identity of the offender in explaining the offensive behavior: "What can you expect from such people? You can't trust them, and this cheating proves it."

Incidentally, favorably disposed observers will emphasize the actor's character in explaining praiseworthy behavior, and unfavorably disposed observers will emphasize the situation.

The importance of the relationship between the observer and the offender is evident in various contexts. It appears in routine settings. Karen Dion (1972) speculated that physical attractiveness would influence how others respond to and evaluate the deviant behavior of an offender. Female college students were asked to give their reactions to the misbehaviors of kindergarten children. Each woman read a series of reports about the children which had presumably been written by their teachers. Actually, each child's record and misbehavior was constructed by the experimenter. Attached to each report was a photograph of the child. Pictures of children who had previously been rated as attractive or unattractive were used. The women perceived the offenses of the attractive children as less serious, less of a cause for concern, and less typical of their everyday behavior, as compared to the same offenses of the unattractive children. An attractive girl who had supposedly thrown rocks at a sleeping dog on the playground was described as having a bad day. In contrast, a homely girl who engaged in the same behavior was described as "quite bratty" and a "real problem" at home and to teachers. The attractiveness of people favorably disposes us to them, and thus our interpretations of their behavior are likewise influenced.

The impact of the relationship between the observer and the offender helps to explain our reluctance to attribute deviant identities to the high and mighty who engage in offensive behavior (although this has changed somewhat recently). In fact, we may not even consider their illegal behavior criminal. Some sociologists have argued that white-collar crime should not be regarded as crime because the offenders did not have true criminal motives (Burgess, 1950; Vold, 1958). As a prominent criminologist lamented: "There is an obvious and basic incongruity involved in the proposition that a community's leaders and more responsible elements are also its criminals" (Vold, 1958, p. 253).

This incongruity is solved by explaining the illegal behavior in terms of external factors—for example, that an act of embezzlement is the result of "nonsharable problems" (Cressey, 1953). Or the dilemma may be resolved by conferring the "sick label" upon the offender. While this explanation maintains that there is an illness residing within the individual, it considerably reduces personal responsibility for the offense.

> "Kleptomania" turns out to be nothing more than a social label hung on "nice people" who steal and withheld from "bad people" who are simply "crooks"! The label is . . . akin to that of "sick alcoholic" which is accorded the middle-class drinker and denied the Skid Road "drunk." (Gibbons, 1977, p. 456)

Until recently most of us were favorably disposed toward those of high status, and consequently, we did not view their offensive behavior as the result of being deviant. Nowadays, however, many of us are skeptical of those with high status and thus are more likely to interpret their offenses as reflecting offensive identities. In fact, the "bias" that once worked to the favor of the well-heeled may now be working somewhat to the advantage of the downtrodden.

Finally, the impact of the relationship between the observer and the offender on attributions of deviance holds not only for relationships between individuals but also for *intergroup* relationships. The behavior of members of some other group, community, religious organization, and so on—an *outgroup*—will be perceived by observers in a similar way as the behavior of those toward whom we are unfavorably disposed. The behavior of members of one's own group—*ingroup* members—will in general be perceived by observers in similar ways as the behavior of those whom we like (Triandis, 1977, pp. 152–153). This finding helps us understand why we are likely to excuse the offensive behavior of members of our own group, but quickly conclude that the offensive behavior of members of other, often rival groups is due to their being offensive people.

Prior Offenses   Finally, the general tendency of observers to attribute a deviant identity to those who engage in deviance is enhanced by prior offensive behavior of the offender. When a person acts in much the same manner on different occasions, the behavior is seen to reflect a personal disposition (Triandis, 1977, p. 145). Thus, if a student is caught cheating several times in a course, the teacher is likely to conclude that the student must be a cheater. As we will see in the next chapter, this interpretative process underlies the harsher reactions to offenders who have a prior history of offenses.

In general, our attribution of a deviant identity is guided by the principle of consistency, which we mentioned earlier. Offensive behavior is associated with offensive people, and praiseworthy behavior is associated with respectable people. However, that is often not the case, and thus we must cast about for explanations which resolve the apparent inconsistency.

A Difference of Opinion

In all probability, the offenders' views of why they engaged in offensive behavior will be quite different from the observers' views. Not too surprisingly, offenders are likely to emphasize external factors in explaining their behavior, whereas observers, as we have noted, tend to emphasize the identity or character of the offender (Jones and Nisbett, 1971). An important difference of opinion exists. How it is resolved will influence how the offender is dealt with. Therefore, offenders are unlikely to be passive participants in the identification process.

Offenders may try to *account* for their offensive behavior in order to make themselves appear to be respectable (Scott and Lyman, 1968). They may do this in two ways. (1) They may try to *excuse* their behavior by admitting that they were wrong but denying full responsibility for the offenses. Consequently, the offenses are not to be taken as accurate indications of what type of people they are. For example, offenders may argue that the offense was accidental or that they did not intend their actions to have an offensive outcome. (2) They may try to *justify* their behavior. While accepting responsibility for their action, they deny its offensive quality. Although in a general sense the act may be offensive, the alleged offenders claim that it was required or permitted under the circumstances. Thus, a police officer may justify the killing of a suspect by claiming that he fired in self-defense. Techniques of neutralization, to be discussed in Chapter 6, are justifications used to reduce the potential wrath of those whom deviants have offended (Sykes and Matza, 1957).

In accounting for one's offenses, an expression of remorse is often important. Those who show no concern about what they did are likely to be more harshly reacted to than those who do (Pepitone, 1975). Our earlier example of the two teenage males brought in by the police for sex offenses illustrates this point. Judge John Sirica's handling of the Watergate offenders does too. In his own account of the Watergate trials, Sirica (1979) explains his sentencing of defendants in terms of whether they did or did not express sorrow, regret, remorse, or contrition for what they did.

Those who did not were given harsher sentences. Thus, in attempting to account for their offensive behavior, deviants often try to present themselves as respectable people and thereby reduce the severity of our reactions toward them.

CONCLUSION

Once we have established standards of respectability and deviance, we must recognize deviance and identify deviants before we can deal with those who offend us. We recognize deviance through checking out and interpreting information in light of our conceptions of deviance. Our conceptions of deviance often include signs and symptoms which we take to be indirect indications of deviance. These indications, as well as characterizations, are acquired through various sources, such as the mass media. In checking out the situation, the visibility of deviance is important. Those who have access to private places are less likely to be recognized than those who do not. As observers become more sophisticated in spotting deviance, offenders become more sophisticated in hiding it. Finally, as information is gathered it is interpreted. Whether our suspicions are confirmed or not will depend on the information we have gathered, our familiarity with the deviant behavior, and the kind of relationship we have with the suspect. Once we decide that an individual has engaged in deviance, we may retrospectively interpret past incidents in a manner that supports our present judgment. In recognizing deviance, however, we are likely to both falsely accuse people of being offensive when they were not and to overlook their deviance when they have been. The latter mistake is more likely.

Although we may recognize deviance, this need not mean that we identify the offender as a deviant. There is an important difference between doing and being. In attributing an identity to people, we are likely to give the greatest weight to their offensive behavior. However, as in recognizing deviance, our relationship to the offender profoundly influences whether we explain the offender's behavior in terms of external factors or personality disposition. Offenders are likely to use the former explanation, and thus an important difference of opinion is created. How this difference is resolved will influence how we deal with the deviant. It is to this issue, dealing with deviance, that we turn now.

PROJECTS

1   Though this technique is not completely satisfactory, as we mentioned in the chapter, try to develop a list of the signs and symptoms that your friends use as indications of various categories of deviance and deviants, such as homosexuality (male or female), prostitution, cheating, drug use, and so on. Try to be as

specific as possible. For example, what is a "swishy" manner, if that is an indication of homosexuality? After drawing up a list for different offenses and offenders, present the list to others in order to see what the characteristics indicate to them. What *combination* of the *fewest* characteristics indicates to most of your respondents that the person so described is engaged in offensive behavior?

2   Analyze the mass media—newspapers, TV, or magazines, for example—in order to determine the typifications that they present about different kinds of deviance and deviants. Have the images presented by the media changed over the years?

3   Talk with or observe official agents as they recognize deviance. What are the signs and symptoms that police officers use during routine patrol, that doctors use for suspecting mental illness, that teachers use for suspecting child abuse (in many states teachers are required to report suspected cases) or learning problems in their students, and so on? How do they gather information? How do they interpret it?

4   There is an important difference between "doing" deviance and being deviant. See if you can write a set of vignettes that "captures" this difference. The vignettes should concern various people engaging in deviance, but with certain features of the situation changed from one vignette to another. The features you vary should be the ones which you feel make a difference in how we attribute deviant identities to people who have engaged in deviance. Remember our hypothetical example of the 68-year-old shoplifter and the 19-year-old shoplifter. Have a group of people read the vignettes. How do they interpret the behavior of the offenders? Do they attribute different identities to different offenders?

5   Follow some newspaper and magazine accounts of a well-publicized trial. Degradation ceremonies focus on both what the accused is alleged to have done and what type of person the accused may be. The prosecution and the defense will each try to present a view of what kind of person the accused is. Examine how the presentations take place. You might want to take note of how motives, personal characteristics, past behavior, or associations with others are used to present the accused as good or evil.

Chapter 5

Dealing With Deviance

We defined deviance in the first chapter as those behaviors, ideas, or attributes which others find offensive, and which, if known about, lead to some kind of reaction. The reaction need not be dramatic, severe, or even easily noticed; but if there is no reaction, the behavior is not deviant to the observer. Thus, our definition of deviance indicates that our reactions are an integral and essential part of the phenomenon of deviance.

Our reactions to deviance are likely to be both complex and widely varying in nature. Emotional reactions are certainly an essential feature. Annoyance, anger, rage, disgust, or loathing may precede and accompany our dealings with the deviant. Those who are sympathetic to the accused may be surprised, apprehensive, or sad about what has and will take place. Although emotions are an essential component in our reactions to deviance, sociologists have given them relatively little attention, primarily focusing, instead, on what we *do* about deviance and to deviants.

As in the past, nowadays there continues to be a wide range of reactions to deviance. Deviant behavior and deviant people are not always and everywhere dealt with in the same way. We warn, ridicule, execute, lock up, fine, fire, educate, treat, counsel, ostracize, expel, punish, pity, and do many other things to and for those who offend us.

For example, "troublemakers" at a certain junior high school in the South are not necessarily suspended. Instead they may go to "jail." First the parents are consulted. If they decide against suspension, the child can be sent for a minimum three-day stay in an "Alternate Adjustment Lab"—i.e., confinement in a small Army quonset hut—where they are required to complete homework assignments. They may earn their release through accumulating points based on good conduct and group participation (Associated Press, 1979). As another example, businesses are beginning to provide rehabilitation programs for alcoholic employees and counseling for those with an "abrasive personality in the office" instead of firing them (Levinson, 1978). Finally, after a ten-year moratorium, we are beginning to execute people again. We deal with deviance in many ways.

In every area of life dealing with deviance is an issue. Whether it be recruiting violations in athletics or in the military, incompetence on the job, crime in the streets or in corporate headquarters, or misconduct in the armed services, deviance and our reactions to it can be found everywhere. Obviously some situations seem more spectacular than others, and social scientists have investigated some situations more than others, but the process is similar. Further, we all are involved in dealing with deviance. Many of us might feel that police officers, mental health officials, inspectors,or judges are the ones who react to and handle deviant behavior and people. True. However, even where we have set up formal agencies and empowered official agents to handle deviance for us, these agencies and agents depend on us for their business. Without our initial reactions to deviance, they would have less work and fewer cases to handle. Further, most deviance in everyday life is not handled by official agencies, such as police, courts, or mental health facilities. We have not established agencies to deal with all forms and kinds of deviance and deviants, though increasingly we do seem to be establishing more formal ways of handling deviance. The coach who suspends a star player for training violations, a teacher who allows a student who cheated in class to stay in the course, parents who reprimand their children, a moviegoer who tells a noisy patron to be quiet, and a boss who fires an incompetent employee are all dealing with deviance. Their reactions are often just as important and crucial for the deviant as are a police officer's reactions to a suspected thief.

In this chapter we will examine several important topics concerning our dealings with deviance. We react to deviant behavior for various *reasons*. It may seem obvious that we react to deviance because we are upset with it and therefore want to punish the deviant. Certainly punishment is one reason for dealing with deviance, but it is not the only one or necessarily the most important one. Further, what we intend by our reactions to deviance may not actually occur. There may also be unintended consequences.

Oftentimes in dealing with deviance we have set up formal mechanisms of social control. We have designated certain people as *control agents* whose duty is to handle deviant behavior and deviant people. Police officers, judges, mental health officials, psychiatrists, and prosecuting attorneys are obvious examples of such agents. These various agents make up different systems for dealing with deviance: the criminal justice system, the juvenile justice system, and the mental health system. Other people are also formally charged with dealing with deviance. Teachers and principals have the formal responsibility of dealing with disruptive students. In many schools, formal hearings are held to decide whether a student will be suspended or not. Teachers and principals may no longer have the sole power. Social workers who are part of a "protective service" division of their agency are expected to handle child abuse and neglect cases. The duties of public health officials include dealing with violations of public health codes by restaurants and other establishments. Most sports leagues and collegiate athletic associations have investigative bodies whose job is to uncover violations and then take action against violators. Throughout society and in various areas of activity we have designated particular people as control agents. We want to examine some important features of their work.

For the past 100 years, prisons, mental hospitals, training schools for juvenile delinquents, and other *total institutions* have been an important and dramatic way in which society has dealt with deviance. We will explore several of their features.

Both control agents and citizens handle deviance in various ways. What influences our reactions to deviance? Why do we imprison some offensive people, but counsel others? Why do we treat some deviants, but punish others? Obviously, we handle different kinds of deviance in different ways, but why? We may also handle what seems to be the same deviance in different ways. It is often complained that our reactions to deviance and deviants are arbitrary and unfair. The rich, the powerful, the well-connected are handled leniently, while the poor, the minorities, the less respectable are treated harshly. People point to Watergate and complain that Richard Nixon was not prosecuted because he was President, while those under him were prosecuted. Similarly, a well-respected high school football player may only be reprimanded for some school vandalism, but a marginal student is suspended for having a can of beer in his car. Are reactions to deviance so easily determined? We need to thoroughly examine our *decision-making* when we deal with deviance because it has created so much controversy among sociologists and concerned citizens.

Finally, it has often been assumed that deviants are relatively passive bystanders when society deals with them. Deviants are reacted to by society, but do not "fight back." Such an assumption is very misleading. Deviants are usually actively involved in some way in our dealings with them. An obvious example can be noted here. Through their defense lawyers, defendants are actively involved in negotiating what the punishment will be. Most cases in the criminal justice system are handled through plea bargaining. Our reactions to deviance *emerge* within the interaction between accusers and the accused. We do not simply "lay on" or apply our reactions to deviant behavior. Rather the reactions arise out of discussion, negotiation, pleas, denials, and so on. Dealings with deviant behavior are created through the activities of both the accusers and the accused.

REASONS FOR OUR REACTIONS TO DEVIANCE

We react to deviant behavior and deviant people for many reasons. Some sociologists do not like to use the concept of reasons or intention, saying it smacks of psychology. Instead, they would say that society's reactions to deviance have many consequences or fulfill many functions. People deal with deviance in different ways for various reasons. However, what they intend by their reactions may not be what actually occurs. There can be unintended consequences as well as intended ones. Specific reactions to deviance may occur for several reasons: revenge, protection, making deviants conventional, keeping conventional people conventional, boundary maintenance, and symbolic appeasement. Our dealings with deviance may also have unintended consequences.

Revenge

Traditionally revenge has been a major reason for our reactions to deviance. We often want to "get even" or "get back at" those who have harmed us or those we care about, or who have damaged that which we hold dear. We feel that the deviant *deserves* what he or she gets. Often we feel better after achieving our revenge, almost like an emotional catharsis, though sometimes we feel ashamed too. Typically, revenge has followed the ancient "eye for an eye and tooth for a tooth" philosophy. Deviants should be punished in equal severity to the degree of damage they caused. For example, the Code of Hammurabi, which dates back almost 4,000 years, provided that if a man knocked out the eye of a patrician, an individual of high status, then his eye would be knocked out, and if he broke the arm of a patrician, then his arm would be broken. Interestingly, if the same offenses were committed against a plebeian, a commoner, only a fine had to be paid (Reid, 1979). One might argue that this is a very early indication of the discrimination which occurs in our dealing with deviance. It seems that in many cases not only do we want to get even, but actually we want to get more than even. We vent our frustration or anger by doing more harm to the deviant than the deviant did to us.

Revenge is not merely an ancient or outmoded reason for our

reactions to deviance. Nowadays we may still seek revenge in reacting to deviants. When especially brutal murders are committed, communities (through the prosecuting attorney) may seek the death penalty as revenge for what was done. Of course, they may seek the death penalty for other reasons as well. Schools and colleges often retaliate against their rivals for the damage their rivals do to them as the "big" game of the year approaches (e.g., the spray painting of slogans on buildings or the stealing of the school mascot). In 1980, legislators in a Southern state introduced an amendment to the state budget that would have barred all Iranian students from attending state-supported colleges and universities. The amendment was proposed as retaliation for the seizure of American hostages in Iran. Revenge remains an important reason for our reactions to deviance, even though we may be less likely nowadays to publicly acknowledge that such is the case.

Protection

Many of our reactions to deviance are designed to protect the community against further harm from the deviant. The harm might be intentional, as in the case of a professional thief, or unintentional, as in the case of a mentally ill individual. We can *incapacitate* deviants in various ways. We can isolate the deviant from us. The isolation can be relatively permanent and total, or it can be temporary and partial. Capital punishment, of course, is a permanent and total isolation of the deviant from us. Banishment or deportation to another country is a kind of isolation. Yet so is the suspending of a disruptive student from the classroom. Religious organizations are often concerned about protecting their members from "heretics"—those who no longer follow the church doctrine. Recently, a feminist who actively voiced support for the Equal Rights Amendment was excommunicated from the Mormon Church (Associated Press, 1979). Excommunication is designed to protect members against ideological and moral contagion by the deviant.

We can also confine deviants in prisons, jails, training schools, mental hospitals, their quarters, and so on, as a way of isolating them from us. We can restrain them by using straitjackets and drugs. While confined to such places and in such ways they cannot harm us, though they may harm other residents or staff who work with them.

We can also protect ourselves from further harm by making it more difficult for the deviant to engage in the offensive behavior in the future. Corporal punishment has often been used for this purpose. Many societies have routinely cut off the hand of a thief or cut out the tongue of a slanderer. Between 1935 and 1956 Denmark castrated 600 sex offenders (Reid, 1979). Of course, we can make it more difficult for the deviant to harm us by protecting ourselves and our living spaces. Thus our reactions to deviance may not be aimed at any specific deviant. Locks and chains on a door, security fences, attack dogs, hidden safes, businesses open by appointment only, classes in self-defense, and escort services are all reactions to deviances designed to protect ourselves and others from harm.

Making Deviants Conventional

Many of our dealings with deviants are designed to promote conventional behavior. We want the offensive people to stop doing whatever it is that bothers us. We may try to achieve this goal in two primary ways: through *threat* or through *rehabilitation.*

Ridicule, suspensions, fines, demotions, imprisonment, and so on, may serve as a threat to offenders that if they engage in the offensive behavior again, they can again expect to be dealt with in an unpleasant way. The rationale is that once punished, the offender will not want to risk being punished again. The use of punishment in reactions to deviants is often justified by its presumed *deterrent* effect. Punishing the deviants will deter them from future offensive behavior. It is partly with this idea of deterrence in mind that some people criticize what they see to be the lax discipline in schools, the coddling of juvenile and adult offenders, "country club" prisons, and so on. They argue that because of such lax handling, deviants will never learn their lesson. Making deviants conventional through threat is based on the idea that even if we cannot change deviants so that they become "truly" conventional people in their beliefs and attitudes, we can at least create enough of a risk so that they will become conventional in their behavior. Evil may still lurk inside them, but at least it will not come out into the open.

Rehabilitation is the other major means for making deviants conventional. Rehabilitation, though, is based on a different approach than threat. Through rehabilitation we try to "convert" deviants to our conventional way of life. We try to change the character of the deviants— what they are "really" like, and not merely their behavior. Through threat we only make people comply with our rules and regulations. Through rehabilitation we hope that they will become true believers.

Rehabilitation is a relatively recent mode of reacting to deviance. In Western society it did not become a major factor in the handling of criminals or the mentally ill until the nineteenth century, and was not firmly established until the twentieth. Even now it waxes and wanes as a justification for different kinds of reactions to deviance. Through treatment, therapy, or training, we try to make deviant people conventional. Nowadays, alcoholics are likely to be handled through treatment programs rather than being merely locked away. Prison inmates may be provided with vocational and educational training as well as work-release and study-release opportunities. The juvenile justice system has traditionally been based on the philosophy that youth need guidance, counseling, and treatment in order to develop as "responsible" citizens. Those arrested for driving under the influence or for simple possession of marijuana are often referred to a community education program. Further convictions, however, may not be dealt with in a rehabilitative way. Later in the chapter we will discuss the development of the rehabilitative philosophy and why we are likely to handle some offenders in a rehabilitative manner but not others.

Keeping Conventional People Conventional

Many of our reactions to deviance are designed to influence others who have not yet engaged in deviant behavior (or at least who are not known to have done so) against engaging in it. We react to deviance in order to keep conventional people conventional (Buckner, 1971, pp. 211–214). Our reactions to the offender serve as a warning to others who might be contemplating a similar course of action that they can expect similar consequences if they are caught. We not only threaten the offender with future unpleasantness, but we also threaten others as well.

Punishment of offenders is often justified on the ground that it is also a *general deterrent* to would-be offenders. People will "think twice" before engaging in an offensive behavior if they know what might happen to them. As an eighteenth-century judge told an accused thief, "You are to be hanged not because you have stolen a sheep but in order that others may not steal sheep" (Kadish and Paulsen, 1969, p. 85, in Reid, 1979, p. 592). Recently, the Saudi Arabian government beheaded more than fifty people who had seized the country's holy shrine. The beheadings were carried out in several cities throughout the country so as to make as much of an impact as possible on other would-be rebels (AP, 1980). In the same spirit, the commissioner of a professional basketball league suspended and heavily fined a player for hitting another player during a basketball game. The commissioner and others felt that fighting among players had gotten out of hand and that something needed to be done about it (*Sports Illustrated,* January 2, 1978).

Three key features may influence how effective reactions are in keeping conventional people conventional and in making deviants conventional: *severity, certainty,* and *celerity.* Severity refers to the harshness of the reaction. Harsh reactions to deviance are thought to be more effective for deterring would-be deviants than lenient treatment. Certainty is the likelihood of a reaction for engaging in deviance. The more certain the reaction, the greater is its effect, presumably, on would-be offenders. If there is a low risk of being punished, few people will be deterred by the punishment even it if is relatively severe. Celerity has received the least amount of attention. It refers to how promptly we react to deviance. If deviants are punished many years after their offensive behavior, such "tardy" punishment may have little impact on the behavior of would-be offenders. If punishment is swift, it may be a more effective deterrent.

Many researchers have recently examined how effective legal punishment is as a deterrent to would-be offenders and to punished offenders. The research is basically inconclusive (Gibbs, 1977), though quite interesting. Most of the research has focused on the effectiveness of legal punishment as a deterrent. However, reactions from family, friends, and others which do not have the official standing of legal punishment may be just as effective, or even more so, in keeping conventional people conventional and in making deviants conventional (Meier and Johnson, 1977). The embarrassment that we imagine our families and friends would experience if they were to find out that we were engaging in deviance may be much more effective in keeping us conventional than the threat of legal sanctions. For example, while civil libertarians complained, the mayor of New York City began in the fall of 1979 to publish and broadcast the names of convicted patrons of prostitutes in the hope that this would deter people from patronizing prostitutes.

> Tired of complaints that streetwalkers were turning once respectable neighborhoods into instant brothels, Koch said the names of convicted patrons would be turned over to the media. He likened it to the use of public stocks to shame malefactors in Puritan times. . . .
>
> Sgt. Richard Klev, of the police department's public morals squad, said the program, while aimed at the streets, had an effect on patrons in houses of prostitution.
>
> "Customers that we arrested during parlor raids were really concerned about having their name publicized," he said. "The first thing they would ask us after we raided the place was, 'This isn't going to be used on that John Hour thing, is it?" (*Columbia Record,* January 28, 1980, p. A-2)

Of course, our reactions to deviance are not the only activities that are designed to keep conventional people conventional. Much of what goes on at home, in school, and in churches is explicitly designed to indicate to us what behavior is acceptable and to promote that behavior. Through explanations, teaching, praise, personal example, and role models, people are taught to be conventional. Interestingly, many of the stories, fairy tales, and religious teachings used in this instruction deal with what happens to people who engage in deviant behavior. By implication, it could happen to us, too. As every little child knows, the "boogeyman" will get them if they misbehave. Thus, our reactions to deviance are part of the promotion of acceptable behavior.

Boundary Maintenance

Our reactions to deviance may also help make clear to other members of the community where the often fine and indistinct line between acceptable and unacceptable behavior lies. Our dealings with deviance inform others of where the boundary of respectability has been drawn. That boundary is part of a group's collective identity. People define their moral boundaries and themselves by referring to "geographical location, a set of honored traditions, a particular religious or political viewpoint, an occupational specialty, a common language, or just some local ways of doing things" (Erikson, 1964, p. 13). Through our reactions to deviance we also proclaim that we are like this but not like that. We do things this way but not that way. As Erikson (1964, p. 15) continues, without deviance and the community's reaction to it, the "community would have no inner sense of identity and cohesion, no sense of the contrasts which set it off as a special place in the larger world."

Further, our reactions to deviance can help reaffirm our commitment to certain standards. In "casting out" the deviant, we reaffirm who we are and what we are like. We bring the members of the community together and thereby maintain or even increase its solidarity (Durkheim, 1964, 1966).

Traditionally, our dealings with deviance were public spectacles. Hangings were in the public square so that citizens could gather and watch. The stocks and pillories of Colonial America were placed in view of the passing public. Our reactions today may occur behind closed walls and doors and are less directly accessible to the public, but the mass media can bring the event to us. Such public reactions, or accounts of them in the mass media, serve to unite the community in its disgust for the deviant (Erikson, 1964).

Reactions to pornography, massage parlors, and other forms of sexual entertainment is a present-day example of how reactions can maintain the moral boundary of the community. The Supreme Court itself has ruled that pornography can only be defined in terms of local community standards. Through picketing the showing of particular movies, by raiding and closing down massage parlors, or by speaking against the issuance of a license for a topless bar, citizens and officials of the community declare that their community is "not the kind of place where such filth is permitted." In so doing, they contrast their community to other communities which allow such activities and therefore are "dens of depravity." San Francisco seems to have been given that title by many.

Symbolic Appeasement: Convincing Others of Our Concern

Sometimes we react to deviance only to appease others. We wish to convince others that we are as concerned and indignant as they are about the deviant behavior. Or we wish to show that we are fully enforcing the rule or law or common understanding that prohibits certain behaviors. In such cases, those who are reacting to the deviant behavior may not be particularly offended by it, but others are offended, and the reactors have to please them. An offense such as gambling in a club or prostitution is often treated informally by the police but may be dealt with more severely if it comes to the public's attention (LaFave, 1965). While the police may feel that they should concentrate on other offenses, they may also realize that they need to satisfy the community. Many people feel that Patricia Hearst, the kidnapped newspaper heiress turned bank robber, was prosecuted and imprisoned as a way of demonstrating that no one is above the law. Many Americans had grave doubts about the fairness of our criminal justice system. Prosecuting Patty Hearst may have restored their faith in it.

Unintended Consequences of our Reactions

Our reactions to deviance may also result in many less easily noticed and unintended consequences. For example, some sociologists argue that our reactions to deviance serve to enhance or solidify a deviant identity and to increase future deviant behavior rather than to lessen it. There is a great deal of controversy about this issue, which we will discuss in Chapter 7, but presumably it would be an unintended consequence of our reactions to deviance. Kai Erikson (1964, p. 15) wonders, though, if discouraging deviance is the "real" function of our prisons, mental hospitals, and other institutions devised for "discouraging" it. Since they seem to perpetuate deviance, he questions whether they are really intended to make deviants conventional.

In a critical examination of prisons, Charles Reasons and Russell Kaplan (1975) argue that imprisonment results in many unintended consequences. For example, it *politicizes* prisoners. Blacks, the poor, and other presumably oppressed groups in prison became sensitive to the distribution and use of power in society. Prisons also provide *jobs* for more than 70,000 persons who might otherwise have a difficult time finding work, according to Reasons and Kaplan. Prisons are a source of *cheap labor* for the state. Whether this is an unintended consequence is questionable. Gresham Sykes (1958) found that the classifications of prison inmates may be changed when it is necessary for more of them to be allowed to go outside of the prison to harvest state crops. Prisons *reduce the unemployment* rate. Prisoners serve as *guinea pigs* for scientific research. Prisons are a means of *birth control*. These and other unintended consequences are an indication that our reactions to deviance often serve many functions of which we may not at first be aware. Depending on one's perspective, these unintended consequences may be pleasant surprises or unwanted results that need to be changed.

CONTROL AGENCIES AND AGENTS

We create agencies to which we formally delegate the authority and responsibility of handling deviance for the rest of us. We empower the agents of these control agencies to manage deviance. Police officers, mental health officials, judges, probation officers, and prosecutors are control agents who come readily to mind. However, health and welfare inspectors, deans of student affairs, and commissioners of athletic leagues are also control agents. The various agencies may be connected to each other within what is called a "control system," where decisions on handling deviants and reactions to them occur at various levels. The criminal justice system, the juvenile justice system, and the mental health system are obvious control systems. Within the criminal justice system, the police, the prosecutor, and the judge may all handle the same case at one time or another. Thus an individual offender is likely to be subjected to many reactions and decisions within a control system. While the criminal justice, juvenile justice, and mental health systems come readily to mind, there are also agencies and even systems which deal with the disabled, the mentally retarded, child neglect, neglect or abuse cases, health and safety violations, and so on. Control agencies and agents are an important aspect of the deviance process.

Although the legal authority to deal with deviance is delegated to control agencies and agents, control agents generally depend on the general public to bring cases of potential deviant behavior to their attention. While we may think that the police, mental health officials, or protective service workers are the "first line of defense" with regard to crime, mental illness, or child abuse, this is not the case. Control agencies and agents tend to be much more *reactive* in their work than we might imagine. Often they respond when summoned by citizens. To a large degree they depend on the actions of citizens in order to have "business" to take care of.

For example, research for approximately a one-month period in Chicago in 1966 showed that almost 93 percent of all incidents processed by the police patrol division were initiated by citizens (Reiss, 1971, p. 97). A study of encounters between the police and juvenile suspects showed that 72 percent of the encounters were initiated by citizen complaints (Black and Reiss, 1970). Mental health facilities depend almost entirely on referrals from the community: from physicians, police, courts, ministers, family members, friends, and even self-referrals (Hollingshead and Red-lich, 1958; chap. 6). In Tennessee, 27 percent of male first admissions to state hospitals between 1956 and 1965 were voluntary admissions, they were initiated by the patient. In fact, 40 percent of those later assessed as mildly impaired were self-referrals (Rushing and Esco, 1977). Thus mental health officials depend on other agencies, on the general public, and even on the deviant to bring them business.

Of course, certain agencies and certain divisions within agencies may be more *proactive* than others. Through their own initiative, agents may "drum up" business without depending on complaints by citizens. Traffic violations are rarely brought to the attention of the police by citizens. Traffic divisions in police departments and other officers who have responsibility for traffic violators are engaged in proactive control (Lundman et al., 1978). Investigative bodies in college athletics are becoming more proactive than in the past. Rather than waiting for word of a possible violation, investigators are actively searching out violators. For example, they are beginning to question the top high school football prospects each year in order to catch colleges which have engaged in recruiting violations. Of course, such investigative bodies still depend on tips from rival schools, reporters, and others. Public schools drum up much of their own business in terms of mental retardation (Mercer, 1973). In fact, public schools are likely to process many children as mentally retarded who are not diagnosed as retarded by other community organizations or professionals. In general, agencies are most likely to be proactive in their work when they deal with deviance that has no easily identified victim. If there are no victims, who will complain to the control agents? For example, the police are most proactive in handling what are called "victimless crimes": drug use, prostitution, gambling, homosexuality, and so on. Corporate bribes to foreign officials or price-fixing and overcharges entail no easily identified victim. We are all victims. Therefore, in these cases control agencies must be proactive in their work. Typically, however, in order to have cases to manage, control agencies depend on the actions of those who are not officially trained or responsible for handling deviance.

The Filtering Process

Within control systems a *filtering process* takes place (Schur, 1971, p. 97). Agents at various levels in the system make decisions about how to handle the offender. These decisions lead basically to two outcomes: the offender is either dismissed from the system or referred on to the next level within the system. For example, a police officer may decide to warn a suspected criminal, thus releasing the suspect from the system, at least temporarily. Or the officer may arrest the suspect. A suspect who is arrested may later be released for insufficient evidence. If not, the prosecuting attorney will probably decide whether the suspect should be prosecuted. A suspect who is prosecuted may be found guilty or innocent, the charges could be dismissed, or the suspect could plead guilty. Due to the various decisions at each level, fewer and fewer offenders are processed further and further into the system. That is what we mean by saying there is a filtering or funneling process within control agencies and systems.

The filtering process is quite evident in the criminal and juvenile justice systems. For example, in a national study of victims of crimes, the attrition of alleged cases of deviance within the criminal justice system was tremendous. Only 49 percent of offenses were reported by the victims to the police. The police responded in 77 percent of the cases when notified. After responding they called 75 percent of the incidents a crime. They made arrests in 20 percent of the cases considered to be crimes. Of those arrested, 42 percent went to trial. And of those who went to trial, the victim felt that there was a proper conviction in 52 percent of the cases. Thus Philip Ennis (1967) and his colleagues began with 2,077 offenses which they felt were legitimate, but ended with 26 cases where the victim felt that a proper conviction had been achieved. Similar filtering occurs in the victimization of college students. Out of 772 offenses recorded in a study at the University of Maryland, only 28 resulted in some kind of sanction or action was pending (Butler, 1977).

These and other studies (Rose and Randall, 1978) indicate several interesting points about the filtering process. First, a large bulk of the filtering occurs outside of formal control agencies. In Ennis's study, victims notified police less than half the time. The failure to report may be increasing. In 1975, victims reported only 32 percent of all personal crimes to the police (U.S. Department of Justice, 1977). Official control agents are simply not made aware of much deviance. Whether victims or observers complain or not is due to many reasons, some of which we will discuss later. Second, what one observer may call deviance, another observer may not. We noticed this conflict in previous chapters. Third, some of the filtering that takes place is due to the inability of control agents to locate offenders and to successfully prove that they are deviant. In other words, control agents do not always "get their man or woman." Fourth, given the enormous number of people who engage in deviant behavior, relatively few are processed all the way through a control system. Finally, in the same way that control agents depend on the actions of the general public to bring them business, control agents at higher levels in the system depend on the actions of lower-level agents for their business.

Conflict Among Control Agents

Because many control agents are making decisions at various levels within a control system, there is likely to be conflict about how the deviant should be dealt with. This conflict stems from several sources. First, the working procedures and philosophy that guide agents may be quite different at various levels within the control system. For example, the assumptions and priorities that guide police officers are likely to be different from what guides judges. Each has a different job to do and faces a different set of circumstances. The police may be more concerned with maintaining order and enforcing the law, whereas judges may be more concerned with abstract notions about justice (Reiss, 1971). We will discuss later this idea of working procedures and philosophy and its importance in control agents' dealing with deviants.

Second, the sorts of deviance and deviant people seen by control agents at each higher level differ from what control agents see at the lower levels. Control agents are likely to select from the total pool of cases those which they feel need additional attention and refer them to the next level.

Control agents at the next higher level also select from the total cases which they see those which they feel need additional handling. Yet they are selecting from a different pool of cases than are the lower-level control agents. Even if they used the same criteria as the lower-level agents, they would be discriminating among cases that lower-level agents had already decided needed additional attention. For example, prosecuting attorneys and police officers may both discriminate between serious and minor cases, but the prosecutors make the distinction among cases that the officers have already decided were serious enough to warrant an arrest. If control agents merely processed everyone who was brought to their attention on to the next level, they would not be serving a useful *gatekeeping* function. Soon others would wonder if the agents were needed at all. If at each level control agents exercise discretion, selecting some cases for further attention and screening others out, agents at lower levels are likely to be upset with some of the decisions made by agents at higher levels.

Finally, agents at higher levels within the control system often are not only deciding how to handle the deviants referred to them, but are also passing judgment on how agents at lower levels handled the deviant. Few agents follow all the rules that are supposed to guide and limit their actions. If they did, they would often be unable to do their jobs. Also, they may see the rules as hindrances and as not relating very well to the everyday problems they face. Further, higher-level agents and lower-level agents are likely to have different training, experiences, and goals. Higher-level control agents may also find fault with how lower-level control agents have done their job. In other words, higher-level control agents are concerned with both controlling the deviant and with how the lower-level agents deal with the deviant.

If lower-level control agents feel that their actions are not being supported by agents at higher levels, they may try to circumvent the higher-level agents. For example, police often use what is called "curbside justice" in controlling juveniles. Police may try to keep juveniles "in line" by harassing them rather than formally handling them through arrest and referral to the juvenile court (Sanders, 1976). If the police feel that the judges are too lenient, they may see informally harassing juveniles as a more effective strategy than turning them over to judges who only create a lack of respect for the police and for the law by "slapping" the juvenile on the wrist (Reiss, 1971). Police officers may also use curbside justice when they feel that later handling by the courts might be too harsh. In either case, they are circumventing the formal mechanisms of the juvenile justice system. The same circumvention of the formal mechanisms of social control occurs in other areas as well: the college teacher who deals with plagiarism personally rather than turning the offender in to the dean of student affairs, or the sergeant who "busts a private's butt" instead of turning the private in.

Such "unauthorized" ways of dealing with deviance may sometimes backfire. A former bank manager was sentenced to a three-year prison term for making eight unrecorded loans totaling almost $90,000. Instead of reporting to his president customers who were late in making loan payments, he paddled them. When several customers threatened to report him to his superiors, he made the unrecorded loans to keep his "victims" quiet (Associated Press, 1979). The unauthorized handling of deviance itself became deviant and led to a cover-up which was also deviant.

Routinizing the Handling of Deviance

While to most of us what goes on within control agencies often seems very dramatic and even exciting, to the experienced agents the work is often quite routine. In fact, agencies and agents develop procedures, philosophies, and assumptions about what they are and should be doing, and about the deviants whom they handle, in order to routinize their work. In large bureaucracies where many people will be processed, an orderly flow of people and cases is essential. Cases and people which can not be easily categorized and then routinely handled create difficulties. They back up what is often an already overloaded system.

The set of perspectives and procedures that allows control agents to more or less routinely handle cases of deviance has been called the "theory of the office" (Rubington and Weinberg, 1978). This "theory," or their working procedures and philosophies, allows control agents to maintain order in their work. Different agencies are likely to develop different procedures and philosophies. Agencies that are part of the same control system (e.g., police, juvenile court, and training schools) or that must work together on particular cases of deviance sometimes disagree over how to handle cases.

The working philosophy and procedures of control agents allow them to routinely handle a wide diversity of people by placing them within a smaller number of categories. If all suspected or "convicted" deviants were handled based on their unique characteristics, control agents could never get their work done.

We all classify people when we interact with them. Except for intimate associates, rarely do we take into account very much of the information that we already know or could learn about other people. It would be difficult to process so much information. How would we use it in deciding what to do? Should we give more weight to some information than to other? For many purposes, using just a few pieces of information in order to classify someone often works reasonably well. For example, most students are not particularly concerned about a professor's culinary likes and dislikes, religious orientation, or child-rearing practices. In deciding whose courses to take, students are likely to pick out information bearing on how difficult, entertaining, or interesting a professor is. The "theories" that students use, developed over years of experience and shared among many students, work reasonably well and therefore continue to be used.

The same holds true for the working procedures, philosophies, and classification schemes used by control agencies and agents. There is nothing particularly mysterious about them. They are developed and modified through years of experience. The "theories of the office" are likely to be taught to new agents as they are brought into the agency. Agents also learn these working procedures and philosophies as they do their jobs and come in contact with more experienced personnel (Harris, 1973). Thus control agents, like citizens at large, typify deviants in order to routinely handle them.

For example, Robert Bogdan (1974) and his colleagues argue that attendants on the wards of state schools for the mentally retarded develop a perspective or orientation which guides them in their work. Attendants are lower-level staff who help take care of the clients and also do custodial and cleaning work. Attendants develop an orientation about their superiors, about their job, and about the residents of the schools. New staff are likely to learn these views during a three-week orientation program where they are rotated from building to building. During the orientation program they come in contact with more experienced attendants who expose them to the perspective which has already been developed. The perspectives of new attendants are reinforced through off-the-job contacts. Many of the attendants spend their free time together at local bars and clubs, and some are related by marriage. Thus new control agents do not reinvent the working procedures and philosophies used by their colleagues; instead, their colleagues socialize them into the already existing procedures and routines.

What do these "theories of the office," or working procedures and philosophies, look like? Sociologists have investigated numerous control agencies, though certainly not all. In many cases, however, they did not investigate the "theories of the office." There is a lot of research to be done. But we do have an idea of the working procedures and philosophies of some control agencies and agents. Let us present a few examples.

"Normal" Crimes   According to David Sudnow (1965), public defenders and prosecuting attorneys often work closely together in order to expeditiously move cases through the court. Both the public defender and the district attorney wish to avoid trials by obtaining guilty pleas from the defendants. Trials disrupt the orderly flow of work. They may also lead to the news media's giving the cases attention. Most control agents would rather pursue their work in anonymity.

Both public defenders and prosecuting attorneys are concerned that defendants pay their "dues." Therefore, reductions in charges against defendants should be enough so that they will plead guilty, but not so great that defendants do not pay their "dues." In the course of handling cases, public defenders and district attorneys develop conceptions of typical types of crimes. Sudnow calls these typical types of crimes "normal" crimes. Conceptions of "normal" crimes are based on the way the crimes are committed and the characteristics of the offenders, victims, and scenes involved. Thus public defenders and district attorneys develop notions of what is a typical or "normal" theft, burglary, assault with a deadly weapon, and so on. For example, a typical burglary is seen as involving "regular violators, no weapons, low-priced items, little property damage, lower class establishments, largely Negro defendants, independent operators, and a non-professional orientation to crime." A normal case of drunkenness involves offenders who are "lower class white and Negro, get drunk on wine and beer, have long histories of repeated drunkenness, don't hold down jobs, are usually arrested on the streets, seldom violate other penal code sections, etc." (Sudnow, 1965, p. 260).

Public defenders and prosecuting attorneys develop unwritten but commonly understood procedures for reducing "normal" crimes to a lesser charge. In the public defender's office that Sudnow investigated, typical burglaries were reduced to petty theft. "Normal" assault with a deadly weapon was reduced to simple assault. Typical cases of child molestation were reduced to loitering around a schoolyard. These "recipes" for reduction of charges were used only for specific cases that public defenders and district attorneys were able to place within their conceptions of typical or normal crimes. The "recipes" for reduction of charges concerning "normal" crimes allowed the public defender and the prosecuting attorney to routinely handle cases.

However, recalcitrant defendants who do not accept the bargain struck between the public defender and the prosecuting attorney upset the routine handling of cases. In these situations, the cases go to trial. Yet even here, the public defender and the defense attorney can routinely manage the case by "putting on a trial." They matter-of-factly assume that the defendant is guilty, but was not reasonable enough to accept the lesser charge. The public defender and the prosecuting attorney each conduct their part of the proceedings with respect for proper legal procedures, but without attempting to degrade the other side. Trials with stubborn defendants who are accused of committing a "normal" crime do not cause the public defender or prosecuting attorney undue trouble. They are simply seen as a waste of time.

However, in cases which arouse public attention and coverage from the mass media, notions of typical or normal crimes are not well developed and guilty pleas are less likely to be bargained. Murders, dope-ring operations, embezzlement, and other less frequent or highly dramatic cases are more likely to lead to a trial. The privacy of the guilty-plea procedures which are reserved only for defendants of "normal" crimes cannot be maintained. Public defenders and defense attorneys must strike a more combative stance. As Sudnow (1965, p. 275) notes, "two persons who regularly dance together must now appear, with the lights turned on, to be fighting." Each side now may impeach the morality and credibility of the other side. Public attention demands such a show. In order to handle the possible friction that such atypical cases could create for future relations between the public defenders and the prosecuting attorneys, the older, more experienced attorneys from each side handle the case. The attorneys who handle the regular cases are kept away in these atypical cases in order to maintain the *routine* relations among them. Routine procedures for handling plea bargaining have also been observed in other jurisdictions.

Dealing with Drunks   In San Diego, city attorneys who handle cases of driving while under the influence (DUI cases) routinely use several criteria in deciding how to handle defendants who initially plead not guilty (Cloyd, 1977). Those who plead guilty at arraignment are sentenced without further adjudication. For those who do not, a city attorney reviews the case in order to determine whether charges should or should not be reduced in order to induce the defense to plead guilty.

Whether the city attorney will offer a reduced charge or not depends on the evidence in the case: the blood alcohol level (BAL), results of the field sobriety test (a test of the suspect's ability to follow directions and control bodily movements), the observed driving pattern of the defendant, and the defendant's record. The BAL is considered the most objective evidence, the field test is next, and then the observed driving pattern. The city attorney may offer to reduce the DUI charge to: (1) driving a motor vehicle on private property while under the influence of alcohol, (2) unable to exercise care for safety due to intoxicating liquor, (3) reckless driving, or (4) two moving violations involving unsafe lane changes. These reduced violations run from most to least severe.

If the BAL is available, there are standards by which the city attorney will routinely offer to reduce the original DUI charge. By law, a BAL under 0.10 requires that the city attorneys prove through other evidence that the defendant was under the influence of alcohol. In such cases, the city attorneys routinely offer to reduce the DUI charge to two one-point unsafe-lane-change violations. If the BAL is between 0.10 and 0.15, in which case it is legally presumed that the defendant is under the influence, the city attorneys will offer a reduction to reckless driving with a suspension of sentence and three years probation. Finally, if the BAL is over 0.15 and under 0.20, the city attorneys will typically not offer a reduced charge but will be open to negotiation.

However, these standard offers of reduced charges, based on the BAL, may be modified depending on the results of the field sobriety test, the officer's description of the defendant's driving, and the defendant's record. For example, if the BAL is between 0.10 and 0.15, but the defendant's driving and the results of the field sobriety test show the defendant to be in poor condition, the city attorney will be reluctant to offer an initial charge reduction. In such a case, the city attorney and the defense attorney will actively negotiate a reduced charge. If the defendant refused to take the BAL, if there are discrepancies among the pieces of evidence in the case, or if the defendant refuses to accept the prosecutor's initial offer, the standard way of handling the case is no longer applicable. Approximately 15 to 20 percent of the DUI cases prosecuted by city attorneys in San Diego are not routine. They require a "significant amount of negotiation" (Cloyd, 1977, p. 401). It is in these cases of negotiation that the *emergent* nature of our reactions to deviance is most easily noticed. We will explore the emergent nature of our reactions to deviance later in the chapter.

Working procedures may allow agents to dispose of a large number of deviants in little time—to do a "high-volume" business. Jacqueline Wiseman (1970, pp. 85–100) found that judges processed drunks as fast as one every thirty seconds, with as many as 250 drunks handled in a few hours. How was that possible? According to Wiseman, judges classified drunks into social types based primarily on three factors: (1) general physical appearance (shaking, trembling, dirty, bloody, etc.), (2) past performance (past record of arrests for being drunk), and (3) social position (job, marital status, permanent address or not, down-and-out appearance).

Based on these three factors, judges created about seven different social types of drunks. Each social type was likely to receive a particular type of sentence. For example, the "middle-aged repeater who has not been up for some time" was likely to receive a suspended sentence with required attendance at alcoholism school or was given to the custody of Christian missionaries. Transients were routinely handled by being given a suspended sentence or probation if they would leave town. However, less than one minute was hardly enough time for the judges, by themselves, to gather and integrate enough material on each defendant, review it, type the defendant, and then sentence the defendant. Consequently, judges often employed an assistant, known to the defendants as "the Rapper," who knew the Skid Row men well and could answer the judges' questions about the men or suggest dispositions. Thus, "the Rapper" assisted the judge in quickly disposing of drunk cases.

Issuing Traffic Warrants   Police officers also develop routine procedures in doing their job. Jerome Skolnick (1966) argues that traffic warrant policemen use a general guideline or theory of the office in performing their duties. Traffic warrant officers have the duty of serving unanswered warrants for parking and moving violations. Warrant officers may arrest the offender, but they are not required to do so. In fact, while automatic arrest is efficient, it is seen as unduly harsh and bad public relations by the police department. Instead, depending on their judgment, warrant officers can give the offender time to make bail.

How do warrant officers handle offenders? According to Skolnick, warrant officers develop a set of criteria in deciding who is trustworthy and who is not—who will post bail later if not arrested and who will not. In general, offenders who have several outstanding warrants are likely to be arrested unless they can post bail. Warrant officers generally view such offenders as having no intention of posting bail if they are let go. And if an offender is released and then does not post bail, that reflects poorly on the warrant officer's judgment.

In simple cases, where there is one warrant outstanding, officers use the general criteria of *stability* in deciding whether or not to arrest an offender. Defendants who own a house or furniture or have a job are considered better risks by warrant officers. Such defendants are unlikely to flee just in order to escape paying $15. Women are handled a little more leniently than men. Traffic officers feel that it is degrading to use coercion on a woman in public. Women who resist create embarrassment for the officers. If the woman has children, the police officer has the responsibility of seeing to it that her children are taken care of, which entails extra work for him. Finally, an officer may feel bad about detaining a group of children—perhaps in a jail, detention facility, or foster home—because their mother could not post a $15 or $20 bail. Thus warrant officers, like other control agents, develop and use working procedures in order to routinely do their jobs.

TOTAL INSTITUTIONS

For the past 100 years, prisons, mental hospitals, residential schools for the mentally retarded, and other total institutions have been an important resource for dealing with deviants. In modern society people tend to work, play, and sleep in different settings and with different participants. Total institutions combine these three activities. In total institutions:

    1 All aspects of life are conducted in the same place and under the same authority.

    2 Each phase of the member's daily activity is carried on in the immediate company of a large batch of others.

    3 All phases of the day's activities are tightly scheduled.

    4 The various enforced activities are brought together into a single rational plan purportedly designed to fulfill the official aims of the institution.

    5 Persons . . . can be supervised by personnel whose chief activity is not guidance or periodic inspection . . . but rather *surveillance*—seeing to it that everyone does what he or she has been clearly told.

   6   There is a basic split between a large managed group, conveniently called inmates, and a small supervisory staff (Goffman, 1961, pp. 6–7).

Prisons, mental hospitals, and other facilities more or less fit this concept of a total institution. For example, in a pre-release center for prisoners, the inmates may work in the community during the day but return to the facility in the evening. Thus, we should not expect institutions that deal with deviants to rigidly possess all the characteristics that Goffman has outlined.

Millions of people each year pass through total institutions. Some stay only a few days or weeks, while others spend a much longer time. For example, on a typical day approximately half a million youths and adults are confined in prisons, jails, and detention facilities (Sykes, 1978, pp. 502). Approximately 150,000 individuals are in public facilities for the mentally retarded on any one day, and there are more than 1.5 million patient-care episodes in mental health facilities each year (U.S. Bureau of the Census, 1979). Thousands of disabled youth are educated in special residential facilities. Total institutions are big business.

The vast number of total institutions can be categorized in various ways. Erving Goffman (1961, pp. 4–5) establishes five types, not all of which are directly relevant to deviance. Some total institutions care for people who are felt to be incapable of caring for themselves and are harmless, such as residential schools for the deaf or the blind, orphanages, and homes for the elderly. Others, such as mental hospitals and TB sanitariums, care for those who are also felt to be incapable of caring for themselves, but are considered to be an unintentional threat to the community. Some are institutions designed to protect the community from intentional harm by deviants, such as prisons, jails, training schools for delinquents, and P.O.W. camps. Some facilities are run as total institutions because it is assumed that through such arrangements the organizations can better pursue their tasks. Army barracks, boarding schools, and ships at sea might fit this type of total institution. Finally, some total institutions are religious retreats from the secular world, such as monasteries or convents. The latter two types of total institutions are not directly related to our dealing with deviance, though certainly deviance may occur within them.

Mortification of Self

Critics of total institutions charge that they often have a debilitating rather than rehabilitating effect on the inmates, clients, or patients. In particular, total institutions are said to *mortify the self* of the residents (Goffman,

1961). Total institutions subdue or deaden the individual's unique self. They humiliate or shame the individual. According to Hawkins and Tiedeman (1975, pp. 286–292), four factors contribute to such degradation and humiliation: *depersonalization, behavior monitoring,* the *record,* and *"being on."* Those confined to total institutions are shorn (often literally) of their unique personalities by being issued standardized clothing, by being referred to by a number or derogatory phrase (e.g., the "puker"), or by being talked about by staff members in their presence as if they were not there. Due to extensive behavior monitoring or surveillance, there may be few places where even the basic necessities of life can be taken care of in private. The self is degraded because it is always open to view. Total institutions record information about their residents—past and present information. Constant surveillance can easily lead to the generation of a great deal of information, most of it relating to the "problem"—whatever led to the individual's confinement in the institution. What is noted in the record influences and supports decisions made by the staff about the resident's treatment and release. If something is in the record it is important. If it is not in the record, it did not happen or is not important. Unless, of course, there was an oversight, in which case it may then be recorded. The resident need not be consulted by the staff. Instead, the staff can look it up in the records. The record takes on a life of its own, and in a bureaucratic organization of forms and paperwork this life may become more important than the resident's life. Finally, compared to those on the outside, residents have relatively little time when they can "let their hair down" and be themselves without worrying what others will think. Instead, they are often on view, and thus must be concerned with the image they are presenting to the staff as well as to other inmates. Consequently, trust becomes a key issue. Can the residents trust the impressions they receive from other residents (or staff for that matter)? Can they trust the impressions they create? Which selves are really them, and which ones are for show? Thus, according to critics, residents of total institutions are degraded and mortified through depersonalization, behavior monitoring, the record, and being on.

A Hierarchy of Staff

If total institutions do have the debilitating effect that their critics charge, one reason may be the organizational set-up of the staff. In total institutions, as in any large organization, a staff hierarchy exists. Those at the bottom of the hierarchy—the guards, attendants, caretakers, and the others who do the dirty work—have the least training, expertise, and authority, and the lowest pay. Yet, typically they have the most direct contact with the residents of the institution. Ironically, the staff at the top of the hierarchy—directors, administrators, wardens, doctors, and so on—who have the most training, expertise, and authority, and the highest pay, also have the least contact with the residents. For example, in a study of psychiatric hospitalization which we mentioned in the previous chapter, Rosenhan (1973) found that physicians and especially psychiatrists were rarely seen on the wards except when they arrived or departed. Otherwise they were in their offices or the glassed-in quarters on each ward—the "cage," as it was called by residents—which contained professional staff.

Further, the lower-level staff are likely to have a different view of the institution than the upper-level staff. The differences are due to the different backgrounds of the two groups, their different training, and the different positions they occupy. The lower-level staff's view of the institution may conflict with the programs that are established by the upper-level staff but are at least partly to be implemented through the activities of the lower-level staff. The lower-level staff, intentionally or unintentionally, may subvert the programs of the upper-level staff because the intentions and demands of the programs conflict with their own view of the institution.

Such is the case in state schools for the mentally retarded, according to Bogdan (1974) and his colleagues. As we noted earlier, attendants' perspectives concern three features of the institution: their *superiors,* their own *work,* and the *residents.* Attendants feel that their superiors do not know what it is like on the wards or what is best for the residents. According to attendants, their superiors are rarely on the wards, but the attendants know the residents well. Attendants are also skeptical of the professionals' jargon and procedures. They question the competence of the professionals, especially those who are foreign-born. Their doubts about competence are enhanced by their knowledge that working at the state school is a low-status job for professionals. According to the attendants, the upper-level staff are underworked and overpaid.

Attendants view their work as just a job. Someone has to do it, and it might as well be them. The rewards of their jobs are primarily extrinsic, derived from the pay and fringe benefits, not from satisfaction with the work itself. Custodial aspects of the work are stressed. Professionals, who are trained to do so, are supposed to work with residents. Attendants minimize their own work by using "brighter" residents to do many of the custodial tasks (e.g., mopping the floors) and to control other residents. While attendants complain that they have too much to do, they goof off a great deal in order to avoid their unsatisfying work.

Attendants view the residents in terms of the trouble or work they cause or in terms of their disabilities. Thus, residents are referred to as a "puker," "soiler," "headbanger," and so on. Attendants are fatalistic about the residents' chances for improving themselves. Little hope is held out for them. However, attendants feel that the residents can be spoiled.

Too much attention will lead to residents who are difficult to control. Thus, it is better to show the residents who is boss and not to lavish too much attention on them.

The attendants' perspective about the state school for the retarded may subvert the intentions of the upper-level staff and administrators who try to implement innovative programs for the residents. New programs are viewed as an additional chore for an already overworked staff, a staff which is not trained to implement the program or paid well enough to do so. Further, most of the residents are viewed as incapable of learning from the new programs. At best the programs simply occupy the residents' time. At worst the programs could spoil them. At one state school a behavior modification program which was designed to reward residents for appropriate conduct, was used by attendants to punish them for annoying behavior. The program became a way for attendants to control the residents' behavior through punishment. Thus, total institutions may have a debilitating effect on the residents in part due to the organizational set-up of the staff.

However, to blame the alleged failures of total institutions only on lower-level staff is much too facile.

> To offer [feeble attempts at] programming as a remedy to a system that by its very nature isolates, desocializes, and dehumanizes . . . [represents] the cruelest lies of this debilitating system. (Bogdan et al., 1974, p. 150)

Harmful or Helpful: A Difference in Interpretation

While many critics charge that total institutions mortify the residents' selves and are debilitating in other ways, the research is not so clear (Hawkins and Tiedeman, 1975, p. 292). We do not intend to marshall all of the evidence for and against that assertion. Instead, we plan to pursue this empirical issue from a different stance. As we noted in Chapter 2, our understanding of deviance is created through the investigative activities of social scientists and other concerned people. Different activities may lead to different understandings. Such seems to be the case when we examine total institutions, particularly mental hospitals.

According to Raymond Weinstein (1979), *qualitative* research in which the investigators interviewed, observed, or masqueraded as patients has led to an overwhelmingly negative portrayal of mental hospitals.

> The hospital is generally pictured as an authoritarian system that forces patients to define themselves as mentally ill, change their thinking and behavior, suffer humiliations, accept restrictions, and adjust to institutional life. Patients, it is argued, have negative attitudes toward mental hospitalization. (Weinstein, 1979, p. 239)

A review of *quantitative* studies, in which the researchers systematically questioned random samples of patients about the hospital and did so with so-called objective tests and validated scales, presents a different picture of mental hospitals. In general, patients who are formally interviewed or questioned stress the "bright, not the dark side of the hospitalization" (Weinstein, 1979, p. 251). In more than three-fourths of the samples tested, half or more of the patients expressed favorable attitudes about mental hospitals. More specifically, patients tended to rate mental hospitals in general more favorably than their own, and to rate the treatment, organization, restrictions, and amenities of their hospitals more favorably than the staff and other patients. Thus, different investigative techniques have led to different understandings about mental hospitals and their patients. Why so?

Researchers using a qualitative approach may rely on the anecdotes and incidents involving the most active and vocal patients. The views of such patients may not reflect the views of the wider patient population. Also, researchers who pose as pseudopatients are not in a position to benefit from treatment, and thus their experiences are not completely comparable to the experiences of the patients who may be benefiting from treatment. Many, if not most, of the qualitative researchers were concerned for the patients' welfare. Such a stance might lead them to interpret critically, perhaps overcritically, what they observed. For many patients a mental hospital is a "temporary haven" from the rigors of the outside world, a place where one's needs are met even if they are met in a restrictive environment (Braginsky et al., 1969). Food, clothing, shelter, and other amenities are provided. No wonder that some patients may have a favorable view of mental hospitals. Many who are readmitted return on their own due to a lack of appealing alternatives on the outside (Weinstein, 1979). The parallel to college students should not be missed. Researchers, however, who come from comfortable environments and who prize autonomy in their professional lives, are likely to be struck by the restrictions and regimentation of the mental hospital. In his own work Goffman (1961, p. x) realizes this possibility. Also, patients who want to leave may tell researchers in an interview or questionnaire how wonderful the mental hospital is in the hope that such answers may help them be discharged. Upon discharge many express negative attitudes. Thus, whether mental hospitals are debilitating places or not seems to depend on whom you ask and their interpretations of the situation. The "facts" may be the same. What is made of them may be different (Essex et al., 1980; Weinstein, 1980).

Decarceration

Since the 1950s, total institutions have been deemphasized as a way of dealing with deviance in America (and England) (Scull, 1977). For example, in the mid-1950s, 560,000 people resided in state and county mental hospitals. In 1974, only 215,000 did. At the end of 1965, 187,000 people resided in public facilities for the mentally retarded. At the end of 1978, only 151,000 did (U.S. Bureau of the Census, 1979). To varying degrees, this deemphasis applies to other kinds of total institutions. However, it may be premature to argue, as Scull has, that prisons are part of this trend too. We have the highest rate of imprisonment—143 people per 100,000 population, since comprehensive records were kept in 1940 (Newsweek, 1981). Nevertheless, this trend of closing down total institutions or emphasizing them less in comparison to community-based alternatives is what Andrew Scull (1977) calls "decarcertaion." Why has it occurred now?

According to Scull, typical answers are either that the psychoactive drug revolution of the 1950s provided psychiatrists with an effective means of dealing with mental illness, or that legislators, judges, and other officials finally began to listen to social scientists and liberal critics who charged that total institutions were harmful, not helpful, places. Scull argues that the drug revolution cannot adequately account for decarceration. In England decarceration had already begun in some mental hospitals before the advent of the new drugs. There is little evidence that the use of the new tranquilizers directly led to the release of patients. The tranquilizers do not cure the patients, but provide relief for symptoms of an assumed underlying illness. And the drug revolution cannot account for the decarceration of other types of deviants, such as criminals and juvenile delinquents. The drugs are primarily a chemical straitjacket which allows for easier management of the mentally ill within and outside the hospital. They may have had some impact on the early release of patients, but they cannot adequately account for the movement toward decarceration.

Neither can the criticisms of total institutions by social scientists, according to Scull. Social scientists in the 1950s and 1960s were not the first to criticize what they felt were the harmful effects of incarceration. In the nineteenth century, both when total institutions were being erected and later when they were widely used, critics in England and America charged that asylums, prisons, and reformatories were harmful places. However, "despite the elaborateness and intellectual force of these accounts of the superiority of community care, and despite the social prominence of many of the advocates of decarceration, their efforts had no substantial impact" (Scull, 1977, p. 112). If criticism of total institutions had no significant impact 100 or 80 years ago, then how could similar criticism today from less prominent people (after all, sociologists are "merely" academicians) have such an impact? It has not, says Scull.

Instead, Scull (1977, p. 128) argues that total institutions, which had once been "convenient way(s) of getting rid of inconvenient people," had become extremely costly by the middle of the twentieth century. For

example, in 1976 maintenance expenditures (i.e., wages, salaries, purchases, food, and so on) in public facilities for the mentally retarded
averaged more than $13,000 per resident (U.S. Bureau of the Census,
1979). In 1975, it cost the state of Maryland almost $16 per day to house an
inmate in a walled prison (Parisi et al., 1979). That is more than $5,700 per
year. As some have suggested, why not send the inmates to college?
Further, during the twentieth century both federal and state governments
developed a wide array of welfare programs, such as social security,
disability payments, unemployment compensation, health care, and aid to
the poor. Such welfare payments have become an increasingly large part of
governmental budgets. They are now alternative sources of support for the
mentally ill and retarded (and their families), who in the nineteenth
century could not have provided for themselves if they had been released
from mental hospitals and facilities for the retarded. Thus, the increase in
welfare programs has made the decarceration movement both possible (by
providing alternative sources of support) and desirable (because government revenues are heavily strained). Decarceration downplays costly total
institutions in favor of hopefully cheaper community alternatives. Thus,
decarceration:

> reflects the structural pressures to curtail sharply the costly system of
> segregative control once welfare payments, providing a subsistence existence
> for elements of the surplus population, make available a viable alternative to
> management in an institution. (Scull, 1977, p. 152)

Unfortunately, according to Scull and others, the community alternatives for deviants are a sham. Few real resources may be provided to those
who are not institutionalized. For example, in the past several years a
national concern has developed about the ghettos of the mentally ill that
have resulted from dumping mental hospital patients into the community
without providing significant adjustment or follow-up services.

Whether Scull is right or not, he suggests that deviance—in this case
the decline of total institutions—cannot be understood apart from the
society in which it exists. The decline of total institutions may be a result of
important changes in the capitalist system in the twentieth century. We
wonder where those changes might lead us in the future.

DECISION-MAKING: WHY WE REACT THE WAY WE DO

We do not deal with deviance in the same way all the time. We react to
different deviant behaviors in different ways. This is not particularly
surprising. Most of us would feel that we should handle classroom cheating
by a student differently from a strong-arm robbery. However, we may also
react to what seems to be the same deviant behavior in different ways. Two

juveniles who have been charged with the same offense—burglary, for example—may be handled in different ways. One may be put on probation while the other may be incarcerated in a state training school. The intriguing question becomes: Why do we handle deviance in the ways that we do? What do we base our decisions on in dealing with deviance?

For the past fifteen years sociologists have devoted a great deal of attention to this issue. Three major approaches have been pursued in explaining our reactions to deviance: the legalistic approach, the societal reaction perspective, and the conflict approach.

Legalistic Approach

Many social scientists, as well as police officers, mental health professionals, and other control agents, argue that what influences society's reactions to deviance is primarily the deviant behavior itself. The *seriousness* of the present behavior and the prior *history or record* of deviant behavior are *claimed* to have the major impact on our reactions to deviance (Hagan, 1974; Tittle, 1975). We take that information into account more so than other kinds. The more serious the deviant behavior is, the more severely does society react to it. Also, the greater the history of prior deviant behavior, the more severely does society react to the transgressor. The seriousness of the present deviance and the past record of deviances are factors which have been enacted into the laws dealing with deviance. Hence, we call this approach to explaining society's reactions to deviance the legalistic approach. Advocates of this approach would not restrict its use to explaining society's reactions to illegal behavior. Most of the research investigating this approach, though, has dealt with society's reactions to crime and delinquency.

Casual observation of the criminal justice system as well as a great deal of research lends some support to this approach. For example, our most severe penalties are reserved for what society considers the most serious crimes. Since 1930 more than 3,800 persons have been executed in the United States. Approximately 86 percent of those executed were convicted of murder, 12 percent for rape, and the remainder for such crimes as burglary, armed robbery, and kidnapping (Sellin, 1967). Americans consider murder and rape two of the most serious crimes that can be committed. A study of Baltimore citizens in 1972 showed that out of 140 specific offenses which the citizens rated, different specific instances of planned and impulsive killing were rated as five of the worst seven offenses, with forcible rape after breaking into a home rated the fourth most serious offense (Rossi et al., 1974). Selling heroin happened to be rated the third most serious offense, with airplane hijacking, armed robbery of a bank, and selling LSD rounding out the top ten.

Specific studies of the workings of the criminal justice, juvenile justice, and mental health systems indicate that the seriousness of the deviant behavior as well as the history or record of prior deviant behavior influence how deviants are handled. For example, the police are more likely to arrest youths or adults who are suspected of committing a felony than those who are suspected of committing a misdemeanor. Those who are suspected of committing a misdemeanor are more likely to be handled informally, with a warning perhaps, though certainly some are arrested (Piliavin and Briar, 1964; Black, 1970; Black and Reiss, 1970). In observing police-citizen encounters in a Midwestern city, Lundman (1978) and his colleagues found that all juveniles suspected of a felony were arrested, whereas only 5 percent of rowdiness cases resulted in arrest. Judges are also influenced by the seriousness of the present deviance and by a record of past deviance in sentencing criminal offenders or disposing of juvenile cases. Those convicted of serious offenses and those who have a prior record of offenses receive more severe sanctions, are more likely to be imprisoned or incarcerated (the term used in juvenile justice), and when imprisoned to receive longer sentences than those who have committed a less serious offense or have no or little prior record (Bernstein et al., 1977; Thomas and Cage, 1977, Cohen and Kluegel, 1978).

Interestingly, victims use similar reasons in deciding whether to report a crime to police. In general, the more serious the crime, the more likely it will be reported. Completed crimes are more likely to be reported than attempted crimes. Crimes involving force are more likely to be reported than those not involving force. For example, in a national victimization study, 62 percent of robbery and attempted robbery victimizations with injury were reported to the police, but only 15 percent of thefts of under $50 were reported. One of the major reasons that victims give for not reporting the victimization to the police is that the "victimization was not important enough" (Hindelang and Gottfredson, 1976).

Similarly, department store managers are more likely to prosecute shoplifters who steal more expensive items. Gerald Robin (1963) found that store managers in Philadelphia stated that the major factor influencing whether they turned shoplifters over to the police for prosecution was the size of the theft. Robin checked their statements and found that of adults who lifted merchandise worth less than $20, only 6 percent were prosecuted; whereas of those who lifted merchandise valued at $60 or more, 94 percent were prosecuted. These findings have been supported by other research (Hindelang, 1974). Of course, the value of the merchandise may not be the only reason for the managers' actions.

Commitments to mental hospitals are also influenced by the seriousness of the deviant behavior. Individuals can *voluntarily* commit themselves to a mental hospital or be *involuntarily* committed by others. Procedures vary from state to state, but in order to have a person involuntarily committed, a citizen who feels that the person is ill may ask that a physician sign commitment papers. Once someone is committed, a hearing is often held within a specified period of time in order to determine whether continued hospitalization is necessary. Most patients are involuntarily committed to mental hospitals. However, the more severely impaired the patient is, the more likely that the patient will have been involuntarily committed. A study of mental hospital commitments in Tennessee indicated that 88 percent of patients whose assessed impairment was severe had been involuntarily committed. Only 60 percent of patients whose impairments were assessed as mild had been involuntarily committed (Rushing and Esco, 1977). Thus, the seriousness of the deviance and a prior history of deviance are taken into account by both control agents and citizens in deciding what to do with a deviant.

Responsibility and Prognosis Eliot Freidson (1966) argues that we take into account responsibility and prognosis in dealing with deviance. In fact, these two factors can help us to understand why the seriousness of the present deviant behavior and a history of prior deviance influence our reactions to deviance in the ways that they do. They can also help us to understand the historical shift in our reactions to deviance from punishment to rehabilitation.

According to Friedson (1966), if we assume that the individual is responsible for his or her deviant behavior, we are likely to punish the individual in some way. If we decide that the individual is not responsible for his or her deviance, we are likely to treat or instruct the individual. Responsibility is a matter of degree. We view people as more or less responsible for their behavior, though observers may certainly differ in how much responsibility they assign to the individual. For example, juveniles are considered less responsible for their behavior than adults, and children under 7 are typically considered not to be legally responsible for their behavior at all. A successful defense of insanity can absolve individuals of responsibility for their deviant behavior. A prior record of deviant behavior is likely to be viewed as an indication that offenders are responsible for their deviant behavior. They know what they are doing and continue to engage in offensive behavior. As we saw in the previous chapter, the issue of responsibility is an important one in the deviance process.

Prognosis also influences how we deal with deviance, according to Freidson. If we feel that the deviant can be cured, that the deviance is only temporary, we are likely to handle the case differently than if we feel that the situation is relatively hopeless, that there will be little change or improvement. In cases where the prognosis is good, segregation of the deviant from the rest of society is likely to be temporary. When the prognosis is poor, however, the deviant is likely to be more permanently or totally segregated from the community, even to the point of execution. One might argue that the prognosis of those who have a long history of prior deviant behaviors and of those who have committed serious deviant acts is likely to be seen as poor. Often, judges will make just that point when they sentence an offender who has several "priors." Thus, both prognosis and responsibility help us to understand why factors in the legalistic approach influence society's reactions to deviance in the ways that they do.

Combining both responsibility and prognosis might lead to the following possibilities. Deviants who were seen as responsible for their behavior would be punished in a limited way if their behavior was viewed as curable. However, they might be executed or given life imprisonment or a lengthy prison sentence if their behavior was seen as incurable. Those who were held not responsible for their deviance might be provided with some kind of treatment or education if the prognosis was good, but protective custody if the prognosis was poor (Freidson, 1966, p. 77). While it would be difficult to place precisely any particular deviant behavior within the categories of responsibility and prognosis (and, of course, observers are likely to differ), Freidson (1966, p. 78) suggests that the "man-in-the-street" might make the following placements. A juvenile would be held responsible for shoplifting, but the behavior would be seen as curable. A sex murderer would be held responsible for his or her behavior, but prognosis would be poor. Individuals with pneumonia would not be held responsible for their illness, but the illness would be seen as curable. Finally, someone with cancer would also not be held responsible, but prognosis would likely be poor. Observers are likely to take into account the specifics of any case in assessing the offender's responsibility and prognosis.

From Punishment to Treatment Earlier in the chapter we mentioned that rehabilitation or treatment of deviants is a fairly recent reason for our reactions to deviance. The increasing use of rehabilitation in dealing with deviance is related to our changing views about deviance and deviants, about their responsibility and prognosis. We are increasingly getting away from viewing deviants as bad and moving toward seeing them as sick (Conrad and Schneider, 1980). Alcoholics are an obvious example of this trend. If we view deviants as sick, we are less likely to see them as responsible for their behavior, and if they are sick, maybe they can be cured. Also, with the rise of the social sciences, there has been an emphasis on explaining people's behavior by reference to social factors in the environment. Instead of viewing deviance as the result of sin or biological factors, as was traditionally the case, social scientists have stressed such influences as poverty, peer influence, poor relations with parents, and so on. This emphasis on social factors has also led to a change in our view of the deviants' responsibility and prognosis. If social factors influence the individual's behavior, then people are not completely responsible for what they do. At the same time, if the social factors can be changed (whereas sin and biological factors cannot be), perhaps people's behaviors will change. Thus an emphasis on social factors leads to a view of offensive people as less responsible for their deviance and as having a better prognosis. Consequently we treat rather than punish the offender (Kittrie, 1971; Hawkins and Tiedeman, 1975).

Societal Reaction Perspective

Sociologists known as societal reaction theorists argue that legal factors alone cannot account for our reactions to deviants. Characteristics other than the offense have an impact as well. Societal reaction theorists call our attention to the accusers and not only to those who are accused (Becker, 1974). They stress that the contingencies leading to society's reactions may lie outside the individual's act and at times even outside the individual (Kitsuse, 1962; Erikson, 1964; Scheff, 1974). For example, the race or sex of offenders may have an impact on how we deal with them. In what might be considered the extreme, some argue that the only difference between deviants and nondeviants is that the former have been assessed, labeled, and reacted to as deviant, while the latter have not (Chapman, 1968, p. 4). The behavior of the two really does not differ. Most societal reaction theorists, however, do not take such an extreme position.

Societal reaction theorists might point to the following situations as examples of what they mean and as indications that much further research is needed. During the Watergate scandal of the early 1970s, the then-President of the United States, Richard Nixon, was not criminally indicted, though there was sufficient evidence to do so. His successor, Gerald Ford, pardoned him for any crimes he might have committed related to the scandal. However, people who served under Nixon did go to prison, with the top officials serving the shortest sentences. As another example, historically blacks and men have been more likely to be executed than whites or women. Of the more than 3,800 executions since 1930, only thirty-two have been women (Sellin, 1967). More than 90 percent of those executed for rape since 1930 have been black. These incidents and many more suggest that how we deal with deviance is not solely based on the deviance of the offender.

Standard "Disadvantaged" Variables   Research in a variety of areas indicates that characteristics other than the deviant behavior itself are also used when we decide what to do with deviance. Much of this research has focused on the importance of standard "disadvantaged" variables, such as the race or social class of the offender (Schur, 1975). For example, research on the commitment of individuals to mental hospitals shows that status resources, such as marital status and education, have an impact on whether the individuals are voluntarily or involuntarily committed to mental hospitals (Rushing and Esco, 1977; Rushing, 1978). In general, patients with greater education are less likely to have been involuntarily committed as compared to those with less education. More than 85 percent of patients who had finished four years or less of school had been involuntarily committed in a study of mental hospital commitments in Tennessee. However, less than 50 percent of the patients with more than twelve years of schooling had been involuntarily committed (Rushing, 1978). Similarly, more than 80 percent of patients who had never married had been involuntarily committed, while approximately only 70 percent of those who were married had been involuntarily committed (Rushing and Esco, 1977). The more resources individuals have, either through greater education or through being married (i.e., family contacts), the more likely they can influence the type of mental hospital commitment to their perceived advantage.

Reactions to illegal behavior are also influenced by characteristics other than the deviant behavior. Though not all the research is in agreement, the race of the juvenile offender seems to have a cumulative effect on the several decision-making levels within the juvenile justice system. The influence of race on society's reactions to delinquency at the stages of arrest, of referral to the juvenile court, and of judicial disposition leads to substantial differences in outcomes for black and white youth (Liska and Tausig, 1979). On the other hand, the social class of the youth does not seem to make as much of a consistent difference.

Although there is a great deal of debate as to whether the race of the offender has an impact on the handling of adult criminal suspects, Hepburn (1978) found that it did influence whether prosecutors issued a warrant for the arrest of a suspect after the suspect had been taken into custody by the police. Blacks who were arrested for what the FBI calls Part II offenses (such as simple assault, forgery, prostitution, drunkenness, and so on, which are considered less serious than the eight Part I offenses) were more likely *not* to have a warrant issued by the prosecutor's office than were whites who were arrested for similar offenses. Hepburn argued that the refusal of the prosecutor's office to issue a warrant is an indication that the police made the initial arrest on less than sufficient grounds. Thus, the prosecutor's issuing warrants for black suspects at a lower rate as compared to white suspects is an indirect indication of the impact of the race of the suspect on the *police officer's* decision to take a suspect into custody.

Citizens also take into account information besides the deviance of the offender in deciding what to do. These decisions may be influenced by our stereotypes about people. Steffensmeier and Terry (1973) conducted a field experiment concerning customers' reactions to staged incidents of shoplifting. Confederates were dressed either as "hippies" or as "straights." "Hippies" wore soiled, patched blue jeans and well-worn shoes, went unshaven or without makeup, and had long, unkempt hair. "Straight" confederates had short, neatly cut or styled hair, were clean-shaven or well groomed, and wore slacks, tie, and a sport jacket or a dress if female. Shoppers in three different stores were exposed to staged incidents of shoplifting. Of course, the experimenters had the cooperation of the store managers. Shoppers were more likely to report "hippie" shoplifters than "straight" shoplifters. A "hippie" appearance served as a master status (Hughes, 1945). "Hippies" were seen as lacking ambition and commitment to middle-class values. They already possessed a negative identity in the minds of many. The appearance of the "hippie" shoplifters and the stereotypes which surround them were highly salient to the customers. Some customers became very excited, even enthusiastic, in reporting the "hippie" shoplifters. Others included such comments as, "That hippie thing took a package of lunchmeat" (Steffensmeier and Terry, 1973, p. 425). Thus, as we noted in the previous chapter, our typifications and stereotypes of deviants not only help us to recognize and characterize offenders, but are also taken into account when we deal with them.

Victims may also take into account information other than the behavior of the offender in deciding how to deal with deviance. Robin (1970) found that a department store was more likely to prosecute male employees who stole $100 or more from the company than females who stole a similar amount (60 percent as compared to 47 percent) and lower-status employees, such as cleaners and stock workers, more so than higher-status workers, such as executives (73 percent to 50 percent).

"Subtle" Reasoning in Dealing with Deviance   While the obvious "disadvantaged" variables, such as race, sex, or social class, may be the easiest to observe and record, there are likely to be other factors, often more subtle ones, which influence our reactions to deviance (Schur, 1975). Researchers have found that the attitude of youthful suspects influences how police officers handle them. While the majority of encounters between police and juveniles are civil, both overly respectful as well as disrespectful youths are more likely to be handled formally by the police than those who are polite and civil (Piliavin and Briar, 1964; Black and Reiss, 1970; Lundman et al., 1978). Being disrespectful and antagonistic is an indication of "bad" character and therefore of a juvenile who is truly delinquent and consequently should be handled formally. Being overly respectful may arouse police suspicions because most youths are not particularly deferential toward the police. Teenagers are one of the least respectful of age groups toward the police (Moland, 1975). Therefore, police may suspect that juveniles who are very deferential toward them may be hiding something. Certainly, the attitude of the suspect does not completely explain police officers' reactions to juveniles, but it does have an impact.

Victims of deviance may also use more subtle reasoning in deciding not to report a crime to police. For example, in the national study of victimization mentioned earlier, while many victims mentioned that the victimization was "not important enough" as a reason for not reporting it to the police, the reason most often given was that "nothing could be done." Victims felt that it would be a waste of their time to report the crime to the police. The victims' reasoning may be quite sound because the clearance rate for crimes (the rate of committed crimes which the police have "solved" by arrest or exceptional means) is often low and has been steadily declining. For example, between 1960 and 1978, the clearance rate for robbery has declined from more than 40 percent to 26 percent. Clearance rates for burglary fell to 16 percent from about 30 percent in the same time period (Webster, 1979). Victims may also state that the offense was a "private matter" or that they "fear reprisal" if they report the offense. These two reasons are likely to be given by rape victims (Hindelang and Gottfredson, 1976). Thus victims take into account more than the seriousness of the offense in deciding whether to report it.

Michael Hindelang (1974) argues that while the standard variables, such as race, social class, or sex, may have had an influence on store managers' prosecuting shoplifters twenty or thirty years ago (see Cameron, 1964), they have relatively little influence now. However, how the store personnel interpret the theft may have a subtle impact on whether the shoplifter is prosecuted or not. For example, if the "items stolen are those which the store personnel believe are to be resold—liquor, cigarettes and perhaps fresh meat—they may take a firmer position in favor of referral" (Hindelang, 1974, p. 590). The way in which the item was taken—was it placed under one's clothing or not—could also have an impact. Thus, more subtle reasons may be used in dealing with deviants than merely their sex or skin color.

Organizational considerations unrelated to the offender may also have an impact on how we deal with deviance. For example, overcrowding of facilities and a backlog of cases is likely to have an impact on how suspected deviants are handled. Many observers have noted that plea bargaining in the criminal courts is a result of such backlogs, though some researchers argue that plea bargaining is also used in courts with relatively little backlog (Heumann, 1977). Nevertheless, an investigation of the factors influencing plea bargaining in a major metropolitan criminal court in New York indicated that a backlog of cases *at the next higher court,* the Supreme Court, had a great impact on plea bargaining in the criminal court. In New York, criminal courts can only dispose of cases involving misdemeanors or violations. To convict a defendant of a felony, the case must be waived to Supreme Court. However, Supreme Court is extremely overloaded. Therefore, defendants prosecuted for felony offenses were likely to receive a more favorable reduction in charge than those charged with misdemeanors. Felony charges were often reduced to misdemeanor charges in order to keep the case in criminal court (Bernstein et al., 1977).

External Threats to the Group   In some suggestive research, Pat Lauderdale (1976) also illustrates the importance of organizational considerations in our dealing with deviants. Working with experimental groups of college students who were discussing a hypothetical case involving a juvenile delinquent, Lauderdale (1976) found that the other members of the group more strongly rejected a fellow member (actually a confederate of the experimenter) who expressed extreme views about the case *after* the group was threatened with disbandment. Members of groups where there was a threat implying that they would be disbanded were less likely to want to include the deviant in a future group and more likely to view the deviant in negative terms, as compared to members of groups where there was no threat. In fact, members of the group where a threat was made even started moving their chairs away from the deviant.

According to Lauderdale, external threats to a group may lead to more severe reactions to deviants even if the deviants' behavior has not changed. When groups are threatened from the outside, the external threat magnifies the internal threat posed by the deviant. Solidarity among the members is likely to decrease following the threat, but it will increase as they encourage one another to meet the threat. Establishing stricter standards and reaffirming a common purpose is a way to combat the threat. As the members rally together to combat the outside threat, the group becomes less tolerant. Offensive behavior that may have been tolerated before the threat will now be viewed as clearly unacceptable. Thus, the once-tolerated deviant is more severely rejected because his or her behavior, which is unchanged, now departs further from the standards of the group, which have become more strict. To somewhat simplify Lauderdale's argument, one might say that the time-worn phrase, "If you are not for us, then you must be against us," applies here.

Lauderdale wonders about the extent to which the impact of an external threat on reactions to deviance may account for the placement of thousands of Japanese-Americans in relocation centers (also referred to as concentration camps) following the Japanese attack on Pearl Harbor. Of course, one could argue that the "obvious" ties and potential sympathy between the Japanese invaders and the Japanese-Americans led to the latter's relocation. What would be more interesting to examine is whether reactions to other deviants who had no "obvious" ties to the invaders—for example, criminals, the mentally ill, or homosexuals—became more severe following the Japanese attack on Pearl Harbor. If Lauderdale's explanation is a sound one, then perhaps small colleges, which nowadays are threatened with closure due to financial strains, might react more severely to students and faculty whose offensive behavior would have been tolerated in the past.

As Russia prepared for the 1980 Summer Olympics, which were held in Moscow, plans were made to send Moscow children to summer camps and to place known dissidents under house arrest or to ship them off to remote regions of the country.

> Almost all dissidents have been cleared out—arrested or banished or persuaded to go on vacation—during the cleanup that began months ago. School children are away in summer camps—"as usual," say authorities, although parents report a good deal more than the usual pressure to get the youngsters out of town. . . .
>
> Security officials are visiting all major places of work and study to lecture on the need for vigilance against foreign subversion . . . (*Columbia Record* July 14, 1980, p. D-2)

Though Russia was not threatened with the end of its society, its leaders did feel threatened by ideological contamination from Western visitors to the Olympics. To meet the outside threat, they reacted more severely toward dissidents who at times had been tolerated in the past.

Conflict Approach

Social scientists who work within a conflict approach (see Chapter 3) also argue, as do societal reaction theorists, that legal factors cannot completely explain how society deals with deviance. However, they criticize societal reaction theorists for not thoroughly pursuing the fundamental conflict between those who have and those who have not, between the owners and the workers, between the classes. This conflict stems from the exploitative relationship between the capitalist owners of the means of production and the workers who produce. As capitalism develops, a larger and larger pool of workers become surplus labor. They are not needed. They lose whatever stake they had in society. Their children do not develop that commitment. They become a "dangerous class." They are dangerous to the extent that they disturb:

   1 capitalist modes of appropriating the product of human labor (e.g., when the poor "steal" from the rich)
   2 the social conditions under which capitalist production takes place (e.g., those who refuse or are unable to perform wage labor)
   3 patterns of distribution and consumption in capitalist society (e.g., those who use drugs for escape and transcendence rather than sociability and adjustment)
   4 the process of socialization for productive and nonproductive roles (e.g., youths who refuse to be schooled or those who deny the validity of "family life")

5 the ideology which supports the functioning of capitalist society (e.g., proponents of alternative forms of social organization) (Spitzer, 1975, p. 642).

Therefore, the criminal justice system, the juvenile justice system, the mental health system, and other social control agencies and systems are the:

> modern way(s) of controlling this surplus population produced by late capitalist development . . . controlling the population that is already oppressed by the conditions of advanced capitalism. And control becomes especially acute in periods when the economic crisis is most obvious: during depressions and recessions. (Quinney, 1979, pp. 417–418)

According to the conflict approach, our dealings with deviance, and especially the government's dealings, are designed to protect the privileged position of capitalists and others who have "made it" in the capitalist society. While much "grand theory" has been put forth by conflict social scientists (some might call it speculation), some interesting research has also been conducted.

For example, Carter and Clelland (1979) argue that the social class background of juveniles will have its greatest impact on juvenile court dispositions in crimes against the "moral order" as compared to the traditional crimes against persons and property. Status offenses, such as disorderly conduct, running away, and incorrigibility, and victimless moral crimes, such as those that involve drugs, alcohol, and sex, threaten the moral order of capitalist society. They must be controlled in order to reproduce and support the capitalist system. Status offenses and victimless moral offenses are indications that youth are not developing the commitment and skills necessary to be productive and responsible producers and consumers in a capitalist society. However, the state cannot depend on the unstable working class and the chronically unemployed to control their own children. Neither the children nor their parents have much of a stake in society and therefore little reason to abide by its rules. The state, however, can still depend on the prevailing system of class domination to guide moral delinquents from the stable working class and higher classes. These youths have a stake in society because they realize that they will reap its benefits if they "play the game." Thus, the juvenile court need not be as harsh toward those who may still be effectively controlled in other ways. Crimes against persons and property are "direct threats to all classes" (Carter and Clelland, 1979, p. 100) and cannot be tolerated, no matter what the class background of the offender. Thus, the social class of the offender should have no impact on juvenile court dispositions in these cases.

In analyzing juvenile court dispositions in a southeastern metropolitan area, Carter and Clelland found that juveniles from the lower class were handled more harshly than those from the other classes for offenses against the moral order as well as traditional property and person offenses. However, the bias against lower-class youth was greatest for offenses against the moral order. Thus, Carter and Clelland's conflict perspective on handling juvenile delinquency was at least partially supported by their research.

Hagan and Bernstein (1979) suggest that the impact of the race of draft registers or their type of resistance on how they were dealt with between 1963 and 1976 depended on the social and political context in which their political deviance occurred. The period from 1963 to 1968 in the city which they studied was an era of *coercive control* in which there were a large number of antidraft demonstrations, editorials which admonished resisters to accept their punishment, and a high use of imprisonment. From 1969 to 1976, when the city practiced *cooptive control*, antidraft demonstrations declined dramatically, editorials challenged the use of severe sanctions for some types of resistance, and probation was most likely to be used. Cooptive control is designed to bring dissidents back into the community, to reduce conflict by making them feel a part of the established order.

Hagan and Bernstein found that during the coercive control period black resisters and Jehovah's Witnesses were more likely to be imprisoned than white resisters, but the *reverse* was true during the cooptive control period. During the coercive control period, passive resisters (e.g., those failing to appear for a physical examination) were slightly more likely to be imprisoned than active resisters (e.g., those who burned their draft cards) but active resisters were much more likely to be imprisoned than were passive resisters during the cooptive control period. White active resisters were the ones most likely to be imprisoned during the latter period. How do these findings make sense? Aren't whites members of the majority, and blacks and Jehovah's Witnesses minorities?

Hagan and Bernstein suggest that minority group members are indeed more likely to be coercively controlled when the country tries to squelch political dissent. Those outside of the majority are seen as most threatening when dissent develops. Yet, when political dissent becomes widespread and even somewhat respectable, "majority group members present an even greater threat than minority group members to governing authority" (Hagan and Bernstein, 1979, p. 120). Minorities might be able to be coopted (i.e., "bought off") through leniency. Majority group members who persist in their deviance are the enemies from within. They threaten the unity of the ruling class. We wonder what the implications of this research are for the recent reenactment of registration for all males 18 and over and for the resistance to that registration by some. Will we see a period of coercive control or cooptive control?

The Continuing Debate

Debate continues as to whether legal factors or extralegal factors have a greater impact on our handling of deviance (Gove, 1975; Krohn and Akers, 1977). Is it the seriousness of the offense or characteristics of the offender and context of the offense which we take into account? Such a debate seems to be misplaced. We agree with Edwin Schur (1975) that societal reaction is a basic process in deviance. A societal reaction perspective and other alternative approaches, such as the legalistic and conflict views, need not be mutually exclusive. Merely weighing the relative impact of legal factors and extralegal factors on our reactions to deviance is not particularly useful. Instead, a broader view of our dealings with deviance suggests that we always react to deviance, but that our reactions develop in different ways out of complex and often changing situations. The task for us becomes to specify or more clearly elaborate how we decide to deal with deviance in all the ways that we do. In the future, perhaps, sociologists will begin to examine the full complexity of our dealings with deviance rather than to narrowly champion one approach or another.

OUR EMERGENT REACTIONS TO DEVIANCE

Our ways of dealing with deviance emerge out of the interaction between the accusers, the accused, and other interested parties. Our reactions are created through discussion, negotiation, pleas, denials, proposals, counter-proposals, and so on. We do not mechanically react to deviants as if we were trained pigeons pecking for food when the light flashes. Further, how deviants are dealt with is not merely the result of actions by the accusers. Sociologists, probably more so than other people, have often assumed that deviants are relatively passive, powerless, and resourceless bystanders who take whatever society dishes out. Such an assumption is misleading. Deviants are typically actively involved in the process which leads to some kind of reaction toward them. Some deviants are more actively involved in the process than others. However, even martyrs *choose* not to defend themselves. It is in problematic and difficult cases, where there is a great deal of uncertainty and negotiation, that the emergent nature of our reactions to deviance is apparent. Even in routine cases, though, accusers and accused are actively involved in deciding what is to be done.

As we mentioned earlier, control agents develop working procedures for routinely handling cases. Even when cases can be handled routinely, the agents are actively deciding which category the case falls into and how it should be handled. If the accused does not cooperate, the active involvement of accusers and accused becomes much more apparent in the creation of our reactions to deviance.

Plea bargaining is one of the clearest instances of our reactions emerging out of the interaction between accusers and accused. Even plea bargaining is often routinely handled, as Sudnow (1965) and Cloyd (1977) make clear. However, as Cloyd notes, between 15 percent and 20 percent of DUI cases processed by the city attorneys for San Diego required a significant amount of negotiation.

Negotiations between the prosecutor and the defense increase when there is an *anomaly:* a piece of information is absent or does not fit with other information. For example, when the BAL score is missing, attention may shift to the field coordination test and the description of the driving. In one case that Cloyd observed, the defense attorney *argued* that the defendant had done well on the field coordination test and that the driving was not poor—the defendant had only driven on the double line, but did not cross it. The defense attorney also *brought out* that the defendant planned to enlist in the Navy. The city attorney was *concerned* that the defendant refused to take the BAL test, *wondered* if the defendant's driving was a menace to the community, and *wanted* to make sure that he could justify a reduction of charges to his superior. Given the circumstances as *presented* by the defense attorney, the city attorney *interpreted* the failure of the defendant to take the BAL as an indication that the defendant was probably just scared, especially considering that he was only 21. Therefore, the city attorney felt *justified* in reducing the DUI charge to reckless driving. Even in this relatively simple case, which probably only took a few minutes at most, both sides were actively involved in reaching a decision about what should be done. Of course, the decision may not always please both sides or either side.

Resources for Negotiation

From the accused's standpoint, *experience, information, power,* and *trouble* are resources that can be drawn on in negotiating a more favorable outcome. Offenders who have more experience about the workings of the control system are better able to negotiate a favorable deal. Those who have been caught and processed through the system before can use that experience to their advantage. Thus criminal offenders with prior records seem to do better in negotiating a reduced charge than those with no priors (Bernstein et al., 1977). Those who have information that control agents desire can often bargain for a better outcome. Such offenders become state's witnesses, testifying against their colleagues in crime. Some observers, however, criticize such deals by pointing to the fact that state's witnesses often are not severely punished. Prosecutors argue, though, that such arrangements may be the only way to "get the goods" on more important offenders. Power, which is the ability to influence others to one's advantage, can be used by offenders in striking a favorable bargain. Knowing the "right" people, buying the best defense, and so on, can be used to the offender's advantage (Swigert and Farrell, 1977). Finally, offenders may be able to achieve a better deal if their prosecution would cause a lot of trouble (Pfuhl, 1980, p. 114). President Ford used this reasoning in pardoning President Nixon. He argued that the prosecution of Nixon would tear the country apart. Individuals who have stolen secret reports may be given a less severe punishment in order to get them to admit their guilt so that the country or company can avoid a public hearing which could disclose other sensitive information. "National security" cases often follow this pattern.

Making a Case: Interpretations and Recommendations

Reactions to deviance emerge out of the attempts of the accuser and the accused to "make a case" for their position. Through interpreting what has happened and then trying to support their version of the events, each side argues that the offender should be dealt with in certain ways. Thus *interpretations* and *recommendations* are two key features of the emergent nature of our reactions to deviance. Accusers and accused may disagree on either or both of these issues, though not always.

Often the interpretation centers on the identity or character of the offender. Is the offender "really" a delinquent, a hard-core criminal, an incompetent, a gay, or did the offender engage in offensive behavior without being "that" *kind* of person? In the previous chapter we looked at the process by which we recognize deviant behavior and identify deviants. Establishing or avoiding a deviant identity is a prelude to how the offender is dealt with. Thus, recognition of deviance, identifying deviants, and then dealing with deviants are tightly interwoven processes. Therefore, much of the emergence of our reactions to deviance stems from the documentation and denials that the offender is "truly" deviant, an issue which we discussed in the previous chapter. Without repeating that earlier discussion, let us briefly relate the issues of interpretation and recommendation to our reactions to deviance.

The interpretation of what the offender is "really" like arises out of the activities of the accusers and the accused. As we saw in the previous chapter, based on their training and experience control agents develop general theories about what offenders are like. Specific interpretations of the accusers, however, arise out of their interaction with the accused. Initial interpretations can be changed as the accusers begin to deal with the accused. For example, as described in the previous chapter, Piliavin and Briar (1964) observed one case in their study of police encounters with juveniles in which the police initially interpreted a male juvenile accused with statutory rape as an "undesirable" kid. However, after talking with the cooperative youth, who admitted to numerous counts of statutory rape, but stated that he planned to marry the girl in question, the police changed their opinion of the juvenile and decided to try and get him "off the hook." Thus a different interpretation, which was in part the result of the offender's activities, led to a different recommendation as to what should be done.

Interpretations, though, may have to be documented or supported in order for the related recommendations to be accepted. This becomes apparent when a judge or jury listens to the competing arguments of the accuser and the accused. For example, Robert Emerson (1969) notes that probation officers and others may try to depict the juvenile offender as basically a normal kid or as a true delinquent in order to persuade the judge that their recommendation should be followed. *Pitches* are designed to show that the juvenile's offense was the "typical product of a normal actor" (Emerson, 1969, p. 106) and therefore the juvenile is a normal kid. They are designed to persuade the judge to go with a more lenient reaction than might otherwise be expected and to present evidence that will justify the leniency. The "sterling" qualities of the youth are emphasized.

Through *denunciations,* probation officers and others depict the juveniles as delinquent and their acts as those committed by a "criminal-like" character. Denunciations are used in order to persuade the judge to give more severe dispositions than might be anticipated. Through successful denunciations probation officers or police may achieve greater control over the juveniles: probation rather than "continuance without a finding" or a suspended sentence instead of just probation. In either case, the moral character of the juvenile is constructed through a selective presentation of information.

Juvenile offenders, though, use "protective" strategies in order to counteract the denunciations of the accusers (Emerson, 1969). They try to account for their behavior through stressing their *innocence* or through using *justifications* and *excuses.* We discussed the latter two in the previous chapter. Successful use of these strategies will lead to a less harsh disposition from the judge. In some cases, however, defensive strategies by the accused may be interpreted as further evidence of deviance. When accused delinquents maintain their innocence even though the evidence in the case is conclusive, that action "appears to court personnel as an unrepentant rejection of culpability and serves only to discredit moral character" (Emerson, 1969, p. 149). Similarly, resistance in words and deeds by persons suspected of mental illness "ironically may be interpreted as further evidence of illness and may be used to justify commitment" (Nuebeck, 1979, p. 355). Deviants need to know when to "shut up" as well as when to "put up." Doing the appropriate one at the correct time may lead to less severe reactions.

CONCLUSIONS

Once we recognize deviance and identify deviants, we deal with the offenders in various ways. Deviants may be imprisoned, ostracized, lectured, dismissed, punished, treated, or handled in many other ways. Our reasons for doing so may be revenge, the protection of the community, to make the deviants conventional, to keep respectable people respectable, to maintain the boundaries of decency, or to appease others. Our reactions, however, may have unintended consequences as well.

While we are all involved in dealing with deviance, we have created official control agencies and empowered control agents to handle much of it for us. These agencies, however, depend on our responses to deviance in order to have business to take care of. Through decisions at various levels within these agencies a filtering system is created. Fewer and fewer offenders are processed further and further into the control system. In processing deviants, control agencies and agents develop theories of the office in order to handle deviants as routinely as possible. Instead of handling deviants on an individual, unique basis, control agents typify deviants and their offenses and handle them in terms of those categories. For the past 100 years, total institutions have been an important and dramatic way of dealing with deviance. While critics claim that such facilities are harmful places, the research is not so clear on this point. In the past twenty to thirty years a movement toward decarceration has begun. It remains to be seen whether this movement will continue and what effect it has had and will have on the lives of deviants.

A great deal of debate among social scientists and concerned citizens centers on how decisions are made in handling deviants. Are legal factors the sole or most important ones? Are our reactions based on extralegal factors? Is the social control of deviants designed to support the interests of capitalists? More research and especially more sophisticated thinking is needed here. We must examine the varieties of our reactions to deviance in the numerous contexts in which they occur. We must also remember that our reactions emerge out of the interaction between the accusers and the accused. However, we do not deal with deviance unless there are people who act in ways that we find offensive. It is to the classical issue of why people engage in offensive behavior that we turn our attention now.

PROJECTS

1   Diagram or outline the procedures for disciplining students (or faculty) on your campus. Think of the disciplinary system as similar to the criminal justice system. How do the disciplinary procedures work? Who is involved in the proceedings? Does much filtering take place? Can you uncover the working procedures and philosophies that help those involved to routinize their work? What are decisions about discipline based on? To what extent do the decisions emerge out of the actions of the accuser and the accused?

2   One way of examining how we deal with deviance is through experiments. Invent a hypothetical situation to which your respondents are to react. Give two sets of respondents slightly different versions of the same hypothetical situation.

For example, if you think that the sex of the offender makes a difference in our reactions to deviance, then in one case the offender should be male, and in another, female. Below is one of the hypothetical situations we use in our courses. Do you think students respond to the examples in different ways?

What would you do as the teacher and why? Some alternatives are listed for you.

> You have just caught a twelfth-grade high school student cheating on a final exam in your class. The student is on the honor roll through hard work, but is not that gifted. The student is on the student council. The student is very sorry and apologizes. You know that the student's parents want the student to get into a prestigious college and have put a lot of pressure on the student to do well.

> or

> You have just caught a twelfth-grade high school student cheating on a final exam in your class. The student has done poorly throughout high school due to a lack of effort and not because of a lack of ability. The student is often truant and rarely does assignments. The student denies cheating and laughs when you ask for an apology.

a Let the student take a make-up test which will be a little bit harder.
b Give the student an F on the test.
c Flunk the student for the course.
d Inform the principal and recommend that the student be suspended.
3 Observe control agents as they do their jobs. You might observe in a court, police officers on patrol (many departments allow you to ride with officers, though you do want to be aware of the possible danger involved), public health inspectors, in a mental hospital, and so on. What is the work of the agents like? Is it exciting or routine? What seem to be the important issues to the agents? Can you begin to uncover what influences their work?
4 Our reactions to deviance emerge out of the interaction between the accusers and the accused. One feature of this interaction is how the accused accounts for his/her behavior. Take a present event or recall a past one in which you were accused of being deviant (e.g., incompetent, cheating, irresponsible, lying, or something more "serious"). Discuss how you tried to account for your deviance.

Becoming Deviant

Why do some individuals rob a liquor store? Why do others smoke marijuana? Why do some business executives bribe foreign officials? How does a young woman become a prostitute? Why does someone commit murder? Why do some coaches illegally recruit athletes? Why do some students cheat on tests and taxpayers on their income tax returns? How do some police officers become involved in corruption? Why do some scientists forge data? Why do some people engage in deviant behavior? Because the question of why some people engage in offensive behavior is so fascinating, most social scientific efforts to understand deviance, at least until recently, have aimed at understanding its causes.

Why has this been so? Primarily for one reason: in order to control it (Cohen, 1966, pp. 33–40; Matza, 1969, p. 87). If deviance was objectively pathological, then it needed to be controlled in some way. It needed to be cured or prevented, to use a medical analogy that is gaining wider acceptance, as we have seen. Cures may not always depend on understanding the causes. However, social scientists and others assumed that with better understanding of the causes, society could better control deviance. Society could prevent deviance from occurring, or from recurring if it has already occurred. Such a heavy emphasis on the causes of deviance to the exclusion of other concerns stemmed from the traditional, absolute, objective, and pathological approach to viewing deviance.

Since the early 1960s sociologists have turned their attention to other features of the phenomenon of deviance. They have become interested in the creation of deviant behavior, in the development of rules and regulations, in the recognition of deviance, in how society deals with deviance, and so on. This growing interest in understanding the various features of the phenomenon of deviance has correspondingly meant a decreased concern with the causes of deviance, though certainly not an abandonment of that issue. However, some sociologists feel that the shift in attention away from the etiology of deviance is unfortunate (Akers et al., 1979).

In this chapter we devote our attention to the important issue of becoming deviant. However, we also want to stress, as the other chapters of this book make clear, that while the cause of deviance is an important issue, it is only one feature to be explored in attaining an understanding of deviance. In the following pages we will discuss some of the major approaches for understanding deviance and some specific attempts within those approaches. We will note their strengths and limitations. We will then present an alternative view of becoming deviant which has been called the *career model* of deviance.

PERSPECTIVES ON DEVIANCE

There are many specific social scientific attempts to understand why people engage in deviance, whether shoplifting, prostitution, burglary, drug use, homosexuality, and so on. We do not plan to cover all of them. To do so would take an entire book, and it still might be only a beginning. Instead, in various ways social scientists have categorized these specific attempts into major approaches. We do not plan to discuss all of these different classification schemes either. Instead, we will briefly explore some of the major ways in which specific attempts to understand why people engage in deviance have been categorized. We will then examine a few of the specific and significant attempts in one of those schemes. We will also examine some of the limitations of the approaches and of the specific attempts.

Attempts at understanding why people engage in deviance may emphasize *kinds of people* or *kinds of situations* (Cohen, 1966, pp. 41–44). Attempts which emphasize kinds of people are likely to focus on events and processes that occurred earlier in the *history* of the now-deviant individual. Such attempts look for biological factors, psychological factors, or social-background factors, such as the attitudes of the parents or their social-class standing, which produce certain kinds of people who engage in deviance (Sutherland and Cressey, 1978, pp. 79–80). Attempts stressing kinds of situations assume that most people are capable of engaging in deviance depending on the situation in which they find themselves. Since those who engage in deviance are not special kinds of people, the dynamics of the particular situation becomes the focus for investigation (Sutherland and Cressey, 1978, p. 79). Many attempts at understanding why people commit deviant acts incorporate both approaches, but tend to emphasize kinds-of-people explanations.

Attempts at understanding why people engage in deviance have also been classified as either *strain* theories, *cultural deviance* theories, or *control* theories (Hirschi, 1969). Strain theories assume that people are basically conventional until some kind of tension, frustration, or strain develops in their life which motivates or propels them into deviance. Cultural deviance approaches emphasize the values and beliefs individuals learn in a social setting. The assumption is that people act according to what they learn, whether it be called deviant or conventional. People do not behave deviantly from or opposite to the values and beliefs they have learned, although others, with a different set of standards, may call their behavior deviant. Control theories assume that everyone is capable of engaging in deviance. Many do, and many more would if they dared. The bonds that tie people to conventional society control their behavior. When the bonds are weak, people are freer to engage in deviance. Thus control theories primarily ask why people do not engage in deviance, rather than why they do engage in deviance.

David Matza (1969) has devised a somewhat similar scheme, using three basic approaches which he calls: *affinity, affiliation,* and *signification.* Affinity is similar to strain theories. People become deviant because of the circumstances they find themselves in. Certain circumstances predispose people to engage in deviance. According to Matza (1969, pp. 94–95), sociologists using this approach have stressed the presumed relationship between poverty and pathology. Poverty is assumed to be frustrating, oppressive, and miserable, and thus leads to deviance. Affiliation is similar to cultural deviance. Because of our associations with others, we may be *converted* to behavior that is novel for us but already established for others (Matza, 1969, p. 101). Signification, though, does not correspond to any of Hirschi's approaches. Signification, the most recent approach among sociologists, refers to the potential impact of banning behavior and denouncing deviants on *further* deviant activities. What has come to be called the societal reaction or labeling approach embodies ideas similar to Matza's signification.

For our discussion we will classify attempts at understanding why people become deviant as either *strain* approaches, *cultural deviance* approaches, *control* approaches, or *societal reaction* approaches. We will now examine specific attempts within each approach aimed at understanding why people engage in deviance. We will also examine some of the limitations of these approaches. This discussion will set the stage for an alternative view for understanding becoming deviant: a career model of becoming deviant.

Strain

There are many specific attempts to explain various forms of deviant behavior that are based on a strain approach. Psychological theories tend to emphasize that some kind of abnormality or defective training leads to crime, delinquency, and mental illness. The motivation for deviance may be repressed complexes, unconscious conflict which gives rise to guilt and anxiety, and a corresponding desire for punishment to atone for the guilt (Vold, 1958). Deviance may be due to neurotic behavior, a defective superego, a search for compensation because of early deprivation or, in girls, because of penis envy (Empey, 1978). Or, frustration may lead to aggression (Dollard et al., 1939). Sociological explanations have also been based on a strain approach. Poverty, social disorganization, broken homes, lack of warmth between parents and children, have all been used to explain various forms of deviance (Sanders, 1976). Perhaps the most significant strain explanation in the social sciences is Robert Merton's (1957) notion of anomie.

Anomie According to Merton, almost everyone in our society grows up believing in similar success goals. Through the mass media, the family, the school, and so on, youths are socialized to want these success goals. In our society, the goals are perhaps very materialistic. In other societies, there are likely to be a different set of goals. However, not all people have equal access to the legitimate means for achieving the goals. In our society the legitimate means are hard work and study, a good education, and then a rewarding job. However, the way society is structured not all have easy access to a good education or a rewarding job. Therefore, some people live in an anomic situation. There is a gap between the goals they and others have been taught to strive for and the legitimate ways for achieving those goals.

Thus, Merton (1957, p. 132) is interested in how "some social structures exert a definite pressure upon certain persons in the society to engage in nonconforming rather than conforming conduct." The acute disjunction between the goals of society and the legitimate means for achieving those goals, one source of anomie, helps to explain the distribution of deviant behavior within society. Merton suggests that there are five possible responses for dealing with an anomic situation.

Conformity is the most prevalent response. Here, people continue to believe in the success goals of society and try to achieve them through legitimate means. *Innovation,* though, leads to deviance. While individuals still believe in the success goals of society, they reject the not-easily-accessible legitimate means and turn to illegitimate means in order to achieve success. According to Merton, those in the lower strata of society are most likely to use innovation. They experience anomie the most acutely. Further, innovation "presupposes that individuals have been imperfectly socialized so that they abandon institutional means while retaining the success-aspiration" (Merton, 1957, p. 149).

Ritualism involves scaling down one's lofty desires, an abandonment of the goals of success, but a continued adherence to the legitimate means for achieving success. Lower-middle-class Americans are likely to use this adaptation, according to Merton. Even if they and their children cannot move up into the middle class, at least in their behavior they can be solid citizens. They can imitate the presumed behavior of the middle class even if they will not be as successful. The notions of following a routine, doing things out of habit, or being in a rut underlie ritualism.

Retreatism is probably the least common response. The individual rejects both the goals of success and the legitimate means for achieving the goals. Because of previously internalizing the legitimate means for success, individuals who "drop out" are morally opposed to using illegitimate means in order to be successful. Retreatists are "*in* the society, but not *of* it" (Merton, 1957, p. 153). Vagrants, vagabonds, tramps, and chronic drunkards are retreating from society, according to Merton.

Finally, some people *rebel* against society. They become alienated from both the present goals of success and the legitimate means for achieving the goals. They believe that a new social order should be created in which different goals and different means for achieving those goals are established. Some might call rebels idealistic. Others might call them strange, weird, or crazy. The utopian communities of nineteenth-century America and perhaps the "hippie" communes of the late 1960s, some of which still survive, would be examples of rebellion.

Limitations and Applications   While Merton's notion of anomie has had a profound impact on thinking, research, and policy concerning deviant behavior, it has several limitations. Some have argued that you need to examine the availability of illegitimate opportunities, and not just the availability of legitimate opportunities, in order to understand patterns of deviance (Cloward and Ohlin, 1960). Further, Merton's approach would be supported if lower-class individuals were the ones most heavily involved in deviance. Official statistics at the time Merton devised his explanation supported that pattern, but more recent research and analysis seriously question whether social class has much of a relationship to illegal behavior (Tittle et al., 1978; Hindelang et al., 1979). The earlier findings that lower-class individuals were more involved in illegal behavior may have been due to citizen and police practices in handling illegal behavior or to sociologists' misinterpreting the data (Hindelang et al., 1979). Further, it does not seem to be the case that many youths experience anomie

(Hirschi, 1969). Compared to the number that are engaged in delinquency, relatively few youths experience a gap between their *aspirations* for success—or what would be goals in Merton's terms—and their *expectations* as to what they believe they will achieve—which parallels Merton's notion of the availability of legitimate opportunities. Thus, even if some youths are living in an anomic situation, not enough experience anomie to explain the fact that most youths, now as in the past, commit illegal offenses as they grow up. Finally, anomie cannot adequately explain deviance that is unrelated to attaining success, such as recreational drug use or sexual deviance.

While Merton's anomie approach may not be particularly useful for understanding deviant behavior in society at large, it may be more useful in certain more limited situations, as Merton himself hints. The primary motivation toward deviance, according to Merton, is the frustration experienced by individuals who expect to achieve, are even told to be successful, but do not have the legitimate resources readily available in order to be successful. Deviance as a solution to anomie might be most likely to occur in situations where success and goals are very heavily emphasized, even more so than in society at large. Certain industries, businesses, and agencies may fit this situation (see Cohen, 1966, pp. 80–82). Thus individual executives may engage in bribes, kickbacks, and other deviant activities in order for their companies to be successful when otherwise they would not be. Perhaps student cheating can be understood in part as the response of students to the feeling that they cannot earn acceptable grades through legitimate means but are expected by parents, friends, themselves, and others to do so. Previous research suggests that the inability to do well legitimately in college (as measured by verbal SAT scores) is related to cheating on term papers, but that inability becomes most important for those with the opportunity to cheat and the support for cheating (i.e., fraternity members) (Harp and Taietz, 1966).

Or, what about the recent scandals in military recruiting and in college athletics which concern both recruiting and eligibility? Although military officials acknowledge that there is pressure on recruiters to meet recruiting goals, they do not feel that such pressure is overbearing. As the brigadier general heading the Army investigation said, "No one is forced to cheat in order to recruit for the Army" (*Columbia Record,* November 19, 1979, p. 4-A). However, the military has fallen below its recruiting goals, and some critics claim that it would have fallen even farther behind if it had not lowered the level of education needed for enlistment. Thus, recruiters have coached potential recruits to help them do well on various examinations, they have changed the names of potential recruits who might be rejected because of a police record, and they have put willing recruits through a second time under different names. In college athletics, athletes' exams may be taken for them by other people, transcripts altered, course credit given without the corresponding attendance and work, and under-the-table payments made, all in the name of winning. A former college football coach has criticized what he considers to be the harsh penalties recently imposed on five Pacific-10 Conference universities. In criticizing the penalties, he acknowledged the pressures to win and the potentially anomic situation coaches find themselves in.

> They hire and fire football coaches on the basis of wins and losses. They don't give tenure like that with a chemistry teacher. If the chemistry teacher was evaluated 12 weekends, on the basis of wins and losses, he'd probably find a way to make sure the students got a little better grade, too. . . . I'm not advocating cheating. I just think the system is messed up. (*Columbia State*, August 14, 1980, p. 3-D)

Thus, anomie may be a useful base for beginning to understand deviance in those organizations and situations where success, achieving goals, or winning is all-important. Even then, anomie will only be a beginning for our understanding of the process of becoming deviant.

Cultural Deviance

Perhaps the two best-known attempts to explain involvement in deviant behavior on the basis of a cultural deviance or *learning* approach are Walter Miller's (1958) notion of lower-class *focal concerns* and Edwin Sutherland's (with Donald Cressey, 1978) *differential association*. Many social scientists and others have suggested that lower-class culture is different from the values, beliefs, and practices of the middle class. At various times members of the lower class have been described as unable to defer gratification (i.e., unable to postpone immediate wants and therefore plan for long-range goals), leaning toward physical punishment for disciplinary purposes, encouraging physical combat to solve disputes instead of reason and diplomacy, less concerned about ambition and effort, and so forth (Cohen, 1955). To what degree the lower class may differ from other classes, and if it does, why, has been sharply debated (Valentine, 1968).

Working within this tradition of class differences in culture, Walter Miller argues that boys who grow up in the lower class are likely to be sensitive to certain issues and concerns that may lead them to engage in delinquent or deviant behavior. Miller argues that the lower class is characterized by six focal concerns: trouble, toughness, smartness (i.e., the ability to outwit others), excitement, fate, and autonomy. Miller does not suggest that these focal concerns are values that lower-class parents teach their children. Instead, they are important dimensions of or issues within lower-class life which youths deal with. In becoming aware of these concerns and in dealing with them, lower-class youths may get in trouble with the law. Thus, due to what they learn and must deal with, lower-class youth may engage in delinquency.

Differential Association   Sutherland's theory of differential association has a much broader focus than merely the behavior of lower-class youth. Sutherland contended that we could not explain deviant behavior in terms of frustrations, biological drives, psychological abnormalities, and so on. Instead, deviant behavior is learned, just as is conventional behavior, through a process of differential association, through interaction with others who influence us in both conforming and deviant ways. The relative or differential amount of conventional and unconventional influences from others leads us to become more or less involved in deviant behavior. To badly restate an old saying, differential association suggests that "birds who flock together are likely to become of the same feather."

In its latest version, which has remained constant since 1947, differential association has nine propositions (Sutherland and Cressey, 1978, pp. 80–82). They are:

1   Criminal behavior is learned
2   Criminal behavior is learned in interaction with other persons in a process of communication
3   The principal part of the learning of criminal behavior occurs within intimate personal groups
4   When criminal behavior is learned, the learning includes (a) techniques of committing the crime, which are sometimes very complicated, sometimes very simple; (b) the specific direction of motives, drives, rationalizations, and attitudes
5   The specific direction of motives and drives is learned from definitions of the legal codes as favorable or unfavorable
6   A person becomes delinquent because of an excess of definitions favorable to violation of the law over definitions unfavorable to violation of the law
7   Differential association may vary in frequency, duration, priority, and intensity
8   The process of learning criminal behavior by association with criminal and anticriminal patterns involves all of the mechanisms that are involved in any other learning
9   While criminal behavior is an expression of general needs and values, it is not explained by these general needs and values, since noncriminal behavior is an expression of the same needs and values

Differential association emphasizes that we are likely to become more or less involved in deviant behavior depending on the mix of influences we receive from others. Proposition (9), which stands by itself, needs additional explanation. Proposition (9) indicates that we cannot use people's desires as an explanation for their deviant behavior because others engage in conventional behavior in order to satisfy the same desires. For example, teenagers who want the latest record album could earn money and buy it or they could shoplift it. The desire for the album cannot explain why some youths obtained it conventionally and others obtained it illegally. According to Sutherland, only differential association can explain it.

Differential association has been tested, scrutinized, and defended for more than forty years. Donald Cressey, a student of Sutherland, refutes many of the criticisms leveled against differential association, such as that it omits consideration of free will, assumes that people are overly rational, does not define its terms well, does not explain the origin of deviant behavior, and so on (Sutherland and Cressey, 1978, pp. 83–95).

Notwithstanding Cressey's refutations, differential association is limited in the following basic ways. It is an explanation of the spread of deviant behavior from one person or group of people to another. It does not attempt to explain why deviant behavior originates in some situations and not in others, but instead takes the existence of unconventional behavior and attitudes for granted and then explores how the behaviors and attitudes spread to others. Sutherland did develop a notion of differential social organization which was to help account for the origin of deviant behavior, but he never made it an integral part of differential association. Differential association assumes that people's behavior is the *result* of influences around them. It leaves little room for people to interact with their social environment instead of being merely a product of that environment (Matza, 1969, p. 107). While Sutherland assumes that deviance is the result of learning motives, techniques, definitions, and so on, that are conducive to unconventional behavior, it may be that people learn these motives, techniques, and definitions *as* they engage in deviance (Pfuhl, 1980). In other words, much of what Sutherland assumes people learn in order to engage in deviance may actually be learned not before, but while they engage in deviance. For example, Howard Becker's (1963) exploration of becoming a marijuana user makes just that point. We will return to Becker's work later in the chapter.

Social Learning: Punishment and Rewards   Social scientists still find sources of insight in Sutherland's differential association. Some have sought to modify it, such as Daniel Glaser's (1956) notion of differential identification, in order to make the basic approach more useful. Perhaps the most promising development is Burgess and Aker's (1966) differential association–reinforcement theory, which has been further elaborated by Akers (1977; and colleagues, 1979). Akers has attempted to develop a social learning theory of deviance which incorporates modern behavioral reinforcement theory into the explanation. Briefly, Akers and his colleagues (1979, pp. 637–638) assume that the "primary learning mechanism in social behavior is operant (instrumental) conditioning in which behavior is shaped by the stimuli which follow, or are consequences of the behavior." Put very simply, if you are involved in deviant behavior but find it unpleasant or unrewarding, you are unlikely to continue in that activity.

Akers and his colleagues (1979) recently tested social learning theory in terms of its ability to explain the use and abuse of alcohol and marijuana by youths. They found that a combination of *differential association* (the attitudes of significant adults and the attitudes and behaviors of significant peers concerning use), *definitions* (the individual's own approval or disapproval of use and general attitude toward the law), *imitation* (admired models and their behavior), and *differential reinforcement* (social and nonsocial rewards and punishment for using or not using the substances) is useful for explaining teenagers' use and abuse of alcohol and marijuana. While Akers's social learning approach is a further extension of Sutherland's differential association, and while it has many useful insights, it seems to suffer from the same limitations as differential association. In general, people are seen as prisoners of their environment and not as interacting with their environment.

Control

Control approaches ask the question: Why are individuals not more involved in deviant behavior than they are? Control explanations seek to uncover those features in society which keep people from engaging in deviant behavior. Since the early 1970s there has been a renewed interest in the possible deterrent effect of legal punishment (Tittle and Logan, 1973; Erickson et al., 1977). As we noted in Chapter 5, three features of punishment have been identified: severity, certainty, and celerity. The first two have received the bulk of attention from social scientists. Punishment as a deterrent is based on the assumption that the threat of certain and severe punishment will keep people from engaging in deviant behavior. The threat will control their activities. However, as we noted in Chapter 5, it is not clear to what extent legal punishment is a deterrent. Further, the anticipated and actual reactions of family, friends, and others may be just as effective, if not more effective, in deterring deviance as the threat of legal punishment. This brings us to Travis Hirschi's (1969) control theory of delinquency. It is perhaps the best-developed control explanation of involvement in delinquency. And while it was developed to explain involvement in juvenile delinquency, it seems applicable to many forms of deviance.

Hirschi (1969) notes that control explanations indicate that people engage in deviance when their bonds to society are weak or broken. In his attempt to explain involvement in delinquency, he suggests that there are four elements that bind people to society: *attachment, commitment, involvement,* and *belief.* By attachment, Hirschi means that the more we are sensitive to the opinions of others and care what others think, the less we will be involved in deviance. If we are attached to others, then as we anticipate engaging in deviance we are likely to realize that such behavior will disappoint them. This anticipated disappointment controls our behavior.

Commitment refers to an investment in conventional activities. The more that individuals invest of their time, energy, and themselves in conventional activities and goals, such as getting a good education, building up a business, getting ahead in life, the less they will risk their investment by committing deviant acts. The concept of commitment assumes that deviant behavior is generally a risk to one's investment. Ambition and aspiration should be important in keeping people conventional.

Involvement is the least important of the four elements that bind us to society. Time and energy are limited. The more "caught up" we are in conventional activities—meetings, deadlines, appointments, and so forth—the less opportunity or energy we have to engage in deviance. The notion is that "idle hands do the devil's work." Thus delinquency prevention programs have stressed the importance of afterschool recreational opportunities, the concern for school dropouts, and the presumed salutary effects of inducting young men into the armed services, which would take up most of their twenty-four hours each day. Involvement is the least important of the four elements because much deviance only takes a short period of time to commit. Thus, even the busiest person has time and energy to engage in deviance. However, involvement tends to be related to the other three elements, especially commitment. It is part of a "package deal" which may bind us to society.

Belief is the fourth element that binds people to society. People more or less believe in conventional morality. The less that people believe they should obey the rules of society, the more they are likely to violate them. A lessened belief in conventional morality frees people to engage in deviance. In general, the more that people are tied to conventional society through any one of the four elements, the more they are likely to be tied to conventional society through the other three elements. The four elements that bind us to society are interrelated.

A great deal of research supports Hirschi's control approach (Hirschi, 1969; Empey, 1978). However, while the various elements of the bond are related to delinquency, they "account for only about 25 percent of the variation between delinquents and nondelinquents" (Empey, 1978, p. 239). In other words, Hirschi's elements are consistently related to deviant behavior, but not as strongly as one might like. Other approaches or factors are necessary in order to understand why people engage in deviance. Further, Hirschi's approach does not explain how the four elements of the bond develop, or once developed, how they become weak. Hirschi merely assumes that they are relatively weak or strong for different people, but does not explain why that is the case. Other approaches would be necessary to supplement Hirschi's on this point. Conger (1976) suggests that it makes a difference what kinds of friends and parents individuals are attached to. Attachments by themselves do not necessarily restrain people from engaging in deviance. For example, attachment to punitive parents may have little impact on controlling one's behavior. Akers and his colleagues (1979) argue that the important features of control theory can be subsumed under social learning approaches. For example, greater attachment to others would lead you to anticipate more negative reactions if you were to engage in deviance than if you were less attached. The anticipated negative reactions would be a possible consequence if your behavior were deviant and would shape your future behavior. Finally, control approaches, like some of the previous approaches, do not give adequate attention to the gradual progression of becoming deviant. Instead, control approaches explain why people are more or less conventional without examining how they arrived at that stage and where they may go from there. We will have more to say about the gradual progression into deviance when we examine a career model of deviance.

Societal Reaction

There is a great deal of writing and research in many substantive areas of deviance that is based on or aimed at testing the following statement: our reactions to offensive people *may lead those people to engage in further deviance, to enhance or solidify a deviant orientation,* rather than to lessen their deviant activities and attitudes. The issue is not why people engage in deviance in the first instance, but rather, that how we deal with deviance may lead to more deviance, not less. As we said in the previous chapter, the societal reaction perspective is also concerned with what influences our reactions to deviants.

The societal reaction perspective has become a dominant approach for research and thinking in deviance since the 1960s. Although its roots go back even further, the development of the societal reaction approach is often traced back to Frank Tannenbaum's (1938, pp. 19–20) statement of the *dramatization of evil:*

> The process of making the criminal, therefore, is a process of tagging, defining, identifying, segregating, describing, emphasizing, making conscious and self-conscious; it becomes a way of stimulating, suggesting, emphasizing, and evoking the very traits that are complained of.

Edwin Lemert (1951) elaborated Tannenbaum's idea through his discussion of *primary* and *secondary* deviance. Offensive behavior that is still seen as part of a socially acceptable role is primary deviance. Due to diverse reasons and situations, people may drink an excessive amount of alcohol, cheat on an exam, do some drugs, and so on. As long as the individuals engaging in the deviance are still viewed by themselves and by the other members of society as acceptable members of society who happen to have engaged in deviance, the deviance is primary. The individuals who engage in the deviance are not seen as deviant by themselves or by others in society—they are acceptable people, *but* they have acted offensively. However, if the deviance or other offensive behavior continues, and if society, no longer tolerant, reacts more severely to the offender, the deviance may become secondary. "When a person begins to employ his deviant behavior or a role based on it as a means of defense, attack or adjustment to the overt and covert problems created by the consequent societal reaction to him, his deviation is secondary" (Lemert, 1951, p. 76). If those who engage in offensive behavior begin to redefine themselves as deviant and to use further deviant behavior as a way of coping with society's reactions to them, though not necessarily successfully coping with those reactions, then that further deviance is secondary.

Secondary deviance is not merely deviance that occurs later or after the first involvement in deviance. It is not necessarily a more serious form of deviance, though it may be. It may be the same form as the primary deviance. Lemert is not particularly interested in primary deviance. We may be, though, but the societal reaction approach does not address why people engage in primary deviance. Perhaps the other approaches we have discussed can help us here.

There is likely to be a gradual progression from primary to secondary deviance, involving a reciprocal relation between the increasing reactions of society and the small accretions in the deviant behavior. Lemert suggests that primary deviation may lead to some social penalties (disapproval, fines, and so on). Further primary deviation may occur, leading to harsher reactions. There may then be more deviation, accompanied by resentment of the offenders toward those who are rejecting them. Finally, the community will stigmatize the individuals as deviant. The individuals may begin to incorporate this view within their self-concepts, and future deviance based on the new self-concept or as a strategy for coping with society's reactions is secondary deviance. Lemert is not suggesting that primary deviance and society's reactions to it necessarily lead to secondary deviance, though many have interpreted him to say so. He is merely suggesting that some deviance is a result of our reactions to initial deviance, and in these cases there is a gradual progression from primary to secondary deviance.

For example, homosexuals who commit suicide because of the anticipated or real reactions to them, such as ridicule, being fired, or the heartbreak of their families who have found out, and then the consequent self-doubt and guilt, have committed a very serious secondary deviance. Less dramatic is the businessman who has had a drinking problem for a while (perhaps because his business is failing), but after his wife leaves him (she has had all she can take) and his creditors no longer extend him credit, he hits the bottle even harder in order to forget, to get revenge, or because he does not care any longer. His business folds and he drinks himself into a hospital. Similarly, after serving time in prison, an ex-convict may find that he cannot get a job, that his family no longer socially supports him, and that he is resentful toward the "system." Having learned from fellow inmates how to ply his trade of burglary better, and with little chance to make it legitimately, the ex-convict returns to crime.

The idea of a *self-fulfilling prophecy* (Merton, 1957) is compatible with the societal reaction position. The self-fulfilling prophecy is the process in which our views about what other people are like lead us to act in such ways toward those people as to make them begin to behave in ways that fit our initial views of them. Through our own actions we have fulfilled the prophecy we held of others. For example, research shows that men who think they are talking with a beautiful woman over the telephone will change their behavior in such ways (become warmer, more humorous, sociable, and so on) that the women begin to act in ways (greater confidence, greater animation, and so on) that fit the stereotypes the men have of beautiful women. The same is true if men feel they are talking with unattractive women (Snyder et al., 1977). As related to deviance, if you believe that visually impaired people are helpless and dependent, might you then act in ways which do not allow such impaired people to be independent?

For and Against The societal reaction approach has created a great deal of controversy in sociology. The controversy at times has taken the form of an ideological debate in which there are both defenders and detractors of the "faith" (Gove, 1975; Suchar, 1978, pp. 224–232; Schur, 1979, pp. 255–261). There has been criticism and refutation of the criticism concerning the societal reaction perspective. Let us first examine some of the research in various areas of deviance—delinquency and crime, disability, drugs, and mental illness—that has addressed the issue of whether our reactions to deviance lead to more or less deviance. Researchers have found evidence both for and against the societal reaction approach.

Research Some researchers have found that youths who have been officially sanctioned in some way—arrested or incarcerated for example— become more delinquent in their orientation, attitude, or behavior, compared to those who have not been officially sanctioned (Gold and Williams, 1969; Gold, 1970; O'Connor, 1970; Jensen, 1972; Farrington, 1977). For example, in one investigation over a four-year period, youths with police contacts, especially white males, showed a statistically significant, though also small, increase in delinquent orientation, compared with those who had no contacts (Ageton and Elliott, 1974). Anthony Harris (1975) found that while short-term stays in prison for youthful offenders led to an initial decrease in the relative expected utility (usefulness) of "going crooked," continued imprisonment reversed that effect.

Other researchers, however, find no support or only ambiguous support for the societal reaction approach as it concerns illegal behavior by youths and adults (Fisher, 1972; Foster et al., 1972; Gibbs, 1974; Giordano, 1976; Hepburn, 1977). For example, Travis Hirschi (1975) suggests that research on the treatment of juvenile delinquents shows that it basically has had no effect, one way or the other. And while many people complain that prisons are schools for crime, Charles Tittle (1975, p. 174) suggests that studies of recidivism do not show that imprisonment leads to "crime in the general case or that it is the most important variable in the production of criminal careers." However, Tittle allows that societal reactions may have some impact on further criminal behavior.

Many sociologists have remarked that the disabled are limited in their opportunities not merely by their physical impairments, but more importantly by the reactions of the nondisabled to them (Safilios-Rothschild, 1970). The disabled tend to be put in a subordinate position by the nondisabled. The disabled have often found it difficult to get an education and later to get a job. When they are employed, it is often in positions far below their capabilities. They may receive few promotions. Their disability becomes a central trait or master status around which the nondisabled focus their actions. Social acceptance of the disabled is often half-hearted at best (Davis, 1961; Goffman, 1963; Higgins, 1980). Agencies serving the disabled may even lead to the disabled's greater deviance.

According to Robert Scott (1969), agencies for the blind are likely to use one of two major approaches in working with their clients. For various reasons most follow the *accommodative* approach, though some use a *restorative* approach. The basic premise of the restorative approach is that:

> most blind people can be restored to a high level of independence enabling them to lead a reasonably normal life. However, these goals are attainable only if the person accepts completely the fact that he is blind, and only after he has received competent professional counseling and training. (Scott, 1969, p. 80)

Agencies which follow the accommodative approach do not disagree that it is desirable for blind people to become independent. However, such agencies feel that because blindness poses tremendous obstacles to independence, only a small fraction of clients can become independent. Therefore, a different approach than the restorative one is needed.

As the name suggests, the accommodative approach assumes that the agency must accommodate itself to the limitations of blindness. The physical set-up of the agency may be altered to fit the handicaps of blindness. Tape recorders which report what floor the elevator is stopping at may be used. Special bells over the front door of an agency may ring in order to let clients know that they are approaching the agency. Cafeterias within the agency may serve only food that blind people can eat easily or staff may cut the food up before it is served. Training within the agency is carried out with blindness in mind so that there are few similarities between a sheltered workshop and a commercial setting. As Scott (1969, p. 85) notes, "The unstated assumption of accommodative agencies is that most clients will end up organizing their lives around the agency." Such an approach makes visually impaired people helpless and dependent rather than independent. However, other researchers suggest that official agents who deal with the disabled "do not channel the behavior of the disabled into deviant careers; rather, much of the effort of these agents is directed toward beneficial outcomes" (Smith, 1975, p. 153).

While there are critics of the view that society's reactions to drug use have led to additional deviance (see McAuliffe, 1975, for a cogent critique), other researchers suggest that our country's policy of making drug use and addiction a criminal offense has led to additional deviance (Goode, 1978, pp. 246–252; Schur, 1979, pp. 249–255). They, and other sociologists, would point to organized crime, which thrives on providing illegal but highly desired drugs, or to street crimes, such as theft, mugging, and prostitution, which are often necessary to support a user's habit. They would point to Britain, where there has long been control over the distribution of drugs, but addiction has been seen as a medical problem. Since drugs were available to addicts for free or for a small amount, organized illegal efforts to supply such drugs, and street crime to support a habit, do not exist on the same scale in Britain as in America.

There is similar conflict as to whether our reactions to the mentally ill further enhance their deviance or not. Thomas Scheff (1975, p. 10) argues that:

> When residual rule breaking is denied, the rule breaking will generally be transitory (as when the stress causing rule breaking is removed: e.g., the cessation of sleep deprivation), compensated for, or channeled into some socially acceptable form. If, however, labeling occurs, the rule breaking that would otherwise have been terminated, compensated for, or channeled may be stabilized; thus, the offender, through the agency of labeling, is launched on a career of "chronic mental illness."

However, others who cite various research state that very rarely, if at all, does labeling lead to the stabilization of symptoms and to careers as mentally ill (Clausen and Huffine, 1975).

Criticism   Not only has there been a great deal of research concerning the societal reaction approach, there have also been criticisms of it (Conover, 1976). Critics wonder if the societal reaction approach is suggesting that our reactions to deviance always lead to continued deviance and whether reactions are necessary for continued deviance. Critics argue that societal reactions are neither a necessary nor a sufficient condition for future, persistent deviance (Mankoff, 1971; Davis, 1980, p. 227). We believe that the critics are correct. However, few societal reaction explanations have suggested that persistent deviance is only, always, or completely due to society's reactions to initial deviance (Schur, 1979, p. 258).

Some criticize the societal reaction approach for emphasizing public labels and reactions and ignoring self-labels (Warren and Johnson, 1972). Thus, most homosexuals are not publicly labeled as such, but members of the gay community do organize their lives around the symbolic labels and meanings of being gay (Warren, 1974). Most research by societal reaction theorists has been focused on the impact of public reactions and negative labels on the offender's future behavior. Howard Becker (1963, p. 31), who has been identified with the societal reaction approach, has stated that "one of the most crucial steps in the process of building a stable pattern of deviant behavior is likely to be the experience of being caught and publicly labeled as a deviant." Yet, Becker (1963, p. 31) also notes that self or symbolic reactions are indeed important in becoming deviant: "even though no one else discovers the nonconformity or enforces the rules against it, the individual who has committed the impropriety may himself act as enforcer." We would simply add that the important self-reactions by the offender need not be ones of punishment.

More importantly, perhaps, societal reaction theorists have tended to see individuals who engage in offensive behavior as relatively passive people who are at the mercy of and are propelled further into deviance by the cruel and uncaring reactions of conventional members of society (Gouldner, 1968; Levitin, 1975). Society has become the "big bad wolf," and the deviants have become unsuspecting and helpless "little Red Riding Hoods." Such a view is simplistic. Deviants are active participants in the process of how we deal with them, as we saw in Chapter 5. Lemert clearly noted this point in his discussion of the reciprocal nature between society's reactions to the offender and the offender's reactions to society. Yet his message seems to have been lost. Thus, to a large extent the societal reaction approach is limited in the same way that the previous approaches we have discussed are limited. All see individuals as pawns moved about life by various hands (i.e., factors) over which they have little control.

Elaborations   If societal reactions do not always lead to continued deviance, then under what circumstances do which reactions lead to additional deviance, or for that matter, less deviance? Instead of debating whether reactions do or do not lead to further deviance, those working within the societal reaction approach need to explore the processes by which specific reactions lead to various outcomes. Do we really believe that being stopped by the police will turn a young juvenile into a hardened criminal? Hopefully not. Yet some social scientists research and write as if that were the case.

Some suggestions have been offered for elaborating or more clearly specifying the societal reaction approach. Thorsell and Klemke (1972) suggest that under several different circumstances our labeling of or reactions to deviance will decrease or stop the offensive behavior rather than enhance it. According to them, future deviance may be avoided if the labeling is done in secret and the person labeled is not a professional deviant. The glare of publicity may have harmful effects. Such reasoning has been used in the traditional ban on printing or broadcasting the names of juveniles who have gotten into trouble with the law. That ban has now been declared unconstitutional, and fewer than five states still have such a ban. Second, if the offenders are sensitive to the beliefs of those who label them, the labels may decrease rather than increase offensive behavior. Does this sound similar to Akers's social learning approach or Hirschi's notion of attachment? The labeling as a deviant which occurs in Synanon, Alcoholics Anonymous, and other self-help groups may be, to some degree, an effective strategy for making deviants conventional (Warren, 1974; Laslett and Warren, 1975). We will take this point up again in the next chapter. Third, the more easily the stigmatization of being labeled deviant can be removed, the more likely the offender will become conventional. In Sweden, the anonymity of released offenders is protected so that the stigmatization of previous deivance does not interfere with the offender's integration into society. Finally, if the reactions are positive and supportive, if they are integrative rather than exclusionary, then continued deviance is less likely. We suspect that societal reaction theorists would argue that most of our reactions to deviance are not supportive, but instead are exclusionary.

Milton Mankoff (1971) makes a distinction between *ascribed* and *achieved* deviance that is similar to the distinction others have made between involuntary and voluntary deviance. Ascribed deviants are those with some kind of impairment, be they blind, ugly, a dwarf, or so on. According to Mankoff, the subordinate statuses these people (as well as women and blacks) are placed in, and the preoccupation they have with their physical or visible traits, is due to the reactions of others and not to their own motives and behaviors. Remember Adam's notion of inferiorized groups, mentioned in Chapter 4? Such ascribed deviants are handicapped or limited in their lives because of the "invidious labeling process" and not because their "physical and/or visible traits prevent them from playing any particular role" (Mankoff, 1971, p. 207; see Safilios-Rothschild, 1970, p. 115, for a similar view). Thus, our reactions to the visibly disabled are necessary for their continued deviance, but the reactions by themselves may not be sufficient. The visibly impaired or tainted may be able to assume more or less conventional roles in the community depending on their power, their socioeconomic status, or the compensatory skills they have developed.

Achieved deviance requires the commission of an act. Drug users, bank robbers, illegal recruiters, cheaters, and so on, are *doing* something that offends others. According to Mankoff, many achieved deviants may continue in their behavior without publicly being reacted to, and many who are reacted to do not necessarily continue in their offensive ways. Thus, Mankoff suggests, our reactions to deviance are more likely to lead to continued deviance when ascribed deviance is involved. However, it is achieved deviance that has most concerned sociologists. The distinction between achieved and ascribed deviance is probably not as clear as Mankoff might wish. For example, which kind of deviance is homosexuality or alcoholism? Or, many kinds of disability may today be seen as ascribed, but in the past were not. They were seen as the result of a sin by the disabled person or the disabled person's parents. Nevertheless, Mankoff's ideas are at least a stimulus for further thought.

Mankoff's suggestion that even our reactions to ascribed deviants may not be a sufficient condition for continued deviance points to the time-worn standbys of *power* and *social status* as resources which can be used to mitigate the effects of society's reactions to deviance (Pfuhl, 1980, pp. 241–244). For example, in an often-cited study, Schwartz and Skolnick (1964) found through an experiment that unskilled workers who had a criminal record would less likely be offered a job than those without such a record. They found that just being accused of a crime, even if you were later found innocent, hurt your chances for obtaining employment. Difficulty in finding a job might then lead to additional crime in order to support oneself. However, in the second part of the research, Schwartz and Skolnick found that doctors who had been sued for malpractice suffered few effects. In fact, several doctors' practices improved, and the biggest loser in court reported the greatest gain. There are several possible reasons for the difference in findings between the two studies: different types of reactions were involved, the studies were carried out in different ways (one was an experiment, and the other collected data about actual occurrences), and so forth. One possibility is that doctors often form a powerful colleagueship in which they support one another. The doctors whose practices improved following the malpractice suit received additional referrals frqm fellow doctors. Unskilled workers do not enjoy such communal support. Also, the doctors were probably able to keep their having been sued hidden from their patients. In the experiment, prospective employers knew about the criminal record of the unskilled worker. Nowadays, many prospective employees must take lie detector tests in order to be hired. Thus, their previous deviance may not remain a secret. Remember Thorsell and Klemke's notion that future deviance may be avoided if the labeling is done in secret. Thus, the power, social class, and colleagueship of the doctors mitigated the possible effects of the malpractice suits.

In general, we are less likely to characterize the offensive behavior of powerful people and those of high standing as particularly deviant (see Chapter 4). Nor are such offenders likely to see their behavior as very deviant (Sutherland, 1949). Consequently, our reactions are unlikely to lead to further deviance by the "high and mighty," though certainly they may continue their deviance anyway. Using a deterrent approach, one could argue that our lack of serious reactions to the offenses of the well-heeled and the well-connected serves as a green light for further deviance.

The societal reaction approach sensitizes us to the possibility that our reactions to offenders may lead to more deviance, not less. However, those who find this approach useful must seriously examine the contexts within which, and the processes by which, various reactions influence the future behavior of offenders.

Toward an Alternative Approach

While there are many more specific attempts to explain why people engage in deviance, we believe that we have outlined the major approaches and some of the significant attempts within those approaches. No doubt, we have not included some attempts that other authors might include. We would like to suggest the necessity for a different view of becoming deviant than is indicated by the previous approaches. To do so, we will briefly examine some of the basic or fundamental limitations which we feel characterize the previous approaches to varying degrees. In contrast, the *career model* of deviance will not be limited in these ways.

To varying degrees, the approaches and attempts we have discussed tend to be *static,* they tend to overlook the *situated* nature of deviance, and they imply that people are *passive* prisoners of their environment. The previous approaches do not suggest the gradual process of becoming deviant. There is no procession from being conventional to engaging in deviance. Apparently, it just happens (Glaser, 1956). One day the individual is a conventional member of society, and the next day the individual is a depraved deviant—a hardcore criminal, a junkie, a whore, and so on. Differential association, social learning, and societal reaction approaches acknowledge that there is change over time, but that change in behavior has not been seriously investigated. Further, there is little acknowledgment from previous approaches that people who engage in deviance may not consistently engage in deviance or may never engage in it again. Much deviance is episodic, but this seems to be overlooked. In being static, these approaches do not adequately handle the changes people make as they become deviant—as they become more or less involved in deviance.

The previous approaches tend to overlook the relatively obvious fact that deviance is committed in specific situations. Deviance, like all of our activities, is *situated*. It occurs in specific contexts. And the contexts may be full of contingencies which those who become involved in deviance deal with to varying degrees of success. The previous approaches rely heavily on kinds-of-people explanations. Such explanations seemingly do not need to be grounded in the everyday circumstances that people find themselves in. Instead, the approaches drift along, often with only the most tenuous connections to the very real and complex situations that people find themselves in and create for themselves. This brings us to the last limitation.

People are not merely pinballs knocked about the game of life by flippers—by factors in their social environment. Rather, people interact with their environment. They create it. For the most part, people choose what they do even if their choices are ones which we wish they had not made. What people choose to do will no doubt be influenced by the past and present situations they find themselves in and by future ones they anticipate being in. Thus, becoming deviant is not simply a matter of being propelled into deviance, though it may seem that way at times to the participants. Instead, those who become deviant are actively involved in the process (Matza, 1969).

The previous approaches that we have examined have limitations. Yet, they also provide useful insights, and we have no intention of throwing them out. Instead, as we develop a career model of deviance, we will refer back to some of the ideas and insights of these approaches and use them where we find them helpful. Our career model, too, has limitations, as will become evident. As always, additional thought and observation are necessary. Yet, that is the challenge of understanding deviance.

CAREER MODEL OF DEVIANCE

A useful alternative to the previously discussed approaches for understanding why people become deviant is the concept of a *career*. The concept of a career was developed in the study of occupations, but it has been usefully applied to understanding how people get into (and out of) deviance. A career is a "sequence of movements from one position to another" within a system by anyone within that system (Becker, 1963, p. 24). Typically, the system of interest has been occupational. Thus, a career for a university professor might have the following sequence: graduate work leading to a Ph.D., first position as an assistant professor for several years, movement to another university but still at the rank of assistant professor, promotion to associate professor and (much) later to full professor and perhaps chairperson, with several sabbatical leaves and consulting positions thrown in. The system of interest, however, could be deviance rather than occupations.

A career model of deviance does not mean that we are only interested in occupations or jobs which are deviant or unconventional, such as prostitution, drug dealing, work as a masseuse, stripping, or burglary. Some forms of deviance may be part of the world of work (Miller, 1978). Those which are should be easily understandable in terms of a career. However, much of deviance is not part of the world of work. Smoking marijuana, being a nudist, illegal recruiting, or being disabled is not a job. Yet, becoming involved in such deviance can also be usefully understood in terms of a career. We are interested in deviant occupations, deviance that occurs within respectable and conventional jobs, and deviance that is unrelated to work. A career model can help us to understand how people become involved in all of these various offensive activities.

A career model of deviance is different from the concept of career deviance. Career deviance indicates that progressive commitment to and involvement in particular offensive behaviors has occurred. Career deviance has been conceptualized as the process of being identified as a deviant by others (i.e., labeled) and by oneself and being excluded from participating in conventional activities (Pfuhl, 1980, p. 161). Career deviance suggests a commitment to deviance as a way of life. Career deviance, though, is only one possible outcome in becoming deviant. For example, not everyone who intends to become a doctor actually does become a doctor. In the same way, trying marijuana may be an early stage toward becoming a career user or it may not be. Not all school skippers become dropouts (Crespo, 1974). People may taste the "forbidden fruit" without eating all of it and then later growing and selling it. Career deviance is only one stage in a career model of deviance.

Deviance as a career suggests that there are various stages or positions that people may achieve in becoming deviant. Some do become career deviants. Some do not. Some remain novices. Others become professionals. There may also be different paths by which people reach these positions. And some may be coming and others may be going, though they momentarily occupy the same position. In the same way that a conventional career can be abandoned or changed, so too can becoming deviant. Those who are heavily involved in deviance may abandon it for conventional activities, or they may switch to another set of offensive activities. A career model of deviance allows for *diversity* in the positions that are achieved and in how they are achieved.

A career model of deviance overcomes the limitations that characterize the other approaches we have discussed. Careers are not static. By the way we define careers, they are a sequence of movements. There is a progression from one position to another. In the same way that a person does not suddenly go from medical school applicant to brain surgeon, a conventional individual does not suddenly become a "hardcore" deviant. Careers also imply a concern with the specific situations within which people become deviant, with the contingencies that people confront as they become deviant. Finally, people make decisions. In interaction with others they choose the paths they take. Those who become deviant are not passive prisoners of their environment any more than those who become conventional. Thus a career model of deviance assumes that people make decisions within various specific situations, and that these decisions may lead to changes in their involvement in deviance.

A career model suggests several features that we should attend to in order to better understand the process of becoming deviant. As defined, a career is composed of a sequence of movements from one position to another. Thus we must attend to that *sequence* for different· forms of deviance. The sequence is likely to be gradual. As in any career, one must *learn the trade.* So it is for becoming deviant. It is a process of socialization where one learns and develops attitudes, techniques, and behaviors as one becomes deviant. Careers are *contingent* on how we deal with potential obstacles and opportunities that we face as we pursue our careers. How we deal with a new boss, a proposed transfer, or a salary cut will influence our career. Becoming deviant, too, has contingencies. And the ways in which we deal with those contingencies will influence our involvement in deviance. The contingencies, of course, occur in concrete situations which involve other people and events. Thus, careers are *situated* within a world created by those involved. We need to attend to all of these features in order to understand deviance as a career.

Finally, a career model is concerned less with *why* people become deviant and more with *how* people become deviant. What are the paths they take? What are the contingencies they face, and how do they deal with them? What are the changes that they make? How does becoming deviant develop?

A Sequence of Movements

Deviance as a career involves a sequence of movements from one position to another within a system of deviance and respectability. One does not go from being square to being hip overnight. Instead, there is likely to be a gradual progression from one activity to another. Social scientists are beginning to document the various stages people may go through in becoming deviant in various areas of offensive activity. Let us briefly give a few examples.

Adolescent Drug Use   Kandel and Faust (1975) suggest that there is a sequence of stages for adolescent drug use. Nonusers do not suddenly become dope fiends. Instead, for those who do finally use drugs like heroin, there is a progression from nonuse to serious involvement. Nonusers who try drugs are likely to first try beer or wine. Some who use beer or wine may then drink hard liquor and smoke cigarettes, though many youths go on to hard liquor without smoking cigarettes. Some at the second stage of drug use will then try marijuana. And some who try marijuana will then go on to other illicit drugs—pills, psychedelics, cocaine, and heroin in that order. Those at each level of involvement in drug use typically have not abandoned the use of drugs at lower levels of involvement. Instead, they add on the next level of use. Marijuana users, for example, are likely to still use beer, wine, hard liquor, and perhaps cigarettes. Smaller and smaller numbers of youths go on to each more-involved level of drug use. For example, more than 90 percent of high school students have tried alcohol; somewhere between 50 percent and 60 percent of seniors have tried marijuana; only one out of ten high school graduates has tried cocaine; and about 1 percent of youth use heroin (Radosevich et al., 1979). Thus, marijuana use does not necessarily lead to heroin use. Many who oppose the use of marijuana have claimed that its use is the first step toward the inevitable use of harder drugs. Not so. However, it is true that most heroin users first became involved with legal drugs (legal for adults; though not for minors), then tried marijuana, then turned to other illicit drugs and finally to heroin. Very few youths become so heavily involved, however. At each stage in the sequence of use, those who use drugs the most frequently and the most recently are the ones most likely to go on to the next stage of use. Finally, according to Kandel and Faust, those at more-involved stages of use are not static in their behavior. Some, followed a few months later, have become less involved and not more involved. Those who do become less involved, however, do not typically give up drugs altogether. Instead, just as they gradually progressed from one level to the next, so do they gradually retrace their paths, slowly decreasing their levels of involvement. Adolescent drug use follows a sequence of movements.

Police Graft   Lawrence Sherman (1974) indicates that there are six stages in a police officer's becoming a grafter (i.e., someone who accepts a bribe). A police officer does not go from being an idealistic rookie to a "hard-bitten" cynical cop who accepts drug money after only one week on the job. And, of course, many police officers do not go through all six stages. Some, tempted by ever increasing levels of graft, may choose an "inside" job, a job within the department that does not expose them to the temptations of the outside world. Others may go only so far—accepting bribes from gamblers and prostitutes, but not from drug dealers. Police officers who do become involved in grafting are likely to go through the following sequence of accepting bribes: (1) minor "perks," such as free coffee and meals from restaurants on the officers' beats; (2) accepting bribes, such as a drink from bar owners who are allowed to stay open after closing hours; (3) bribes from motorists who have been stopped for a traffic violation or from construction bosses who illegally leave materials on a sidewalk; (4) payoffs from gambling operations; (5) bribes from prostitutes, pimps, or madams; and (6) bribes from drug dealers. Thus, there is a gradual sequence in becoming a police grafter, from accepting quasi-legitimate perks to accepting payoffs from drug dealers.

Developing a Gay Identity   Finally, Richard Troiden (1979) notes that there are four stages whereby men who have acquired a gay identity do so. The four stages of Troiden's model should be seen as an *ideal* type that each individual instance of becoming gay will fit more or less well. In order, the four stages are: *sensitization, dissociation and signification, coming out,* and *commitment.* During childhood and approximately before the age of 17, those who later become gay acquire experiences they they will use *later* to interpret their feelings as homosexual. Before age 13 gay men became sensitized to feeling *different* from other children—perhaps alienated, a sense of gender inadequacy, or something else. Between the ages of 13 and 17 a sense of *sexual difference* is experienced. The male teenager may feel less interest in the opposite sex than what he believes he should feel or may have "undue" interest in other males. By approximately age 17, then, those who later acquired a gay identity became aware of or sensitized to being sexually different from other young men.

During the second stage these young men dissociate their same-sex sexual interest and activity from who they are fundamentally. They "explain away" their sexual behavior with and sexual interest in other men. They were drunk, experimenting, or it was something they would outgrow. However, to try to discount their behavior and interest serves to signify, to make them face the possibility that they are homosexual. Thus, during the second stage of acquiring a gay identity, the homosexual aspect of the sexual behavior, feelings, and doubts becomes recognized even if it is seen as only temporary or not part of their "true" selves.

During stage 3, those who become gay identify themselves to themselves as homosexual. For Troiden's respondents this self-definition occurred at an average age of 21.3, though defining one's sexual feelings as homosexual, a product of the second stage, occurred at an average age of 19.7. Many who later acquired a gay identity experienced some confusion regarding their sexual identities in their late teens. They labeled their sexual feelings as homosexual, but did not immediately label themselves as homosexual. Meeting other gay men was the most common situation leading to a self-definition as homosexual. Involvement in the homosexual subculture was likely to occur at the same time as the self-definition as a homosexual or a few months later. As these men *came out* and gained more information about homosexuality, they began to define themselves and homosexuality in a positive way instead of in the overwhelmingly negative way that they had viewed it before (e.g., as mental illness, which, as we noted in Chapter 4, was and to some degree still is the general public's view).

Becoming committed to homosexuality as a way of life is the final stage in acquiring a gay identity. Commitment implies that homosexuality is valued as much as if not more than heterosexuality or bisexuality, and that the one who is committed would remain homosexual if faced with the opportunity to become otherwise. While Troiden feels that taking a lover is only part of becoming committed, he found that those of his respondents who had one or more lovers entered their first relationship on the average two and one-half years *after* defining themselves as homosexual. Thus commitment to a gay identity develops after self-definition as homosexual.

The various examples we have presented—becoming a drug user, a police officer's accepting graft, and acquiring a gay identity—indicate that there is a sequence of movements from one stage or position in becoming deviant to the next. Not all within a particular system of deviance will move through all the stages. Those who have reached higher levels of involvement may later abandon the system altogether. The stages themselves should not be seen as something absolute and objective. Instead, they are a convenient way of classifying people's progress along the various paths to becoming deviant. It may be difficult to place any particular person at one of the stages. An individual may be between stages or straddling more than one. Becoming deviant is more fluid than the concept of stages or positions implies. However, stages and sequences of positions serve as a useful framework for organizing the many movements of people who become deviant.

A Gradual Progression From our examples it should be apparent that the sequence of movements from one position to another is *gradual*. People make decisions, they interpret their activities and the activities of others, and they choose courses of action depending on the circumstances. This all takes time. For example, according to Kandel and Faust (1975), students may try beer, wine, or cigarettes around the age of 12, but not try marijuana, on the average, until the age of 14. Thus, there is gradual process of several years from being a nonuser to trying marijuana, and more time will elapse before greater levels of drug involvement are achieved. Troiden (1979) notes that those who acquired a gay identity in their early twenties (the average age at which his respondents had their first love affair was almost 24) first felt different from other children before they were adolescents. From first sensations to commitment as a gay seems to be more than a ten-year process. Barbara Heyl (1979) notes that it may take years for a novice prostitute to become a professional, and this does not even include the progress from being a member of the "square" world to being a novice. (We will more thoroughly discuss Heyl's research on becoming a prostitute at the end of the chapter.) Similarly, it may take years for some people who become visually impaired to think of themselves or act like helpless, dependent blind persons. In fact, as we will see shortly, the process of becoming blind may actually begin years before individuals become visually impaired (Scott, 1969). Becoming deviant is typically a gradual process that may involve years of effort by both conventional and deviant folks.

Learning the Trade

A career model suggests that as people become deviant, as they move into deviance and from one position to another, they learn values, beliefs, techniques, rationalizations, and so forth, as part of the process. They learn the trade. The sequence of movements that we have just discussed is only possible if people learn the trade of deviance. However, unlike Sutherland's differential association explanation, which implies that the principal part of the learning occurs before people engage in deviance, a career model suggests that one learns as one becomes deviant as well as before one becomes deviant.

For example, Howard Becker (1963) suggests that deviant motives are not learned prior to becoming a marijuana user and that such motives are not what propel people into marijuana use. Recent research on the smoking of marijuana by college students supports Becker's position (Ginsberg and Greenley, 1978). As people become involved in using marijuana, typically in the company of others, they develop motives or conceptions about marijuana and how it can be used. More specifically, Becker contends that in order to go from a willingness to try marijuana to being able to use the drug for pleasure (i.e., a beginning user), individuals must learn three aspects of the use of marijuana. First, they must learn the *technique* of smoking marijuana. Nowadays many who have yet to use marijuana know the techniques because they are widely displayed in the mass media. At the time of Becker's research in the late 1940s and early 1950s, use of marijuana, and therefore knowledge of how to smoke it, was much more limited. Those who learn to use marijuana for pleasure must also develop the ability to *perceive the effects* of smoking marijuana and to be able to associate those effects with doing dope. Finally, in order to become a beginning user for pleasure, individuals must learn to interpret the effects as *enjoyable*. Such experiences as dizziness, thirstiness, hungriness, and misjudging time and distance could be interpreted as unpleasant. To learn to enjoy them is a socially acquired taste. According to Becker, all three features of learning to use marijuana for pleasure occur in interaction with others, usually experienced users, who can help point out to the experimenters what is happening to them.

Similarly, Rasmussen and Kuhn (1977) indicate that in the process of becoming a successful or professional masseuse, women learn several techniques and skills. They learn to be disinterested in the sex they are having with customers. They become able to take an objective view of the job, performing sex for money, without becoming emotionally involved. To be objective, though, may discourage customers. Therefore, professional masseuses learn to fake involvement. And even though the customers may realize that the involvement is only a pretense, they willingly suspend their disbelief while they get what they paid for. Masseuses learn to pick up clues by which they can decide what type of woman the customer prefers and therefore how to satisfy him. They learn to market themselves to prospective customers through their attire, body language, seduction rhetoric, and services provided. They also learn how to check out customers in order to uncover those who are actually undercover agents. And perhaps most important of all, they are likely to develop a conception of themselves (e.g., "I am not a common prostitute" or "I only do 'locals' ") which allows them to neutralize their own possible feelings of guilt and shame as well as the anticipated negative reactions of others. Later we will speak of this issue, the contingency of shame which those who become deviant often face.

Individuals often learn the trade as they become deviant. They learn in interaction with other offenders. However, one may begin to learn the trade in *anticipation* of becoming involved in deviant activities at a later time. Much of socialization is anticipatory learning. Those who later become marriage partners, parents, old people, or even doctors, lawyers, or Indian chiefs, often develop conceptions of what those positions and jobs entail before they assume them and at times even before they think of assuming them. For example, Cloward and Ohlin (1960) argue that much of that lower-class delinquency which seems to be "for the hell of it" according to Albert Cohen (1955), in which there is an apparent disregard for the item itself, can actually be understood as very purposeful, rational behavior. Stealing the items may be a way for juveniles to express solidarity with the adult criminals whose operations they hope later to become members of. Stealing "for the hell of it" is also practice. It provides the opportunity to acquire needed skills. The items themselves may not be particularly important, but the stealing is, in terms of the youths' anticipating becoming members of adult criminal gangs.

Conventional Learning in the Service of Deviance   Other kinds of preparation for becoming deviant may not be intentionally tied to anticipation of future deviant behavior. In fact, the so-called preparation may only later be reinterpreted as preparation once the people become deviant. As we mentioned before, deviance and respectability are interwoven features of society. Knowledge and skills learned in one realm are often easily transferable to the other. Thus, much of what we learn as conventional members of society may play an important part in our later becoming deviant. For example, Donald Cressey (1953) argues that criminal violation of financial trust, or what is commonly called embezzlement, only occurs when persons in a position of financial trust (1) think of themselves as having a financial problem that cannot be shared with others, (2) become aware that this problem can be secretly solved by trust violation, and (3) are able to apply to their situation a verbalization that enables them to violate their trust without seeing themselves as violators. Cressey argues that embezzlers become aware that they can solve their problems through trust violation from stories about embezzlers in the mass media, from the company, which may bond its employees, and from the dishonest practices of others. Further, the skills required for embezzlement are often the same skills necessary for faithfully performing one's job. The verbalizations or rationalizations applied to the anticipated trust violation by embezzlers are not different from what people conventionally say and do on their jobs—"everyone cheats a little" or "the money is just being borrowed." What we learn as conventional members of society may stand us in good stead when we become deviant.

What we learn as conventional members of society may even subtly support our becoming deviant even though we had not intended to become the kind of people that others find offensive. Scott (1969) suggests that those who are visually impaired become blind people (i.e., helpless, dependent people for whom blindness has become the overriding concern) through three major processes. The latter two processes occur after a sighted person becomes visually impaired. These two processes are the awkward interaction which often occurs between the visually impaired and the sighted, and the handling of visually impaired clients in agencies for the blind. We spoke of the second of these two processes earlier in this chapter when we discussed the accommodative approach in agencies for the blind. The first process occurs during childhood, youth, and into adulthood when, as sighted people, those who later become impaired acquire experiences about the blind. These experiences and information are typically used to characterize the blind as helpless and dependent. Later, those who become visually impaired may apply this typification to themselves and thus enhance their becoming helpless, dependent, blind people. Much the same could be said for becoming disabled or deviant in general.

Thus, learning the trade is an important issue in becoming deviant. Much of it occurs as one becomes deviant. However, some of it may occur in anticipation of becoming deviant. And some of the skills, knowledge, and beliefs involved in becoming deviant are acquired as conventional members of society.

Contingencies

Careers are contingent on how we deal with the possible obstacles and opportunities that we face as we create our careers. In becoming a police officer, one may face some of the following contingencies: few openings due to budgetary considerations or hiring practices, exams, and tests; low salary and perhaps little respect; internal investigations of corruption; danger; the emotional pressure of being an officer; shake-ups in the department; opportunities for advancement, bribery temptations; and old age. How individuals deal with these contingencies influences the careers they create for themselves. The same is true for deviance. How we cope with contingencies has an impact on the paths we take into and out of deviance. Becoming deviant is full of contingencies.

Shame   For many, the primary (the most important as well as often the first) contingency in becoming deviant is *shame* (Douglas, 1977). According to Douglas, rules are enforced primarily by feelings of shame and guilt. We are shamed by others. Or, we may shame ourselves (i.e., feel guilty) to the extent that we have "bought into" or internalized the rules that we have broken or anticipate breaking. Many people may engage in deviant behavior once or twice, but then not again. The deviant behavior was too highly shaming for them to continue it. Douglas (1977, p. 63) argues further that "most wickedness, almost all of it, is only thinking, never action, because the thinking elicits too much fear of shame or actual shame." Does this remind you of Hirschi's notion of attachment? Think of former President Carter's admission in *Playboy* (November 1976) of his lusting after other women "in his heart." Certainly, he is not the only one who has thought about offensive activities, whether it be lust or something else.

Thus, because of the contingency of shame, much of deviance occurs only in the imagination, and that which does occur is often episodic and sporadic. However, if conventional behavior is powerfully enforced through the threat of shame, how do people get started, and once started, how do they continue to become deviant?

Techniques of Neutralization   Gresham Sykes and David Matza (1957) argue that those who break rules neutralize the anticipated negative reactions (i.e., shame) from others and even from themselves through five specific techniques of neutralization. In their discussion they focused on juvenile delinquency. According to Sykes and Matza, juveniles who break laws are not in complete opposition to conventional society. They have "bought into" conventional morality to some degree, and therefore they must deal with the anticipated shame that their delinquent behavior may cause. As juveniles realize, even laws have legitimate exceptions. Juveniles, however, extend, modify, and distort the legally acceptable justifications, so that while the justifications are still acceptable to them, they are no longer acceptable to conventional society. These techniques allow the juveniles to affirm to themselves that they are conventional members of society, but that in this particular case they had a legitimate reason for not acting conventionally. While these techniques are developed or learned before the youths engage in illegal activities (and to that extent are different from rationalizations, which are developed after the fact), they can be used after the involvement in delinquency in order to explain to others the youths' seemingly unacceptable behavior.

The five techniques of neutralization are: denial of responsibility, denial of injury, denial of the victim, condemnation of the condemners, and appeal to higher loyalties. Juveniles may deny that they are responsible for their behavior. They may claim instead that they are more acted upon by forces over which they have no control (e.g., a broken home or a deprived childhood) than actors. Or, youths may argue that what they did really harmed no one. No damage was done. The vandalism was harmless mischief, and the stolen car was just borrowed for a good time. If damage was done, the juveniles may claim that the people who were harmed were not really victims. Instead, the so-called victims were a bully, a crooked store-owner, or a spiteful teacher who got what they deserved. The teenagers may also condemn those who condemned them. They may criticize police, teachers, or parents for not being without fault themselves. Therefore, such adults are hypocrites for condemning the youths when they have their own shortcomings. By focusing attention on those who condemn them, juveniles who break the law deflect attention from their own behavior, and in comparison their offenses do not seem so unacceptable. Finally, youths may appeal to higher loyalties. They may convince themselves and later justify to others that they needed to stand up for their friends, and in doing so became involved in delinquent activities. Can you see how these five techniques of neutralization are elaborations or distortions of legitimate justifications for what would otherwise be rule-violating behavior?

Through these techniques and due to other reasons, many juveniles are likely to *drift* into and out of delinquency (Matza, 1964). They are not committed to criminal values. Yet, at times they become relatively free of the restraint of conventional values. At those times, they are drifting between freedom and control, between criminal and conventional behavior. Through *preparation* (i.e., previous experiences of being involved in the illegal activities) or through *desperation* (trying to overcome the fatalistic view that one has no control over one's environment) they may choose to commit delinquent acts.

While Sykes and Matza focused on juveniles in their discussion of techniques of neutralization, similar techniques are employed by others who engage in deviance. Remember Cressey's discussion of embezzlers and the verbalizations they use in order to retain a respectable image of themselves. Taylor and Bogdan (1979) examined how administrators in human service organizations—in particular, state schools for the mentally retarded—neutralized themselves from outside criticism—from criticism which points at the disparity between what is supposed to take place in their facilities and what actually takes place. Administrators too may deny that they are responsible for the unacceptable conditions. Instead, a lack of money is the problem, or the attendants are incompetent, but cannot be fired due to civil service regulations. They may claim that even if conditions are not as good as everyone would like, the residents still receive better care than they would get elsewhere. Injury is denied. At times administrators may talk as if the scars and lacerations of the residents were due to their retardation. "What else can you expect will happen to such people?" is the rhetorical question that they ask. Critics of the state schools are seen as naive or self-serving. Administrators appeal to the responsibilities of being a mature professional. Loyalty to this image also serves to neutralize the criticisms of others. Administrators may argue that their facility is better than other facilities or better than it was. They deny criticism by *comparing* their facilities with other present or past ones. Finally, administrators may deflect criticism of their facilities by arguing that the future will bring new approaches and new results. Thus, juveniles who engage in delinquency are not the only ones who neutralize the negative reactions of others.

Evading and Managing Shame   Douglas (1977, p. 63) argues, however, that talk cannot truly neutralize or rationalize feelings of shame and guilt. Feelings are more powerful than talk. Rationalizations only work to the extent that others have a reason for sharing in the pretense that the rule-breakers are still conventional people. Rationalizations are important as a tenuous social bridge between the rule-breaker and conventional people. It can collapse whenever the conventional members of society no longer decide to share in that social fiction.

Instead, Douglas (1977) argues that those who "successfully" become deviant deal with potential feelings of shame through evasion and deception. They evade them through *self-seduction,* and they deceive others so as not to bring about their wrath. When shame feelings cannot be evaded, they may be managed through *aggressive countermoralism* or through *counterpride displays.*

Self-seduction is a slow, gradual, stepwise process in which one deceives oneself as to exactly what one is doing or becoming. Thus, college-educated women who are about to become masseuses have over a number of years gradually gone from being virgins to engaging in casual sex to finally engaging in group sex with pride. Yet, sex for money is still highly shameful. How do they deal with the shame? They may talk with insiders who perhaps act as if there is no shame. They hint at or talk indirectly about what they plan to do, using words which are not heavily loaded with shame. Yet, they still may feel shame. Thus, in small stages, each with its limits, which are later exceeded, the women become masseuses. They may begin by sincerely believing that they will only give massages. Or they may set a limit—"hand jobs" or "locals" only. Later, they may make an exception to the rule, and even later the exception may become the rule (Rasmussen and Kuhn, 1977). As they become more involved they may develop an ideology or perspective about their work—they are therapists who help men with sexual problems. This perspective gives them pride in their work or at least allows them to reject (neutralize?) those who reject them. Even later, though, they may have de-shamed sexual behavior enough so that they no longer need to deceive themselves that they are "sex therapists." Instead, they begin to admit to themselves that they are hookers. By deceiving ourselves about our feelings or about where we are headed, while also increasing the temptation of the activity (e.g., it's fun, well-paying, and so on), we can seduce ourselves into deviant behavior.

However, not all shame feelings can be evaded through deception. Those that arise must be managed in order for people to continue in their deviant ways. Through aggressive countermoralism, those who are shamed may aggressively shame the shamers. A prostitute may shame "respectable" women for selling their bodies to their husbands in order to live well. Most of the time we only subtly shame the shamers, with a sneer, a smirk, or a curse under our breath. Notice the similarity to Sykes and Matza's condemnation of the condemners. Through counterpride displays, the shamed person takes pride and displays pride in that which aroused feelings of shame. Thus, the prostitute who is shamed by others for doing sex for money may take pride in being the best at such a job, and may even flaunt that stance to "squares." By combining a countershame and counterpride display into one comeback, a female impersonator silenced a heckler who demanded that the impersonator address him as "sir." "Tris replied, with elaborate sarcasm in his voice, "Sir . . .? I'm more 'sir' than you'll ever be and twice the broad you'll ever pick up" (Newton, 1979, p. 66).

Whether talk is as ineffective as Douglas claims, or whether it is not, his discussion of evading shame and guilt points to an important contingency, *conventional morality,* which those who become deviant must deal with. Freaks deal with middle-class morality (Wieder and Zimmerman, 1976), nudists with the morality of clothed society (Weinberg, 1966), and so on. Those who become deviant are likely to develop an ideology or perspective that justifies their behavior. Nudists explain their activities in terms of friendliness, relaxation, and freedom, even though they realize that clothed society is likely to see them as sex fiends (Weinberg, 1966). Similarly, as Becker (1963) suggests, in order to become regular marijuana users, individuals must deal with the conventional view that users are slaves to the drug. Those who cannot do this are unlikely to become regular users for pleasure. Effective rationales might be that the drug use is under control because the user has stopped for a week or two, or simply that to be aware of the possible problem is to be in control of it. Stripteasers may claim that they provide a harmless outlet for the sexual needs of "degenerates" or educational services for the women who attend their performances (Skipper and McCaghy, 1971). In the same way that those who pursue a legitimate career must come to terms with some of the unenjoyable or dehumanizing aspects of their work, so too must those who become deviant. And coming to terms with the shaming aspects of deviance will take time. Rarely can conventional morality be brushed aside easily. To a large degree that is why increasing involvement in deviance is a gradual process.

Secrecy   While shame is perhaps the most important contingency that those who become deviant must face, it is not the only one. The possibility of being caught or being exposed is an issue which many who become involved in deviance must face. Some confront the issue by severing all ties with conventional society, or as many as possible, and associating only or primarily with fellow deviants. Others engage in deviance in places where their identities will remain anonymous. Thus, respectable members of the community may seek impersonal sex in restrooms or in nocturnal visits to parks (Delph, 1978). Only sociologists and muggers are likely to intrude in those places. Or, again according to Becker (1963), in order to become regular users of marijuana, occasional users must develop the belief, usually acquired through a fortuitous circumstance, that they can smoke marijuana and while still under its effects keep their use secret from others. Those who cannot effectively deal with secrecy are unlikely to become heavily involved in deviance, or if they do, probably will be caught. In the following chapter we will explore in detail how deviants deal with the issue of secrecy.

Performance   Careers entail doing things. And how well we do them will influence the paths our careers take. Thus performance is another contingency that arises in becoming deviant. This is most evident in terms of work that is unconventional or deviant. For example, some strippers become headliners—the stars of the show, others are co-features who are under headliner status, and others are line girls, and they are paid accordingly (Skipper and McCaghy, 1970). Or, Cloward and Ohlin (1960) argue that lower- and working-class youths who do not have easy access to legitimate opportunities may turn to drugs after they have *failed* at illegitimate activities, such as theft for profit or gang fighting. Or, age catches up with everyone—the athlete, the singer, the dancer, and the deviant. Middle-aged homosexuals may have a difficult time in attracting a sexual partner. Consequently, they may not frequent gay bars, which primarily serve a young clientele (Warren, 1974). With increasing age, male homosexuals decrease their involvement in the gay community and increase the time they spend with heterosexuals (Weinberg, 1970). They may do so out of an increased self-acceptance and a lessened sense of distinctiveness from straights (Troiden, 1979), or perhaps they do so out of the inability to successfully compete in the sexual marketplace. For this second reason male street and bar hustlers in the gay community often have a short career (Miller, 1978). "Aging" prostitutes (perhaps women in their thirties) who want to stay in the business may realize that their income and status already are or will likely be declining. No longer able to successfully use their own bodies, such prostitutes may contemplate becoming madams, manager-hostesses of a prostitution operation (Heyl, 1979). Thus, one's performance and how one copes with declining performance also influence the paths that are taken in becoming deviant.

Situated Nature of Deviance

Careers are situated. By this we mean that people prepare for, obtain, and then work at certain jobs in concrete situations. What they do has its fullest meaning within the specific situations in which they carry out their activities. One becomes a professor through attending specific schools and later being a professor (i.e., doing the things that professors do) in particular institutions. For example, lecturing makes sense in a classroom, but the same activity may take on an entirely different meaning at a party. Because it may, "wise" professors confine their lecturing to classrooms. Or, to look at it another way, can one be a secretary without the accouterments of the secretarial situation—offices, co-workers, business machines, and so forth? Perhaps so, but it is difficult. Personal secretaries who travel with a wealthy individual are often thought of as something other than secretaries because their activities do not seem to occur within the expected situation. Finally, if the activities that make up a career are situated, then people are sometimes working within (or at) their careers and sometimes are not. Even the most dedicated of us do not work all the time. We confine our career activities to certain times and situations. Becoming deviant is also situated.

Becoming deviant occurs within a set of circumstances—a time, a location, a special gathering of people, perhaps—and a certain view of the situation (some might call it willingness) (Pfuhl, 1980, p. 57). Deviance, just like careers, does not occur in limbo or in the Twilight Zone, though we often speak as if that were the case. We speak as if those who become deviant are engaging in their forbidden activity all the time, any time. Not so. For example, one provides sex for money in certain circumstances. People may provide sex for money in many circumstances, but not in all circumstances. As a prostitute in London said more than twenty-five years ago, "When I go off business I won't take anyone else. It's the same as if you opened a shop, if someone came in half an hour after you had closed you wouldn't serve him" (Rolph, 1955, p. 77, in Heyl, 1979, p. 226). Or as a masseuse said, "I only do those customers that I especially like" (Rasmussen and Kuhn, 1977, p. 30).

One becomes deviant and does deviance in concrete situations. Some of the contingencies of becoming deviant are the other people and their activities and interests which are part of the situation. This is readily apparent in terms of deviant work—strippers, prostitutes, female impersonators, con artists, burglars, and so on. How well individuals deal with pimps, managers, the audience, the victim, and the others who appear in the situation influences to what extent they become and continue to be deviant (Miller, 1978).

In this regard, the generally rising rate of predatory crimes since World War II may be due in part to the changing circumstances of our lives (Cohen and Felson, 1979). Most crimes require a convergence or coming together of "likely offenders, suitable targets and the absence of capable guardians against the crime" (Cohen and Felson, 1979, p. 588). Broadly speaking, these are the characteristics of the situation within which crime takes place. Instead of emphasizing characteristics of offenders in order to explain rising rates of rape, robbery, assault, larceny, or other predatory crimes, the changing circumstances of our lives may be more important. For example, since the war people have been spending more of their time away from home. Yet, predatory crimes are most likely to occur away from our homes. Also since 1960 there has been a tremendous increase in the production of small, durable goods. For example, television sets are much lighter now than in the past. Suitable targets, one of the necessary items in order for crime to occur, have increased dramatically in the past twenty years. Thus, much of the rising rate of crime may not be due to an increase in how "prone" people are to commit crimes, but to an increase in those features of the situation which are conducive to crime.

Similarly, rather than appealing to an inclination to commit murder, we can also understand criminal homicide as a *situated transaction* (Luckenbill, 1977). Such an event is a chain of interaction between two or more people (and an audience perhaps) which lasts while the people are in the presence of one another. Transactions that lead to homicide escalate into *character contests* in "which at least one, but usually both [participants] attempt to establish or save face at the other's expense by standing steady in the face of adversity" (Luckenbill, 1977, p. 177). Such transactions are likely to occur during social occasions characterized by several features: nonwork or leisure-time occasions; "permissive" settings, such as the home or a tavern where both conventional and unconventional activities which are often pleasurable may take place; and the parties involved are likely to know each other or be in the company of those whom they know. The homicide occurs through a sequence of six stages:

1   An activity of the victim that is later interpreted by the offender as a personal affront, for example, an extramarital affair
2   The interpretation by the offender of the victim's activity as personally offensive
3   Retaliation by the offender which indicates to the victim that the victim is an unworthy person—a verbal or physical challenge to the victim
4   Behavior by the victim which is seen as standing up to the offender's challenge and therefore implies that violence is an acceptable

solution to the confrontation; for example, a refusal to comply with the offender's demands

    5 Commitment to battle by the victim and the offender—the securing of weapons or mobilizing weapons already in hand

    6 Once the victim falls, the offender terminates the transaction by fleeing or by remaining, either voluntarily or involuntarily, due to the restraints of others

Thus homicide may occur within certain settings through the situated interaction between offenders and victims.

Becoming a Prostitute

While a great deal of research has addressed various aspects of becoming deviant, relatively little has *thoroughly* explored becoming deviant in terms of a career model. As you can see from our previous discussion, we have used ideas and examples from various areas in order to describe and illustrate how people become deviant. In the following pages we will present a brief summary of Barbara Heyl's (1979, pp. 197–235) analysis of becoming a prostitute, an analysis which is illuminating in its thorough use of a career approach to understanding becoming deviant.

    According to Heyl, there are four stages in becoming a prostitute. Women start as "squares," then move to (1) *willing to try,* (2) *novices,* (3) *professional prostitute,* and (3a) *madam*—which is a career option for a professional prostitute. These stages are "ideal types"—a synthesis of various features into a typical "square," "novice," and so on. Any particular woman who is becoming a prostitute will more or less fit the ideal type at each stage. The four stages can be described along five dimensions which serve to differentiate them from one another.

    The first dimension, *interaction partners,* refers to the relative degree of contacts that women have with people who are square and with people "in the racket." Those in the prostitution business refer to themselves as "in the life" or "in the racket" and refer to those who are not as "squares." Squares would have contact only with other squares, whereas those at Stage 1, "willing to try," would have mixed relationships. Those further involved in prostitution would progressively lessen their contact with the square society. The second dimension is *employment.* In which "world" does the woman work? Again there is a progressive movement from only legitimate jobs, to being unemployed or marginally employed for those "willing to try," to perceiving the racket as temporary, and finally to viewing it as a full-time activity. The third dimension is the women's *perception of prostitution.* How does she view it? Squares see it in the traditional, negative way, but as women move into the racket they first suspend their conventional view and then learn new evaluations of prostitution, such as, "How can it be so evil when so many straight men pay for it?" The fourth dimension refers to the rules or *norms* which women hold regarding sexual behavior—how often it should be done, what acts can be engaged in, and what role the woman should play. Again, squares hold the conventional view that intercourse outside of marriage is wrong, that only a limited number of acts are acceptable, and that women should be passive, following rather than initiating and leading. As women move toward becoming professional prostitutes they increasingly feel that they must be socially and sexually aggressive with the "tricks," and that a wide variety of acts are acceptable and desirable for business. With the pimp, however, they are expected to be passive. The frequency of sex is expected to increase dramatically. However, the madam is expected to refrain from or have very little sexual contact with her customers. The final dimension is the *actual* frequency and degree of predictability of sexual behavior, the *timing of sexual encounters*. The square woman's sexual behavior is likely to be relatively infrequent and nonroutine. As one moves into the racket, frequency and predictability increase. Sex becomes a brief, frequently scheduled activity. With pimps or business partners, however, it still remains nonroutine.

How do women move from one stage to the next? Heyl suggests that *subjective preconditions, situational contingencies* (and also subjective contingencies for those moving from being a square to being willing to try), and *subjective responses* are necessary for women to move from one stage to the next. Women who begin the movement need not go through all the stages. If they are to go on to later stages, though, they must "undergo the situational and subjective changes described in the phases" (Heyl, 1979, p. 205). While women who have moved into the racket world may later become less involved, they clearly cannot erase their previous experiences. These previous experiences will be felt as women return to the square world as well as if they later return to the racket. From a large population of eligible women—square women primarily between the ages of 15 and 30, and more specifically between 17 and 21—a relatively small and continually decreasing number will move through the four phases.

In Phase 1, from square to "willing to try," several subjective preconditions must exist in order for square women to become willing to try prostitution. Women must strongly feel dissatisfied and tense. These feelings may be due to home difficulties, being alone in a strange city, or being financially strapped in boring jobs. Women must then view their problems as capable of being improved through acquiring more money and perhaps social support. The third subjective precondition is that the women see themselves as capable of satisfying men sexually. Women who have had many sexual partners may see themselves as capable, but so too may those who have had only one.

Certain situational contingencies are likely to occur in this first phase. There is likely to be a "turning point"—a moment perceived by the individual as marking the end of one life pattern and the beginning of another which as yet may be unknown. For potential prostitutes, moving to a new, strange city may be the turning point. Old relationships may be disrupted. Consequently, commitment to prior people and responsibilities is lessened. One senses a feeling of freedom, a freedom from those who hold traditional values. The turning point makes women more aware of their problems, which tend to be seen as economic. It is now, when the women are without supportive relations and under economic strain, that contact with racket people will have an impact. Contact with such people, who may profit from recruiting new women into "the life," lays the groundwork for women to begin to redefine prostitution in a favorable manner: good income, social rewards, and the positive definitions of racket people. If they still experience financial difficulties and an "estrangement from conventional sources of support" (p. 214), they may be open to continuing contact with people in the racket. As the contact continues, they may begin to contemplate "trying" prostitution in a way that does not threaten their self-image. They see themselves as able to satisfy men sexually, and they are told that they could make a lot of money. They're willing to try it.

In Phase 2, the woman moves from "willing to try" to novice. It may be a short step from being willing to try to working as a novice in prostitution—perhaps a few months or only a few days—but it is not automatic. Those who become novices must have continued contact with racket people, and it is through them, frequently, that their first opportunity to work as a prostitute develops. After their first trick, the feedback from the racket people is important. Racket people help the fledgling prostitutes to interpret their experiences positively. The fledglings have proof that they can make money at this business. Less important, but also crucial, is social support from the tricks, the pimps, or the madam, some or all of whom may compliment or encourage their activity. These monetary and social rewards help the fledglings to overcome whatever unpleasant experiences they have their first day as a prostitute—experiences related to the fact that they are no longer contemplating prostitution but have engaged in it. In order to become a novice prostitute, the women must come through their initial experience with confidence that they are capable of performing well and making money, and that what they did is acceptable. If so, they may "go into prostitution for a while."

Phase 3 covers the period from novice to professional prostitute. It may take years for a novice to become a professional prostitute. A professional prostitute is an "experienced, skilled and working prostitute who is an accepted member of the prostitution world" (Heyl, 1979, p. 219). Prostitution is the professional prostitute's full-time occupation. She is skilled at her job, knows how to keep regular customers and how to avoid and manage arrests, and maintains her personal hygiene. She takes pride in her work and develops an ideology that supports it. While she may have friends who are conventional in every respect, and while she shares in many of the values of conventional society (especially those concerning the importance of money), her life is "organized around the techniques, contacts, customs, and language through which she earns her income" (Heyl, 1979, p. 221).

In order for a novice to become a professional prostitute, she needs additional training and coaching in the skills and orientation of prostitution. It is important for her to develop the belief that her sexual behavior with customers is just part of her job and does not interfere with her relationship with her pimp or lover. Sex with the customers becomes devoid of emotion. Training that isolates the novice from her previous, conventional lifestyle will be most effective in helping the novice to become a professional. Training in a house of prostitution serves well to isolate the novice from previous contacts. In order for the novice to continue in the racket, she must continue to be rewarded financially and socially—money, friends, and excitement and status in a new world can all be rewarding. This additional training, isolation from previous contacts, and rewards from prostitution may enable some novices to begin to see themselves as part of the racket world. And while the novice may not hold all members of that world in high esteem, some novices realize that they all share common problems and experiences. Arrests for prostitution may accelerate the women's identification with the racket world and their estrangement from conventional society. Finally, continued success as a prostitute, perhaps in different settings or on their own, builds self-confidence. Based upon these experiences and the self-confidence that they have made it and can continue to make it in the racket, some prostitutes decide to make a career of prostitution.

Phase 4 is the movement from professional prostitute to madam. A madam is the manager-hostess of a prostitution operation. Not all professional prostitutes become madams, but most madams have been professional prostitutes. Becoming a madam is one alternative for aging prostitutes who want to remain in the racket. House prostitutes, who work for a madam, are more likely than others to recognize the financial gain of becoming a madam, as well as to develop the feeling that they have the skills to be a madam. Those who do not want to remain in the racket, do not recognize the rewards of being a madam, or do not feel that they have the skills to manage a prostitution corporation, do not become madams.

The prospective madam must have the resources and the opportunity to acquire a setting for a prostitution operation. She needs help from racket people—to find prostitutes and perhaps to build up a clientele. Like other business people she will have competition that challenges her operation. And again like other business people, she will need to deal with the demands of all the various individuals who are involved in or impinge upon her operation—customers, prostitutes in her employment, police, perhaps a landlord, and to some degree the pimps and other madams in her area. In setting up her operation, she becomes aware of the increased responsibility and complexity of her position. Yet, if she is to become a madam, she must derive satisfaction from that responsibility and from being her own boss. She is the madam of the house now.

CONCLUSION

Until recently social scientists interested in deviance were primarily interested in why people engage in deviance. A search for causes might help in the search for cures and controls. Various approaches have been developed to explain involvement in offensive activities. Strain approaches assume that people are conventional until some kind of strain or tension develops which propels them into deviance. Cultural deviance approaches assume that people conform to the influences around them. However, these influences may be conventional or deviant. Control approaches are based on the idea that people would engage in deviance or in more deviance if they dared. They dare not to to the extent that their behavior is controlled by bonds tying them to conventional society. The societal reaction perspective focuses on the possibility that how we react to and handle deviance may lead to more, not less, deviance. All of these approaches are both useful and limited in their ability to help us understand the causes of deviant behavior.

To supplement them, we explored a career model of deviance. Such a perspective is more concerned with how people become deviant than with why they become deviant. A career model instructs us to look for the gradual sequence of movements that people make in becoming deviant. In becoming deviant, individuals must learn the trade and must cope with contingencies, of which shame is perhaps the most important. Finally, careers are situated. We decide to do deviance in specific contexts. Change the context and we may not do the deviance.

Becoming deviant is a never-ending process. It is not something that is simply achieved and then is maintained with no additional effort. Becoming deviant must be worked at as constantly as becoming respectable. Just as athletes can rarely rest on their laurels, on what they did last season or even the day before, neither can those who are becoming deviant. Athletes must prove themselves each time they perform. Those who become deviant must decide and act each time they contemplate doing deviance. Even those who are heavily involved in deviance face anew the issue of doing deviance the next time. They may become deviant (i.e., do deviance) the next time, the next one hundred times, but not the time after that. Thus, becoming deviant should not be seen as a journey in which some reach their destinations and others fall by the wayside, and in which some of those who reach their destinations become disenchanted and return. Certainly this metaphor contains some insight into becoming deviant, but it also contains some distortions. Instead, we see becoming deviant and becoming respectable as part of the same, endless, ever-changing creation.

To be sure, we all are likely, to various degrees, to treat deviance as a status that can be achieved and, once achieved, is difficult to get rid of. We assume that deviance is persistent. We often feel that it is a quality of an individual which cannot be shed like the skin of a snake when it molts. The most ardent exponents of this belief will remind us that even when a snake has shed its skin, it grows a new one and is still a snake. Those who are involved in deviance may share society's view of them. And why shouldn't they? They are part of society. They may agree that some people have deviance in them just as others have show business in their blood. To this, all we can say is that the show only goes on when the performers perform. And those who do perform deviantly must cope with conventional society, with those who find their activities offensive. We turn to that issue now.

PROJECTS

1 Most of us are involved in deviance in various ways and to various degrees. Trace your own career path—whether the career involves doing drugs, premarital sex, cheating, delinquency, or so forth. What were the stages or levels of involvement that you went through? What skills, techniques, and ideas did you learn or develop as you became more involved? How did you manage shame and other contingencies? What are the specific situations in which you decided to do deviance? If you are no longer involved, describe how you abandoned deviance.

2 Many people, if you approach them in the right manner, are willing to talk about their involvement in deviance. You might think of working up a *life history* of someone who is involved in deviance—i.e., to write a biography of the individual's life as it centers around deviance and respectability.

3 Sociologists are forever doing questionnaire studies aimed at understanding what factors influence our involvement in deviance. Some of these studies are enlightening, and some are not. Pick an area of deviance that you are interested in—sexual behavior, drug use, employee theft, or whatever. What factors do you think might be related to involvement in that deviance? By examining previous research on the topic, or through combining your own or others' experiences about that area of deviance with your understanding of the various approaches discussed in the chapter, you will be able to settle on some possible factors. Develop a questionnaire that will provide information about people's involvement in deviance and how they stand on these factors that you think are related to involvement. Pass the questionnaire out to an appropriate sample of people. What do your results show?

Chapter 7

Coping With Conventional Society

Just as conventional society deals with deviant behavior and people, so those who are offensive, in turn, cope with conventional society. Deviants are not the passive rule-breakers that some sociologists have assumed them to be. They may deny, counter, or conceal their deviance. For example, the member of Congress who becomes too sick to attend an investigative hearing on his alleged wrongdoings is coping with conventional society's reactions to him. The gay office worker who passes as straight is coping with the anticipated reactions of straight society. Some deviants cope by joining a self-help group, such as Alcoholics Anonymous, Gamblers Anonymous, or a weight-loss organization. They attempt to become conventional people. Others become deeply involved in a community of deviants—a gay community, or a deaf community, for example. The members look to one another for social support, a sense of belonging, and the opportunity to be who they are. Some deviants may attempt to change the rejection, pity, or indifference of co-workers, acquaintances, and family. Others, fed up with being what they feel are second-class citizens, create or join a "liberation" movement—gay liberation, "prostitute power," or a disability awareness group in order to change society's policies toward them and its definitions of deviance. If these liberation movements are successful, then we have come full circle in the phenomenon of deviance, back to the creation of deviance.

All these ways and more are how deviants deal with their deviance and with society's reactions to them. The deviant's way of coping with conventional society is the final feature of the phenomenon of deviance. Some sociologists have developed classification schemes for the various strategies used by offensive people in order to bring a little order to what would otherwise be great disorder (Goffman, 1963; Humphreys, 1972, pp. 135–156). The typology of nine techniques by Rogers and Buffalo (1974) is a useful beginning for our discussion in this chapter.

FIGHTING BACK

Joseph Rogers and Douglas Buffalo (1974) outline nine different strategies that deviants may use in "fighting back" or coping with society's reaction to them as deviant. These strategies are: acquiescence, repudiation, flight, channeling, evasion, modification, reinterpretation, redefinition, and alteration. Deviants may move from one strategy to another in combating the reactions of conventional society.

Some deviants may *acquiesce* to the validity of the label of deviance. They accept the accusation that they are indeed alcoholics, prostitutes, or drug addicts—that they are unworthy people. There are variations in acquiescence. It may become the kind of resignation to one's lot, or self-hatred, that has long been alleged among oppressed groups—blacks, women, Jews—as well as among homosexuals, who have also been oppressed (Humphreys, 1972; Adam, 1978). Others may become "true believers," embracing the correctness of the designations used to describe them. This stance may be a prelude to other strategies, such as alteration (e.g., members of Alcoholics Anonymous). Some deviants may conclude that it is futile to contest the imposition of the label. Others may extract compensation for wearing the label of deviance. Thus blind beggars "accept" the label of helplessness and dependence, but only in return for a fee (Scott, 1969).

Deviants may *repudiate* the accusation that they are offensive. In claiming to be innocent, however, the accused may intensify or highlight the salience of the label. The alleged deviant's confrontations over the accusation and handling of deviance may be interpreted by others as further evidence of offensiveness. If successful, though, the protests may obliterate the negative characteristics ascribed to the deviant. Rogers and Buffalo suggest that successful repudiation requires a great deal of resources. However, as an unsuccessful contender for the Republican Presidential nomination in 1980 learned, successful repudiation in the courts concerning wrongdoing does not mean successful repudiation in the minds of potential voters. The "mere" fact of having been accused lingers on (Schwartz and Skolnick, 1964).

Other deviants may *flee*. Running away, suicide, or starting over again in a new locale with a new name are attempted flights from conventional society. Those who flee, however, will likely have to cope with their prior history as deviant. Only with difficulty can "fresh starts" fully escape soiled pasts. The management of information about those pasts, part of the issue of *passing* (Goffman, 1963), becomes an important issue which we will take up later.

Channeling is a fourth technique for coping with the reactions of conventional society. Not only do some deviants accept the imputation that they are deviant, but they use the label (and what it means) as an important and positive feature of their identity. Becoming an AA member is one way of channeling deviance. "Black is Beautiful" is an expression of pride and self-identity for an oppressed group. Using one's height or lack of it to become an actor or an athlete is a way of giving positive expression to what may have been a belittling experience as a child or youth.

Some deviants *evade* society's reactions by rejecting them through denials, excuses, justifications, and accounts (Scott and Lyman, 1968). Sykes and Matza's (1957) techniques of neutralization, which can be used in order to become deviant, as we noted in the previous chapter, could also be used to counteract the accusations of conventional people who have been offended. Ironically, the professional explanations or diagnoses of why offenders engage in deviance "may be converted into excusing behavior by offenders" (Rogers and Buffalo, 1974, p. 111). The sociologist may argue that a "bad home situation" leads to delinquency, and juveniles involved in delinquency may use the same explanation to excuse their behavior. Evasions are likely to be used during the initial confrontation between the accusers and the accused when it is decided what should be done with the accused.

Through *modification* deviants attempt to substitute an image of themselves that is less offensive than the one implied by the initial accusation. The accused alcoholic claims to be a heavy social drinker; the "chicken" claims to have been sick; or the gay claims to be bisexual. Deviants attempt to alter the impression that others have of them even if they may not be able to completely escape a negative label.

Through *reinterpretation* the moral image of the behavior is changed— the "facts" are accepted, but their meaning is reinterpreted. As Rogers and Buffalo note, the "enemy of the Crown" is reinterpreted as being a loyal American patriot. Participants in sit-ins and protest marches, such as the late Dr. Martin Luther King, Jr., are troublemakers and law breakers to some, but may interpret their own behavior as a crusade for justice and equality. Reinterpretation is a reflection of the relativity of deviance. The same behavior may take on entirely different meanings for different audiences.

Redefinition occurs when society's views of deviance have been changed. What was once considered offensive is now tolerated or even considered conventional. Social movements often aim to redefine what is and is not considered immoral, illegal, or deviant. Redefinition speaks to the historical relativity of deviance. Thus, those involved in deviance may be important participants in the creation of deviance and respectability.

Alteration is an attempt by deviants to become conventional. Through therapy, self-help groups, surgery, or individual abstinence, deviants may seek to alter that which offends others. Self-alteration may be difficult, however, because in many cases conventional people doubt that deviants can change their "true nature." In Chapter 4 we mentioned the idea of persistence: "once a deviant, always a deviant." Because of this, alteration may be only partly successful. The deviants become *ex-deviants* in the minds of others and perhaps even in their own minds. It is as ex-deviants, then, that those who have altered their deviance must contend for the remainder of their lives. For example, Senator Thomas Eagleton, who was chosen by Senator George McGovern as his running mate in the 1972 Presidential campaign, was not able to escape the label of ex-deviant—in this case of having, as he admitted, checked into a hospital three times in the 1960s for nervous exhaustion and fatigue, and of twice having undergone electroshock treatments (Altheide, 1976, pp. 141–155). Eagleton eventually stepped-down from the Democratic ticket.

STRATEGIES FOR SURVIVAL

Rogers and Buffalo's discussion of nine strategies for "fighting back" gives us an idea of the variety of ways in which deviants may cope with conventional society. It provides a useful beginning for our examination of this issue. However, we would like to use a slightly different framework in investigating coping strategies. Some deviants *contend* with the immediate accusations of conventional others. The denials, neutralizations, and accounts used to counter the accusations of deviance are particularly important in the emergent nature of how we deal with deviance—the interaction between the accuser and the accused as to what should be done. Since we discussed the strategy of countering accusations in Chapters 4 and 5, we will *not* pursue it here. Other deviants utilize various strategies in an effort to *live with* their deviance, trying to navigate through conventional society with as little difficulty as possible. Issues of passing and covering arise here (Goffman, 1963). Still other deviants, however, seek to *become conventional* through changing either themselves or the attitudes of others.

These three general approaches are not mutually exclusive, since any individual deviant may use a shifting combination of strategies from each of them. For example, those who are living with their deviance through being members of a deviant community may also develop an ideology (a set of ideas) to justify their behavior to themselves and to conventional people. They may also attempt to change public policy toward them. For ease of presentation we have separated the three basic approaches that deviants use in coping with conventional society, but in everyday life, depending on the situation, the individual deviant may use a variety of strategies. However, individually as well as hisorically on a collective basis, we suspect that deviants who seek to become conventional through redefining what is deviant have first contended with their accusers when possible and then have tried to live with their deviance. Born out of desperation and hope, becoming conventional through changing the attitudes of others would be the last strategy in a progression of attempts to cope with conventional society (Humphreys, 1972, pp. 135–156; Adam, 1978, pp. 122–124). Certainly, not all deviants complete this sequence of attempts, just as not all become equally involved in deviance.

Living With Deviance

Offensive people who live with their deviance attempt to navigate through conventional society with as little difficulty as possible. They neither contend with the accusation that they are deviant nor attempt to become conventional; instead, they attempt to live as satisfying a life as possible. One way for deviants to minimize trouble is to control the information that conventional people have about them. Thus, *managing stigmas* becomes an important issue for many deviants. Others join a *voluntary organization* or become members of a *community of deviants.* Such groups may help to create or solidify an individual's identity as a deviant. Members can provide support for one another and share problems and coping techniques. Within such groups deviants may carry on their offensive activities with a minimum of interference from the outside. Through individual or collective strategies, deviants may try to minimize the troubles they face as disreputable people in conventional society.

Managing a Stigma   Deviant people are stigmatized. A stigma is a deeply discrediting trait, a failing, shortcoming, or handicap (Goffman, 1963). It is a negative discrepancy between *virtual* and *actual* social identity. A virtual social identity encompasses the characteristics that we expect others to possess. An actual social identity encompasses the characteristics that people do possess. Those who fall short of what we expect are stigmatized. We generally expect people to be conventional, able-bodied, and of sound mind. Deviants, however, diverge from these expectations. They are stigmatized.

As we noted in earlier chapters, deviance is relative. So are stigmas. A characteristic that is stigmatizing in one situation may be quite expected in another. For example, having a high school diploma is not discrediting among cab drivers, but among teachers having no higher academic degree would be quite discrediting. Being gay is expected in certain bars. Being gay and an elementary school teacher is heavily stigmatized. Characteristics that discredit people in one situation may confirm their unusualness in another.

The stigmatized are likely to face the issue of *social acceptance*. Will they be accepted by conventional people for what they are, or will their stigmas become master statuses? Will they be accorded the respect and regard which they feel their other attributes warrant, or will the disrespect due to their tainted characteristics become overwhelming? How will they be treated if others know of their deviance?

Stigmas may be either *discredited* or *discreditable*. Discredited characteristics, such as a visible disability, are easily noticed or are already known about. For example, others may know that a certain colleague is a drug addict or a former mental patient. In either case, discredited people are concerned with managing the tension, awkwardness, and uncertainty that are likely to occur when encountering others. The discreditable, however, possess stigmas that are not easily noticed or are not known to others, but *could* become known. A drug user, an ex-convict, a gay, or someone who engages in extramarital affairs all could be found out. Discreditable people are thus concerned with managing information—with concealing information or revealing it to others.

Passing Many discreditable deviants are likely to pass as if they were not. They are likely to present an image of themselves as conventional. Fear or uncertainty about what might happen if conventional people knew of their deviance leads them to cope with being deviant by concealing it. Even with the gay liberation movement of the past decade, many gays are still "in the closet" to various degrees depending on the audience—their own selves, fellow gays, family, straight friends, co-workers, and so forth (Ponse, 1977). Ill-prepared students may attempt to conceal their lack of preparation from their professors, and the mentally retarded may at times try to create a cloak of competence (Edgerton, 1967). Members of oppressed groups, whether deviant or not, may at times try to pass as one of the oppressors. It is not surprising that light-skinned blacks have passed as white. Passing is one way of living with a stigma.

Goffman suggests that there are several strategies that discreditable people are likely to use in passing as "normal." Some may attempt to *conceal or obliterate* the signs or indications of their stigmas. Name changes may disguise the infamous. Contact lenses or a hearing aid in the frame of eyeglasses may help the visually or hearing impaired to pass as otherwise. Drug users who shoot up in areas other than the arm are trying to conceal needle marks, the telltale signs of their activity.

Others may use *disidentifiers* in order to present the appearance of respectability. Disidentifiers are "props" which are typically taken as signs of being conventional. Disidentifiers attest to the unusualness that conventional people expect. Thus, an unwed mother and father can pass as a respectable couple by getting married (Pfuhl, 1978). A burglar may dress in a business suit when casing and burglarizing a fancy neighborhood (Sanders, 1977). Or gays may ask friends of the opposite sex to pretend to be their spouse or lover in order not to arouse the suspicions of straight colleagues. A 52-year-old lesbian used this strategy in order to account for her distress at the ending of a long relationship with her female lover. For years, she took a male, gay friend to parties, where they pretended to be living together. Her business associates did not know that the man was gay. During her traumatic breakup with her female lover, she took a *different* gay fellow to a party:

> And this just threw everyone into a tizzy, you know, and I said well, Tom [her long-time 'accomplice'] and I have been having problems, so they would think that all this emotional crisis that I had was over him (Ponse, 1977, p. 58).

Disidentifiers allow deviants to blend into the conventional world.

Discreditable deviants may conceal their stigmas by presenting the signs of their failing as signs of a different, less stigmatized attribute. The hard-of-hearing may pass themselves off as daydreamers or as aloof; students who failed to do their homework may pass themselves off as careless students who lost their homework. The latter attempt is rarely successful more than once or twice, however.

Deviants may enlist the aid of conventional people in their "charades." They may disclose their failings to a few who they feel will be sympathetic to them. Close friends and family members can help a deviant to successfully maintain a pretense of conventionality.

Some conventional people become "wise." Those who work around deviants—such as a bartender in a gay bar or a staff member in a rehabilitation institute—and those who have a family member or close friend who is deviant may be more tolerant toward deviants, and less stigmatizing, than would be expected of conventional members of society. They have some "insider" knowledge of the life of the deviants and therefore may be granted *courtesy membership* by the deviant group. These wise people are not full members of the deviant group because they are not deviant themselves and have not fully experienced the condemnation of conventional society. Yet, due to their sympathy and understanding, they are partially accepted by the deviants. These wise members may aid in the deviants' passing as respectable people. However, those who are wise may find that they have not only a courtesy membership within a deviant group, but a *courtesy* stigma in the eyes of conventional society. Those who have some kind of relationship with stigmatized people, whether they are wise or not, may also be somewhat discredited. Conventional people may downgrade the friend of a homosexual or the spouse of a mental patient. We are judged by the company we keep. Thus, some straight people may hesitate to become too close to a deviant, or to help a deviant in coping with conventional society, for fear of how conventional society will react to them. The epithet "nigger lover" illustrates the dilemma.

Members of conventional society may also aid a deviant to pass as respectable through *counterfeit secrecy* (Ponse, 1977). Conventional people may ignore or overlook an individual's deviant status in order to keep the social interaction flowing smoothly. They act as if nothing is out of the ordinary. As long as the implicit is not made explicit through naming or direct confrontation, both the deviant and the conventional people can continue as if nothing is amiss. Counterfeit secrecy enables cordial, but superficial relationships to continue. Thus the family of a gay may know, but never talk about or acknowledge, that the member is gay.

Finally, the discreditable can *avoid* intimate contact with conventional society. The less contact deviants have with conventional society, the less likely will conventional society discover their stigmas. The prostitute who spends most of her time with racket people simply has fewer occasions during which she needs to pass as conventional. Becoming a member of a deviant community may in part be due to a desire to avoid stigmatization by conventional society.

Pitfalls in Passing   Those who pass face several contingencies or possible pitfalls. They may experience in-deeper-ism, "the pressure to elaborate a lie further and further to prevent a given disclosure" (Goffman, 1963, p. 83). Adulterers must make up convincing stories to tell their spouses. In doing so, they may have to include an increasing number of events, people, appointments, and so on, in order to be consistent. In-deeper-ism may collapse under the weight of building such an enormous lie. Also, in concealing a stigma a deviant may inadvertently give the impression of having other failings. A hard-of-hearing person may offend others by being rude or stubborn, and a convict on study-release may seem unfriendly because he never participates in afterclass beer parties. Those who pass leave themselves open to hearing what others really think of deviants like them. Conventional people may deride "fags," "four-eyes," and dope "fiends" in front of passers who are thought to be conventional. Passers are also likely to "be on" (Goffman, 1963, p. 14), to plan ahead for possible pitfalls or take into account features of the situation that conventional people need not attend to. The casualness of social interaction is lost to them. Thus, one lesbian noted that she lost a great deal of spontaneity in her speech because she always had to think thirty seconds ahead about what she was going to say (Ponse, 1977, p. 58). Being on guard takes a toll on "natural," uninhibited interaction.

Finally, passers can be found out. They can be exposed. Not only is their stigma disclosed, which can be humiliating, but the fact that they tried to conceal it can also be damaging. We may interpret a deviant's attempt to pass as a further indication of deviance, of a lack of honesty and trustworthiness. We may also interpret an attempt to pass as an indirect indication that the deviant does not consider us trustworthy. Most of us like to believe that we are reasonably tolerant, and we may be upset if we discover that the deviant who was passing did not think enough of us to share the truth. Deviants who pass cast doubts on the moral character, trustworthiness, and empathic qualities of the people from whom they conceal the stigmas.

Covering   Once a stigma has been disclosed or exposed, discreditable deviants become discredited. Other deviants had no option. Their failings were easily noticed. Discredited people face the issue of managing an awkward, tense situation with conventional individuals. Covering is the attempt by discredited people to reduce the impact or obtrusiveness of their stigma—to make it loom less large when encountering conventional people. If they succeed in doing this, their interactions with conventional people will become less awkward and inhibited. Strategies used in passing can be adapted to covering. What will conceal a stigma from those who do not know may lessen its impact for those who do.

Through covering, additional negative traits that may be associated with stigmas can be concealed. Blind people who wear dark glasses signify that they are visually impaired, but they may also be covering abnormal eyes or unsightly scars from unsuccessful operations. Others try to assimilate themselves as much as possible into conventional society. Visually impaired people may avoid holding a book a few inches from their eyes when in the presence of others. An artificial hand may draw less attention than a metal prosthetic, even if the latter is more effective for grasping and holding. Gays may dress conservatively even if others are aware of their identity. Ex-cons may not dwell on their previous life of crime. Through covering, deviants may minimize the impact of their offensive behavior and characteristics.

Organizations of Deviants

Various deviant organizations, such as the National Association of the Deaf, the Mattachine Society (for gays), Little People of America (which we will discuss shortly), and clubs for former mental patients, strive to improve the everyday lives of their members (Sagarin, 1969). Through attending meetings and conventions or reading the organization's publications, members learn how to cope better with an often hostile world. For example, the *18 Wheeler,* a gay newsletter published on the East Coast, publishes tips for homosexuals who wish to cruise (i.e., pick up) truckers (Corzine and Kirby, 1977). The *Deaf American* presents information on insurance at reasonable rates and on teletypewriters or TTYs, devices which enable deaf people to call one another, gives addresses and meeting times of churches and clubs for the deaf, and provides stories about deaf people. These and other publications inform subscribers of the latest paraphernalia, devices, and events of concern to them. Such publications may also be an integral part of deviant communities and not just deviant organizations. Attendance at meetings and conventions, and reading the organization's publications, helps deviants to develop a sense of solidarity with fellow sufferers.

The leaders of these organizations may become spokespeople for fellow sufferers to the conventional world (Goffman, 1963). Through their writings, speeches, and other presentations, they may attempt to present a more favorable image of their fellow deviants to the wider society. Or, they may attempt to influence policy decisions. To that extent, such activities are aimed at changing the deviant status of the organization's members. Thus, a deviant organization may enable its members to live a more satisfying life in conventional society and may also strive to change the standards and policies of conventional society that make its members deviant. As we noted earlier, deviants are likely to be using many strategies in coping with conventional society.

Little People of America Little People of America (LPA), a voluntary association of short people, midgets, and dwarfs, illustrates how such organizations can help their members to cope with the difficulties of being deviant (Weinberg, 1968; Sagarin, 1969). Dwarfs are disproportioned little people, often with short fingers, arms, and legs, a large head and bowed legs, but with a normal trunk. Midgets are normally proportioned short people. There may be some antagonism between the two groups. Midgets may stigmatize dwarfs for being misshapen, much as normally-heighted people literally and figuratively look down upon short people.

The stated goals of LPA are: (1) to increase medical knowledge regarding the physical condition of being short—doctors may be guest speakers at LPA meetings; (2) to lessen the inconvenience of being short—advertisements and tips on insurance problems, information on how to obtain brake and accelerator extensions and how to deal with clothing and housing problems; and (3) to overcome employment difficulties (Weinberg, 1968).

While LPA fulfills these stated functions, its most important service is a *social one.* Its meetings provide the opportunity for short people to meet one another. Meetings at the local level are social occasions where short people, who often might otherwise be isolated, develop acquaintances, make friends, and even find spouses. Sixty-five percent of the members who were asked why they joined LPA indicated that they joined for the chance to meet other little people. Members noted that they had met their spouses or had gained "friends, happiness, and a million dollars worth of living" from joining LPA (Weinberg, 1968, p. 68). However, those who are specifically interested in relationships with the opposite sex are likely to be less satisfied with the organization than are those who are interested in friendship in general with other little people.

Some members become very dependent on LPA for their social activities. Others pursue relationships outside of the organization. The social relationships within LPA may take on a sense of urgency at the conventions and meetings. The standard sequence of dating, going steady, being engaged, and getting married may be accelerated. After having been isolated in a normally-heighted world, little people meet a field of eligible mates. The common fate of short stature and loneliness may override the importance of having similar interests and beliefs in the dating and mating game. Consequently, more experienced members may advise new members to go slowly and not to rush into some kind of commitment based only on surface similarities. Those who rush in and find no suitable mate or who fail in their courtship may leave the organization in frustration.

Little People of America provides the occasion for short people to find companionship. In doing so, it forces little people who might otherwise not have faced it to acknowledge their own condition. For some new members it is a shock to see other short people. They may never have met another little person before. Nonmembers may avoid members who contact them in order to tell them about the organization. Parents of nonmembers may turn away members who come calling. To mingle with other short people provides a mirror in which to observe oneself. One gets a glimpse and maybe even a good look at how, as a short person, one must appear to normally-heighted people. Without such a mirror one may be able to avoid fully acknowledging one's complex feelings about being short. Those feelings remain partially hidden.

Little people are not born with an identification with other short people, nor do they immediately acquire one on becoming a member of LPA. Within LPA, members find "social opportunity, social knowledge, and social support" (Weinberg, 1968, p. 70). They can share their problems with others and learn how others cope with them. Through this organization, little people develop an identification with one another. They develop social solidarity with one another where previously it did not exist.

Deviant Communities

An organization of deviants may take up relatively little of its members' time and commitment. Thus, deviants may also create and become members of a community of deviants. Membership in such communities may be part of the process of becoming deviant as well as one way in which deviants cope with conventional society. Deviant communities are unlikely to be merely residential neighborhoods geographically bounded by streets, railroads, and rivers, as in the case of ethnic neighborhoods. While deviants may cluster in certain neighborhoods—for example, in some cities there are "gay ghettos" (Levine, 1979)—typically they are scattered throughout a city. Through marriages (both real and symbolic), friendships, clubs, bars, religious organizations, publications, a special argot, and so on, deviants may create a community. Gays create such communities (Warren, 1974; Ponse, 1978), as do the deaf (Higgins, 1980). Being a member of a deviant community is one way for deviants to cope with a world that is typically hostile, or at best, indifferent.

Membership in a deviant community provides a sense of belonging and wholeness that is typically lacking for deviants in the larger world. As one member of a Midwestern deaf community commented:

> At a club for the deaf, if I see a deaf person whom I don't know, I will go up to that person and say, "Hi! What's your name?" I would never do that to a hearing person. (Higgins, 1980, p. 39)

A member of a West Coast gay community noted:

> You get in a gay bar, I think, it gives you a chance to really let your hair down, and say, you know that you don't have to put on any kind of facade, no one there is looking for you to be any one else but yourselves. (Warren, 1974, p. 32)

A deviant community provides a setting in which its members can live more satisfying and less troubled lives. Sexual as well as social relations can be pursued in the gay community. Easy and uninhibited communication becomes the rule, not the exception, for members of the deaf community. The shame of being deviant is lessened or rejected, and instead self-awareness and pride may develop. As Becker (1963) noted of deviant groups, membership in a deviant community enhances a deviant identity. Becker does not mean that members of a deviant community feel more offensive, but rather that they are more likely to see themselves as a gay person, a deaf person, or whatever. The members will create and share a set of perspectives about what the world is like and how to deal with it. They develop an ideology that rationalizes their behavior and characteristics and repudiates the critical morality of conventional society. Put simply, a deviant community provides a setting in which its members can feel that they are conventional, or at least much more so than they are in the outside world.

Membership   Not all who are deviant, however, become members of a deviant community. Many gays are firmly in the closet with the door tightly shut (Troiden, 1979). Most hearing-impaired people are not members of a deaf community (Higgins, 1980). Many of them scorn those who are members of deaf communities, just as hearing people stigmatize those who cannot hear well. Being deviant does not naturally make one a member of a deviant community. Membership in a deviant community is not an *ascribed* status, something granted merely by virtue of being deviant. It must be achieved through the activities and attitudes of those who aspire to be members. For example, as we noted in the previous chapter, the third phase in becoming gay is "coming out," a process of self-definition which is likely to occur as one becomes involved in the gay community. The final phase, "commitment," indicates that homosexuality has been adopted as a way of life. As Troiden (1979, p. 372) concludes:

> Those who do acquire them [gay identities] exhibit the following characteristics: homosexual behavior, homosexual attractions, homosexual self-conceptions, social as well as sexual affiliation with the gay world, and same-sex romantic attachments.

All of these must be acquired and developed during a "tenuous" process "fraught with ambiguity, confusion, and uncertainty" (Troiden, 1979, p. 373). Thus, membership in a deviant community must be achieved. To illustrate, we will present an extended example of membership in the deaf community.

Membership in the Deaf Community   Membership in the deaf community is not reserved only for those who are profoundly hearing-impaired. In fact, while a hearing impairment is a necessary condition for membership in a deaf community, many members are not severely hearing-impaired. With a hearing aid some can use a telephone reasonably well, if also somewhat haltingly. Instead, membership is achieved through (1) identification with the deaf world; (2) shared experiences of being hearing-impaired; and (3) active participation in the community's activities. Most hearing-impaired people do not seek membership in deaf communities and would not be warmly accepted by the members. Others have been members for as long as they can remember.

Identification with the deaf world is typically an outgrowth of being educated in a special program for the deaf as a child or adolescent. For this reason, those who lose their hearing after adolescence are unlikely to become members of a deaf community. Their identities formed and developed while they were hearing persons. Having lost their hearing as adults, they see themselves as hearing people with a hearing loss, not as deaf people, and they do not feel they have very much in common with those who have been impaired from an early age. However, children and youths with mild or moderate hearing losses may be today, and have been in the past, educated in special programs—residential schools, for example—along with more severely impaired students. No other programs were available for these less impaired children. The influence from and experience with deaf teachers and students in the programs led to a beginning identification of these hearing-impaired youths with the deaf world. Additional associations within the deaf community further strengthen an identification with the deaf.

Shared experiences of being hearing-impaired relate to the deaf person's being an outsider in a hearing world—"our childhood, our education, our problems, and all that" as one member of a deaf community noted (Higgins, 1980, p. 44). These shared experiences concern particularly the loneliness of being left out, being teased by neighborhood acquaintances or stared at by passers-by. Such experiences involve the frustration and embarrassment of not understanding or being understood by family members, acquaintances, clerks, co-workers, and so on. The deaf community, however, like other deviant communities, is not merely a symbolic group created through shared experiences and orientations. Deaf people become members and in turn collectively create the community through participation with one another in clubs, religious organizations, informal gatherings, sports activities, and so on. Identification with the deaf world and shared experiences of being hearing-impaired provide the soul for the community, whereas participation with fellow members provides the body (Higgins, 1980).

Structure   While members of conventional society often stereotype deviants as homogeneous, members of deviant communities make distinctions among one another. These distinctions are used in structuring relationships, in establishing friendships, in deciding what clubs to attend, and so on. Heterogeneity is created out of what conventional people see as homogeneity.

Members of deviant communities grew up within, and to various degrees still live within, the larger, conventional world. They are socialized to some degree within the dominant culture. They learn its values and beliefs. Deviant communities and their subcultures are continuous with the dominant culture of conventional society, even if we, as members of the dominant culture, see a radical disjunction between their world and ours (Plummer, 1975, p. 157). For example, money and what it can buy is important among professional prostitutes, just as it is among business people, doctors, and yes, professors too (Heyl, 1979). Therefore, characteristics that members of conventional society use to differentiate each other may also be used by members of deviant communities in making distinctions among one another.

For example, within the male gay community *class* and *caste* are important (Warren, 1974, pp. 80–90). Occupational prestige, income, and education are important in the gay world just as they are in the straight world. Distinctions are made among "elite" or upper, "career" or middle, and "deviant" or lower classes. Elite gays are likely to be employed in stable professional and business occupations, to be "middle-aged" (late twenties and older for the gay world), and to interact with one another primarily in private homes. Within the gay world, they live the elegant life-style. Career gays are younger (teens to thirties), do not have stable occupations, and may spend typical working hours as well as leisure time cruising bars. They may participate in gay liberation activities, "flout convention," or act outrageously (Warren, 1974, p. 84). Deviants, who we will turn to later, are troublesome gays, such as transvestites, child molesters, and sadomasochists who are not fully accepted within the "normal" gay community. Caste or ethnic and racial differences are also important in the gay community. Communities are structured along ethnic and racial lines—all white, all black, and all Chicano communities—and some are composed only of interracial couples.

Members of deviant communities also use other characteristics in order to differentiate among one another. These characteristics are related to their unique position as outsiders in conventional society. For example, skin color has played an important, but now diminishing, role in the black community (Udry et al., 1971). Traditionally, blacks with light skins enjoyed a more favorable status in the black community than those with dark skins. In the deaf community, members make distinctions between *speakers,* who are a numerical minority, and *signers.* This distinction has to do with communication preferences and skills. While both speakers and signers can sign, the latter are much more skilled and fluent, and they embrace sign language as an integral aspect of their identity. Speakers use it to supplement their speaking and lip-reading. To fellow speakers they would be unlikely to sign. The distinction and at times antagonism between signers and speakers relates to the long-standing, though now rapidly changing, emphasis on speech and lip-reading, and the concomitant rejection and degradation of sign language, in the education of deaf children. Hearing educators tried to create hearing people out of deaf children. Often this failed because deaf children failed to understand what was going on about them. Thus, signers view speakers as either trying to hide or disown their deafness or as hopelessly under the influence of misguided educators (Higgins, 1980, chap. 2).

Deviance Among the Deviants   These distinctions may become important enough to be used not merely in helping to structure relationships among members of the community but in defining what is and is not acceptable behavior within the community. Deviant communities, like conventional communities, create definitions of deviance. For example, the secret, sociable gay community that Carol Warren (1974, pp. 131–135) studied in California limits membership to "normal queers"—gays who are not drag queens or liberationists, who do not engage in "bizarre" sexual behavior, and who do not flaunt their preferences throughout the straight world. Respectable members may do those forbidden things for fun or may tease about them, but they are not committed to them. Within this gay community, transvestites, transsexuals, pedophiles, and sadomasochists are considered deviant or trashy, just as they are in straight society. This gay community also defines as deviant bisexuals and gays married to straights, people who might be more acceptable within straight society. Married gays and bisexuals show bad faith and a lack of commitment to the gay community. They are not fully part of the community, though they may be accepted as sexual partners. Bisexuals are viewed as copping out from the choice of being gay *or* being straight. Married gays are assumed to have wed out of spite for a gay lover or because of family pressures. Because of their affiliation with the straight world, which stigmatizes gays, bisexuals and married gays are stigmatized in the gay world.

In order to understand what is deviant in a deviant community or group, we cannot merely examine the group. We must also take into account its position in the larger world that condemns it—often both its historical position and its present social position. In other words, we must view the deviant community in context. What is deviant in a deviant community is often a reflection of how the community is coping with conventional society. For example, begging by the blind and peddling by the deaf are offensive to their respective groups (Higgins, 1979). Each activity is seen as playing on the misguided sympathy of the nondisabled, a sympathy based on the historical image that the nondisabled have had of the disabled—of being helpless, dependent, and incompetent. This image has been the traditional basis for the inferior status of these two disabled groups. The blind and the deaf, however, disavow (Davis, 1961) their helplessness and dependence. Since begging and peddling are viewed as reinforcing that image in the minds of the nondisabled who control activities, such as jobs, in which the disabled wish to share. Thus, begging and peddling spoil the collective identities of the blind and the deaf, and in so doing support the historically subjugated position of these two disabled groups. Thus, deviant groups and communities also develop standards of acceptable and unacceptable behavior. In some cases, deviant groups may develop rules and regulations that are more strict then those of conventional society.

Respectability Among Nudists   Members of clothed society may be titillated by the idea of nudist camps, and may view them as immoral and depraved places, but some nudist camps have rules for their members that are more strict than the rules of clothed society. In an investigation of Midwestern nudist camps, Martin Weinberg (1965, 1976) found that nudist camps constructed and sustained to a large degree the following morality: (1) nudity and sex are unrelated; (2) there is nothing shameful about the human body; (3) nudity supports freedom and natural pleasure; (4) nudity promotes physical, mental, and spiritual well-being. The first two aspects of nudist morality are the ones that are most at odds with clothed society's view of nudity. Weinberg found that nudist camps sustained this morality through two major strategies: *organizational precautions* and *norms of interpersonal behavior.*

Most camps took precautions about who could visit and who could join. Since single people, especially men, were viewed as a threat to nudist morality, some camps excluded unmarried people, particularly men, or had a limited quota. Camps that allowed singles sometimes charged them more in order to discourage them. The higher fee was still relatively low compared to the cost of other kinds of resorts, so instead of discouraging possibly unwanted singles, it may have only created resentment among the single members of the nudist camps. Certification by camp owners and letters of recommendation were sometimes required of prospective members. The number of trial visits before joining was sometimes limited, and a time period during which guests may remain clothed was usually established. These organizational precautions were designed to screen out undesirable people, those who were not oriented toward the camp's morality.

In the nudist camp, members were expected to abide by the following rules: (1) no staring; (2) no sex talk or "dirty" jokes; (3) no or only limited body contact (e.g., no nude dancing); (4) no alcoholic beverages (in American camps); (5) photography is controlled (e.g., pictures are to be taken only with the subject's permission); (6) no accentuation of the body, such as sitting with one's legs apart or shaving one's pubic area; and (7) no unnatural attempts at covering the body.

Nudist camps attempt to routinize nudity. If they are successful, nudity becomes taken for granted—"no big deal." As the strategies supporting the nudist morality indicate, the views of clothed society have an impact on what is and is not acceptable in nudist camps. Nudists realize that clothed society views them as weirdos and perverts who engage in orgies. Since nudists do not agree with this image, they establish rules and regulations designed not to give it even the slightest support in their own minds or in the imagined minds of clothed society. Further, while nudists claim that nudity and sex are unrelated, they are sensitive to the possible breakdown of that stance. Witness the bans on alcohol, sex talk, and dancing. They may also interpret what might otherwise be considered harmless behavior as inappropriate. Thus, running one's hand along the arm of an opposite-sex person might be called "mauling." Being sensitive to clothed society's view of them and to the possibility that the "base," "animal" instincts of their fellow members may appear, nudists in many ways are quite prudish. Behavior that would be acceptable in clothed society is forbidden in nudist camps. Thus, their rules and regulations, their definitions of deviance, can only be understood in the context of their relationship to the larger, clothed society which condemns them. Their rules and regulations, of course, help them to cope with conventional society.

Becoming Conventional

In addition to contending with their accusers or trying to live with a deviant identity, deviants may also employ various strategies designed to change their deviant status. They may try to change their own behavior through abstinence, therapy, or self-help groups. Some deviants who adopt this strategy do not differ much with conventional society over the offensiveness of their behavior. They agree and desire to "mend their ways," to come back from "beyond the pale" in order to become conventional members of society. Others *disavow* their deviance (Davis, 1961). They do not concur with the conventional wisdom that they should be ashamed of themselves and instead try to change the specific reactions of the conventional people with whom they have contacts—they try to have others treat them as "normal." Finally, through collective action some seek to change society's definitions of deviance, to have society change its policies, laws, and regulations concerning them. Not content to merely establish an untainted identity on a one-to-one basis with conventional others, they seek to redefine what is respectable or deviant. They seek to *vindicate* themselves. If successful, new standards of what is and is not acceptable will have been created.

Reentry into Conventional Society   Some deviants attempt to reenter conventional society. Interestingly, while a great deal of research has been aimed at understanding why people engage in deviance, very little has examined the "hows" and "whys" of attempting to "leave the life" and return to conventional society (Heyl, 1979). Perhaps we feel that those involved in deviance, like old soldiers, just fade away.

Reentry into conventional society may be beset with a wide variety of problems. The magnitude of the problems is likely to depend on how much the offender was involved in deviance. Unlike the triumphant soldier returning from a glorious victory, deviants will probably not receive a universally warm welcome, even if they claim to be ex-deviants. Just as contingencies must be faced in becoming deviant, so must obstacles be surmounted in returning to conventional society. For example, Jacqueline Wiseman (1970) notes that Skid Row men may face the following problems when they decide to "make it" in sober society: employment difficulties, problems of living arrangements, sociability, and women.

The Skid Row man's union membership may have lapsed. He cannot get a job that requires either a security clearance or bonding. He cannot work around heavy machinery because of insurance premiums. His age, lack of current experience, and the long gap in his employment record all add to the difficulty of finding a job. If he finally does get work, it is likely to be low-paying and requiring little responsibility or skill. As a result, he may be torn between fear of failure (he has not worked for years) and anger at being exploited.

Based on the jobs they get, Skid Row men can usually only afford cheap quarters. They have difficulty obtaining lodgings even in stable working-class neighborhoods because of their appearance and of being single. It may be easier to find housing on Skid Row, but that is where they find alcohol as well. Those who desire to stay sober try to avoid old drinking companions. However, because Skid Row men feel that AA members are "holier-than-thou," and because they have little in common with the co-workers on their new job, viewing them as squares, they are likely to live in isolation when they attempt to reenter sober society. Consequently, they may receive little support for the adjustments they are making and the problems they are facing. Finally, while Skid Row men would like to meet "decent women," they have had so little recent experience that they may feel shy or awkward in approaching them. The support of such women, however, could aid in the return of Skid Row men to sober society.

Thus, it may be extremely difficult for Skid Row men to reenter conventional society. However, they can get off the "loop"—the cycle of hospitals, missionaries, and other institutions that Skid Row men travel periodically—in three other ways. They may become live-in workers at hospitals, rest homes, or other nonprofit institutions. They may go into alcoholic rehabilitation as a profession, working at various levels in treatment centers, halfway houses, or Alcoholics Anonymous. What was a "vice" in the outside world (excessive drinking and familiarity with the lives of alcoholics) becomes a "virtue" in alcoholic rehabilitation (Wiseman, 1970, pp. 237–238). Finally, death is the third way off the loop.

The problems in going straight faced by felons released on parole are similar to those of Skid Row men trying to get "off their drunk" (Irwin, 1970, pp. 105–148). Parolees face the initial shock of being on the outside for the first time in years. The sights, sounds, and smells may be disorienting and overwhelming. Everyday activities, such as ordering food in a restaurant, crossing the street, catching a bus, or keeping track of time, may seem strange to the felon. The parolee may be lonely, with little support from family and friends. Straight former friends may have little in common with the felon. The family may have adjusted to the absence of the felon, whose return becomes a disruption. Or as Ray (1964) found in the case of heroin addicts who were kicking the habit, family and friends may be skeptical of the abstainer's motives and behaviors and in so doing help lead to a relapse. A job and living arrangements must be secured. The first is not an easy task (Schwartz and Skolnick, 1964). The parolee's record becomes an albatross around his neck which is difficult to shed. A satisfying job may be even harder to secure. For those not returning to wives or girlfriends, satisfying relationships with women may be difficult to establish. Like the drunk, the felon has had little recent experience with a "good old lady" (Irwin, 1970, p. 139). Further, his lack of recent exposure to women, except through magazines and movies, may lead him to develop unrealistic expectations of what women are available. Thus, reentry into straight society is as full of potential pitfalls as reentry into sober society.

Coming Home   While it is untrue that those who have gone away can never come home again, it is probably true that those who return are different, and so is the world to which they are returning. For deviants, reentry into conventional society is typically a gradual process involving a sequence of adjustments. It is a gradual withdrawal of one's self, one's commitment, and one's time from deviance, and the formation of new commitments, attachments, and identities within conventional society. For those heavily involved in deviance, such changes are likely to be profound. For those marginally or episodically involved, fewer, less dramatic shifts in orientation will be necessary. Not all deviants travel the whole sequence. Some may choose deviance again. And of those who have chosen to return to "the life," some may yet try again to become conventional (Irwin, 1970, pp. 143–148).

Recent research on the uneasy homecoming of Vietnam veterans seems applicable to the attempt of deviants to reenter conventional society (Faulkner and McGaw, 1972; Heyl, 1979, chap. 7). Deviants, like the veterans, may go through stages in the reentry process: (1) moving from the deviance (or the war in the case of veterans); (2) moving back into the conventional world; and (3) an attempt toward reintegration into conventional society. Moving through these stages entails successfully coping with the problems of reentry that we previously discussed.

Moving from deviance is a process of disengagement, of breaking ties to a previous way of life. This may be difficult. Just as Vietnam veterans are different people because of their experiences—the adventure, the centrality of the war in their lives, the killing, the trauma—so are deviants. The alcoholic, ex-convict, or prostitute cannot suddenly forget the experiences, activities, and attitudes that developed while they were involved in deviance. Further, deviant friends may be left behind and perhaps missed. Or if not left behind, they may tempt the would-be conformer to return to "the life." According to Heyl (1979) previous ties must be severed if the deviant is to reenter conventional society. However, as deviants leave the deviant world, they are not yet part of conventional society. Instead, they are in a "limbo" between these two worlds (Heyl, 1979, p. 173).

As deviants leave "the life," they move back into conventional society. However, because deviants have a set of experiences and perspectives different from those of conventional people, the deviants are coming back to a world which, even if it has not changed, is different from the one they left. It is different because they see it in a different light. Yet, the conventional world has not stood still either. This quickly becomes apparent to convicts released after many years of imprisonment. As a former madam discovered on leaving the profession after more than twenty years in it, conventional values regarding male-female relationships had changed dramatically since the 1950s. Her idea of conventional values was out of date (Heyl, 1979, p. 157).

For some deviants (for example, the felons mentioned earlier), the initial reentry is too fast and too much of a shock. The same was true for many Vietnam veterans, who in a matter of days had made an abrupt transition from war to conventional society. A winding-down period may be necessary as deviants leave "the life" behind. Halfway houses and work- or study-release from prison are attempts to provide for a smoother transition. For others an adjustment to the everyday and often boring as well as frustrating routine of conventional society—appointments, bills, deadlines, and minor foul-ups—must be made. Those who were heavily involved in deviance may not have much recent experience in these mundane activities. The deviants are trying to leave their former experiences and activities behind, but these experiences and activities still remain salient features of who they are. Yet, it is difficult to share them with conventional others who have not had the same experiences and would likely stigmatize the returner when told about them. Social support from conventional people, however, is important. Conventional acquaintances can help the returning deviant with the everyday tasks that must be performed. More importantly they can serve to reinforce the deviant's newly developing self-identity as a conventional individual, as someone who can make it in the square world.

Reintegration into society requires the deviant to firmly establish new commitments and attachments to conventional society or to reestablish old ones. A job, family responsibilities, and conventional friends can all aid deviants to get their "heads" back into the conventional world. Initial success in getting back into and becoming part of conventional society provides further impetus for the returning deviant to become conventional. This success may be a steady, well-paying job (Irwin, 1970, pp. 134–135), or it can be good grades for those who go back to school, as it was for one madam who left the profession (Heyl, 1979, p. 167).

While the support of conventional others can facilitate reentry into conventional society, those who have succeeded say that the personal responsibility of the person making the reentry attempt is essential (Irwin, 1970, p. 112; Faulkner and McGaw, 1977). Many reentered deviants say that blaming conventional society for its antagonism, pettiness, and two-faced actions is a cop-out. In the end, reentering deviants must take responsibility and look out for themselves. They must make an existential choice to become conventional. As some addicts put it, "No dope fiend will clean up his act until he has hit his own personal low" (Warren, 1974, p. 310). Similar philosophies have been stated in other areas of deviance (Carroll, 1961; Sagarin, 1969). Other people, however, may be able to help the deviant experience that low and work through it. Thus, becoming conventional is just as much a matter of choosing and doing as is becoming deviant.

Reentry into conventional society need not be an isolated enterprise even if deviants claim that it ultimately depends on the deviant's own choices. Many self-help groups have been created to help change the behaviors of their members and to provide support for those who are reentering conventional society.

Self-Help Groups   There are many self-help groups that deviants can join. Self-help groups are designed to change their members (Sagarin, 1969). In the cases of Alcoholics Anonymous, Weight Watchers, and Gamblers Anonymous, respectively, drinking, obesity, and gambling are recognized by the members as offensive to the wider society and to themselves. The intent of these groups is not to vindicate the activity, to make it conventional, but to promote conventional behavior among their members.

Though we often speak and act as if a deviant identity, deviant behavior, and deviant life-style go together—each a part of the other— such is not necessarily the case. In fact. self-help groups capitalize on the very fact that we can separate identity, behavior, and life-style. Identity refers to how we and others view and feel about ourselves. Behavior is what we do. Life-style is a somewhat vague concept referring to the "way of life" (Laslett and Warren, 1975) associated with specific behaviors but not comprising those behaviors. To use a stereotypical example, professional athletes play some kind of sport, but their life-style may include a "whirlwind" of travel, endorsements, glamour, adulation from little kids and members of the opposite sex, and so on. Self-help groups may *not* try to change all three—identity, behavior, and life-style—in attempting to make their members conventional.

Weight-Loss Groups   Barbara Laslett and Carol Warren (1975) have investigated the philosophy and the organizational activities aimed at causing weight loss within an unnamed weight-loss organization. Since this organization is similar to Alcoholics Anonymous and Gamblers Anonymous (see Sagarin, 1969, for a discussion of the latter two groups), the following discussion is applicable to other self-help groups.

The weight-loss organization contended that fat people are and always will be fat on the "inside." The fat person's essential identity is as a fat person. Thus, the world is divided between fat people and "civilians," those who are essentially slender. However, while one's identity as a fat person cannot be changed, one's behavior can be. Unlike AA, where total abstinence from alcohol is stressed, the weight-loss group promotes a strict program of eating. Abstinence, of course, would be impossible. Faithfully following such a program, which is itself a change in behavior for the members (many of whom eat "uncontrollably"), can lead to a change in appearance. The fat person can become thin on the outside. The deviance becomes invisible. However, "for the fat person who has become thin, weight loss is always potentially reversible and is an ever-dangerous invisible stigma which threatens the individual" (Laslett and Warren, 1975, p. 72).

Thus, negative or stigmatizing labels are used by the weight-loss organization to reinforce what is taken to be the essential identity of overweight people. The reinforcement of a deviant identity, however, is aimed at changing the deviant's behavior so that the individual's eating and appearance will become conventional. In turn, a change in behavior will likely lead to a change in the life-style of fat people. The weight-loss group stresses to its members that the lives of fat people are full of embarrassing and demeaning experiences: being stuck in a chair or behind the wheel of a car, the inability to find flattering clothes (or any clothes, for that matter), or the reluctance to go different places and join in different activities. According to the weight-loss group, with reduced weight fat people will enjoy a wider range of activities, more energy, better self-esteem, better job situations, and in general a more satisfying life.

Weight loss, however, entails a lifelong commitment to a weight-loss program. Diets are not enough, and a weight-loss program must become an integral part of the members' lives. Therefore, the weight-loss organization promotes itself as an integral aspect of its members' lives. Members, however, do not always successfully lose weight. They may lose thirty pounds, but later gain forty. Consequently, the weight-loss organization stresses that the present is all that counts. The next meal is what matters. Members need not concern themselves with the past or the future. Failures are not really failures at all. Present "failures" soon become events of the past and not an indication of the present possibility of success or failure. Through this contradiction between a lifelong program and a focus only on the present, the weight-loss organization has constructed a "foolproof" philosophy. Success is due to the organization's program. Failure is due to the members' responsibility, to their being essentially fat people. However, "failures" can always become successes. Thus, former members are welcomed back into the organization, and present members are encouraged to make a lifelong commitment to the organization. In this regard, overweight people have recently complained that the entire "weight-loss industry" is fleecing fat people. The industry is making a great deal of money off people who are tyring to lose weight and are often trying to do so because of the industry's advertising (Pfuhl, 1980, p. 280).

Strategies to Promote Weight Loss   The organization's philosophy is promoted through specific strategies and programs. First, an ingroup-outgroup stance is fostered. Fat members are contrasted with fat nonmembers, and fat "foodalcoholics" (fat people in general) are contrasted with thin "civilians." Fat nonmembers are potential members. If they are not attempting to become thin, they are "slothful and immoral" (Laslett and Warren, 1975, p. 76). If they are using diet pills or other weight-reducing programs, they are bound to fail. Members can serve as role models to nonmembers. Through the efforts of members and the organization's advertising, fat nonmembers are potential recruits.

Thin civilians are the fat members' "enemies." Whether they are husbands who say that they like "cuddly" women, children begging for cookies and cakes, or friends who suggest that a member "try a piece," civilians present temptations to the members. Therefore, members are encouraged to quarantine themselves mentally, if not physically, from thin civilians. Group rituals of weighing members, graduation ceremonies through the various phases of the program, special pins and certificates, hand clapping for those who lost weight or were trying, as well as exhortation by the organization's lecturers, serve to develop an ingroup solidarity.

The change agents within the weight-loss organization are an important element of the organization's strategies for producing behavioral change. The lecturers and other staff are former fat people on the outside who are now only fat on the inside. They provide a model which members can identify with and proof that fat people can take it off and keep it off. The lecturers attempt to create this identification through *stigma displays* and *deviance displays*. Stigma displays are the presentations by the lecturers of their essential selves as fat persons, once visible but now invisible. "Before" and "after" pictures, anecdotes, and sad tales of a life of misery are presented by lecturers in order that members can see the similarities between themselves and their troubles and the former selves and troubles of the lecturers. Through deviance displays lecturers depict the lifelong temptation of food. While they may fail at times and succumb to the temptation of food (i.e., they "pig" out), the organization provides them with the support and knowledge to deal with it. Members too may succumb, but commitment to the organization's philosophy and program will help them overcome momentary setbacks. Thus, through stigma displays lecturers hold out the possibility to members that they too can become thin on the outside. Through deviance displays lecturers indicate the essential identities of fat people and the necessity for a lifelong commitment to the organization. Through emphasizing the deviant identities of its members, the weight-loss organization attempts to promote conventional behavior and, in turn, a conventional life-style.

Whether the weight-loss organization is successful in promoting a change in the behavior and outward appearance of members is not clear. The organization claims not to keep systematic records. Indications of success or failure are sparingly provided. Lecturers may announce gross total weight loss for the class, but often without mentioning weight gain as well. In one class where weight gain was noted, it almost equaled the total gross weight loss. Thus, a few pounds of net weight loss were "shared" among more than fifty members of the class. The organization prohibits social or medical research by outsiders. Consequently, while claims may be made for the success of the weight-loss programs, evidence to support the claims is not readily available. As Altheide and Johnson (1980) note, claims, statistics, and information created and dispensed by organizations should be treated as bureaucratic propaganda. They are designed to serve the purposes of the organization. Nevertheless, many deviants who attempt to become conventional swear by the self-help group to which they belong.

Deviance Disavowal   Becoming or rebecoming conventional is likely to be a more difficult task than becoming deviant. As we discussed in the previous sections, deviants may not only have to change their behavior, but may also have to become involved in conventional, often mundane activities with which they may not have had any recent experience. Becoming conventional, however, is not only a matter of changing one's own behavior or characteristics. Reentry may be also or primarily a matter of changing the attitudes and reactions of specific conventional people who still treat one as deviant. Changing the attitudes of others who are encountered enables deviants to become conventional at least to a few members of the wider society.

Disavowing one's deviance is likely to be a salient issue for those who are physically or mentally impaired. Many of these stigmatized people are unable to change that which stigmatizes them. Abstinence, willpower, or membership in self-help groups simply will not make them nondisabled. At the same time, though, they may not desire to pass either because they cannot (i.e., they are discredited) or because they see no reason for passing. Except for their impairment, which is only one part of their total being, they see themselves as "normal" people. The nondisabled, however, are unlikely to treat them that way (Safilios-Rothschild, 1970; Higgins, 1980). Consequently, if the disabled are to become conventional members of society, they will have to change the orientations of others toward them. Deviance disavowal is that attempt.

Even deviants who can and do change their behavior in an attempt to reenter conventional society are likely to still have to disavow their deviance, in this case being an *ex-deviant:* an ex-con, a former prostitute, or someone who once "did drugs." Thus, those who try to change their behavior in order to become conventional may also be involved in deviance disavowal, just as are the disabled, who cannot change their impairment. While Fred Davis's (1961) examination of deviance disavowal is focused on the visibly handicapped, his analysis applies to other deviants as well. The following discussion will try to make this clear.

Davis (1961) suggests that a visible handicap is a threat to relaxed, uninhibited, "normal" social interaction in four ways: as a *focal point* of the interaction; through its *inundating potential;* because of a *contradiction of attributes;* and because it is an *ambiguous predictor.* These threats can also be created by deviance which is not a visible handicap. The visible handicap may narrow the focus of a sociable encounter. Most ordinary sociable encounters have a diffuse or general focus. However, the visible handicap is likely to be uppermost in the participants' minds. Although the able-bodied may not tactlessly refer to the handicap, they may have to "work at" ignoring it. The disabled often realize this, as when the nondisabled awkwardly catch themselves suggesting to a blind person that they go to the movies or to a wheelchair-bound individual that they go for a stroll in the park. A similar narrowing of focus may occur when the offensive person is an ex-deviant.

Most sociable encounters are casual, light-hearted affairs full of laughter, joking, and teasing. A visible handicap can inundate such encounters with feelings and emotions that are out of place, that "put a damper on the party." The visibly handicapped as well as the ex-deviant may arouse fear, pity, repugnance, or morbid curiosity in the minds of conventional people. Thus the basis for sociable encounters is disrupted.

The nondisabled may be unsettled by the contradiction of attributes possessed by the visibly handicapped: the paraplegic who is a beautiful woman, the blind man with a law degree, the facially disfigured individual who is warm and generous. As we noted in Chapter 4, a cluster of negative traits is assumed to characterize deviants. Yet, the former prostitute may be going to college and doing well. The ex-con may be a devoted family man. To resolve these discrepancies, conventional people may ignore the positive attributes of the visibly handicapped or the ex-deviant, give less credence to the positive qualities, or assimilate them in a patronizing way to the handicap or former deviance. Thus, the attractive wheelchair-bound woman elicits comments such as "How strange that someone so pretty should be in a wheelchair" (Davis, 1961, p. 124). Or a former _____ (you fill in the blank) may be told that it is nice that they are trying to make something of themselves by going to night school or to college.

Finally, handicaps are likely to be ambiguous predictors of an impaired person's ability or desire to participate in various activities. The nondisabled may wonder if the disabled can or want to participate in dancing, going to a movie, or whatever. Even if they cannot, should they be asked? If the disabled refuse an invitation, are they being polite or merely expressing their preference? Conversely, the disabled may wonder if the invitation is genuine or if it was extended out of sympathy. If they accept, will their participation lessen the other people's enjoyment? Ambiguity—what to do and what to make of it—envelops encounters between the disabled and the nondisabled. The same can be said for ex-deviants who are trying to reenter conventional society. For example, should the former alcoholic be invited to a cocktail party, a "night on the town," or anyplace where alcohol is served?

The Process of Normalization   Many visibly handicapped people strive to overcome such awkward and unsatisfying interactions with the nondisabled. Through a three-stage process some are able to disavow their deviance and thereby have others treat them as normal. According to David (1961), the stages are: *fictional acceptance; breaking-through;* and the *institutionalization of a normalized relationship.* In our society, the visibly handicapped, and also the ex-deviant attempting to reenter conventional society, may be accorded superficial acceptance. "Manners" dictate that we treat others more or less as equals and as normal. However, this acceptance is a fiction which has "mixed blessings." It provides at least a basis for social interaction, but not a very deep or satisfying one. However, it may serve as the beginning for breaking through to the next stage of deviance disavowal.

In moving beyond fictional acceptance, the visibly handicapped attempt to present themselves in ways which do not imply that they are deviant. They may try first to put the nondisabled at ease by referring to their handicap, using taboo terms or making fun of their shortcomings. In doing so, they give expression to the nondisabled's focus on the handicap while also conveying the message that it need not be the only focus. Then, through displaying (in words and deeds) abilities and characteristics which are "normal," the disabled may be able to break through the fictional acceptance to where the handicap is no longer given so much attention. The nondisabled begin to see the disabled as similar to themselves rather than as radically different. There is a shift in focus from the handicap to the conventional abilities and behaviors of the impaired. The visibly handicapped, however, may have difficulty breaking through in large gatherings, where the nondisabled may assume that someone else will talk with the handicapped; when children or the elderly are present, because the former's inquisitiveness and the latter's sympathy can be awkward to handle; or when they are in physically awkward situations (e.g., being lifted for those confined to a wheelchair), which can discredit their attempt to be treated as anyone else would be.

Those who have broken through may now find themselves in a delicate position. They do not wish to lose their hard-won normality. Yet if the relationship is to continue, it may be necessary to acknowledge small, qualifying exceptions and to teach the nondisabled how to handle them. The visibly handicapped are "normal, but . . ." For example, wheelchair-bound individuals are restricted in various ways and must show the nondisabled how to help them navigate stairs, doorways, and other pedestrian obstacles. Similar amendments to normality may exist for ex-deviants reentering conventional society—the restrictions of an ex-con on parole; the dietary requirements of someone formerly overweight; or places which are personally off limits for a former addict. These qualifications may be underplayed in the earlier phases of establishing a relationship, as the disabled person or the ex-deviant attempts to be treated as an equal.

According to Davis, if the institutionalization or routine establishment of a normal relationship occurs, it is likely to occur in two ways. First, the nondisabled may completely overlook the very real limitations of the disabled to the point of being thoughtless. Friends may arrange activities for the disabled in which the disabled cannot comfortably participate. For example, the wheelchair-bound individual is taken to a small, crowded restaurant with narrow aisles and narrow restroom facilities. The "buts" are overlooked instead of being matter-of-factly recognized and dealt with appropriately. The relation between the disabled and the nondisabled has become "overnormalized." Or, the nondisabled may give up some of their own normality and join the visibly handicapped in a "half-alienated, half-tolerant" view of the conventional world (Davis, 1961, p. 131). The nondisabled joins the disabled in a marginal position. They are within the larger society, but do not fully endorse the larger society's standards of respectability. Each views the larger world with a jaundiced eye. They may recognize that conventional members of society are narrow-minded, hypocritical, or two-faced. Thus, the companion of the blind person realizes that sighted business people may give charitable donations to a blindness agency, but may not provide job opportunities for the blind. The friend of the ex-junkie realizes that respectable people may depend heavily on tranquilizers and stimulants to get through the day. The friend of the prostitute acknowledges that others sell their bodies but call it marriage or that "pillars of the community" pay for the services of prostitutes. In giving up part of their normality, the conventional person comes to see the unusualness of the disabled or the ex-deviant as not so unusual after all.

The Vindication of Deviance   The interpersonal attempts of deviants to be treated as normal by members of conventional society may be successful. However, if the deviant is to be treated consistently as a normal person, such attempts must be undertaken with each new member of conventional society. Thus, this interpersonal approach entails fighting a continuing series of little battles. A "war," in contrast, may be a much more difficult undertaking, with many setbacks, but if it succeeds, a general redefinition of what is respectable and what is deviant will have taken place. For example, despite many setbacks—arrests, fines, and imprisonment—the efforts of writers, magazine publishers, and movie makers in the past thirty years have been successful in making sexually explicit material relatively easily available. Of course, some might complain that the success of these efforts is unfortunate. Nevertheless, through these efforts, and through larger societal changes, such as an increasingly educated population, shifting sex roles, and the historical increase in interest in sexual materials and gratification during periods of dissatisfaction and turmoil, sexually explicit material has become (almost) commonplace (Winick, 1977).

Deviants may seek to redefine beliefs and practices (i.e., policies) on a societal wide scale. They seek to vindicate their deviance, to have their offensiveness become conventional. As several observers have noted, the vindication of deviance is fundamentally a political process (Horowitz and Liebowitz, 1968; Humphreys, 1972, pp. 141–172; Pfuhl, 1980, pp. 285–287).

Gay liberation organizations, COYOTE (an organization designed to decriminalize prostitution), NORML (the National Organization for the Reform of Marijuana Laws), and a variety of organizations for the disabled desire to change the views of conventional members of society. As the civil rights movement has shown, however, attitudes may be slow in changing. Therefore, various change-oriented organizations and politically active deviants may be initially more interested in altering public policy. Changes in public policy, in rules and regulations, may provide the basis for a later change in the attitudes of conventional members of society. Deviants may not be loved, but through changing public policy they have begun to vindicate their deviance.

As Erdwin Pfuhl (1980, pp. 274–285) notes, the alteration of public policy by deviants is likely to involve tactics and strategies similar to those used in the creation of deviance by conventional people. Personal troubles and dissatisfaction must be transformed into a public or collective issue for a group of deviants. For example, Laud Humphreys (1972) suggests that a turning point for gays was the riot that ensued after the New York police raided Stonewall Inn, an afterhours gay bar in New York City, on June 27, 1969. Within a month after the riot, the Gay Liberation Front had organized in New York City. Word of the riot and the slogan "gay power," which had appeared earlier, spread unevenly, but eventually across the country. In other cities, such as St. Louis, confrontation with the police helped mobilize gays into a more active, political stance. While such mobilization may seem sudden, it may be based on years of activity by less militant groups. Among gays, homophile organizations have existed in the United States since World War II and a few short-lived ones before then. Yet the riot galvanized the feeling of gays that they were intolerably oppressed, and also that change was conceivable (Humphreys, 1972, p. 48). The civil rights movement of the late 1950s and the 1960s was proof to other oppressed groups that change was possible. Through newsletters, magazines, and gatherings, fellow deviants are kept informed of what is happening, and their active participation in changing public policy is developed. Spokespeople for the deviant group are likely to seek to spread its views to the conventional society through the mass media. Demonstrations, parades, or sit-ins may be staged, more for their symbolic value than for their immediate consequences. If picked up and disseminated by the mass media, the newsworthy events provide a widespread hearing for the deviants' positions. In order to influence public policy, deviants may attempt to set their particular concerns within a broader framework with which conventional members of society can identify. For example, NORML repeatedly emphasized that enforcement of laws concerning marijuana diverted law enforcement resources away from more serious offenses. Similar positions have been taken by those who favor the decriminalization of victimless crimes—drug use, prostitution, gambling, sex among consenting adults, and so on. This is very similar to the process by which potential rule-makers create myths within which they set the allegedly offensive activity (see Chapter 3). Thus deviants attempt to create a public issue out of the personal troubles of their fellow sufferers and then gain legitimacy for that issue among conventional members of society.

Victories are hard-won and are often slow in coming. Setbacks are to be expected. Since 1970 avowed homosexuals have been elected to public office, state and local governments have enacted legislation to protect the civil rights of gays, and discriminatory employment and housing policies have been altered. However, other cities in the late 1970s repealed gay rights ordinances, and one large Protestant church, at its once-in-four years governing conference, overwhelmingly rejected efforts to soften its policy toward homosexuals (Associated Press, 1980). Similarly, it took several years for the federal government to write regulations implementing the Vocational Rehabilitation Act of 1973, several sections of which pertain to the civil rights of the disabled. And it will now be up to the courts to interpret the law and the regulations as they apply to individual cases. From the standpoint of the disabled, the results have been mixed, and will probably continue to be so. Nevertheless, through the collective actions of deviants who are attempting to vindicate themselves, change is possible.

Social Change   Societies are not static. One only needs to look around to notice that beliefs, behaviors, attitudes, and relationships among people are changing. Change may occur through various processes—demographic trends, wars, shortages of basic resources, technological innovations, and so on. Deviance, too, can be a force for change. Many of the important changes in society have occurred through the vindication of deviance. Such changes have resulted from disreputable people successfully challenging the larger social order. Whether it is in the arts, sports, science, or everyday life, those who question the prevailing social order are likely to be considered deviant. If they are successful, however, a new social order has been created.

For example, as Howard Becker (1974) suggests, art should be seen as the ongoing, collective production of a network of people. These people work within artistic conventions—the customary ways of doing things. Conventions include the materials and abstractions to be used, the way the two will be combined, the dimensions of an appropriate work, and the relations between artists and audience. Conventions may change gradually or abruptly and disruptively. When conventions are attacked, so are the aesthetic beliefs—the standards by which artistic beauty and effectiveness are judged. However, people feel that their aesthetic beliefs are "natural, proper and moral" (Becker, 1974, p. 773), not merely arbitrary. Therefore, an

> attack on a convention and an aesthetic is also an attack on a morality. The regularity with which audiences greet major changes in dramatic, musical and visual conventions with vituperative hostility indicates the close relation between aesthetic and moral belief. (Becker, 1974, pp. 773–774)

For example, popular music is certainly quite different today from what is was twenty or thirty years ago. The rock-and-rollers of the 1950s were viewed as immoral and sinful. For example, when Elvis Presley first appeared on television, the cameras only showed him from the waist up.

> Critics loathed him; preachers called him sinful; in Miami, he was charged with obscenity; in San Diego, the city fathers voted to ban him unless he omitted from his act all "vulgar movement." A Baptist pastor in Des Moines declared him "morally insane." (Palmer, 1976, pp. 271)

Later, when the Beatles came to America, many people thought that England, with these long-haired (by the standards of the 1960s) musicians, had invaded America for the first time since the War of 1812. Dance and jazz musicians berated the competence of the Beatles. They were condemned for not composing and performing songs in the conventional eight-bar sections, and only later was it realized that they were deliberately composing nine-bar phrases (Becker, 1978). Nowadays, Punk and New Wave music is deviant. Yet, if it successfully challenges the conventional musical styles and taste, a new convention will have been created. One might argue that changes in music and art generally result from a respectable-conventional form being challenged by a different, often deviant, form. If the deviant form is successful, it becomes the conventional music or art of the often short-lived future (Becker, 1978).

Science, too, has its revolutions, According to Thomas Kuhn (1970), these revolutions often occur when younger scientists in a particular discipline (and usually in a particular specialty or subspecialty of a discipline) question the framework or paradigm used to understand events.

An anomaly is observed, an event which the younger scientists cannot explain in accordance with the prevailing paradigm. The anomaly could be ignored, or the prevailing paradigm could be tinkered with in order to make the anomaly "fit," or, if the younger scientists are not as committed to the prevailing paradigm as the older scientists, the paradigm may be questioned. If this happens, the younger scientists may actually be creating a new paradigm, a different set of ideas and assumptions about the world at hand. This competing paradigm may be resisted by more established scientists. The younger scientists become renegades to their scientific brethren and perhaps even to the larger social order. The establishment of a new framework for explaining events may be resisted for years and even decades by those who are committed to an earlier, presently well-respected paradigm. Conversion to the challenging viewpoint is difficult but may slowly be achieved, the older scientists who are wedded to the conventional paradigm may simply die. If the revolution is successful, scientists in the discipline concerned will be practicing normal science again (i.e., routine, everyday puzzle-solving within an accepted paradigm), but in a different framework, one that earlier was deviant. No matter what the field, creative deviance, where people are searching for new ways of living or trying to adapt to new situations, is a powerful force for social change (Douglas, 1977).

Resisting Social Change   However, the guardians of the prevailing social order—the traditional values, beliefs, and behaviors—are unlikely to surrender to the deviant challengers without resisting (Douglas, 1977, p. 77). The intrusion of the deviants will probably be resisted for several reasons. Deviance is concerned with morality. We evaluate ourselves in part by comparing ourselves to others. To the extent that others lose in this comparison we gain, and vice versa. Those who are members of the conventional moral order are likely to feel morally superior to those who are deviant. This moral superiority and self-worth may be threatened and even toppled if the deviants succeed in vindicating their position (Douglas, 1970).

Conventionalists may not only lose in terms of self-esteem if the deviants successfully establish their position. They may also lose materially. For example, the growing demand by the disabled to be treated equally in all areas of life will require that vast amounts of money be spent on educational programs, building renovations, transportation modification, and so on, for the benefit of the disabled. This money would otherwise go to the benefit of the nondisabled. As educational and job opportunities are opened (forced open, perhaps) to the disabled, opportunities for the nondisabled may be lessened, especially in an era of financial worries. We have already seen this happen in the area of race relations as blacks have made significant gains in the past decades. Or as Becker (1974, p. 774) notes in terms of art, "When new people successfully create a new world which defines other conventions as embodying artistic value, all participants in the old world who cannot make a place in the new one lose out." For example, if a dance world is organized around the conventions and skills of ballet, some people are likely to learn these conventions and skills. In doing so they may become famous, wealthy, and happy as they perform with the best dance companies and in roles written for them. However, if a new dance convention is successfully promoted in which those who have made it in the presently accepted convention are not skilled, their high status is threatened (Becker, 1974). Thus deviance is likely to threaten people's self-esteem, their material status, and, of course, their sense of what is moral and immoral.

Let us present an interesting example of how deviance can be an important force for social change and how it is likely to be resisted by those who are threatened by the change. The following discussion of the gun as a trigger for social change is based on Henry Barbera's (1977) insightful analysis.

The Decline of the Knight in Shining Armor   The gun was first used in the fourteenth century. The early guns were crude, cumbersome, and extremely large. Powder problems limited their effectiveness as weapons of warfare. During the fifteenth century this changed as guns were made lighter and portable, and as powder problems were solved through the invention of corned gunpowder. The gun became an important weapon of warfare and subsequently of social change.

Until the development of the gun, warfare in medieval Europe was the province of knights mounted on horses. Warfare between feudal knights was personal. The combatants faced one another. It was guided by chivalrous notions of how warfare should be waged: no surprises or deceptions. The outcome of the knightly duel was seen as the result of divine judgment.

Guns, however, democratized warfare. Commoners, without the noble and specialized training of the knight, and without the resources of the knight, but armed with guns and later with cannons, could fell an entire line of knights on their white chargers. The lowly foot soldier with a gun became more important than the knight mounted on a horse. Deception and death at a distance prevailed. The outcome of combat was no longer viewed as the result of divine judgment, but became the result of personal merit. The new foot soldiers fought for cash and for the state, and no longer merely for an overlord who conditionally gave his cavalry land and enough peasants to farm the land. The noble knight's seemingly entrenched position in his castle and as lord of the fief was severely threatened. The knights railed against the gun—it was the work of the devil, it was dishonorable, those who used it were not chivalrous. Some cut off the hands and plucked out the eyes of captured gunners. Yet their opposition was to no avail. The knight's time was slipping slowly into darkness.

With the increasing demands for guns arose the importance of new types of men—factory owners, financiers, traders, miners, foundry workers, engineers, and so on—the pioneers of what we now call the military-industrial complex. These were urban, sometimes middle-class folks, and they were often at odds with the knights, who were land-based. To equip "modern" soldiers required a great deal of resources. The cost could not be borne by any individual, but could be borne by the developing state. During the Middle Ages feudal groups were often more powerful than the state (i.e., the king). Over centuries of struggle the kings gained central power. The gun aided in this acquisition of power as it rendered vulnerable the feudal castles and walled towns of individual barons. As power became centralized in the state, the increasingly vast resources of the king further enabled the state to equip its army. Well-equipped armies then enabled the modern European states to conquer the world. Spears and arrows were no match for guns and cannons. Thus, the gun was offensive to the feudal knights' way of life. They strongly resisted its use. Yet its triumph aided in the development of modern states with centralized authority which later conquered the world.

CONCLUSION

Deviants cope with conventional society in various ways for different reasons. As we noted in Chapters 4 and 5, they may contend with the initial accusations that they are deviant. Others try to live with their deviance with as few troubles as possible. Through passing or covering, they try to manage their stigmas. Some join voluntary organizations of fellow deviants, whereas others become members of deviant communities. Membership in these groups is likely to enhance one's identity as a deviant. Members develop and share with one another a perspective about what the world is like and how to cope with it. A sense of belonging and wholeness develops for members which is typically lacking for deviants in the larger, conventional world that condemns them.

Some deviants attempt to become conventional through various strategies. Some try to change their own offensive behavior or characteristics and reenter conventional society. Some join self-help groups in an attempt to become respectable. Others disavow their deviance. They seek to become conventional through changing the attitudes of the conventional people they encounter. Finally, through collective action, such as demonstrations, lobbying, and so forth, some deviants attempt to change society's definition of respectability and deviance. They attempt to vindicate their position. In doing so they are likely to threaten the moral and materialistic interests of those who are "making it" in conventional society. Yet, if the deviants are successful, they will have profoundly changed society. The future of deviance and respectability will be altered. It is to that uncertain future that we turn our attention.

PROJECTS

1 Erving Goffman suggests that although some people are stigmatized in almost all encounters, all of us are occasionally stigmatized. Therefore, we all employ strategies of passing and covering. Analyze your own routine, and sometimes not-so-routine, passing and covering. For example, how do you pass as a well-prepared student in class when you may not be? Teachers, of course, face a complementary problem. What about casual drug use? For some audiences (perhaps your parents), passing or, probably, covering is an important strategy to use. Compare your techniques with some friends in order to develop a description of passing and covering in routine, everyday situations.

2 Ex-deviants often have a difficult time reentering conventional society. One reason is that their trustworthiness is still questioned. The issue of trust and prior deviance often appears in finding a job. Through application questions and polygraph tests many employers delve into the background of prospective employees. The employers are interested not only in the applicant's qualifications, but in the applicant's previous respectability. Do a survey in your community of the questions that employers ask of applicants. Contact a wide variety of employers in order to gather the information. You may want to personally interview for job openings or talk with those who have interviewed as well as obtain application forms from the employers. Do various types of employers ask certain types of questions?

3 Examine a change or set of changes in a field of interest to you—the arts, athletics, business, science, and so on. This could be a change that occurred in the past or one that is presently taking place. You may have been or may be involved yourself (e.g., new procedures where you work). Through both scholarly and popular works, investigate the change. If you were involved, use your own observations. How did deviance play a part in the change? Was the deviance resisted? By whom? Why?

Chapter 8

The Future of Deviance

If thirty years ago a sociologist had told the public that homosexuals would be coming out of the "closet" en masse in the 1970s and 1980s, that laws would be passed to ensure their civil rights, and that known homosexuals would be elected as government officials, the sociologist probably would have been thought crazy. So too if the sociologist had predicted that the tobacco industry would be on the defensive due to widespread antismoking sentiment and new regulatory laws, that "respectable" movies would regularly depict people in the nude, and that husbands could be found guilty of raping their wives. Although views about what is deviant may change dramatically over time, predictions to that effect are likely to meet with skepticism from the general public. Moreover, sociologists and other concerned citizens have often fallen woefully short of accuracy in predicting the future of deviance. We have enough difficulty knowing what is happening now.

In this chapter we will examine the future of deviance. We will do so from two perspectives. First, in the future what will social scientists be investigating when they examine deviance, and what issues will they face in the course of their investigations? As we noted in Chapter 2, our understanding of deviance is created through the activities of concerned investigators. What will their activities be in the future? Second, aside from the activities of social scientists, what will be some of the trends in the phenomenon of deviance? Will there be any major changes, as have occurred in the past several decades, and can we begin to glimpse them now? We will speculate about some possibilities.

Predicting the future is, of course, a difficult, if not impossible, task. It is not merely coincidental that some of the most stimulating foresight about the future of our society has been shown by science fiction writers, not by academicians. Science fiction writers creatively explore the future possibilities based on past and present experiences. Some might argue, however, that science fiction writers are not constrained by the responsibilities that tie academicians to small, workable problems and restrict them from going too far beyond their data. "Wild" guesses are not praised among scientists. Thus, social scientists certainly do not have a monopoly on insight into the future. Finally, we should remember that predictions are much like campaign promises. They may make good reading, but how often do they come true?

INVESTIGATING DEVIANCE

Before we examine the possible future of the sociological investigation of deviance, we need to briefly examine where that investigation has been and where it is now: its past and present. We will also discuss some reasons for the changes in the sociological perspective on deviance. This analysis will allow us to tie together several important points made throughout the book. It will also set the stage for our examination of future trends in the investigation of deviance.

Past and Present

Traditionally both social scientists and citizens at large viewed deviance as objectively given. Offensive behaviors were inherently pathological. Consequently, the aim of social scientists was to understand the causes of the pathology (later called "deviance") in order to control, cure, or prevent it. Neither small-town Americans nor small-town American sociologists realized that what they thought was inherently or obviously deviant was a reflection of their own positions in society.

Gradually, sociological views of deviance changed. Foreshadowed by earlier works of Tannebaum (1938) and Lemert (1951), what is called the labeling, societal reaction, or interactionist perspective developed in the early 1960s. It is a major view today in the sociology of deviance, though it certainly has its critics. Societal reaction sociologists call our attention to the accusers and not only to the accused (Becker, 1963, 1974). Rules were no longer taken for granted by these sociologists even though they might still be by the general public. As the societal reaction perspective developed, two issues were emphasized. First, there was a concern with who would be labeled as deviant. Societal reaction theorists argued that the alleged offense was only one item used by accusers in deciding how to deal with an alleged deviant (see Chapter 5). The second focus was on the impact of the labeling or reaction on the offender's future attitudes and behavior. Rather than improve the attitudes and behavior of the deviant, the reactions of society may enhance future deviance (see Chapter 6). As we have noted, these two themes have generated a great deal of controversy.

Societal reaction sociologists examined the actions of the accusers and the accused toward one another—their interaction. This interactionist perspective was humanistic and empathic. In particular, it tried to understand the situation from the viewpoint of those who were reacted to as deviant (Becker, 1967; Spector, 1976). At times this resulted in an "underdog" perspective, with deviants seen as having few resources for contending with societal reactions. At times the deviant was characterized as a victim (Gouldner, 1968).

The societal reaction approach did not develop overnight. At first it met with great hostility from other sociologists. Early papers in the 1950s and 1960s based on such an approach were not warmly received at sociological meetings. The papers found their way into print only after being harshly rejected by many established journals (Spector, 1976). Though the societal reaction perspective is no longer on the defensive, the questioning and criticism continue today, as they should.

Reasons for the Change   The societal reaction perspective developed in the 1950s and 1960s because of several factors: changing times and changing sociologists; perceived flaws in the earlier, objectively given approach; and complementary developments in other areas of sociology.

Times had changed. Sociologists of the late 1950s and 1960s had lived through the witch hunt led by Senator Joseph McCarthy in the early 1950s in which numerous public officials and citizens were falsely accused of being Communists or Communist sympathizers. Those accused were "blacklisted" in the arts, professions, politics, and so on. Only years later were some exonerated. The civil rights movement was the current concern. The Nazi extermination of Jews and the internment of over 100,000 Japanese-Americans in relocation camps by our own government were recent history. Sociologists and others became sensitive to the systematic oppression of even American citizens. Thus societal reactions and the consequences of these reactions in various contexts of conflict were an important part of the lives of sociologists.

Further, sociologists had changed. Those who would later be identified as societal reaction theorists, as well as other sociologists, were no longer just from small-town, Protestant backgrounds. Rather, many were from big cities, where they were exposed to a wide variety of life-styles and behaviors. Some were *marginal* people—not part of mainstream society themselves: ethnic-Americans, jazz musicians, ex-convicts, sons of barmaids. Changing experiences led to changing views of deviance.

Flaws in the research of earlier approaches were gradually identified. Societal reaction theorists questioned the logic of using official data, such as police statistics or psychiatric records, in determining the causes of deviance. Sociologists became aware that not all deviance, not even all "serious" deviance, comes to the attention of official agents. Some of it is hidden. Some is not reported by victims or observers. Even much that is reported is handled informally and therefore does not show up in official records. Official records, particularly those on crime, delinquency, and mental illness, may show more about the procedures of control agencies than about the causes of deviance (Kitsuse and Cicourel, 1963). For example, psychiatric explanations of captive deviants (prison inmates, mental patients, and so on) have been criticized as revealing more about the limited sample and the preconceptions of the researcher than about the actual characteristics of the deviants (Szasz, 1970; Chapman and Chapman, 1971; Gibbons, 1977). Traditional conceptions of deviance could not handle these apparent problems.

Emerging at the same time as the societal reaction perspective were parallel developments in sociology: the rise of ethnomethodology, the development of the dramaturgical view of social life, and a renewed interest in conflict sociology. If not directly contributing to a change in the sociology of deviance, each of these developments certainly provided an atmosphere which was conducive to and supportive of such changes.

Ethnomethodology treats the "objective reality of social facts *as* an ongoing accomplishment of the concerned activities of everyday life" (Garfinkel, 1967, p. vii). No matter how objective the social world around us appears to be, it is created and it exists through the activities of people. Rules and norms are not taken for granted by ethnomethodologists and therefore cannot be used to explain people's behavior. Ethnomethodologists recognize, however, that both sociologists and the public at large explain and describe what people do in terms of these taken-for-granted rules, norms, and shared understanding. Everyday activities, such as the playing of children or telephone conversations, are analyzed because ethnomethodologists are interested in "how members of society go about the task of *seeing, describing,* and *explaining* order in the world in which they live" (Zimmerman and Wieder, 1970, p. 289).

Dramaturgical analysis, as highlighted by Erving Goffman's works (e.g., *Presentation of Self in Everyday Life*), emphasizes that impression management is an integral feature of social interaction. Whether for honorable or deceitful purposes (and who is to say which is which?) actors manage the image they present to others. In turn, how an audience responds influences future presentations. Both ethnomethodology and dramaturgical analysis question the objectively given basis of social life. People continually create their realities.

While harmony, homogeneity, and consensus were dominant themes in sociology from the 1930s to the 1950s, conflict and power became important issues in the late 1950s (Dahrendorf, 1958, 1959; Wrong, 1961; Gouldner, 1970). One only had to be aware of the many wars in the twentieth century, the racial conflicts, and the conflicts between business and labor to realize that consensus did not exist in all spheres of life. Consequently, sociologists developed a renewed interest in conflict. If conflict is ubiquitous, then it must be important in deviance. It must be important in how society creates rules regarding offensive behavior and decides to whom the rules will be applied. Inequality and conflict in the criminal justice system, the very old (though not necessarily entirely accurate) notion that there are separate systems for the rich and for the poor, prompted sociologists to study not just the accused, but also the accusers. These parallel developments in sociology—in ethnomethodology, dramaturgical analysis, and conflict sociology—both accompanied and supported the rise of the societal reaction perspective in deviance.

Limitations in the Societal Reaction Perspective— Since societal reaction theorists are not in complete agreement, there is really no single societal reaction perspective. Rather, there are variations on a general theme. Nevertheless, as the societal reaction perspective is presently conveyed in textbooks (and certainly not all textbooks use the approach), serious limitations exist (Warren and Johnson, 1972).

The societal reaction perspective tends to be limited in scope. Interpersonal processes are stressed. Cultural, structural, and organizational conditions that may have an impact on deviance are not thoroughly pursued (Scull, 1977). Though rules are no longer taken for granted, typically their application but not their creation has been emphasized. There is no reason why the latter could not also be explored using an interactionist perspective (Schur, 1975).

The interactionist perspective has been shortsighted in other ways. Although numerous authors have acknowledged that deviance is not confined to exotic situations (Cohen, 1966; Rushing, 1969; Scarpitti and McFarlane, 1975) presumably dramatic types of deviance, such as prostitution, homosexuality, and drug use, remain predominant. The pathological interpretation of earlier approaches, however, was often replaced by an "underdog sentimentality." Deviants were frequently characterized as passive victims. Their active participation in the societal reaction process was overlooked (Levitin, 1975).

Recently sociologists have called for the inclusion of other types of deviance. Rather than limiting their attention to "nuts, sluts, and per-verts", sociologists should also examine deviance by the more powerful officials in corporations, government, and the military (Liazos, 1972). As one can see, however, the dramatic nature of deviance is still emphasized.

Just as societal reaction theorists felt that they needed to move beyond the traditional approach to deviance, we felt that it was important to move beyond the "traditional" societal reaction approach to deviance. We continue to find much that is useful in the societal reaction approach, but we also feel that it too is limited in various ways. Thus, this book has been a further development in the changing sociological views of deviance. Like deviance itself, those views are dynamic. They change from the past to the present to the future.

The Future

Now that we have a (brief) understanding of the historical development of the sociology of deviance, where will the investigation go from here? Several issues in the study of deviance are likely to be important in the future. Some of these issues will be continuations of present trends. How long the trends will continue is difficult to say.

The view that deviance is a process of interrelated activities and issues will continue to be dominant in the study and understanding of deviance. The widening of our investigative scope in the past twenty years has allowed social scientists to explore issues that were ignored or taken for granted in the past. It has led to greater diversity in perspectives and concerns. The study of deviance seems to have been invigorated by this broadening of its focus. While the merits of the societal reaction perspec-tive, which led to this broader scope of inquiry, continue to be debated, the necessity of such a broader scope seems to be well recognized. Current research efforts and discussions are focused on many important elements of the phenomenon of deviance—the creation of deviance (i.e., of laws, regulations, and standards of respectability), the recognition and identifi-cation of deviants, reactions to and dealing with deviance, the causes of deviance, and how deviants cope with conventional society—and will continue to be in the future.

Recent textbooks, many of which seem to embrace a societal reaction or interactionist perspective, are testimony to the concern of sociologists that students be exposed to recent developments in the investigation and understanding of deviance (Montanino, 1977). We consider this book to be an outgrowth of those recent developments and in particular to be part of an even more recent trend of books which examine the processes or phenomenon of deviance in a systematic way (Hawkins and Tiedeman, 1975; Goode, 1978; Schur, 1979; Pfuhl, 1980).

While the view of deviance as a set of interrelated issues and processes will be an important part of future inquiries, there may be a continuation of at least one aspect of the traditional study of deviance. As we noted in Chapter 1, deviance was traditionally conceptualized and presented as dramatic, exotic, and bizarre. In some ways that still remains the case today, even though many of the other features of the traditional approach have been abandoned. At least in textbooks and perhaps more so in classroom presentations, it may remain the case for years to come. Every department is eager to attract its share of students. With dwindling enrollments at universities and colleges, and with students coping with economic hard times by enrolling in courses that lead to marketable skills (e.g., business administration), sociology departments and other disciplines in the liberal arts and humanities are feeling the pinch. In order to combat the potentially disastrous loss of students, sociology departments may try to entice students into the courses they offer. Courses concerning deviance may do so by titillating students with the bizarre and dramatic. Certainly deviance is that, but it is also much more.

While the various processes of deviance will continue to receive attention, a renewed emphasis on causes may occur in the decade ahead. Some sociologists, in bemoaning the relative lack of causal research in the past decade, have already implicitly called for such a renewed emphasis (Akers et al., 1979). The renewed emphasis on causal research will be part of the continuing cycle in the study of deviance, whereby issues and approaches regain importance after years of neglect. A renewed emphasis on causes may reflect the growing conservative movement in America. As we will discuss shortly, a conservative drift may have a profound impact on the phenomenon of deviance. One outgrowth of a conservative shift would seem to be a greater emphasis on the control and containment of deviance. This in turn would imply a renewed search for the causes of deviance. Increased understanding of why people engage in deviance may lead to the development of more effective prevention and control strategies.

A greater emphasis on the control and containment of deviance has also stimulated renewed emphasis on the possible deterrent impact of punishment (Meier and Johnson, 1977). Even if we cannot uncover the causes of deviance, we may still be able to control it more effectively if we can understand how law and punishment deter people from engaging in deviance. To use a medical analogy, doctors do not always wait for a full understanding of the development of a disease or illness before they try to prevent or treat it. So too with officials and scholars concerned about deviance.

The federal government can stimulate and support a possibly renewed emphasis on the causes and control of deviance through its policies of funding social science research. According to critical criminologists, the federal government, through such agencies as the Law Enforcement Assistance Administration, has in the past funneled millions of dollars into research aimed at improving law enforcement, criminal justice, and control. Such improvement might buttress the capitalist system, which is threatened from within by the "dangerous classes" of the disenfranchised, the chronically unemployed, and so on. Consequently, until recently "conventional" crime, such as burglary, robbery, or drug dealing, has been the focus of efforts by social scientists. Crimes by the government, by corporations, or in professions received little funding and little attention (Quinney, 1979). It will be interesting to see what the government's funding policies become and what impact they have on the study of deviance.

Finally, part of the renewed emphasis on causes and control seems to be related to the resurgence of interest in the biological basis of behavior in general and of deviance in particular. We will have more to say about this later.

Deviance Among the High and Mighty   In the past there was considerable reluctance to include within the sociology of deviance the illegal or offensive behavior of respectable people as they performed their respectable jobs. For example, for several years following Edwin Sutherland's (1949) introductory investigation of white-collar crime, criminologists debated whether it was really crime or not (see Gibbons, 1977, pp. 329–330). Objections to viewing white-collar crime as crime were that offenders did not define themselves as criminals, violators did not possess criminal motivation, relatively few criminal sanctions were applied to violators, and so on. Recently, political scientist James Q. Wilson's (1975) *Thinking About Crime* had nothing to say about corporate crime, bribery, fraud, and corruption, apparently because these offenses do not pose a threat of physical harm or loss of life. Deviance at the top has historically been overlooked.

Recently social scientists, journalists, law enforcement officials, legislators, and the general public have devoted more attention to deviance among the high and mighty. There is increased concern about understanding and controlling offensive behavior among the well-respected. The twenty-first-century sociologist who looks back to write about today's "wayward" Americans:

> may be as likely to focus on deviations among those who manage the institutions of our society, on problems of fraud, bribery, and corruption of public trust, as on those street crimes that are currently perceived as virtually coextensive with "the crime problem." (Wheeler, 1976, p. 530)

Social scientists have realized that they can no longer afford the luxury of concentrating on deviance among the powerless if they want to fully understand the phenomenon of deviance. Admonitions from fellow sociologists who criticized their colleagues for overlooking deviance at the top may have helped to spur this new inquiry (Gouldner, 1968; Liazos, 1972;

Thio, 1973; Quinney, 1979). With increased concern among law enforcement officers and government officials about top-level deviance, as witnessed by the recent undercover operations of the FBI, such as the Abscam probe of political corruption, which led to the indictment of several members of Congress, social scientists are likely to continue and even increase their own investigations in this area. Textbooks and edited collections are appearing in order to bring the social scientists' interest in deviance at the top to their students (Douglas and Johnson, 1977; Geis and Meier, 1977; Johnson and Douglas, 1978; Erman and Lundman, 1978).

Even the medical profession is coming under scrutiny from all angles. Ivan Illich (1976) argues that medicine itself is a threat to our health and independence. Duane Stroman (1979) estimates that more than 2 million unnecessary operations are performed each year. After two years of observing surgery, emergency room activities, and staff meetings, Millman (1977, p. 17) found that the medical review of a patient's death becomes a retrospective justification of the errors made and an absolution of any blame for the physician instead of a thorough search for mistakes with the intent of preventing their recurrence. Some of the severest critics of medicine are physicians themselves. One accuses his colleagues of arrogant misuse of power, unwarranted surgery, misuse and abuse of drugs, and other offensive behaviors (Mendelsohn, 1979). Perhaps nothing is sacred any longer.

Much of what popular writers and social scientists have written about deviance at the top expresses a righteous indignation and condemnation of the perpetrators.

> It is becoming increasingly apparent that the real weakness of America lies not with its addicts and homosexuals, or even with its gun-wielding murderers and robbers. It lies with the moral pretention and hypocrisy of some of its controllers and policy-makers. These persons are the *"new"* deviants and the targets of the new reformers, who in championing the rights of the weak and disadvantaged have become the conscience of the United States. (McCaghy, 1976, p. 390)

Perhaps the sociologists of deviance will repeat in part the earlier tendency to characterize deviance from a moralistic and pathological stance. Such simplistic indignation will not be helpful in understanding offensive behavior in respectable places.

A focus on the new deviance—political corruption, business fraud, corporate crime, medical malpractice, and so on—is not merely a broadening of the sociological interest in deviance. More importantly, it is an acknowledgment that deviance is a pervasive and integral feature of major institutions and organizations as well as of our everyday lives. However, as we noted in Chapter 4, privacy tends to accompany power. Thus social scientists will continue to struggle, as do law enforcement officials, journalists, and government investigative committees, to get behind closed doors in their examination of deviance among the high and mighty.

Continuing Concerns   While pursuing deviance among the high and mighty, social scientists may continue to investigate routine deviance as well. For example, whereas crime in general may be seen as a fairly dramatic form of deviance, some recent research has focused on a routine if still harrowing form of street crime, mugging (Lejeune and Alex, 1973; Lejeune, 1977). While most research on voyeurism has examined the lone, presumably pathological peeper, routine peeping among construction workers has received some attention (Feigelman, 1974). Instead of doing research on the facially disfigured or those with missing limbs, social scientists have recently investigated those who are temporarily disabled or who are hearing-impaired, disabilities which might be considered less dramatic (Levitin, 1975; Higgins, 1980). More than ten years ago Norman Denzin (1970, p. 121) called for a return to the study of routine forms of deviance:

> We must return to the mundane and routine forms of behavior to establish a solidly grounded theory of deviance. In short, a complete theory of deviance must account for misconduct that does not come to the attention of broader agencies of social control.

Denzin's call has not gone completely unheeded. However, as shown in the previous chapters by the relative lack of research examples concerning routine forms of deviance, there is a need for additional work in this area. An understanding of deviance will be complete only if it explains both routine and dramatic forms of deviance and the issues surrounding them, *and* if both deviance and respectability are understood within the same framework. As we noted in Chapter 1, deviance and respectability are tightly interwoven. They are the opposite sides of the same coin. In the past, particular theories were developed to explain deviant behavior. Today, social scientists are questioning whether such an approach is useful. For example, Ronald Akers's social learning theory of deviance is just as much an explanation of respectable behavior as of deviant behavior. We hope that attempts to understand deviance will also be attempts to understand respectability. Such an approach would put the study of deviance back into the mainstream of sociological inquiry, where it originated.

Increasing concern about confidentiality and the rights of minors and patients of all kinds has led to increased difficulty in researching deviance. The increase in concern was due to what were perceived as the widespread abuses of disseminating information contained in patients' records and to experimenting on or studying patients and minors. Nowadays self-report studies on the involvement of high school students in delinquency require the approval of the students and their parents, as well as school administrators. In the past, the principal's approval was often enough. Similarly, in order to investigate issues in the mental health system, approval from various review boards and the consent of the patients and staff who are to be involved in the research may be necessary. While it has always been difficult to study deviance among the high and mighty, it is now becoming increasingly difficult to study deviance among those who are relatively powerless. Social scientists will need perseverance in order to investigate deviance in the future (Klockars and O'Connor, 1979).

Not only in the area of deviance, but in the study of it as well, conflict will be a watchword. As always, there will continue to be disagreement about what research results mean. More fundamentally, however, there will be conflict about the field itself and how it should be investigated (Posner, 1980). For example, while we support Denzin's call for an examination of routine forms of deviance, others question the usefulness of such a strategy. Don Gibbons and Joseph Jones (1975, pp. 49–51) argue that an "omnibus" definition of deviance brings together behaviors, such as murder and the breaching of table etiquette in a sorority, whose connection to one another is not readily apparent; that it includes trivial offenses; that a new field of inquiry would be needed if such a framework were used; and that such a conceptualization of deviance would lead to its analysis being almost all of sociology. While Malcolm Spector (1976, p. 74) states that "labeling theory is well established, if not the current orthodoxy," a session at the 1977 annual meeting of the American Society of Criminology was entitled "The Demise of Labeling" (Montanino, 1977). Conflict among sociologists about what they should be studying, how they should be studying it, and what their results mean will characterize the future of deviance.

Finally, in the future sociologists may abandon the term "deviance" for one which they feel more accurately depicts their orientation. Some see "deviance" as conveying an unnecessarily negative connotation (Neubeck, 1979, pp. 16, 22). It implies that there is indeed something wrong with the people who are deviant and therefore they should mend their ways. Further, it shifts our focus away from the social system, away from the arrangements of social institutions and practices which are conducive to or foster behavior that others consider offensive. It emphasizes the pathological qualities of individuals (i.e., "you pervert!"), instead of the larger system in which people live and in which their lives are constrained. Others argue that the concept is one-sided, emphasizing the troubles deviants cause for conventional people and tending to neglect the problems conventional people create for deviants (Simmons, 1969, p. 10). We have tried to avoid these connotations in our use of the term "deviance."

However, neither we nor other social scientists can completely overcome the images called to mind by terms that are part of everyday life. The term "social pathology" gave way to "deviance." Perhaps "deviance" will give way to some other term that does not carry with it unwanted baggage.

FUTURE TRENDS IN DEVIANCE

In addition to involving our thoughts on what social scientists will be investigating in the years ahead, our look into the future of deviance must also touch upon the shape of deviance to come. We see two important trends that will characterize deviance in the future. One is a return to the biological basis for offensive behavior. No doubt many social scientists will be skeptical of a renewed interest in a biological perspective on deviance. They will resist it. Yet, we feel that a biological revival is likely to occur in the years or decades ahead. Second, there has been in the past few years, and continues to be, a conservative shift in America. Some will welcome this shift in orientation. Others will not. Nevertheless, the conservative shift has already had an impact on deviance and may have a profound impact on deviance in the future.

Deviance and Biology Revisited

A biological renaissance, which began in the 1970s, is well under way today. Tremendous developments in understanding the nature of life, such as the work on recombinant DNA or "gene splicing" to create new forms of life, testifies to this renaissance. The Supreme Court's decision in 1980 that such new forms of life can be patented will spur additional research efforts and interest. The biological renaissance includes a renewed interest in the biological bases for social behavior and, in particular, for deviant social behavior.

In recent years social scientists have become involved in a controversial revitalization of biological explanations of social behavior. Many of the new *sociobiological* theories come not from sociologists but from biologists, physicians, and practitioners affiliated with social control agencies, and to a lesser extent from psychologists and anthropologists. Harvard zoologist Edward O. Wilson became the center of attention with his publication of *Sociobiology: The New Synthesis* (1975) and *On Human Nature* (1978). He argues that much of human behavior, such as selfishness, aggression, homosexuality, fear of strangers, and even human ethics or values, is to a large extent programmed into our genes. Wilson's evolutionary-genetic reinterpretation of human behavior has reactivated the long-standing battle between scientists who view human behavior as a social product and others who believe that biology is destiny.

Opposition to Wilson's perspective should, of course, be anticipated. Sherwood Washburn (1978, p. 54), a leading anthropologist, argues that a "strong case can be made that the founders of social science would have been better off if they had never heard of biology or evolution." Yet, he concedes that in the future the understanding of human behavior may be advanced by anthropologists who have some knowledge of human biology but avoid the mistakes of the past, such as simplistic and unwarranted comparisons between human and animal behavior. To the social scientist, Wilson's sociobiology has the familiar ring of early biological determinism, which attributed deviance to inborn traits of genetic inferiority or mental defectiveness. Further, an emphasis on genetics was once used to justify poverty, racism, and programs of eugenic sterilization. It is not surprising, then, that the debate about sociobiology concerns ethical as well as scientific issues (Caplan, 1978; Gregory et al., 1978).

We would expect social scientists to be reluctant to return to a search for the biological bases of deviant behavior. The legacies of Lombroso's atavistic criminal, Goddard's Kallikak family, and the more recent XYY chromosome episode are reminders of the errors social science has fallen into because of the temptation to look for simple biological causes and solutions to complex human behavior and problems.

The editors of a recent collection of Danish studies, *The Biosocial Bases of Criminal Behavior,* are aware of the prevailing skepticism of their social scientific audience. They recognize that their findings:

> may alarm social causation theorists because of our rather firm findings of the importance of genetic and physiological factors in crime. On the other hand, geneticists may be disturbed by the fact that these findings are so dependent on social variables for the salience of their expression. (Mednick and Christiansen, 1977, p. x)

In the foreword to this Danish collection, Marvin Wolfgang, a leading American criminologist, acknowledges the pitfalls of the previous biological understandings of deviance. Yet, he suggests, a revival of the biological approach can be useful now due to our more sophisticated and technologically fascinating research tools. Wolfgang (1977, pp. v–vi) supports this particular return to a biological approach by declaring that Danish record-keeping on criminality is the best in the Western world, that the editors are among the "most respected students of social psychology and sociological criminology," and that the research is based on the "best canons of science." He notes that this recent attempt to understand the biological importance of deviant behavior is not a "cyclical return to biosociality, not a revival of Lombroso, Hooten, Schlapp and Smith or Sheldon. The studies reported here are new and exciting, buttressed by control groups and experimental analyses" (Wolfgang, 1977, p. v).

And what do the studies show? They provide varying degrees of support for the biological bases of deviance, from a distinctive relationship between the criminality of biological fathers and their sons who were adopted by other families (pp. 127–141) to no evidence of aggressive criminality among XYY chromosome men (pp. 165–187). Perhaps the most novel contribution is the evidence that specific differences in the autonomic nervous system are related to the efficiency with which juveniles internalized social norms. The "insensitivity" or "inability to learn from experience" that has often been attributed to delinquents and psychopaths is demonstrated to be a physiologically based deficiency in learning processes or a diminished response to punishment or pain (chaps. 1, 2, 12, 13, 17). As Mednick and Christiansen (1977) note, the lack of success of social causation theories of crime and deviance and the inability to reduce crime will open the door to new biological approaches. It remains to be seen how far the door will be opened.

Biochemical Demons Others have called for a broader or more balanced biosocial theory of deviance which provides an "integration of both genetic and environmental determinants of behavior" (Baldwin and Baldwin, 1980). Such theories would consider the behavioral consequences of nutrition, toxins, foreign chemicals, drugs, stress, levels of exercise, sensory stimulation, and other biochemical demons.

The potentially adverse effects of food additives, such as preservatives and dyes, and toxic levels of heavy metals, such as lead and mercury, have become a popular and somewhat controversial topic. Numerous interested persons, including public health officials, physicians, and nutritionists, as well as officials who deal with deviants, have commented that chemical deficiencies and imbalances and brain toxicity contribute to deviance of all kinds (Hippchen, 1977, 1978). Vitamin deficiency and vitamin dependency (i.e., requirement of vitamins in excess of normal amounts) are alleged to create severe perceptual distortions and violent behavior and can lead to antisocial or criminal conduct. Some researchers have found that an extremely high percentage of criminals, alcoholics, and children with learning disabilities suffer from vitamin dependency, food allergies, or hypoglycemia (Hoffer, 1975). Treatment for such "imbalances" involves megavitamin therapy (i.e., extremely large doses of vitamins) and the elimination of foods thought to contain toxic or allergenic substances. Bold claims are made for the effectiveness of such therapy. Recovery rates of 70 percent for "hardcore" alcoholics, 80 percent success with schizophrenia, and 80 percent success with drug users are presented as common (Hippchen, 1977). Other researchers question the effectiveness of such treatment and argue that megavitamin therapy may be harmful rather than helpful.

Not too surprisingly, critics charge that the claims of success are not supported by sound scientific procedures (Gaensbauer, 1979). Further, proponents of the "biochemical demon" approach sometimes overstate their case. Hoffer (1975) maintains that vitamin B-3 dependency is the primary cause of restlessness among today's youth, leading them to delinquency, crime, and schizophrenia. Moralistic ideas abound. For example, one proponent argues that:

> Instant gratification has become acceptable. Loss of mores, lying, cheating, whoring and boozing are the "in" thing now, and why not? The government encourages this by overtaxing the hard-working, and by making more government jobs. They throw good money after bad. This encourages illegal strikes: unions demand and get exorbitant settlements. Welfare is a way of life. . . . Why did this sad chain of events happen now and not 50 years ago? . . . We can link the entire degenerative process of our bodies and our society to the excessive use of flour, sugar, and starch. (Green, 1978, p. 278)

Even though recent thinking and research concerning the possible connection between environmental and chemical contaminants and a variety of offensive behaviors and problems has been criticized, we should expect to see more work in this area. Novel research, such as surveys of the relationship between the levels of lead in the baby teeth of urban children and their performance in school, is being conducted (Fogel, 1980). Sophisticated technology now enables the California court system to analyze an offender's hair in order to determine whether toxic metals are contributing to the offender's behavior (Schauss, 1979). Various nutritional and vitamin therapies are becoming widely practiced. The demons of deviance are becoming biological ones once again. And if they can be identified, perhaps they can be exorcised.

Back to Basics in Psychiatry Professions that deal with deviance, such as psychiatry, are also returning to their biological beginnings. During the past two decades psychiatry has been severely criticized, often by psychiatrists. Thomas Szasz (1961, 1974, 1978) has questioned the validity of psychiatric doctrine, diagnostic procedures, and even the concept of mental illness. Another psychiatrist, E. Fuller Torrey, observes that psychiatry is becoming expendable. Today, less than half as many medical school graduates go into psychiatry as did in 1970 (*Time,* April 2, 1979, p. 74). During the 1960s and 1970s psychiatry seemed to identify itself more with the social sciences than with medicine. Its effectiveness was questioned. Yet with the development of drugs that relieve psychiatric symptoms and allow many mental patients to return to constructive lives in the community, psychiatry seems to be on the upswing. The catchphrase has become: "Getting back to our roots in medicine" (*Time,* April 2, 1979, p. 80).

The first antipsychotic drug was discovered by accident. It was used to reduce the stress of surgery. However, when it was used to calm schizophrenics, it was also found to reduce their disordered thinking and delusions and to help them overcome their emotional withdrawal. This raised some interesting questions. If chemicals could be used to drastically alter aberrant thinking, then perhaps the problem behavior was caused by abnormal brain chemistry. This prompted deliberate research into the biochemistry of the brain (*Newsweek,* November 12, 1979, p. 99).

Today, psychiatry has entered a new era. Instead of viewing mental illness as the result of some early psychic trauma, psychiatrists are now more likely to be interested in the chemicals that transmit impulses in the brain and the nerve sites that receive the messages. The newest theories of mental disorder are based on the belief that the problem is a result of mix-ups in the infinitely complex interplay of brain chemicals.

More than twenty brain chemicals, which transmit messages such as pain, emotion, and physical stimulation, have been discovered. Many scientists think these chemical neurotransmitters are the key to understanding many mysteries of the mind. An overproduction or a surplus level of some of them is thought to result in greater levels of excitation and perceptual distortion, while deficient levels are associated with depression, apathy, and insensitivity (Van Praag and Bruinvels, 1977). The antipsychotic drugs work by either blocking or reducing the effects of message transmitters found at surplus levels or by enhancing or prolonging the effects of neurotransmitters existing at deficient levels. These drugs are being hailed not only for their effectiveness in dealing with mental illness, but even more so because they signal the beginning of a new era in understanding and controlling human behavior (*Newsweek,* November 12, 1979, p. 104; *Time,* April 2, 1979, p. 82). The back-to-basics movement in psychiatry is a further reflection of the medicalization of our understanding of deviance and of our means of dealing with it (Conrad and Schneider, 1980). And as we noted in Chapter 2, the biological perspective of deviance was initially developed by physicians. Thus, the renewed emphasis on the biological bases and control of deviance is a reflection of an old concern.

A Conservative Drift in Deviance

While for the immediate future there may be continuing tolerance of alternative life-styles (e.g., living together without being married or being gay), we suspect that a countering current of conservatism in America may have a profound impact on deviance in the future. If a conservative approach to dealing with deviance continues to develop, it will be part of a broader conservatism in the country. As compared to the "Great Society" liberalism of the 1960s, politicians and the public have shifted rightward. The increasing difficulty faced by proponents of ERA in their efforts to have that amendment ratified is testimony to the conservative mood of the country. While the Supreme Court, headed by Chief Justice Warren

Burger, cannot be characterized as simply a conservative, strict-constructionist court, in many areas its decisions have departed from the liberal decisions of the Warren Court of the 1960s. Its recent decision that the states and the federal government are not required by the Constitution to pay for abortions even though abortion is legal under certain circumstances reaffirmed its 1973 decision and reflects a continuing conservative mood in the country. The rise of born-again Christians among American adults is further testimony to the "back-to-basics" movement in the country. The surprisingly large gains made by Republicans in the 1980 elections are the most recent indication of the conservative shift. The shift should not be seen as something new, however. Instead, it is evidence of a renewed emphasis on an ever-present conservative orientation. It is part of a continual change in emphasis among conservative, liberal, and other orientations to our lives. Nevertheless, a conservative drift in America is bound to have an impact on the phenomenon of deviance.

A conservative drift in how we view and handle deviance is already evident in a number of areas. In the 1970s we returned to the use of the death penalty for those convicted of capital crimes. The execution of Gary Gilmore in 1977 was the first execution in the United States in ten years. By the mid-seventies, criminologists had begun to feel that incarceration for treatment and rehabilitation was a failure. During the 1960s many studies seemed to indicate that humanistic, reform-oriented efforts to change the behavior of criminals was not reducing the "crime problem" (von Hirsch, 1976; Wheeler, 1976). Recidivism rates remained high. Some blamed this failure on social scientists' lack of knowledge. Others blamed it on the kinds of people that officials were trying to work with. Still others accounted for the failure in terms of the enormity of the problem and the lack of resources to tackle the job. Thus, the rehabilitation ideology is on the wane. In its place, incapacitation is being suggested as the main reason for imprisonment (van den Haag, 1975; Wilson, 1975). To a great degree, Americans support these changes. Since 1945, Americans have increasingly become more punitive toward criminals, as indicated by their support for harsher penalties such as the death penalty (Stinchcombe et al., 1980).

Similarly the gay rights movement suffered some setbacks in the late 1970s as several cities throughout the country repealed their "gay rights" ordinances. Voters in other cities, however, refused to do so. The conflict over homosexuality is not finished. After a much debated vote in 1974 the American Psychiatric Association decided that homosexuality should not be defined as a disorder. It was removed from the profession's diagnostic manual. A survey of APA members several years later, however, indicated that many still viewed homosexuality as unhealthy. Sixty-nine percent of the first 2,500 respondents believed that homosexuality was usually a "pathological" adaptation, while 18 percent disagreed. Three-fifths felt that homosexuals were less capable of mature, loving relationships as compared to heterosexuals, and 70 percent believed that homosexuals' problems had less to do with their stigmatization by society and more to do with their own inner conflicts. Finally, 43 percent of the psychiatrists agreed that homosexuals were a greater risk than heterosexuals when holding positions of great responsibility (Bawer, 1977).

Recently, in the prestigious *American Bar Association Journal,* a psychiatrist called for protecting the rights of the mentally ill. The psychiatrist argues that in trying to reform archaic mental health systems, well-intentioned young lawyers and civil libertarians have inadvertently increased the suffering of the mentally ill and their families. The law assumes that people are rational in their activities, whereas psychiatry often deals with people whose actions are seemingly illogical and governed by irrational forces. The two disciplines make fundamentally different assumptions about people.

> When irrational forces so tether the rational capabilities of the human being, "freedom" and "individual rights" become sardonic and cruel jokes unwittingly perpetrated by clinically untutored persons. (Shwed, 1978, p. 566)

Thus, the psychiatrist argues that his profession is unnecessarily constrained in its ability to help the mentally ill because of new, too narrowly defined requirements for involuntary admissions, misunderstanding of electroconvulsive treatment or "shock" therapy, right-to-treatment legislation, which reformers proudly point to but which is undermined by a lack of funds and understaffing, and so on. Conservative criticism of how we handle deviants and of the alleged failure of liberal trends in handling deviants is growing.

Reasons for the Drift   The possible conservative trend in viewing and handling deviance may be understood in part by appealing to Lauderdale's (1976) research on deviance and moral boundaries. As we noted in Chapter 5, Lauderdale suggests that when a group is threatened from the outside, it will more severely reject offensive people who had previously been tolerated. In meeting the outside threat, members become more strict in their standards, and this leads to a greater rejection of marginal members who do not mend their ways. One might argue that America is being threatened by economic problems, by Soviet expansion, by our declining stature in the world, by a concern over the capabilities of our leaders, by a sense of impotence, and so on. If that is so, and if Lauderdale's research is applicable outside of the laboratory, we can expect less tolerance of deviance in the years ahead. Conflict sociologists such as Richard Quinney (1979) argue that as the problems of late capitalist development worsen (e.g., as the surplus population steadily grows larger, requiring increasingly more oppressive control measures), the state will become even more repressive in order to combat the threat from within. Either way, the "gains" made by deviants in the past decades may not be duplicated in the decades ahead and may even be eroded away in various places. Some have argued that this has already happened to black Americans, a group whose subordination makes its experience similar in certain respects to the experience of deviant groups. Because deviance is an integral part of our lives, general trends in our society are bound to involve deviance as well.

CONCLUSION

Deviance is a complex phenomenon created through the activities and ideas of many people. It is ever-changing, as witnessed by the shift from a traditional, objective approach to understanding deviance to the more recent subjectively problematic, interactionist perspective. The changes in deviance grow out of changes in sociology and in the larger society. Because deviance is ever-changing and because our understanding is just beginning, it is difficult to know what lies ahead. Many of the recent trends in the investigation of deviance are likely to continue into the future. The phenomenon of deviance will continue to be seen as a process of interrelated activities and issues. Increased interest in deviance among the high and mighty will continue, as will conflict about where social scientists should put their attention. We may even see the abandonment of the term "deviance" for some other, presumably less loaded word.

Two profound trends in deviance seem to be emerging. First, as part of a larger biological renaissance, we are experiencing a rejuvenation of the concern for the biological basis of offensive behavior. Second, there seems to be an emerging conservative drift in America which has already had profound implications for deviance and may have more in the future. We need not merely wait, though, to see what happens in the future. Instead, we can continue to broaden and deepen our understanding of deviance. In doing so, we will increase our understanding of ourselves.

PROJECTS

1 Examine both popular and social scientific pronouncements about deviance from an earlier time (e.g., writings, speeches, interviews, and so on). You might like to sample works from ten years ago, twenty years ago, or even longer ago. What observations were made then about the future of deviance? What kinds of information or ideas were the predictions based on? Did the observations come true? If not, then with the benefit of hindsight explain why they did not.

2   Based on your understanding of deviance and your knowledge of the world
    around you, what do you see as the future of deviance? Make a list of what you
    believe will be issues in deviance in the immediate future or in the more distant
    future. For example, while we have witnessed the relative decline of total
    institutions in the past twenty years, might there be a renewed emphasis on total
    institutions with a continuing conservative shift in America? What are your
    thoughts about the future of deviance?

Glossary

Absolute Fixed, unchanging, and unquestioned. Part of the traditional approach to studying deviance.

Accounts Explanations used by deviants in order to make themselves appear to be respectable (i.e., to justify or excuse their offensive behavior).

Achieved deviance Those who are offensive because of what they do.

Acquiescence To accept the validity of the label of deviance (the accusation) that society has conferred upon the individual.

Actual social identity The social characteristics that people possess.

Alteration To change that which others find offensive about an individual.

Anomie A gap between the success goals of society and the available, legitimate means for achieving those goals.

Ascribed deviance According to Mankoff (1971) those with some kind of impairment, such as being blind or a dwarf, who are put in subordinated statuses not because of what they do, but because of our reactions to them.

"Being on" A heightened concern with the impression one is making on others.

Boundary maintenance The process by which the moral line between acceptable and unacceptable behavior for a community is created and sustained.

Career model A view of becoming deviant which focuses on the sequence of movements from one position to another that people make as they become deviant, how they make the movements, and the issues they face in making the movements.

Causality An emphasis on the causes of deviance.

Celerity How promptly the deviant is responded to.

Centrality One of six features of stereotypes of deviants whereby we treat the deviance as the most important feature of the offender's life.

Channeling To use the label of deviance as an important and positive feature of one's identity.

Clustering One of six features of stereotypes of deviants in which deviants are characterized by a group or cluster of negative traits.

Cognitive consistency The interpretation that good is associated with good and bad with bad. Generally we are comfortable with, and try to maintain, a consistent interpretation of the world.

Conflict A view of society which stresses the disagreement and differences among its members.

Consensus A view of society which emphasizes the agreement and harmony among its members.

Context The social environment, composed of the audience, the actor, and the situation, in which deviance is defined.

Control theories Explanations which focus on features of the social environment that keep people from engaging in (additional) deviance.

Counterfeit secrecy While conventional members may know that someone is stigmatized, they act as if they do not.

Countermoralism Shaming those who shame you (countershaming).

Counterpride displays Taking "undue" pride in that which others shame you for.

Courtesy stigma A stigma that is acquired because of an individual's relationship to someone who is already tainted.

Covering Attempts to minimize the impact or obtrusiveness of a discredited stigma.

Cultural deviance theories Approaches which emphasize that people behave according to what they learn or are exposed to, whether it be called deviant or conventional.

"Dangerous class" In a conflict approach those who are surplus labor—i.e., those who are not needed in the economy as producers (the chronically unemployed and underemployed)—are viewed as losing any stake in society they may have had. They become dangerous to the present capitalist system.

Decarceration The movement toward relatively less use of total institutions in dealing with deviance in favor of other alternatives.

Depersonalization To treat impersonally, as one of a batch of people.

Designation of deviance The indication that offenses are problems of a certain kind—a sin, a crime, or a sickness.

Determinism The view that a factor or a set of factors causes or makes something else happen (e.g., poverty causes crime).

Deterrence That which discourages or prevents offensive behavior due to the fear of the consequences.

Deviance Behavior, ideas, or attributes which some, though not necessarily all, people find offensive.

Deviance disavowal   The process by which stigmatized people attempt to have individual members of conventional society treat them as "normal."

Deviance displays   Presentations by lecturers in weight-loss organizations which indicate the essential "fat" identity of overweight people and the necessity for a lifelong commitment to the organization (i.e., one can always "pig-out").

Differential association   An explanation for deviant behavior which focuses on the relative amount of conventional and deviant influences that people are exposed to.

Differentiation   The separation or distinction between deviants and conventional people.

Differential law enforcement   Giving greater or less attention to different citizens.

Differential visibility   The relative visibility of people's involvement in deviance (evidentness).

Discreditable   Not easily noticed and not yet known about, but could become found out.

Discredited   Known about or easily noticed shortcoming.

Disidentifiers   "Props" which attest to the conventionality of the person using them (e.g., a "wedding" ring used by an unmarried couple who check into a motel).

Disjunctiveness   One of six features of stereotypes of deviants in which we emphasize a radical separation or difference between what deviants and conventional people do and are.

Dramaturgical analysis   The investigation of social life in terms of the impressions that people create for one another, how they are created, why they are created, and the consequences of their creation.

Ethnomethodology   An orientation for understanding social behavior which examines how people accomplish the activities in which they engage and how people create order in those activities.

Evade   To excuse or justify one's actions which are condemned by society.

Evidentness   How easily perceived (through any of our senses) the deviance is.

Exaggeration   One of six features of stereotypes of deviants in which the most extreme instances of people and behavior are seen as typical of all that is placed into the same category.

Flee   To "run away" from the accusers.

Filtering process   The set of decisions by control agents which leads to fewer and fewer offenders being processed further and further through the control system (e.g., the criminal justice system).

Homogeneity   One of six features of stereotypes of deviants in which those in the same category are seen as all alike.

Identification   The decision (and the process by which that decision is made) as to what *kind* of person someone "really" is. Identification is concerned with *being* and not just *doing*.

Incapacitate   To make a deviant incapable of harming others.

Industrialization   The increasing development of industry and business as the foundation for the country, as opposed to an agricultural society.

Integral   An important part of; intimately tied to.

Master status   That feature of an individual (e.g., being black) which others heavily emphasize, to the exclusion of other characteristics, in dealing with the person.

Method of suspicion   The orientation used by officials to routinely suspect some groups of people more than others of being involved in deviance.

Modification   To substitute a less offensive label for the one which society is conferring upon the offender.

Moral entrepreneurs   Those individuals who seek to define what is respectable and what is deviant for the rest of us.

Mortification of self   Subduing the individual's unique self; humiliating or shaming the individual.

Multiple perspectives   The various views of the people involved in a particular situation.

Myth   A story developed by potential rule-makers which describes the evil that troubles them in terms of a moral framework already accepted by the audience toward whom the story is addressed (e.g., dope use is bad because users become criminals, rapists, and crazy people).

"Normal" crimes   Typifications of certain common and routine crimes used by public defenders and prosecutors in deciding how to handle an offender.

Objective view of deviance   An approach which sees such behaviors as crime, drunkenness, or "improper" sexual behavior as inherently deviant. The very nature of the act makes it offensive.

Official observations   The collection of information based on official (e.g., police) records or from officially designated deviants.

Passing   Presenting oneself as a kind of person that one is not.

Pathology   Harmful, diseased, or aberrant condition in an organism. Society has often been viewed as a social organism.

Persistence   One of six features of stereotypes of deviants which emphasizes that "once a deviant, always a deviant."

Personal identity   The unique biography of an individual to which we attach a name.

Phenomenon of deviance   The interrelated activities of people concerning that which is offensive (such as creating standards of respectability, recognizing deviance, dealing with deviance, and so on).

Primary deviance   Offensive behavior engaged in by a person whom others and the individual see as still a conventional member of society.

Proactive   Through one's own initiative offenders are sought out.

Psychopath or sociopath   A diagnostic category (often a "catchall" category) used to refer to people who are thought to be extremely insensitive to the feelings of others, who do not learn from experience, who are impulsive, and who feel little remorse after doing wrong.

Reactive   Responding to offenders because of the complaints of others.

Redefinition   Speaks to the historical relativity of deviance; a vindication of that which was once deviant.

Reinterpretation   While the "facts" are accepted, the meaning of the allegedly deviant act is changed.

Repudiate   To reject the label of deviance.

Retrospective interpretation   The reinterpretation of past incidents involving a person, in light of a present belief about the person's deviance, in order to support the present belief that the person is deviant and was always like that or was "on the road" to it.

Routinization   Making the handling of deviants orderly and commonplace.

Rule-making   The process by which standards of respectability are created.

Ruling elite   The people who directly or indirectly control the important activities of a society—the economy, the government, and so on.

Secondary deviance   Offensive behavior used to adjust to, retaliate against, or cope with the increasingly less tolerant reactions of others. Those engaged in the offenses are now viewed by others and perhaps by themselves as offensive types of people.

Self-fulfilling prophecy   The process by which, based on our views about what others are like, we act toward others in a manner that causes them to behave in a way that fits our initial view of them.

Self-report studies   Studies based on information supplied by people about themselves (e.g., a questionnaire concerning involvement in delinquency).

Self-seduction   A gradual, stepwise process by which we deceive ourselves as to exactly what we are doing and where we may be heading.

Signification   An approach that emphasizes the potential impact of banning behavior and denouncing the offender on further deviant activities (compatible with the societal reaction approach).

Situated transaction   The interaction between two or more persons which lasts while they are in one another's presence.

Social control   Activities designed to deal with deviance in some way.

Social identity   The general social characteristics of a person, such as age, sex, and occupation, as well as character attributes, such as honesty and friendliness.

Societal reaction   A perspective which focuses on how we handle deviants: the influences on our reactions to deviants and the impact of our reactions.

Sociobiology   The joining of biology and social science for understanding the social behavior of people.

Sociopath   Same as Psychopath.

Status degradation ceremonies   Official ceremonies, such as trials or commitment proceedings, in which the moral identity of the offender is at stake. If the ceremony is "successful," the offender becomes a devalued type of person.

Stereotypes   Typifications concerning people (*see* Typifications).

Stigma   A negative discrepancy between virtual and actual social identity; a failing, shortcoming, or deeply discrediting trait.

Stigma displays   In weight-loss organizations, presentations by lecturers who were once fat themselves, designed to show the similarities between their former selves and troubles and the members' selves and troubles.

Strain theories   Approaches which emphasize that people are conventional until some kind of tension or frustration develops which motivates them to engage in deviance.

Subculture   A group of people who share a common orientation about the world (and that orientation as well); the orientation would have distinctive features as well as features similar to those of the larger culture in which the group lives.

Subjectively problematic view of deviance   An approach which sees deviance as a complex phenomenon of social creation. What is offensive depends on people's interests and activities.

Subordinate status   A position whose occupant must answer to someone above, to a superior; a position with relatively little power.

Symbolic appeasement   An indication to others that one is just as concerned about an issue that troubles them as they are.

Techniques of neutralization   Justifications that offenders use in order to claim that they are conventional members of society but had a legitimate reason for what they did. These techniques can be used to "free" future offenders from the constraints of conventional society before they engage in deviance, or they can be used afterward as rationalizations to account for their deviance.

Theory of the office   The set of perspectives and procedures used by control agents in doing their jobs and in dealing with deviants.

Total institutions   Facilities in which all of the clients' activities are carried out in the same place under the same authority.

Typifications   "Simplified, standardized categories or labels used to place other people and things" (Hawkins and Tiedeman, 1975, p. 82). Characterizations or descriptions of the people or objects that we place into a category, and the indications or signs by which we can recognize people and objects that "belong" in the category.

Urbanization   The increasing concentration of people in cities.

Vindication   Making respectable what was previously deviant.

Virtual social identity   The social characteristics that we expect others to possess in a given situation.

Voluntary deviance   People know what they are doing, and know that it is offensive, but choose to behave offensively anyway.

Bibliography

Adam, Barry D. 1978. *The Survival of Domination: Inferiorization and Everyday Life.* New York: Elsevier.

Ageton, Suzanne S., and Delbert S. Elliott. 1974. "The Effects of Legal Processing on Delinquent Orientations." *Social Problems* 22:87–100.

Akers, Ronald L. 1977. *Deviant Behavior: A Social Learning Approach.* 2d ed. Belmont: Wadsworth.

Akers, Ronald L., et al. 1979. "Social Learning and Deviant Behavior: A Specific Test of a General Theory." *American Sociological Review* 44:636–655.

Altheide, David L. 1976. *Creating Reality: How TV News Distorts Events.* Beverly Hills, Calif.: Sage.

Altheide, David L., and John M. Johnson. 1980. *Bureaucratic Propaganda.* Boston: Allyn & Bacon.

Baldwin, John D., and Janice I. Baldwin. 1980. "Sociobiology or a Balanced Biosocial Theory?" *Pacific Sociological Review* 23:3–27.

Barbera, Henry. 1977. "The Gun: Trigger for Social Change." In Edward Sagarin (ed.), *Deviance and Social Change,* pp. 155–170. Beverly Hills, Calif.: Sage.

Bawer, Theodore (ed.). 1977. "Sexual Survey #4: Current Thinking on Homosexuality." *Medical Aspects of Human Sexuality* 11:110–111.

Becker, Howard S. 1963. *Outsiders: Studies in the Sociology of Deviance.* New

York: Free Press. 1967. "Whose Side Are We On?" *Social Problems* 14:239–247. 1974. "Art as Collective Action." *American Sociological Review* 39:767–776. 1974. "Labelling Theory Reconsidered." In Paul Rock and Mary McIntosh (eds.), *Deviance and Social Control,* pp. 41–66. London: Tavistock. 1978. "Arts and Crafts." *American Journal of Sociology* 83:862–889.

Berk, Richard A., Harold Brackman, and Selma Lesser. 1977. *A Measure of Justice: An Empirical Study of Changes in the California Penal Code, 1955–1971.* New York: Academic Press.

Bernstein, Ilene Nagel, William R. Kelly, and Patricia A. Doyle. 1977. "Societal Reaction to Deviants: The Case of Criminal Defendants." *American Sociological Review* 42:743–755.

Bernstein, Ilene Nagel, et al. 1977. "Charge Reduction: An Intermediary Stage in the Process of Labelling Criminal Defendants." *Social Forces* 56:362–384.

Best, Joel. 1979. "Economic Interests and the Vindication of Deviance: Tobacco in Seventeenth Century Europe." *Sociological Quarterly* 20:171–182.

Bieber, Irving, et al. 1962. *Homosexuality.* New York: Basic Books.

Bischof, Ledford. 1964. *Interpreting Personality Theories.* New York: Harper & Row.

Black, Donald J. 1970. "Production of Crime Rates." *American Sociological Review* 35:733–748.

Black, Donald J., and Albert J. Reiss, Jr. 1970. "Police Control of Juveniles." *American Sociological Review* 35:63–67.

Bogdan, Robert, et al. 1974. "Let Them Eat Programs: Attendants' Perspectives and Programming on Wards in State Schools." *Journal of Health and Social Behavior* 15:142–151.

Bonnie, Richard J., and Charles H. Whitebread II. 1974. *The Marihuana Conviction: A History of Marihuana Prohibition in the United States.* Charlottesville: University Press of Virginia.

Braginsky, Benjamin M., Dorothea D. Braginsky, and Kenneth Ring. 1969. *Methods of Madness: The Mental Hospital as a Last Resort.* New York: Holt.

Brown, Roger. 1965. *Social Psychology.* New York: Free Press.

Bryant, Clifton, D. 1979. *Khaki-Collar Crime: Deviant Behavior in the Military Context.* New York: Free Press.

Buckner, H. Taylor. 1971. *Deviance, Reality and Change.* New York: Random House.

Burgess, Ernest W. 1950. "Comment." *American Journal of Sociology* 56:32–33.

Burgess, Robert L., and Ronald L. Akers. 1966. "A Differential Association–Reinforcement Theory of Criminal Behavior." *Social Problems* 14:128–147.

Butler, Richard R. 1977. "Criminal Victimization Survey of University of Maryland Students." Unpublished manuscript, Institute of Criminal Justice and Criminology, University of Maryland, College Park.

Cameron, Mary Owen. 1964. *The Booster and the Snitch: Department Store Shoplifting.* New York: Free Press.

Caplan, Arthur L. (ed.). 1978. *The Sociobiology Debate: Readings on Ethical and Scientific Issues.* New York: Harper & Row.

Carroll, John S. 1979. "Judgments Made by Parole Boards." In Irene Hanson Frieze, Daniel Bar-Tal, and John S. Carroll (eds.), *New Approaches to Social Problems,* pp. 285–308. San Francisco: Jossey-Bass.

Carroll, Thomas J. 1961. *Blindness: What It Is, What It Does, and How to Live With It.* Boston: Little, Brown.

Carter, Timothy, and Donald Clelland. 1979. "A Neo-Marxian Critique, Formulation and Test of Juvenile Dispositions as a Function of Social Class." *Social Problems* 27:96–108.

Cavan, Ruth Shonle. 1961. "The Concepts of Tolerance and Contraculture as Applied to Delinquency." *Sociological Quarterly* 2:243–258.

Chambliss, William J. 1973. "The Saints and the Roughnecks." *Society* 11:24–31. 1974. "The State, the Law, and the Definition of Behavior as Criminal or Delinquent." In Daniel Glaser (ed.), *Handbook of Criminology*, pp. 7–43. Chicago: Rand McNally.

Chapman, Dennis. 1968. *Sociology and the Stereotype of the Criminal.* London: Tavistock.

Chapman, Loren J., and Jean P. Chapman. 1967. "Genesis of Popular But Erroneous Psycho-Diagnostic Observations." *Journal of Abnormal Psychology* 72:193–204. 1971. "Test Results Are What You Think They Are." *Psychology Today* (November): 18–22, 106–107.

Chase, Allan. 1977. *The Legacy of Malthus.* New York: Knopf.

Clausen, John A., and Carol L. Huffine. 1975. "Sociocultural and Social-Psychological Factors Affecting Social Responses to Mental Disorder." *Journal of Health and Social Behavior* 16:405–420.

Cloward, Richard A., and Lloyd E. Ohlin. 1960. *Delinquency and Opportunity: A Theory of Delinquent Gangs.* Glencoe, Ill: Free Press.

Cloyd, Jerald W. 1977. "The Processing of Misdemeanor Drinking Drivers: The Bureaucratization of the Arrest, Prosecution, and Plea Bargaining Situations." *Social Forces* 56:385–407.

Cohen, Albert K. 1955. *Delinquent Boys: The Culture of the Gang.* New York: Free Press. 1966. *Deviance and Control.* Englewood Cliffs, N.J.: Prentice-Hall.

Cohen, Lawrence E., and Marcus Felson. 1979. "Social Change and Crime Rate Trends: A Routine Activity Approach." *American Sociological Review* 44:588–608.

Cohen, Lawrence E., and James R. Kluegel. 1978. "Determinants of Juvenile Court Dispositions: Ascriptive and Achieved Factors in Two Metropolitan Courts." *American Sociological Review* 43:162–176.

Cole, Stephen, and Robert Lejeune. 1972. "Illness and the Legitimation of Failure." *American Sociological Review* 37:347–356.

Collins, Randall, and Michael Makowsky. 1972. *The Discovery of Society.* New York: Random House.

Conger, Rand D. 1976. "Social Control and Social Learning Models of Delinquent Behavior: A Synthesis." *Criminology* 14:17–40.

Conover, Patrick W. 1976. "A Reassessment of Labeling Theory: A Constructive Response to Criticism." In Lewis A. Coser and Otto N. Larsen (eds.), *The Uses of Controversy in Sociology*, pp. 228–243. New York: Free Press.

Conrad, Peter. 1976. *Identifying Hyperactive Children: The Medicalization of Deviant Behavior.* Lexington, Mass: Heath.

Conrad, Peter, and Joseph W. Schneider. 1980. *Deviance and Medicalization: From Badness to Sickness.* St. Louis: Mosby.

Cory, Christopher. 1979. "The Biology of Martyrdom." *Psychology Today* 13 (November): 39, 43.

Corzine, Jay and Richard Kirby. 1977. "Cruising the Truckers: Sexual Encounters in a Highway Rest Area." *Urban Life* 6:171–192.

Cowen, Emory L., et al. 1967. "Development and Evaluation of an Attitude to Deafness Scale." *Journal of Personality and Social Psychology* 6:183–191.

Cowen, Emory L., Rita P. Underberg, and Ronald T. Verrillo. 1958. "The Development and Testing of an Attitude to Blindness Scale." *Journal of Social Psychology* 48:297–304.

Craig, Maude M., and Selma J. Glick. 1963. "Ten Years' Experience with the Glueck Social Prediction Table." *Crime and Delinquency* 9:249–261.

Crespo, Manuel. 1974. "The Career of the School Skipper." In Jack Hass and Bill Shaffir (eds.), *Decency and Deviance,* pp. 129–145. Toronto: McClelland & Stewart.

Cressey, Donald R. 1953. *Other People's Money: A Study in the Social Psychology of Embezzlement.* New York: Free Press.

Cromer, Gerald. 1978. "Character Assassination in the Press." In Charles Winick (ed.), *Deviance and Mass Media,* pp. 225–241. Beverly Hills, Calif.: Sage.

Currie, Elliott P. 1968. "Crimes Without Criminals: Witchcraft and Its Control in Renaissance Europe." *Law and Society Review* 3:7–32.

Dahrendorf, Ralph. 1958. "Out of Utopia: Toward A Reorientation of Sociological Analysis." *American Journal of Sociology* 64:115–127. 1959. *Class and Class Conflict in Industrial Society.* Stanford, Calif.: Stanford.

Davis, Fred. 1961. "Deviance Disavowal: The Management of Strained Interaction by the Visibly Handicapped." *Social Problems* 9:120–132.

Davis, Nanette J. 1980. *Sociological Constructions of Deviance: Perspectives and Issues in the Field.* 2d ed. Dubuque, Iowa: William C. Brown.

Davison, Gerald C., and John M. Neale. 1978. *Abnormal Psychology: An Experimental Clinical Approach.* 2d ed. New York: Wiley.

Delph, Edward William. 1978. *The Silent Community: Public Homosexual Encounters.* Beverly Hills, Calif.: Sage.

Denzin, Norman K. 1970. "Rules of Conduct and the Study of Deviant Behavior: Some Notes on the Social Relationship." In Jack D. Douglas (ed.), *Deviance and Respectability: The Social Construction of Moral Meanings,* pp. 120–159. New York: Basic Books.

Deutscher, Irwin. 1973. *What We Say/What We Do.* Glenview, Ill.: Scott, Foresman.

Dickson, Donald T. 1968. "Bureaucracy and Morality: An Organizational Perspective on a Moral Crusade." *Social Problems* 16:143–156.

Dion, Karen. 1972. "Physical Attractiveness and Evaluation of Children's Transgressions." *Journal of Personality and Social Psychology* 24:207–213.

Dollard, John, et al. 1939. *Frustration and Aggression.* New Haven: Yale.

Dominick, Joseph R. 1978. "Crime and Law Enforcement in the Mass Media." In Charles Winick (ed.), *Deviance and Mass Media,* pp. 105–128. Beverly Hills, Calif.: Sage.

Douglas, Jack D. 1970. "Deviance and Respectability: The Social Construction of Moral Meanings." In Jack D. Douglas (ed.), *Deviance and Respectability: The*

Social Construction of Moral Meanings, pp. 3–30. New York: Basic Books. 1976. *Investigative Social Research: Individual and Team Field Research* Beverly Hills, Calif.: Sage. 1977. "Shame and Deceit in Creative Deviance." In Edward Sagarin (ed.), *Deviance and Social Change,* pp. 59–86. Beverly Hills, Calif.: Sage.

Douglas, Jack D., and John M. Johnson (eds.). 1977. *Official Deviance: Readings in Malfeasance, Misfeasance, and Other Forms of Corruption.* Philadelphia: Lippincott.

Douglas, Jack D., Paul K. Rasmussen, and Carol Ann Flanagan. 1977. *The Nude Beach.* Beverly Hills, Calif.: Sage.

Durkheim, Emile. 1964. *The Division of Labor in Society.* Trans. George Simpson. New York: Free Press. 1966. *The Rules of Sociological Method.* Trans. Sarah A. Solovay and John H. Mueller. Ed. George E. G. Catlin. 8th ed. New York: Free Press.

Edgerton, Robert B. 1967. *The Cloak of Competence: Stigma in the Lives of the Mentally Retarded.* Berkeley: University of California Press. 1976. *Deviance: A Cross-Cultural Perspective.* Menlo Park, Calif.: Cummings.

Elliott, Delbert S., and Suzanne S. Ageton. 1980. "Reconciling Race and Class Differences in Self-Reported and Official Estimates of Delinquency." *American Sociological Review* 45:95–110.

Emerson, Robert M. 1969. *Judging Delinquents: Context and Process in Juvenile Court.* Chicago: Aldine.

Empey, LaMar T. 1978. *American Delinquency: Its Meaning and Construction.* Homewood, Ill.: Dorsey.

Ennis, Philip H. 1967. *Criminal Victimization in the United States: A Report of a National Survey.* Chicago: National Opinion Research Center.

Erickson, Maynard L., Jack P. Gibbs, and Gary F. Jensen. 1977. "The Deterrence Doctrine and the Perceived Certainty of Legal Punishments." *American Sociological Review* 42:305–317.

Erikson, Kai T. 1964. "Notes on the Sociology of Deviance." In Howard S. Becker (ed.), *The Other Side: Perspectives on Deviance,* pp. 9–21. New York: Free Press. 1966. *Wayward Puritans: A Study in the Sociology of Deviance.* New York: Wiley.

Erman, M. David, and Richard J. Lundman (eds.). 1978. *Corporate and Governmental Deviance: Problems of Organizational Behavior in Contemporary Society.* New York: Oxford.

Essex, Marilyn, et al. 1980. "On Weinstein's 'Patient Attitudes toward Mental Hospitalization': A Review of Quantitative Research." *Journal of Health and Social Behavior.* 21:393–396.

Farrington, David P. 1977. "The Effects of Public Labeling." *British Journal of Criminology* 17:112–125.

Faulkner, Robert R., and Douglas B. McGaw. 1977. "Uneasy Homecoming: Stages in the Reentry Transition of Vietnam Veterans." *Urban Life* 6:303–328.

Fiegelman, William. 1974. "Peeping: The Pattern of Voyeurism Among Construction Workers." *Urban Life* 3:35–49.

Fisher, Sethard. 1972. "Stigma and Deviant Careers in Schools." *Social Problems* 20:78–83.

Fogel, Max L. 1980. "Warning: Auto Fumes May Lower Your Kid's IQ." *Psychology Today* 13 (January): 108.

Foster, Jack D., Simon Dinitz, and Walter C. Reckless. 1972. "Perceptions of Stigma Following Public Intervention for Delinquent Behavior." *Social Problems* 20:200–209.

Fox, Richard G. 1971. "The XYY Offender: A Modern Myth?" *Journal of Criminal Law, Criminology and Police Science* 62:59–73.

Fox, Vernon. 1976. *Introduction to Criminology.* Englewood Cliffs, N.J.: Prentice-Hall.

Freedman, Jonathan L., and Anthony N. Doob. 1968. *Deviancy: The Psychology of Being Different.* New York: Academic Press.

Freeman, Roger D., Susan F. Malkin, and Jane O. Hastings. 1975. "Psychosocial Problems of Deaf Children and Their Families: A Comparative Study." *American Annals of the Deaf* 120:391–405.

Freidson, Eliot. 1966. "Disability as Social Deviance." In Marvin B. Sussman (ed.), *Sociology and Rehabilitation,* pp. 71–99. Washington, D.C.: American Sociological Association.

Gaensbauer, Theodore J. 1979. Review of Leonard J. Hippchen (ed.), *Ecologic-Biochemical Approaches to Treatment of Delinquents and Criminals* (New York: Van Nostrand Reinhold, 1978). *Crime and Delinquency* 25:509–511.

Galliher, John F., and Allyn Walker. 1977. "The Puzzle of the Social Origins of the Marihuana Tax Act of 1937." *Social Problems* 24:367–376.

Garfinkel, Harold. 1956. "Conditions of Successful Degradation Ceremonies." *American Journal of Sociology* 61:420–424. 1967. *Studies in Ethnomethodology.* Englewood Cliffs, N.J.: Prentice-Hall.

Geis, Gilbert, and Robert F. Meier (eds.). 1977. *White-Collar Crime: Offenses in Business, Politics, and the Professions.* New York: Free Press.

Gergen, Kenneth J. 1972. "Multiple Identity: The Healthy, Happy Human Being Wears Many Masks." *Psychology Today* 5 (May): 31–35, 64.

Gibbons, Don C. 1977. *Society, Crime, and Criminal Careers.* 3d ed. Englewood Cliffs, N.J.: Prentice-Hall.

Gibbons, Don C., and Joseph F. Jones. 1975. *The Study of Deviance: Perspectives and Problems.* Englewood Cliffs, N.J.: Prentice-Hall.

Gibbs, Jack P. 1977. "Social Control, Deterrence, and Perspectives on Social Order." *Social Forces:* 408–423.

Gibbs, Jack P., and Maynard L. Erickson. 1979. "Conceptions of Criminal and Delinquent Acts." *Deviant Behavior* 1:71–100.

Gibbs, Leonard. 1974. "The Effect of Juvenile Legal Procedure on Juvenile Offenders' Self Attitudes." *Journal of Research in Crime and Delinquency* 11:51–55.

Ginsberg, Irving J., and James R. Greenley. 1978. "Competing Theories of Marijuana Use: A Longitudinal Study." *Journal of Health and Social Behavior* 19:22–34.

Giordano, Peggy C. 1976. "The Sense of Injustice? An Analysis of Juveniles' Reactions to the Justice System." *Criminology* 14:93–111.

Glaser, Daniel. 1956. "Criminality Theories and Behavioral Images." *American Journal of Sociology* 61:433–444. 1978. *Crime in our Changing Society.* New York: Holt.

Glueck, Sheldon, and Eleanor Glueck. 1956. *Physique and Delinquency.* New York: Harper & Row. 1959. *Predicting Delinquency and Crime.* Cambridge, Mass.: Harvard.

Glueck, Sheldon, and Eleanor Glueck (eds.). 1972. *Identification of Predelinquents.* New York: Intercontinental Medical Book.

Goddard, Henry H. 1912. *The Kallikak Family.* New York: Macmillan. 1920. *Human Efficiency and Levels of Intelligence.* Princeton: Princeton University Press.

Goffman, Erving. 1959. *The Presentation of Self in Everyday Life.* Garden City, N.Y.: Doubleday/Anchor. 1961. *Asylums.* Chicago: Aldine. 1963. *Stigma: Notes on the Management of Spoiled Identity.* Englewood Cliffs, N.J.: Prentice-Hall.

Gold, Martin. 1970. *Delinquent Behavior in an American City.* Belmont, Calif.: Brooks/Cole.

Gold, Martin, and Jay R. Williams. 1969. "The Effect of Getting Caught: Apprehension of the Juvenile Offender as a Cause of Subsequent Delinquencies." *Prospectus* 3:1–12.

Goldstein, Kurt. 1950. "Prefrontal Lobotomy: Analysis and Warning." *Scientific American* 182 (February): 44–47.

Goode, Erich. 1978. *Deviant Behavior: An Interactionist Approach.* Englewood Cliffs, N.J.: Prentice-Hall.

Goring, Charles. 1913. *The English Convict: A Statistical Study.* London: H. M. Stationery Office.

Gouldner, Alvin W. 1968. "The Sociologist as Partisan: Sociology and the Welfare State." *American Sociologist* 3:103–116. 1970. *The Coming Crisis of Western Sociology.* New York: Avon.

Gove, Walter R. (ed.). 1975. *The Labelling of Deviance: Evaluating a Perspective.* New York: Russell Sage.

Graham, Billy. 1979. Interview on "Donahue," WGN-TV, Chicago, October 11. Donahue Transcript #10119.

Green, R. Glen. 1978. "Treatment of Penitentiary Inmates." In Leonard J. Hippchen (ed.), *Ecologic-Biochemical Approaches to Treatment of Delinquents and Criminals,* pp. 269–283. New York: Van Nostrand Reinhold.

Gregory, Michael S., Anita Silvers, and Diane Sutch (eds.). 1978. *Sociobiology and Human Nature.* San Francisco: Jossey-Bass.

Griffin, Brenda S., and Charles T. Griffin. 1978. *Juvenile Delinquency in Perspective.* New York: Harper & Row.

Gusfield, Joseph R. 1963. *Symbolic Crusade: Status Politics and the American Temperance Movement.* Urbana: University of Illinois Press.

Haber, Lawrence D., and Richard T. Smith. 1971. "Disability and Deviance: Normative Adaptations of Role Behavior." *American Sociological Review* 36:87–97.

Hagan, John. 1974. "Extra-Legal Attributes and Criminal Sentencing: An Assessment of a Sociological View." *Law and Society Review* 8:357–383.

Hagan, John, and Ilene N. Bernstein. 1979. "Conflict in Context: The Sanctioning of Draft Resisters, 1963–76." *Social Problems* 27:109–122.

Hagan, John, and Jeffrey Leon. 1977. "Rediscovering Delinquency: Social History,

Political Ideology and the Sociology of Law." *American Sociological Review* 42:587–598.

Hall, Jerome. 1952. *Theft, Law, and Society.* 2d ed. Indianapolis: Bobbs-Merrill.

Hallowell, A. Irving. 1959. "Fear and Anxiety as Cultural and Individual Variables in Primitive Society." In Marvin K. Opler (ed.), *Culture and Mental Health: Cross-Cultural Studies,* pp. 41–62. New York: Macmillan.

Hanks, Jane R., and L. M. Hanks, Jr. 1948. "The Physically Handicapped in Certain Non-Occidental Societies." *Journal of Social Issues* 4:11–20.

Hansson, Robert O., and Beverly J. Duffield. 1976. "Physical Attractiveness and the Attribution of Epilepsy." *Journal of Social Psychology* 99:233–240.

Harp, John, and Philip Taietz. 1966. "Academic Integrity and Social Structure: A Study of Cheating Among College Students." *Social Problems* 13:365–373.

Harris, Anthony R. 1975. "Imprisonment and the Expected Value of Criminal Choice: A Specification and Test of Aspects of the Labeling Perspective." *American Sociological Review* 40:71–87.

Harris, Marvin. 1974. *Cows, Pigs, Wars and Witches: The Riddles of Culture.* New York: Random House.

Harris, Richard N. 1973. *The Police Academy: An Inside View.* New York: Wiley.

Hartjen, Clayton A. 1978. *Crime and Criminalization.* 2d ed. New York: Holt.

Hawkins, Richard, and Gary Tiedeman. 1975. *The Creation of Deviance: Interpersonal and Organizational Determinants.* Columbus, Ohio: Merrill.

Hepburn, John R. 1977. "Official Deviance and Spoiled Identity: Delinquents and Their Significant Others." *Pacific Sociological Review* 20:163–179, 1978. "Race and the Decision to Arrest: An Analysis of Warrants Issued." *Journal of Research in Crime and Delinquency* 15:54–73.

Heumann, Milton. 1977. *Plea Bargaining: The Experiences of Prosecutors, Judges, and Defense Attorneys.* Chicago: University of Chicago Press.

Heyl, Barbara Sherman. 1979. *The Madam as Entrepreneur: Career Management in House Prostitution.* New Brunswick, N.J.: Transaction.

Higgins, Paul C. 1979. "Deviance Within a Disabled Community: Peddling Among the Deaf." *Pacific Sociological Review* 22:96–114. 1980. *Outsiders in a Hearing World: A Sociology of Deafness.* Beverly Hills, Calif.: Sage.

Hindelang, Michael J. 1974. "Decisions of Shoplifting Victims to Invoke the Criminal Justice Process." *Social Problems* 21:580–593. 1978. "Race and Involvement in Common Law Personal Crimes." *American Sociological Review* 43:93–109.

Hindelang, Michael J., and Michael Gottfredson. 1976. "The Victim's Decision Not to Invoke the Criminal Justice Process." In William F. McDonald (ed.), *Criminal Justice and the Victim,* pp. 57–78. Beverly Hills, Calif.: Sage.

Hindelang, Michael J., Travis Hirschi, and Joseph G. Weis. 1979. "Correlates of Delinquency: The Illusion of Discrepancy Between Self-Report and Official Measures." *American Sociological Review* 44:995–1014.

Hippchen, Leonard J. 1977. "Contributions of Biochemical Research to Criminological Theory." In Robert F. Meier (ed.), *Theory in Criminology: Contemporary Views.* pp. 57–63. Beverly Hills, Calif.: Sage.

Hippchen, Leonard J. (ed.). 1978. *Ecologic-Biochemical Approaches to Treatment of Delinquents and Criminals.* New York: Van Nostrand Reinhold.

Hirschi, Travis. 1969. *Causes of Delinquency.* Berkeley: University of California Press. 1975. "Labelling Theory and Juvenile Delinquency." In Walter R. Gove (ed.), *The Labelling of Deviance: Evaluating a Perspective,* pp. 181–203. New York: Sage.

Hirschi, Travis, and Michael J. Hindelang. 1977. "Intelligence and Delinquency: A Revisionist Review." *American Sociological Review* 42:571–587.

Hoffer, Abram. 1978. "Some Theoretical Principles Basic to Orthomolecular Psychiatric Treatment." In Leonard J. Hippchen (ed.), *Ecologic-Biochemical Approaches to Treatment of Delinquents and Criminals,* pp. 31–55. New York: Van Nostrand Reinhold.

Hofstadter, Richard. 1955. *Social Darwinism in American Thought.* Boston: Beacon Press.

Hollander, E. P. 1958. "Conformity, Status and Idiosyncrasy Credit." *Psychological Review* 65:117–127.

Hollingshead, August B., and Frederick C. Redlich. 1958. *Social Class and Mental Illness: A Community Study.* New York: Wiley.

Hooton, Earnest A. 1939. *Crime and Man.* Cambridge, Mass.: Harvard.

Hoover, John Edgar. 1961. *Uniform Crime Reports 1960. U.S. Department of Justice.* Washington, D.C.: U.S. Government Printing Office. 1971. *Uniform Crime Reports for the United States 1970. U.S. Department of Justice.* Washington, D.C.: U.S. Government Printing Office.

Horowitz, Irving Louis, and Martin Liebowitz. 1968. "Social Deviance and Political Marginality: Toward a Redefinition of the Relation Between Sociology and Politics." *Social Problems* 15:280–296.

Hughes, Everett C. 1945. "Dilemmas and Contradictions of Status." *American Journal of Sociology* 50:353–359.

Humphreys, Laud. 1972. *Out of the Closets: The Sociology of Homosexual Liberation.* Englewood Cliffs, N.J.: Prentice-Hall.

Illich, Ivan. 1976. *Medical Nemesis: The Expropriation of Health.* Toronto: Bantam.

Ingraham, Barton L., and G. W. Smith. 1972. "The Use of Electronics in the Observation and Control of Human Behavior and Its Possible Use in Rehabilitation and Parole." *Issues in Criminology* 7:35–53.

Irwin, John. 1970. *The Felon.* Englewood Cliffs, N.J.: Prentice-Hall.

Jensen, Gary. 1972. "Delinquency and Adolescent Self-Conceptions: A Study of the Personal Relevance of Infraction." *Social Problems* 20:84–103.

Johnson, John M., and Jack D. Douglas (eds.). 1978. *Crime at the Top: Deviance in Business and the Professions.* Philadelphia: Lippincott.

Johnson, Weldon T., Robert E. Petersen, and L. Edward Wells. 1977. "Arrest Probabilities for Marijuana Users as Indicators of Selective Law Enforcement." *American Journal of Sociology* 83:681–699.

Jones, Edward E., and Keith Davis. 1965. "From Acts to Dispositions: The Attribution Process in Person Perception." In Leonard Berkowitz (ed.), *Advances in Experimental Social Psychology,* Vol. 2, pp. 219–266. New York: Academic Press.

Jones, Edward E., and Richard E. Nisbett. 1971. *The Actor and the Observer: Divergent Perceptions of the Causes of Behavior.* Morristown, N.J.: General Learning Corp.

Kadish, Sanford H., and Monrad G. Paulsen. 1969. *Criminal Law and Its Processes.* Boston: Little, Brown.

Kandel, Denise, and Richard Faust. 1975. "Sequence and Stages in Patterns of Adolescent Drug Use." *Archives of General Psychiatry* 32:923–932.

Kanouse, David E., and L. Reid Hanson, Jr. 1972. "Negativity in Evaluations." In Edward E. Jones et al. (eds.), *Attribution: Perceiving the Causes of Behavior,* pp. 47–62. Morristown, N.J.: General Learning Corp.

Kelley, Harold H. 1971. *Attribution in Social Interaction.* Morristown, N.J.: General Learning Corp.

Kidder, Louise H., and Ellen S. Cohn. 1979. "Public Views of Crime and Crime Prevention." In Irene Hanson Frieze, Daniel Bar-Tal, and John S. Carroll (eds.), *New Approaches to Social Problems,* pp. 237–264. San Francisco: Jossey-Bass.

Kinsey, Alfred C., Wardell B. Pomeroy, and Clyde E. Martin. 1948. *Sexual Behavior in the Human Male.* Philadelphia: Saunders.

Kinsey, Alfred C., et al. 1953. *Sexual Behavior in the Human Female.* Philadelphia: Saunders.

Kitsuse, John I. 1962. "Societal Reaction to Deviance: Problems of Theory and Method." *Social Problems* 9:247–256. 1972. "Deviance, Deviant Behavior and Deviants: Some Conceptual Problems." In William J. Filstead (ed.), *An Introduction to Deviance: Readings in the Process of Making Deviants,* pp. 233–243. Chicago: Markham.

Kitsuse, John I., and Aaron V. Cicourel. 1963. "A Note on the Uses of Official Statistics." *Social Problems* 11:131–139.

Kittrie, Nicholas N. 1971. *The Right to Be Different: Deviance and Enforced Therapy.* Baltimore: Johns Hopkins.

Klockars, Carl B., and Finbarr W. O'Connor (eds.). 1979. *Deviance and Decency: The Ethics of Research with Human Subjects.* Beverly Hills, Calif.: Sage.

Kluckhohn, Clyde, and Dorothea Leighton. 1946. *The Navaho.* Cambridge, Mass.: Harvard.

Krohn, Marvin D., and Ronald L. Akers. 1977. "An Alternative View of the Labelling Versus Psychiatric Perspectives on Societal Reaction to Mental Illness." *Social Forces* 56:341–361.

Kuhn, Thomas S. 1970. *The Structure of Scientific Revolutions.* 2d ed. Chicago: University of Chicago Press.

LaFave, Wayne R. 1965. *Arrest: The Decision to Take a Suspect into Custody.* Boston: Little, Brown.

LaPiere, Richard T. 1959. *The Freudian Ethic.* New York: Duell, Sloan & Pearce.

Laslett, Barbara, and Carol A. B. Warren. 1975. "Losing Weight: The Organizational Promotion of Behavior Change." *Social Problems* 23:69–80.

Lauderdale, Pat. 1976. "Deviance and Moral Boundaries." *American Sociological Review* 41:660–676.

Lehtinen, Marlene W. 1979. "Controlling the Minds and Bodies of Prisoners— Without Prisons." *Barrister* 6:11–13, 54–55.

Lejeune, Robert. 1977. "The Management of a Mugging." *Urban Life* 6:123–148.

Lejeune, Robert, and Nicholas Alex. 1973. "On Being Mugged: The Event and Its Aftermath." *Urban Life* 2:259–287.

Lemert, Edwin M. 1951. *Social Pathology: A Systematic Approach to the Theory of Sociopathic Behavior.* New York: McGraw-Hill.

Levine, Martin P. 1979. "Gay Ghetto." *Journal of Homosexuality* 4:363–377.

Levinson, Harry. 1978. "Abrasive Personality at the Office." *Psychology Today* 11 (May): 78–80.

Levitin, Teresa E. 1975. "Deviants as Active Participants in the Labeling Process: The Visibly Handicapped." *Social Problems* 22:548–557.

Liazos, Alexander. 1972. "The Poverty of the Sociology of Deviance: Nuts, Sluts, and Preverts." *Social Problems* 20:103–120.

Lindesmith, Alfred R. 1965. *The Addict and the Law.* Bloomington: Indiana University Press.

Liska, Allen E., and Mark Tausig. 1979. "Theoretical Interpretations of Social Class and Racial Differentials in Legal Decision-Making for Juveniles." *Sociological Quarterly* 20:197–207.

Lofland, John. 1969. *Deviance and Identity.* Englewood Cliffs, N.J.: Prentice-Hall.

Luckenbill, David F. 1977. "Criminal Homicide as a Transaction." *Social Problems* 25:176–186.

Lundman, Richard, Richard E. Sykes, and John P. Clark. 1978. "Police Control of Juveniles: A Replication." *Journal of Research in Crime and Delinquency* 15:74–91.

McAuliffe, William E. 1975. "Beyond Secondary Deviance: Negative Labelling and Its Effect on the Heroin Addict." In Walter R. Gove (ed.), *The Labelling of Deviance: Evaluating a Perspective,* pp. 205–242. New York: Sage.

McCaghy, Charles H. 1976. *Deviant Behavior: Crime, Conflict, and Interest Groups.* New York: Macmillan.

Mankoff, Milton. 1971. "Societal Reaction and Career Deviance: A Critical Analysis." *Sociological Quarterly* 12:204–218.

Markle, Gerald E., and Ronald J. Troyer. 1979. "Smoke Gets in Your Eyes: Cigarette Smoking as Deviant Behavior." *Social Problems* 26:611–625.

Martindale, Don. 1961. *The Nature and Types of Sociological Theory.* Boston: Houghton Mifflin.

Matza, David. 1964. *Delinquency and Drift.* New York: Wiley. 1969. *Becoming Deviant.* Englewood Cliffs, N.J.: Prentice Hall.

Mednick, Sarnoff A., and Karl O. Christiansen (eds.). 1977. *Biosocial Bases of Criminal Behavior.* New York: Gardner Press.

Meier, Robert F., and Weldon T. Johnson. 1977. "Deterrence as Social Control: The Legal and Extralegal Production of Conformity." *American Sociological Review* 42:292–304.

Mendelsohn, Robert S. 1980. *Confessions of a Medical Heretic.* New York: Warner Books.

Mercer, Jane R. 1973. *Labeling the Mentally Retarded.* Berkeley: University of California Press.

Merton, Robert K. 1957. *Social Theory and Social Structure.* Rev. ed. Glencoe, Ill.: Free Press.

Meyerson, Lee. 1948. "Physical Disability as a Social Psychological Problem." *Journal of Social Issues* 4:2–10.

Miller, Gale. 1978. *Odd Jobs: The World of Deviant Work.* Englewood Cliffs, N.J.: Prentice-Hall.

Miller, Walter B. 1958. "Lower Class Culture as a Generating Milieu of Gang Delinquency." *Journal of Social Issues* 14:5–19.

Millman, Marcia. 1977. "Masking Doctors' Errors." *Human Behavior* 6:16–23.

Mills, C. Wright. 1943. "The Professional Ideology of Social Pathologists." *American Journal of Sociology* 49:165–180. 1959. *The Sociological Imagination.* London: Oxford.

Mischel, Walter, 1968. *Personality and Assessment.* New York: Wiley.

Moland, John, Jr. 1975. "Social Status and Black-White Perceptions of Police Behavior." *Journal of Social and Behavioral Sciences* 21:13–29.

Montanino, Fred. 1977. "Directions in the Study of Deviance: A Biographic Essay, 1960–1977." In Edward Sagarin (ed.), *Deviance and Social Change,* pp. 277–304. Beverly Hills, Calif.: Sage.

Murphy, Fred J., Mary M. Shirley, and Helen L. Witmen. 1946. "The Incidence of Hidden Delinquency." *American Journal of Orthopsychiatry* 16:686–696.

Musto, David F. 1973. *The American Disease: Origins of Narcotic Control.* New Haven, Conn.: Yale.

Neubeck, Kenneth J. 1979. *Social Problems: A Critical Approach.* Glenview, Ill.: Scott, Foresman.

Newton, Esther. 1979. *Mother Camp: Female Impersonators in America.* Chicago: University of Chicago Press.

Nuehring, Elane, and Gerald E. Markle. 1974. "Nicotine and Norms: The Re-Emergence of a Deviant Behavior." *Social Problems* 21:513–527.

O'Connor, Gerald G. 1970. "The Impact of Initial Detention Upon Male Delinquents." *Social Problems* 18:194–199.

Palmer, C. Eddie. 1977. "Microecology and Labeling Theory: A Proposed Merger." In H. Paul Chalfant, Evans W. Curry, and C. Eddie Palmer (eds.), *Sociological Stuff,* pp. 12–17. Dubuque, Iowa: Kendall/Hunt.

Palmer, Tony. 1976. *All You Need Is Love: The Story of Popular Music.* Ed. Paul Medlicott. London: Weidenfeld, Nicholson & Chappell.

Parisi, Nicolette, et al. (eds.). 1979. *Sourcebook of Criminal Justice Statistics—1978.* Albany, N.Y.: Criminal Justice Research Center. Washington, D.C.: U.S. Government Printing Office.

Pepitone, Albert. 1975. "Social Psychological Perspectives on Crime and Punishment." *Journal of Social Issues* 31:197–216.

Pfohl, Stephen. 1977. "The 'Discovery' of Child Abuse." *Social Problems* 24:310–323.

Pfuhl, Erdwin H., Jr. 1978. "The Unwed Father: A 'Non-Deviant' Rule Breaker." *Sociological Quarterly* 19:113–128. 1980. *The Deviance Process.* New York: Van Nostrand.

Piliavin, Irving, and Scott Briar. 1964. "Police Encounters with Juveniles." *American Journal of Sociology* 70:206–214.

Platt, Anthony M. 1977. *The Child Savers: The Invention of Delinquency.* 2d ed. Chicago: University of Chicago Press.

Plummer, Kenneth. 1975. *Sexual Stigma: An Interactionist Account.* London: Routledge.

Ponse, Barbara. 1977. "Secrecy in the Lesbian World." In Carol Warren (ed.), *Sexuality: Encounters, Identities, and Relationships,* pp. 53–78. Beverly Hills, Calif.: Sage. 1978. *Identities in the Lesbian World: The Social Construction of Self.* Westport, Conn.: Greenwood Press.

Posner, Judith. 1980. "On Sociology Chic: Notes on a Possible Direction for Symbolic Interaction." *Urban Life* 9:103–112.

Powis, David. 1977. *The Signs of Crime: A Field Manual for Police.* New York: John Jay Press.

Prescott, James W. 1979. "Alienation of Affection." *Psychology Today* 13 (December): 124.

Quinney, Richard. 1970. *The Social Reality of Crime.* Boston: Little, Brown. 1979. *Criminology.* 2d ed. Boston: Little, Brown.

Radosevich, Marcia, et al. 1979. "The Sociology of Adolescent Drug and Drinking Behavior: A Review of the State of the Field: Part 1." *Deviant Behavior* 1:15–35.

Rasmussen, Paul K., and Lauren L. Kohn. 1977. "The New Masseuse: Play for Pay." In Carol Warren (ed.), *Sexuality: Encounters, Identities, and Relationships,* pp. 11–32. Beverly Hills, Calif.: Sage.

Reasons, Charles E. 1970. "A Developmental Model for the Analysis of Social Problems: Prostitution and Moral Reform in Twentieth Century America." Paper presented at the Pacific Sociological Association meeting, Anaheim, Calif. 1974. *The Criminologist: Crime and the Criminal.* Pacific Palisades, Calif.: Goodyear.

Reasons, Charles E., and Russell L. Kaplan. 1975. "Tear Down the Walls? Some Functions of Prisons." *Crime and Delinquency* 21:360–372.

Reid, Sue Titus. 1979. *Crime and Criminology.* 2d ed. New York: Holt.

Reiss, Albert J. 1971. *The Police and the Public.* New Haven, Conn.: Yale.

Rennie, Ysabel. 1978. *The Search for Criminal Man: A Conceptual History of the Dangerous Offender.* Lexington, Mass.: Lexington Books.

Revitch, Eugene. 1978. "Sexually Motivated Burglaries." *Bulletin of the American Academy of Psychiatry and the Law* 6:277–283.

Robin, Gerald D. 1963. "Patterns of Department Store Shoplifting." *Crime and Delinquency* 9:163–172. 1969. "Employees as Offenders." *Journal of Research in Crime and Delinquency* 6:17–33. 1970. "The Corporate and Judicial Disposition of Employee Thieves." In Erwin O. Smigel and H. Laurence Ross (eds.), *Crimes Against Bureaucracy,* pp. 119–142. New York: Van Nostrand Reinhold.

Robison, Sophia. 1936. *Can Delinquency Be Measured?* New York: Columbia.

Roby, Pamela A. 1969. "Politics and Criminal Law: Revision of the New York State Penal Law on Prostitution." *Social Problems* 17:83–109.

Rogers, Joseph W., and M. D. Buffalo. 1974. "Fighting Back: Nine Modes of Adaptation to a Deviant Label." *Social Problems* 22:101–118.

Rolph, C. H. (ed.). 1955. *Women of the Streets: A Sociological Study of the Common Prostitute.* London: Secker & Warburg.

Rose, Vicki McNickle, and Susan C. Randall. 1978. "Where Have All the Rapists Gone? An Illustration of the Attrition-of-Justice Phenomenon." In James A. Inciardi and Anne E. Pottieger (eds.), *Violent Crime: Historical and Contemporary Issues,* pp. 75–89. Beverly Hills, Calif.: Sage.

Rosenhan, D. L. 1973. "On Being Sane in Insane Places." *Science* 179 (January 19): 250–258.

Rossi, Peter H., et al. 1974. "The Seriousness of Crimes: Normative Structure and Individual Differences." *American Sociological Review* 39:224–237.

Rubington, Earl. 1978. "Variations in Bottle-Gang Controls." In Earl Rubington and Martin S. Weinberg (eds.), *Deviance: The Interactionist Perspective*, pp. 383–391. New York: Macmillan.

Rubington, Earl, and Martin S. Weinberg. 1978. *Deviance: The Interactionist Perspective*. 3d ed. New York: Macmillan.

Rushing, William A. (ed.). 1969. *Deviant Behavior and Social Process*. Chicago: Rand McNally.

Rushing, William. 1978. "Status Resources, Societal Reactions, and Mental Hospital Admission." *American Sociological Review* 43:521–533.

Rushing, William, and Jack Esco. 1977. "Status Resources and Behavioral Deviance as Contingencies of Societal Reaction." *Social Forces* 56:132–147.

Safilios-Rothschild, Constantina. 1970. *The Sociology and Social Psychology of Disability and Rehabilitation* New York: Random House.

Sagarin, Edward. 1969. *Odd Man In: Societies of Deviants in America*. Chicago: Quadrangle. 1975. *Deviants and Deviance: An Introduction to the Study of Disvalued People and Behavior*. New York: Praeger.

Sagarin, Edward, and Fred Montanino (eds.). 1977. *Deviants: Voluntary Actors in a Hostile World*. Morristown, N.J.: General Learning Press.

Sanders, William B. 1976. *Juvenile Delinquency*. New York: Praeger. 1977. *Detective Work: A Study of Criminal Investigations*. New York: Free Press.

Sarbin, Theodore R., and Jeffrey E. Miller. 1970. "Demonism Revisited: The XYY Chromosomal Anomaly." *Issues in Criminology* 5:195–207.

Scarpitti, Frank R., and Paul T. McFarlane (eds.). 1975. *Deviance: Action, Reaction, Interaction*. Reading, Mass.: Addison-Wesley.

Schauss, Alex. 1979. Interview on "Donahue," WGN-TV, Chicago, November 5. Donahue Transcript #11059.

Scheff, Thomas J. 1963. "Decision Rules, Types of Error, and Their Consequences in Medical Diagnosis." *Behavioral Science* 8:97–107. 1966. *Being Mentally Ill: A Sociological Theory*. Chicago: Aldine. 1974. "The Labelling Theory of Mental Illness." *American Sociological Review* 39:444–452. 1975. "Schizophrenia as Ideology." In Thomas J. Scheff (ed.), *Labeling Madness*, pp. 5–12. Englewood Cliffs, N.J.: Prentice-Hall.

Schneider, Joseph W. 1978. "Deviant Drinking as a Disease: Alcoholism as a Social Accomplishment." *Social Problems* 25:361–372.

Schuessler, Karl F., and Donald R. Cressey. 1950. "Personality Characteristics of Criminals." *American Journal of Sociology* 55:476–484.

Schur, Edwin M. 1971. *Labeling Deviant Behavior: Its Sociological Implications*. New York: Harper & Row. 1975. "Comments." In Walter R. Gove (ed.), *The Labelling of Deviance: Evaluating a Perspective*, pp. 285–294. New York: Wiley. 1979. *Interpreting Deviance: A Sociological Introduction*. New York: Harper & Row.

Schwartz, Edward E. 1946. "A Community Experiment in the Measurement of Juvenile Delinquency." In *National Probation Association Yearbook, 1945*, pp. 157–181. New York: National Probation Association.

Schwartz, Richard D., and Jerome H. Skolnick. 1962. "Two Studies of Legal Stigma." *Social Problems* 10:133–142.

Scott, Marvin B., and Stanford M. Lyman. 1968. "Accounts." *American Sociological Review* 33:46–62.

Scott, Robert A. 1969. *The Making of Blind Men: A Study of Adult Socialization*. New York: Russell Sage.

Scull, Andrew T. 1977. *Decarceration: Community Treatment and the Deviant; a Radical View*. Englewood Cliffs, N.J.: Prentice-Hall.

Seidman, David, and Michael Couzens. 1974. "Getting the Crime Rate Down: Political Pressure and Crime Reporting." *Law and Society Review* 8:457–493.

Sellin, Thorstein. 1967. "Executions in the United States." In Thorstein Sellin (ed.), *Capital Punishment*, pp. 31–35. New York: Harper & Row.

Shaw, Clifford R., and Henry D. McKay. 1942, 1969. *Juvenile Delinquency and Urban Areas*. Chicago: University of Chicago Press.

Sherman, Lawrence. 1974. *Police Corruption*. New York: Doubleday.

Shoemaker, Donald J., Donald R. South, and Jay Lowe. 1973. "Facial Stereotypes of Deviants and Judgments of Guilt or Innocence." *Social Forces* 51:427–433.

Shwed, Harvey J. 1978. "Protecting the Rights of the Mentally Ill." *American Bar Association Journal* 64:564–567.

Simmel, Georg. 1903. "The Metropolis and Mental Life." In Kurt H. Wolff (ed.), *The Sociology of Georg Simmel*, pp. 409–424. New York: Free Press, 1950.

Simmons, J. L. 1965. "Public Stereotypes of Deviants." *Social Problems* 13:223–232. 1969. *Deviants*. Santa Barbara, Calif.: Glendessary Press.

Sirica, John J. 1979. *To Set the Record Straight: The Break-in, the Tapes, the Conspirators, the Pardon*. New York: Norton.

Skipper, James K., Jr., and Charles H. McCaghy. 1970. "Stripteasers: The Anatomy and Career Contingencies of a Deviant Occupation." *Social Problems* 17:391–405. 1971. "Stripteasing: A Sex-Oriented Occupation." In James M. Henslin (ed.), *Studies in the Sociology of Sex*, pp. 275–296. New York: Appleton-Century-Crofts.

Skolnick, Jerome H. 1966. *Justice Without Trial*. New York: Wiley.

Skolnick, Jerome H., and J. Richard Woodworth. 1967. "Bureaucracy, Information, and Social Control: A Study of a Morals Detail." In David J. Bordua (ed.), *The Police: Six Sociological Essays*, pp. 99–136. New York: Wiley.

Smith, Richard T. 1975. "Societal Reaction and Physical Disability: Contrasting Perspectives." In Walter R. Gove (ed.), *The Labelling of Deviance: Evaluating a Perspective*, pp. 147–156. New York: Russell Sage.

Smith, Samuel. 1911. *Social Pathology*. New York: Macmillan.

Snyder, Mark, Elizabeth Decker Tanke, and Ellen Berscheid. 1977. "Social Perception and Interpersonal Behavior: On the Self-Fulfilling Nature of Social Stereotypes." *Journal of Personality and Social Psychology* 35:656–666.

Spector, Malcolm. 1976. "Labeling Theory in *Social Problems:* A Young Journal Launches a New Theory." *Social Problems* 24:69–75.

Spitzer, Steven. 1975. "Toward a Marxian Theory of Deviance." *Social Problems* 22:638–665.

Srole, Leo, et al. 1962. *Mental Health in the Metropolis: The Midtown Manhattan Study*. New York: McGraw-Hill.

Steffensmeier, Darrell J., and Robert M. Terry. 1973. "Deviance and Respectability: An Observational Study of Reactions to Shoplifting." *Social Forces* 51:417–426.

Stinchcombe, Arthur L. 1963. "Institutions of Privacy in the Determination of Police Administrative Practice." *American Journal of Sociology* 69:150–160.

Stinchcombe, Arthur L., et al. 1980. *Crime and Punishment: Changing Attitudes in America.* San Francisco: Jossey-Bass.

Stroman, Duane F. 1979. *The Quick Knife: Unnecessary Surgery, U.S.A.* Port Washington, N.Y.: Kennikat Press.

Suchar, Charles S. 1978. *Social Deviance: Perspectives and Prospects.* New York: Holt.

Sudnow, David. 1965. "Normal Crimes: Sociological Features of the Penal Code in a Public Defender Office." *Social Problems* 12:255–276.

Sutherland, Edwin H. 1949. *White Collar Crime.* New York: Dryden Press.

Sutherland, Edwin H., and Donald R. Cressey. 1978. *Criminology.* 10th ed. Philadelphia: Lippincott.

Swigert, Victoria Lynn, and Ronald A. Farrell. 1977. "Normal Homicides and the Law." *American Sociological Review* 42:16–32.

Skyes, Gresham M. 1958. *The Society of Captives.* Princeton, N.J.: Princeton. 1978. *Criminology.* New York: Harcourt Brace Jovanovich.

Sykes, Gresham, and David Matza. 1957. "Techniques of Neutralization: A Theory of Delinquency." *American Sociological Review* 22:664–670.

Szasz, Thomas S. 1961. *The Myth of Mental Illness: Foundations of a Theory of Personal Conduct.* New York: Harper. 1970. *The Manufacture of Madness: A Comparative Study of the Inquisition and the Mental Health Movement.* New York: Harper & Row. 1974. *Ceremonial Chemistry: The Ritual Persecution of Drugs, Addicts, and Pushers.* Garden City, N.Y.: Doubleday/Anchor. 1978. *The Myth of Psychotherapy: Mental Healing as Religion, Rhetoric, and Repression.* Garden City, N.Y.: Doubleday/Anchor.

Tannenbaum, Frank. 1938. *Crime and the Community.* New York: Ginn.

Taylor, Ian, Paul Walton, and Jock Young. 1973. *The New Criminology: For a Social Theory of Deviance.* London: Routledge.

Taylor, Steven J., and Robert Bogdan. 1979. "Defending Illusions: Human Service Administrators in Organizations That Abuse People." Paper presented at the American Sociological Association meeting, Boston.

Terry, W. Clinton, III, and David F. Luckenbill. 1976. "Investigating Criminal Homicides: Police Work in Reporting and Solving Murders." In William B. Sanders and Howard C. Daudistel (eds.), *The Criminal Justice Process: A Reader,* pp. 79–95. New York: Praeger.

Thio, Alex. 1973. "Class Bias in the Sociology of Deviance." *American Sociologist* 8:1–12. 1978. *Deviant Behavior.* Boston: Houghton Mifflin.

Thomas, Charles W., and Robin J. Cage. 1977. "The Effect of Social Characteristics on Juvenile Court Dispositions." *Sociological Quarterly* 18:237–252.

Thorsell, Bernard A., and Lloyd W. Klemke. 1972. "The Labeling Process: Reinforcement and Deterrent?" *Law and Society Review* 6:393–403.

Tittle, Charles R. 1975. "Labelling and Crime: An Empirical Evaluation." In Walter R. Gove (ed.), *The Labelling of Deviance: Evaluating a Perspective,* pp. 157–179. New York: Sage.

Tittle, Charles R., and Charles H. Logan. 1973. "Sanctions and Deviance: Evidence and Remaining Questions." *Law and Society Review* 7:371–392.

Tittle, Charles R., Wayne J. Villemez, and Douglas A. Smith. 1978. "The Myth of Social Class and Criminality: An Empirical Assessment of the Empirical Evidence." *American Sociological Review* 43:643–656.

Toby, Jackson. 1965. "An Evaluation of Early Identification and Intensive Treatment Programs for Predelinquents." *Social Problems* 13:160–175.

Triandis, Harry C. 1977. *Interpersonal Behavior.* Monterey, Calif.: Brooks/Cole.

Troiden, Richard R. 1979. "Becoming Homosexual: A Model of Gay Identity Acquisition." *Psychiatry* 42:362–373.

Udry, J. Richard, Karl E. Bauman, and Charles Chase. 1971. "Skin Color, Status, and Mate Selection." *American Journal of Sociology* 76:722–733.

U.S. Bureau of the Census. 1979. *Statistical Abstract of the United States: 1979 (100th ed.).* Washington, D.C.: U.S. Government Printing Office.

U.S. Department of Justice. 1977. *Criminal Victimization in the United States 1975: A National Crime Survey Report.* Washington, D.C.: U.S. Government Printing Office.

Valentine, Charles A. 1968. *Culture and Poverty: Critique and Counter-Proposals.* Chicago: University of Chicago Press.

van den Haag, Ernest. 1975. *Punishing Criminals.* New York: Basic Books.

Van Praag, H. M., and J. Bruinvels. 1977. *Neurotransmission and Disturbed Behavior.* Utrecht: Bohn, Scheltema, & Holkema.

Vold, George B. 1958. *Theoretical Criminology.* New York: Oxford.

von Hirsch, Andrew. 1976. *Doing Justice: The Choice of Punishments.* New York: Hill & Wang.

Voss, Harwin L., and David M. Peterson (eds.). 1971. *Ecology, Crime, and Delinquency.* New York: Appleton-Century-Crofts.

Walzer, Stanley, Germaine Breau, and Park S. Gerald. 1969. "A Chromosome Survey of 2400 Normal Newborn Infants." *Journal of Pediatrics* 74:438.

Ward, Russell. 1979. "Typifications of Homosexuals." *Sociological Quarterly* 20:411–423.

Warfield, Frances. 1948. *Cotton in My Ears.* New York: Viking.

Warren, Carol A. B. 1974. *Identity and Community in the Gay World.* New York: Wiley. 1974. "The Use of Stigmatizing Social Labels in Conventionalizing Deviant Behavior." *Sociology and Social Research* 58:303–311.

Warren, Carol A. B., and John M. Johnson. 1972. "A Critique of Labeling Theory from the Phenomenological Perspective." In Robert A. Scott and Jack D. Douglas (eds.), *Theoretical Perspectives on Deviance,* pp. 69–92. New York: Basic Books.

Washburn, Sherwood L. 1978. "Animal Behavior and Social Anthropology." In Michael S. Gregory, Anita Silvers, and Diane Sutch (eds.), *Sociobiology and Human Nature: An Interdisciplinary Critique and Defense,* pp. 53–74. San Francisco: Jossey-Bass.

Webster, William H. 1979. *Crime in the United States 1978.* U.S. Department of Justice. Washington, D.C.: U.S. Government Printing Office. 1980. *Crime in the United States 1979.* U.S. Department of Justice. Washington, D.C.: U.S. Government Printing Office.

Weinberg, Martin S. 1965. "Sexual Modesty and the Nudist Camp." *Social Problems* 12:311–318. 1966. "Becoming a Nudist." *Psychiatry: Journal for the Study of Interpersonal Processes* 29:15–24. 1968. "The Problems of Midgets and Dwarfs and Organizational Remedies: A Study of Little People of America." *Journal of Health and Social Behavior* 9:65–71. 1970. "The Male Homosexual: Age-Related Variations in Social and Psychological Characteristics." *Social Problems* 17:527–537. 1976. "The Nudist Management of Respectability." In Martin S. Weinberg, *Sex Research: Studies from the Kinsey Institute,* pp. 217–232. New York: Oxford.

Weinstein, Raymond M. 1979. "Patient Attitudes toward Mental Hospitalization: A Review of Quantitative Research." *Journal of Health and Social Behavior* 20:237–258. 1980. "The Favorableness of Patients' Attitudes toward Mental Hospitalization." *Journal of Health and Social Behavior* 21:397–401.

Wheeler, Stanton. 1976. "Trends and Problems in the Sociological Study of Crime." *Social Problems* 23:525–534.

Wheeler, Stanton, et al. 1968. "Agents of Delinquency Control." In Stanton Wheeler (ed.), *Controlling Delinquents,* pp. 31–60. New York: Wiley.

Wieder, D. Lawrence, and Don H. Zimmerman. 1976. "Becoming a Freak: Pathways into the Counter-Culture." *Youth and Society* 7:311–344.

Williams, Colin J., and Martin S. Weinberg. 1970. "Being Discovered: A Study of Homosexuals in the Military." *Social Problems* 18:217–227.

Wilson, Edward O. 1075. *Sociobiology: The New Synthesis.* Cambridge, Mass.: Belknap Press, Harvard. 1978. *On Human Nature.* Cambridge, Mass.: Harvard.

Wilson, James Q. 1975. *Thinking About Crime.* New York: Random House.

Winick, Charles. 1977. "From Deviant to Normative: Changes in the Social Acceptability of Sexually Explicit Material." In Edward Sagarin (ed.), *Deviance and Social Change,* pp. 219–246. Beverly Hills, Calif.: Sage.

Wirth, Louis. 1938. "Urbanism as a Way of Life." *American Journal of Sociology* 44:1–24.

Wiseman, Jacqueline P. 1970. *Stations of the Lost: The Treatment of Skid Row Alcoholics.* Englewood Cliffs, N.J.: Prentice-Hall.

Wolfgang, Marvin E. 1977. Foreword to Sarnoff A. Mednick and Karl O. Christiansen (eds.), *Biosocial Bases of Criminal Behavior.* New York: Gardner Press.

Wrong, Dennis H. 1961. "The Oversocialized Conception of Man in Modern Society." *American Sociological Review* 26:183–193.

Yarrow, Marian Radke, et al. 1955. "The Psychological Meaning of Mental Illness in the Family." *Journal of Social Issues* 11:12–24.

Yochelson, Samuel, and Stanton E. Samenow. 1976. *The Criminal Personality: A Profile for Change.* Vol. 1. New York: Jason Aronson.

Zimmerman, Don H., and D. Lawrence Wieder. 1970. "Ethnomethodology and the Problem of Order: Comment on Denzin." In Jack D. Douglas (ed.), *Understanding Everyday Life,* pp. 285–295. Chicago: Aldine.

Addenda:

MacNamara, Donal E. J. 1969. "Convicting the Innocent." *Crime and Delinquency* 15:57–61.

Ray, Marsh B. 1964. "The Cycle of Abstinence and Relapse among Heroin Addicts." Pp. 163–177 in Howard S. Becker (ed.), *The Other Side: Perspectives on Deviance.* New York: The Free Press.

Name Index

Adam, Barry D., 49, 81, 82, 177, 203, 206
Ageton, Suzanne S., 36, 38, 39, 84, 173
Akers, Ronald L., 154, 161, 168, 169, 171, 177, 243
Alex, Nicholas, 246
Altheide, David L., 58, 205, 226

Baldwin, Janice I., 250
Baldwin, John D., 250
Barbera, Henry, 234
Bawer, Theodore, 254
Becker, Howard S., 3, 11, 35, 42, 56, 58, 60, 61, 82, 146, 168, 176, 180, 186, 192, 193, 213, 231–234, 238, 239
Berk, Richard A., 50, 51, 53, 58
Bernstein, Ilene Nagel, 143, 150, 153, 155
Best, Joel, 68, 70
Bieber, Irving, 26, 34
Bischof, Ledford, 25
Black, Donald J., 125, 143, 148
Bogdan, Robert, 130, 137, 138, 190
Bonnie, Richard J., 60, 62

Braginsky, Benjamin M., 139
Briar, Scott, 108, 143, 148, 156
Brown, Roger, 47, 101
Bruinvels, J., 252
Bryant, Clifton D., 46
Buckner, H. Taylor, 11, 121
Buffalo, M. D., 203–205
Burgess, Ernest W., 111
Burgess, Robert L., 168
Butler, Richard R., 127

Cage, Robin J., 143
Cameron, Mary Owen, 149
Caplan, Arthur L., 249
Carroll, John S., 109
Carroll, Thomas J., 222
Carter, Timothy, 152, 153
Cavan, Ruth Shonle, 44
Chambliss, William J., 42, 50, 53, 58–60, 92
Chapman, Dennis, 146
Chapman, Jean P., 106, 240

Subject Index